Creek Mary's Blood

Dee Brown

CREEK MARY'S BLOOD

a novel

HOLT · RINEHART · AND · WINSTON
NEW · YORK

7131883

Martin F. Schmitt

SCHOLAR, MAN OF COURAGE & FRIEND

The author wishes to express sincerest thanks to David Gerber for his initial encouragement, continued amiable goading, and good counsel during the writing of this book.

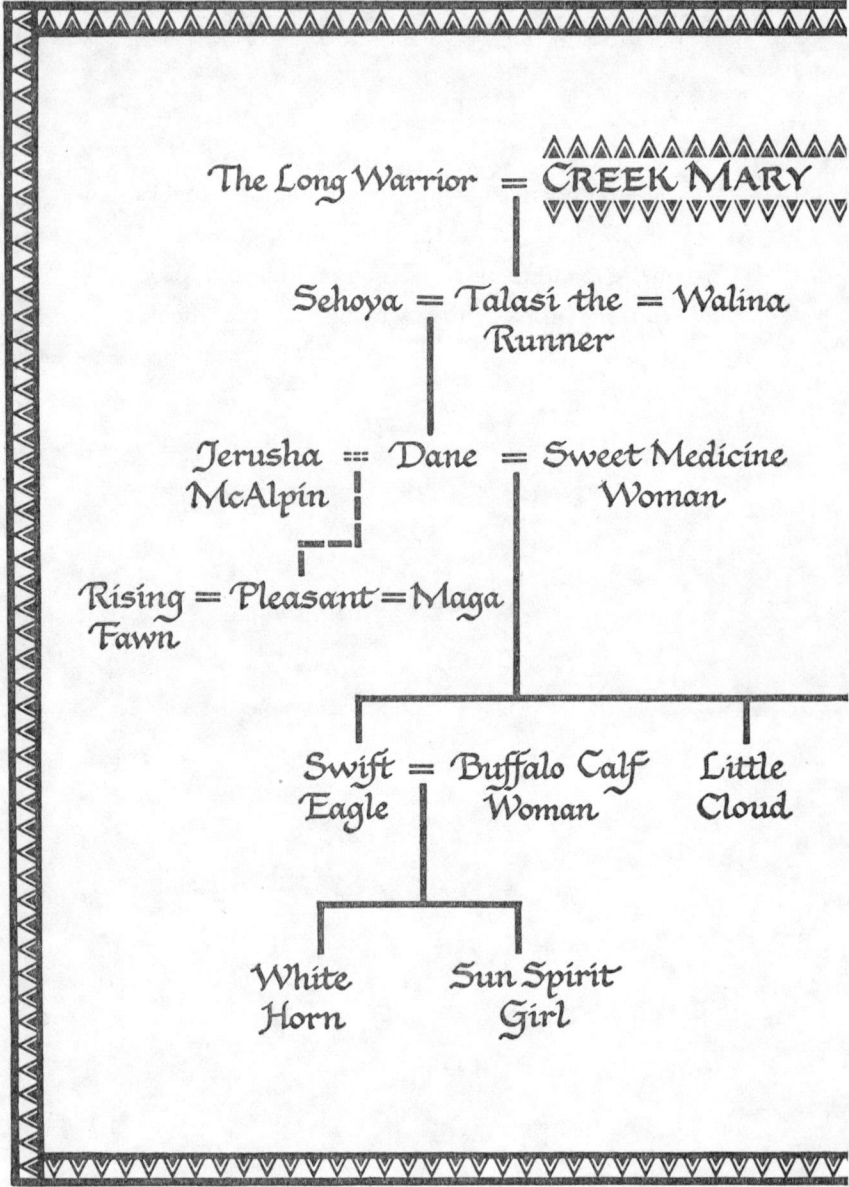

The Long Warrior = CREEK MARY

Sehoya = Talasi the = Walina
          Runner

Jerusha = Dane = Sweet Medicine
McAlpin   Woman

Rising = Pleasant = Maga
Fawn

Swift = Buffalo Calf   Little
Eagle   Woman   Cloud

White   Sun Spirit
Horn   Girl

AMAYI) = John Kingsley

Opothle = Suna-lee Rogers

Priscilla

William = Tatsuwha

Saviah Manning = Jotham = Griffa McBee

Amayi = Bull Bear   Susa   Young Opothle   Meggi

Mary Amayi   two sons

A·Karl

Book One

THE EASTERNERS

1

The Montana landscape is always startling when one comes there straight from the East. It was early morning when I stepped off the train at the little brown-stained depot into an immense space of frosted yellow grass and blue sky. I had scarcely lifted my bag before the train was on its way, the locomotive swirling steam and sulfurous smoke and cinders in its wake. The depot was deserted, but old Dane had sent explicit directions, and as soon as I found my bearings I started up the dirt road that led to his cabin, a mile and a half away.

As I walked, I wondered if I had not been rather foolish in traveling such a distance to ask an aged Indian a few questions about his legendary grandmother. I had known her name, Mary Kingsley, or Creek Mary, or simply Amayi, since the days of my Georgia youth. Later at the university I had tried to write a paper about her, but the records were scanty. She was a full-blood Muskogee, or Creek Indian, daughter of Machichi, a famous chief who had been killed in a skirmish with colonists. After Machichi's death, Mary's people at Bluff Village regarded her as their leader, the Beloved Woman.

By all accounts she was a great beauty who had charmed all the male colonists of Georgia, from General Oglethorpe down to trader John Kingsley, whom she married. Proud and hot-tempered, she had turned on the colonists for taking too much of her people's land. At the head of a mighty force of Creek warriors she stormed into Savannah, determined to drive the British into the sea, but in some way she was betrayed. After that, she vanished, and was mentioned only once more in the annals of Georgia, and that was an undocumented fragment concerning a

Danish sea captain who was said to have fallen in love with her
and went mad searching for her through the swamps and pine-
lands of coastal Georgia.

Over the years I had almost forgotten Creek Mary as I made
my way from one newspaper job to another, moving northward
from Georgia to Washington, a tolerable sort of journalist but
growing cynical, as I suppose we all do. A day or so after Teddy
Roosevelt's inaugural I drew an assignment to a White House
luncheon. I went with no particular enthusiasm. We had been
writing about Roosevelt and the inaugural for several days and
were weary of the subject.

As it turned out the luncheon was in honor of Mary Dane, a
young Indian woman from Montana, the first of her race and the
first of her sex to graduate from Columbia Medical College.
Teddy was in his usual ebullient form, gesturing wildly and slapping his hands sharply together to emphasize his remarks, his
voice rising often to an emotional treble. But I'm afraid I was
negligent of my duties that day. Not one note did I take of the
President's little speech. I was too absorbed in Mary Dane. Her
skin was of a dark honey color; her eyes were a somber black.
She was not only exceptionally beautiful, there was about her an
impulse of life—not a warmth, but a driving force that I imagined could be felt by every one of the forty or so people at the
luncheon tables. I believed that she was aware of each separate
one of us, but her dark eyes were directed most often to a very
old Indian man seated to her left front.

His walnut face was grooved with deep wrinkles. His long
white hair fell over the shoulders of his plain blue-serge coat. He
wore a maroon scarf loosely around his neck, and his bony old
man's nose and the way he held his head proudly erect gave him
more the air of a Spanish grandee than a Montana Indian. Most
of the time his eyes were closed, but when he opened them and
looked at Mary Dane they were very bright, and he would smile,
keeping his thin lips closed.

Suddenly there was Roosevelt handing Mary Dane a scroll of
some sort, and everyone stood and began applauding. In the
midst of it the old Indian uttered a suppressed whoop, and cried

out above the clatter: "Creek Mary's blood!" At first I was not certain of what he had said. I fumbled around for a moment, letting the word-sounds run through my head again. A rather large woman jostled past me, blocking my efforts to push forward to reach the old Indian before attendants hurried him and Mary Dane out through the side door. In the hubbub all I could learn was that they were rushing to board a train. It was not a very good reportorial performance on my part.

I went back to the office and composed my piece for the morning paper, but all evening I kept hearing the old man's voice rising above the applause, and wondering if I had imagined those three words: *Creek Mary's blood.* The next day I learned from a White House secretary that he lived on or nearby a Cheyenne reservation. No one seemed to know his first name. He was Mary Dane's grandfather, Mr. Dane, and his address was simply Dundee, Montana. It made no sense to me, an old Cheyenne Indian named Dane living two thousand miles north by west of the lush green coast of Georgia and having any knowledge whatsoever of my long-vanished Creek Mary.

But I decided to write a letter of inquiry to Mr. Dane at Dundee, Montana, and to my surprise a brief reply came back quite promptly. He assured me that he was indeed a descendant of my Creek Mary, her grandson in fact. Although he had lived with the Cheyennes for many years, he was not of their blood. He was pleased that I knew of his grandmother, and thanked me for writing to him. That was all.

Of course I wrote to him again, asking him to tell me what had happened to Creek Mary after her bold assault upon the city of Savannah. His second reply was as brief as the first. There was much to tell, he said, so much that he could never put it all into a letter. Besides, his old fingers had stiffened with the years and he found it difficult to write. Why did I not pay him a visit? He would tell me whatever I wanted to know.

And so here I was on a frosty morning in spring, trudging up a Montana dirt road pockmarked with hoofprints and rutted by the steel tires of wagons and buggies. Why had I come so far, taking leave without pay from a job that was insecure at best?

Perhaps it was the letters he had written to me, the ink script so carefully handprinted in bold and steady characters. He capitalized most of the nouns; his lowercase *s*'s resembled *f*'s; he used *y* for *i* in a couple of words; he doubled the *l*'s and *t*'s in words that we spell with single letters. This was not misspelling; it was almost perfect eighteenth-century English. He had been taught to read and write by his grandmother, Creek Mary, who had learned her English from eighteenth-century British missionaries in Carolina before the tribe crossed the Savannah River into Georgia. I could guess that much. It was like reading a manuscript from the nascent period of our republic, and I was beguiled by this link with the past, to a time so far distant from the modern now of 1905. For me, Creek Mary had come to life again, and I knew that in her youth her beauty must have been similar to that of Mary Dane's.

His cabin lay in a sprawling valley, with an upthrust of range far off to the northwest. A small stream bordered by cottonwoods and willows flowed just beyond it. A few Herefords that had come to drink there lifted their heads to stare at me. It was a lonely place.

He must have seen me coming. He stepped outside, lifting his face to the sun, waiting. I shouted a good morning to him, and he nodded. He was wearing a gray wool shirt, striped snuff-colored jeans, and old scarred cowboy boots. His long hair, silvery in the sunlight, was no longer loose as he had worn it at the White House, but was parted in the middle with a tightly woven braid hanging over each shoulder. The smooth parchment covering his nose and cheeks stretched out into a network of wrinkles, but his bright eyes belied his years. As I came up he offered his hand, and then gestured for me to go inside.

After the bright sunlight the interior of the cabin seemed dark. Three hickory rocking chairs faced a fireplace where a few orange coals glowed beneath a smoke-blackened coffeepot. He took my coat, hung it over the back of one of the rockers and motioned for me to sit there.

I broke the silence first. "Thank you for inviting me out here."

"It is good to have a visitor," he said. "All my Cheyenne

friends are dead except a few old women, most too feeble to journey out. The younger people are too busy. Do you drink coffee?" His accent struck me as being faintly British, not harsh in the way so many Northern Plains Indians speak.

While he poured the coffee I glanced at the rough bookshelves built under the window of the wall just to the left of his chair—a large dictionary with its boards hanging loose, a three-volume encyclopedia badly worn, *The Laws of Montana, Diseases of Cattle,* Catlin's *North American Indians* in two volumes with the gilt decorations fading, some yearbooks of the U.S. Department of Agriculture in purple bindings, a badly scuffed *Works of Shakespeare,* and a brand-new six-volume brown-leather set of Theodore Roosevelt's *Winning of the West,* probably a gift from the President at the time of Dane's recent visit to the White House.

He handed me a large tin cup of coffee, the metal already so hot that I had to rest it on the arm of the rocker. "Would you mind telling me how old you are?" I asked.

"Ninety-one," he replied.

"You are certain of this?"

"I am certain." His tone was slightly nettled. "We of the so-called 'Five Civilized Tribes' live by your calendar. The old ones of the Cheyenne people mark time by events. Some had winter-count calendars on buffalo skins, all lost in the wars. But of what importance is age by years? My grandmother was probably ninety-five by your calendar when she died. We who have Creek Mary's blood live forever, like the coyotes."

And that is how he began telling me about her. He had known her himself only as an aging woman, but he could visualize her in her early twenties, as could I, through his granddaughter. When Dane was a child eager for stories, seated beside his grandmother or held in her lap, he had listened many times to tales of her days of great glory as the Beloved Woman of the Bluff Village Creeks.

It was a fine summer morning and she went for a ride on the

fast-footed Choctaw pony that John Kingsley had obtained for her in trade. She let the pony trot along easily under the live oaks, passing a succession of pathways that forked off to various small vegetable plots cultivated by the Creeks outside their village. When she came to a level meadow she removed her cape of red English cloth and fastened it to the saddle. Then she put the pony into a fast gallop, feeling the air flow cool over her naked breasts, bracing her neck against the tug of her long hair streaming behind her like a black pennon. The grass ended against a thicket of trees where a clear brook ran swiftly toward the river. Of its own accord the pony slowed and stopped with its forefeet in the stream. She let it wet its nose in the water, and she was at once aware of a heavy quietness. The thicket was filled with silent birds. She knew that the day was too young for birds not to be filling the air with calls and chatter and music.

Without alarm she wondered at the meaning of this, as she often wondered on the meanings of the actions of all living beings—birds, animals, plants, and men and women. She watched the first cloud puffs forming in a sky that was a rich blue after a cleansing night shower.

"Because this was a day that was to have much meaning for her," Dane said, "she told me many times what she was wearing that morning. Besides the cape of red English cloth, she wore a knee-length skirt of the softest deerskin, and moccasins and leggings embroidered with beads of every color. She also wore a ring that General Oglethorpe had given her, a ring that bore a sparkling jewel of some kind. Around her neck would have been the gorget with the silver Danish coin that you may have seen my granddaughter wearing that day in the White House. The coin was Creek Mary's 'medicine,' what you would call an amulet, a charm against evil. She was never without it."

"Why would she place so much faith in a Danish coin?"

"Ah." His eyes brightened. "There was a Danish gentleman in her life. I think she told no one much about him but me, long after she gave me my name."

"So that— Of course. Dane." I could see that he was pleased by my recognition. "In my feeble searches into her history," I volunteered, "I found mention of a Danish sea captain, said to have died of madness in a futile search for her."

"I have no knowledge of that," he said.

As she and the Choctaw pony rested at the brook in the golden morning, there was a sudden fluttering of birds in the highest limbs of the live oaks, and then from beyond the thicket came a scream of rage and pain. Reaching for her cape, she quickly wrapped it around her shoulders and forced the pony into the woods, bowing her head before the slap of leaves and vines until the frightened animal brought her into a clearing. This was Tolchi's farm plot, young Tolchi whose wife had recently died. Mary had known him all her life. The screams came again from across the clearing, and she saw them then, nearby his log shelter.

Tolchi was bound facing a tree, and a stout white man was flogging his naked back with a leather whip. Her pony had come to a halt, but without hesitation she made it leap into a charging gallop. The stout man heard the thud of hooves and swung around in surprise. As horse and rider swept down upon him, his fleshy face showed a mixture of anger and fear. One hand still held the whip upright; his blue porcine eyes widened in disbelief at the onrushing horse and rider. Then as she swept past him she tore the whip from his grasp. She spun the pony around and brought the heavy leather down upon the man's thick mat of hair. He spat out a vicious oath, but she turned back upon him, cutting one side of his face open with the tail of the whip. He screamed, stumbled, and crawled a few yards, blinded by his own blood, wiping the flow on his sleeve. Then he struggled to his feet and ran like an awkward ox for his horse.

She held her pony until he was mounted, and then she lashed the flank of his horse. The big man was almost unseated by the sudden thrust of his mount, but he clung desperately to the animal's mane, shouting curses back at her as he disappeared down the trail that led to Savannah.

Turning back to Tolchi, she dismounted and with some difficulty released him from the ropes. The young man's back was covered with bloody welts from his neck to his waist. "Why?" she cried. "Why, Tolchi, why?"

Tolchi said that he had been away hunting deer in the north. During his absence the intruder had moved into his cabin and staked off the land. When Tolchi returned, the man had ordered him off his own farm plot, claiming that it was his by a grant from the King of Great Britain and the Trustees of Georgia. "Others came with him," Tolchi told her. "I saw them cutting trees to build cabins all along the Upper Ogeechee."

"So once again they are breaking the promises of Oglethorpe's treaty." Her voice was high and angry. "For the last time I've warned the English that they can have no more of our land. This time we will strike not at the separate invaders of our land but at their town, at Savannah itself."

She tried to help Tolchi into his cabin, but he brushed her arm away. His loss of dignity was more painful than the wounds on his back. She found bear's grease in an earthenware jar and rubbed it gently over the welts. "You must see Checote and have him bathe these cuts with that liquid he makes from tulip-tree bark. As soon as that is done, I want you to take my pony and ride as swiftly as you can to Menewa's village. Tell Menewa that his warnings of the treachery of white men have come true. Tell him the Beloved Woman of his tribe needs him and his warriors."

"I have no time to waste with that old conjurer Checote," Tolchi replied. "I shall ride straight to Menewa."

With Tolchi riding behind, they went on together to the edge of Bluff Village. She dropped easily to the ground. "Tolchi." She touched his leg gently as he eased into the saddle. "Go bring Menewa and his warriors back to me." As soon as he galloped away, she strode into the village, her anger still so high that she paid no heed to the greetings of the children playing and laughing in the pathways, and they knew that something was troubling their Beloved Woman.

John Kingsley's trading post was a long low building of logs set to one side of Bluff Village on the high riverbank. In contrast to the windowless Creek houses, that half of the building which served as living quarters had several openings in the sides so the log shutters could admit air. They were wide open now to the summer breeze off the river. From earthen tar pots set at strategic points around the building, curls of black smoke drifted in the warm air to discourage mosquitoes. On the river side, Kingsley had built a crude veranda that was roofed with brown palmetto fronds. He was seated there, with his feet propped on an empty rum cask, when Creek Mary came striding across the grass.

He glanced from her across to the empty enclosure of staked saplings where she kept her pony. "Where's the Choctaw?" he called out. At the sound of his voice the cry of a child came from inside. Mary neither looked at him nor replied to his question, but crossed the veranda to the post's entranceway without slowing her steps. Kingsley turned his head as she passed, swearing softly to himself. He was a handsome man with curly reddish hair and a short beard, but he was beginning to grow stout around the middle. When he heard her footsteps again, he stood up. She was carrying a naked child with its head resting against her shoulder.

"You could have taken him from the cradle," she said accusingly.

"But Edward only now started crying," Kingsley replied.

"His name is Opothle," she said firmly.

He shrugged. "Have it as you will." He kicked at the rum cask. "Where's the pony? Did you have trouble?"

"Tolchi has the pony."

"Tolchi! He came in here last night with a few deerskins. He still owes me fifty."

Her face darkened with quick anger. "They all owe you, don't they? You've made slaves of all my young men. For you they've killed so many deer that now they must travel almost to Cherokee country to find enough skins to trade. To trade for cloth for their women, for rum that should be forbidden, for gunpowder and shot to kill more deer."

"Would you and they want to go back to a life without my trade goods?" he asked sharply. "Become savages again?"

"Savages? Who are the savages? You should have seen that fat-arsed old fussock of a white man I found lashing Tolchi's back into bloody flesh."

Kingsley's face showed concern. "You did have trouble then. Tolchi must have brought the punishment on himself."

She uttered one of those eighteenth-century oaths she had learned from the British. "You're all alike, you English, and the French, and the Spaniards. It is always we, the people you call 'Indians,' who are the wrongdoers. That ruddy pirate was trying to steal Tolchi's cabin and farm plot."

"Did he have papers from Savannah?"

"Papers be damned! Tolchi's ground is Muskogee ground. I sent the bloody bastard scuttering back to Savannah. Then I sent Tolchi for Menewa."

"Menewa! That troublemaker. The man from Savannah may simply have made a mistake of location."

She swung her arms in a gesture of disgust. "He did not come alone. Others of his kind are blazing trees up the Ogeechee."

Kingsley sighed, blowing air through his sullen lips. "You could go down to Savannah alone and straighten it all out. You were always able to do that with Oglethorpe."

"Oglethorpe has gone back to England, where he should be. When Menewa comes with his warriors, we'll frighten Oglethorpe's man Stephens and all the Savannah land-thieves into following Oglethorpe's example."

"William Stephens is an honorable man," Kingsley said. "You wouldn't try to use force?"

The child began crying again, and Mary soothed it with her voice. Disdaining a reply to her husband's question, she turned her back on him and left the veranda.

"Your temper's up," Kingsley muttered. "You'll have a cooler head tomorrow."

But Creek Mary refused to sleep in his bed that night, and she was never to sleep there again.

2

"Menewa came to Bluff Village as Creek Mary said he would," Dane said. "She described for me many times the arrival of his finest warriors from the Creek confederacy, almost three hundred of them, naked and painted for battle. Some came in dugout canoes, some on horseback, armed with a few old flintlock rifles, their war clubs, and their bows and arrows. They filled the town and spread out along the bank of the river. That night Mary's warriors, fifty or so, joined them in a dance. Some had rum that they mixed with their sagamité, and the celebration became quite noisy. John Kingsley locked himself in his trading house and refused to take part."

Dane did not know what the full relationship was between Mary and Menewa. Forthright though she was about her past, she was always a bit reticent when it came to that "crazy war hunter," as she often called him. He was considerably older than she, but handsome and muscular into his later years. Twice more during her life she was to become closely involved with Menewa.

By first daybreak following the dancing and feasting, Mary and Menewa were pounding on the door of her husband's trading post, awakening him and young Opothle. After feeding the child, she directed some of her warriors to carry several kegs of powder and boxes of English biscuits, as well as an assorted lot of

smoked venison and hams, down to Kingsley's trading boat at
the river landing. Kingsley stood by watching helplessly, trying
to calm his nerves by smoking a curved Dutch pipe. Feeling
rather sorry for him, she invited him to join them on the expedition to Savannah. After all, they were using his trading boat for
transport and supplies. "It's madness, it's madness," Kingsley
kept repeating, and then they fell into one of their bitter quarrels
that ended when an old Creek woman arrived to take care of
Opothle during Mary's absence.

At the last minute Kingsley decided to go along. He joined
Mary and Menewa on the prow of the trading boat, which was
an ingenious adaptation of an Indian barge—a platform set upon
a pair of large dugouts with a box-shaped shelter at the center of
the raftlike craft. Mary wore elaborately embroidered deerskins
and was armed with a foot-long British cavalry pistol fitted into
a leather belt that Kingsley had made for her.

And so the expedition started for Savannah. About forty warriors were crowded onto the boat, propelling with poles and pad-
dles, while a hundred canoes served as escorts. A line of horsemen wound in and out of view along the parallel trail. They
faced into a rising sun that tinted the gentle waves of the river
crimson and gold.

Hour by hour the vegetation grew thicker and more virides-
cent as they floated along on the river that was named for an
outcast subtribe of Shawnees—the Shawano—corrupted to Savannah by the British. The surrounding curtain of green ranged
from dark lacquered magnolia leaves to pale marsh grass. The
fragrance of blossoms was overwhelmingly sweet at times, and
then the waters widened and darkened, extending into swamps
that smelled of mud and decaying vegetation. When they left
the high walls of cypress and live oaks, draped with Spanish
moss, the sun burned down like fire. Those who were not pad-
dling or poling drowsed in the heat. Late in the afternoon the
wind shifted and the stagnant air was replaced by a fresh breeze
bearing a faint briny odor of the sea. At the first high bank, they
stopped and camped for the night, gathering armloads of long
moss that had been blown there by the winds. Mary and Me-

newa cautioned the warriors to maintain silence through the
night. Savannah was only a short distance away by land, and
they did not want the inhabitants to know of their coming.

Afterward she accused Kingsley of slipping away to Savannah
during the night and then returning, after warning the authorities of the approach of the Creeks. He denied doing this, yet
when the flotilla and file of horsed Creeks came into view of
Savannah, lines of scarlet-coated militia, mounted and on foot,
were waiting for them on the embankment above the landing.

"Redcoat soldiers," Mary said in disgust. "The bloody Jacks!"
She raised her cavalry flintlock and fired into the air. From all
around the crowded boat a dozen old muskets echoed her example. Menewa's horsemen coming along the trail halted, waiting
for a signal to explain the firing. The dugouts on the river were
suddenly motionless. On shore, officers and sergeants began
barking orders. The affair was approaching a climax.

"William Stephens!" Kingsley shouted in a high excited voice.
"Mr. William Stephens!"

"I hear you, Mr. Kingsley," came a reply from above. "If you
wish to avoid the slaughter of your people, have them lay down
their arms."

"They mean you no harm. We're coming ashore for a parley,
sir." As the boat edged against a quay, Kingsley caught his wife's
arm and forced her to step ashore onto the landing.

"Menewa," she whispered, glancing back at the Creek chief-
tain, her eyes questioning him.

"We've lost surprise," Menewa said simply.

Dane stopped his story and went to attend the logs in the fireplace. "Perhaps I should explain to you the philosophy of a
Creek war party," he said. "They and the Cherokees of the old
days, most of the woods tribes, considered surprise to be an es-
sential part of the game. They went to a great deal of trouble to
surprise the enemy, but if a war party was discovered before it
could attack, there was nothing left to be done but exchange
shouted insults before returning home to try again at some later

time. If Custer had been a Creek, there would have been no bloodshed that day he came to the Little Bighorn—because he lost surprise. He would have turned his men around and gone back to his fort."

"The battlefield is near here, isn't it?" I interrupted.

"Yes, I saw some of the fighting."

"I'd like to hear about that."

He made a shower of sparks with his poker. "We'll come to it."

His thoughts were still another century back in time, recollecting what his grandmother had told him of her day of decision. Mary knew all about the Creek military principle of surprise, but she was not bound by this, and regardless of the attitude of her male counterpart, Menewa, she had no intention of retreating before the redcoated militia of Savannah. After John Kingsley had forced her into a parley, she led the way up the embankment to confront the President of the Georgia Trustees, William Stephens. The latter obviously had dressed in his best for this occasion—a shiny black cocked hat resting on a powdered wig, a light blue long-tailed coat, ruffled sleeves, white stockings, silver-buckled shoes, a ceremonial sword at his side.

"You come bearing arms, Mr. Kingsley," Stephens addressed the trader in a grand tone of voice. "I'm waiting patiently for your explanation."

"John Kingsley bears no arms," Mary interrupted. "It is I and Menewa of the Creek confederacy who so challenge you and your soldiers."

Stephens raised his eyebrows in mock surprise. "Madam, I am unsettled by what you say. We of Savannah have always counted the Beloved Woman of the Creeks as our truest friend."

"No more so," she retorted. "Friends do not steal from one another. You and your spider-shanked Lords have gone too far this time in sending your beggars out to take our land."

Stephens forced a smile. "I assure you, madam, that if illegal land-taking has been done, redress shall be made."

"I have heard such words before." She slipped her flintlock pistol from its leather case, pointing it at his ample belly. "Now step aside, sir. I intend to lead my people into Savannah and take possession of the town."

"If you are jesting, madam," Stephens managed to reply through his tightening jaws, "you show poor taste in drawing that weapon. If you are in earnest, my office forces me to no choice but to order my militia to fire upon your people."

"He's telling you truth, Amayi," Kingsley cried. He reached for the pistol, but she knocked his hand aside. "The militia are too well armed," he continued desperately. "They'll destroy you."

"Listen to your husband, madam," Stephens warned. "Let us not break our long friendship with blood. If you cock that weapon, it will serve as a signal. My soldiers will kill or wound half your warriors in a matter of moments."

Although Mary disliked bloodshed, she knew its occasional necessity, and she was not one to flinch from violence when there was no other recourse. Yet at the same time she had no intention of seeing Creek blood spilled when it would gain nothing. She knew that she had pushed Stephens to the brink of some desperate action. His eyes and the throb of his throat muscles betrayed his fear. She also knew that Menewa was right. This time they could not seize Savannah and force the colonists into flight. Yet she was still unwilling to take the traditional course and turn away, as the male warriors would have done, and go back upriver to await another day, another try. She wanted to show William Stephens that the Creeks had no fear of these invaders of their land, that the colonists were there by sufferance only, and that if they wished to stay they must leave their Creek neighbors alone.

She allowed her husband to believe that it was he who persuaded her to command her warriors to disarm themselves and leave their weapons at the guard post on Bay Street. As this was being done, she tried to find Menewa in the crowd, wanting him by her side for the entry into Savannah. At last she discovered him, far down on the quay, standing very alert in front of the trading boat. She called out to him. He made no reply except to indicate by gestures that he would not disarm his warriors but that he would hold them on the river awaiting her return. As she turned away from Menewa she felt a sense of abandonment, a faint foreboding, and just then she heard her husband accepting an invitation to dine with President Stephens.

She led her little band of warriors up into the town of many squares, where great live oaks spread black patterns of shade over adjoining houses. The older warriors could remember visiting the place when a Yamacraw Creek village stood there in the time before the British came. She was annoyed at Stephens's insistence upon accompanying her. What she had visualized as a triumphant procession through Savannah had turned into a mere promenade, and the presence of Stephens, with his authority fully intact, made it difficult for her to keep her composure. When he proudly pointed out several new buildings under construction, she responded: "I share your pride, sir, in these fine houses because this high ground once sited a Creek village. When you have completed the town, we may make it Creek once again."

"Ah, madam, in this vast country there is land and land enough to spare for everyone. I've heard you say so yourself, to General Oglethorpe."

"If I said such words," she retorted, "Oglethorpe put them into my mouth."

Creek Mary was no stranger in the fine house on Telfair Square where she and John Kingsley went to dine with President Stephens. She had lived there for a time while acting as James Edward Oglethorpe's interpreter in meetings with the Creeks. With her usual frankness she later told Dane that she had bedded with the founder of Georgia on several occasions, although she felt no particular affection for him and laughed at his remorseful piety after these meetings. She also told her grandson that the great man was afflicted with bad teeth and a foul breath.

On this evening she was not, therefore, awed by the glitter of power, the waxed flooring, the liveried black servants, the chandeliers filled with candles, the huge dining table laid with expensive china and silverware. In addition to Mary and Kingsley, the President had invited members of the Georgia colony board, and as she quickly foresaw, the dinner developed into an inquisition.

One of the board members, a bewigged sour-faced man, began it with a whining statement about the original land treaty. His watery pale-blue eyes never once were fixed upon Mary. As she later told Dane, he seemed to be addressing either the ceiling of the dining room or his God. The humorless board member declared that in the general view the lands upriver were never considered to be Creek lands but were a part of the Georgia colony that General Oglethorpe had generously reserved for Creek use until such time as the lands were needed for settlement.

As the man droned on, Mary felt her fury rising. She squeezed her silver wine goblet hard enough to bend it, then lifted it and drained the contents with one gulp. A servant behind her refilled it immediately.

"A fig on General Oglethorpe and his treaties," she shouted, and for the first time the startled board member looked at her. "The truth is the reverse of what you have said, sir. The Creeks through my father ceded this land to you in good faith. If you break that faith, and you have done so many times already, you must leave this land." She stamped a moccasined foot on the floor. "The earth that this building rests upon is ours."

The board members regarded her with solemn faces. Only President Stephens smiled slightly as he lifted a folded document from beside his plate. He unfolded it, the heavy sheets crackling in the sudden silence. "I have here a copy of the last land treaty, signed by representatives of the Cherokees. It is the position of the Crown that the lands you claim along the Savannah were never Creek lands at all, but were Cherokee lands. The Cherokees were paid a handsome sum."

"Then you were cheated, sir," she said, emptying her goblet again. "Any Cherokee who ever dared venture into that country would soon find a Creek warrior hard upon his arse."

One of the board members repressed a titter by clearing his throat. Stephens ignored Mary's remark and lifted another sheaf of papers. "Here, madam, I have the current accounts of your husband, Mr. John Kingsley, with whom you have a trading partnership registered with the Crown. For the past several

months these accounts have shown a steadily growing indebt-
edness of the members of your village, a rapid falling behind in
promised payments of deerskins and furs for trade goods already
given to your people. How can this debt be extinguished except
by an exchange of lands for it?"

She pushed her chair back, rising to her full height, her dark
eyes flashing. "Before you people came among us," she said in
full voice, "we did not know that men could be so base. I beg
the Maker of Breath to defend us from your manners, your laws,
and your power. By God, sirs, you know as well as I that the
trade goods are not worth a tenth of the price that is put upon
them, and that the deerskins are worth ten times the value you
put upon them in trade."

"You forget the many gifts, madam, that we have presented to
you and your people," Stephens interrupted.

"Oh, yes, you have given us gifts, only to demand each time
another cession of our lands, so that these gifts are dearly
bought." She sank back into her chair, sipping again at the wine.
"I ask you to speak no more of our lands. You are already too
close to us. You are like the fires we set in our fields each autumn
to burn away the weeds. If we were not there to stop the fires,
they would destroy everything. Like the fires, you would overrun
our fields and forests if we did not stop you. I advise you to be
satisfied with what we have given you and not to demand more."

Her voice, grown husky, faded away. A small bearded man
near the end of the table clapped his hands together. "God
knows, madam, you are a whole-souled patriot and I admire you
for it."

Stephens nodded. "Yes, with such spirit as you show us,
Madam Kingsley, we are most certainly obliged to make a
friendly accommodation with you and your people."

Mary took a swallow of wine, rolling it with her tongue, and
then laughed her loud and lusty laugh. "Don't go pissing down
my back," she said.

Stephens's face reddened. The bearded man who had ap-
plauded opened his mouth in surprise. The sour-faced man stared
at the ceiling. John Kingsley was whispering something to her.

"I might put some belief in your promises," she went on, "if women were present among you. It is the custom among our people for women to speak in our councils. Why do you white men scorn women? Why do women not sit alongside you in your councils? Were you not born of women?"

The silence that followed was broken by a clatter outside the dining-room entrance. Long afterward, Mary told Dane that she could not clearly remember from that moment the exact sequence of events. She had drunk too much wine. The candlelit room was beginning to swirl. She was aware that Tolchi and another young warrior had forced their way into the outer room but were being held there by a militia guard. Tolchi was calling to her, trying to tell her something about the stout man who had seized his cabin and farm plot, the one she had lashed with his own whip. This man evidently had raised a mob and was threatening the unarmed Creeks who had been roaming through the streets. The other warrior was a messenger from Menewa. Was the Beloved Woman a prisoner? he wanted to know. Did she need Menewa's help?

"No, no, no!" John Kingsley was shouting. "Tell Menewa that all is well, that we shall rejoin him soon."

Above Kingsley's voice, Stephens was ordering a militia officer to investigate the disturbance in the streets, and then beyond the hubbub outside, from the direction of the river, came the sounds of gunfire, the irregular pop-pop of muskets.

"God in Heaven!" Stephens shouted. "It's those armed rascals on the river!" He kicked his chair back and came striding down the dining room, a finger pointing at Mary and Kingsley. "You have gulled me," he said angrily. "You plotted this rebellion. Guardsmen, arrest this pair of conspirators and place them in confinement!"

Mary protested, resisted with all her being, kicked shins and shouted every British epithet she could command, and denounced the militia for interfering with the Queen of All the Creeks. Kingsley offered no resistance, devoting his energies to attempts to soothe her as they were rushed through the streets to a building just above the river that was used as militia headquarters. There they were locked into a windowless evil-smelling room with hard wooden shelves for bunks.

"Oh, but I was well fuzzled," she told Dane long afterward. "Never again did I swig wine or rum as I did on that night."

Early the next morning guards unlocked the door and summoned John Kingsley. He told her not to fear, that he would soon have her free. After he was taken away, she sat on the hard bunk in the dark. Her head ached but she felt no remorse, only a dull anger and a fear that harm might have come to Menewa. Yet she could remember no sounds of firing after those first irregular bursts from the river.

At last Kingsley and the guards returned. "Come along," he said curtly. "We're going home."

The brightness of the morning blinded her and made her eyeballs ache. "Last night," she asked, "were any of the warriors killed?"

"No. They're on the river. Waiting for you. Their weapons have been returned to them. By the way, William Stephens sends his apologies and promises to protect your people from further land seizures by the colonists."

She smiled. "Then we won a victory after all."

"There are conditions, of course."

"What conditions?"

They were descending the wooden steps to the quay. A sea vessel had anchored alongside the trading boat during the night, and was already taking on barrels of tar and turpentine. Only two or three canoes were left of the hundred or so that Menewa's warriors had brought down, and the file of mounted warriors was nowhere in view.

"Where is Menewa?" she asked.

"He fled early last night. After firing off a few muskets."

"Menewa *fled?*"

"Decamped." Kingsley pushed her aboard the trading boat. "I suppose he thought you had gone over to the enemy."

The words were like a slap in the face. She had felt betrayed when she first realized that Menewa had left her; now Kingsley made her feel that she was the betrayer.

Although she asked him several times on the journey upriver what conditions Stephens had demanded of the Bluff Village Creeks, he put her off on one pretext or another until they were back at the trading post. After she had bathed her young son, she confronted Kingsley in the office room. "What were the promises of Stephens? What conditions did he ask of us?"

Kingsley put his Dutch pipe aside and unfolded a document. "He set it all down in writing, all in order, so that there will be no further disputes."

"What is that map drawn there?" she asked.

"We will move Bluff Village up to the Double Branch, leaving the land between here and the Branch open to settlement by the colonists. As you can see by the map, all lands north and west of the Branch will be forever Creek, inviolate to the colonists."

She laughed. "This paper is worthless. I did not sign it."

"I signed for you," he said firmly, "in the interests of peace."

"By what right do you sign for me?"

"English law gives me that right. I am your husband. Your property is my property."

"But I have no property. This land is Creek land."

He sighed and spread his hands. "You are a woman, Amayi. You don't understand these matters."

"Damn you and the Georgia Lords!" she cried. "I am a *miko*, a chief, but because I am a woman, they look upon you, a white man, as being above me. Why do they think a piece of flesh hanging between their legs gives them rights over women? Over a *miko* of the Creek Nation? The Creeks will yield no more land, not one grain of sand!"

He reached out in a fit of anger and caught both her shoulders, shaking her. "Don't be a fool. For bringing those armed Indians into Savannah, they could have charged us with treason, shipped us to England, and hanged both of us. When you wedded me, you became a British subject as I am, liable to the laws forbidding armed rebellion against the King."

"I renounce my British allegiance!" she shouted, pulling away from his grasp. She turned her back on him, her chin held high, and started out of the office room.

"There's no changing anything now," he called after her. "You may as well resign yourself to yielding this land and moving upriver. Either we move voluntarily or the Georgia militia will move us forcibly."

She turned in the doorway and said scornfully: "You always were one to kiss the arses of the Lords, John Kingsley. How much gold did they give you?"

Darkness had fallen when she went outside. The frogs were setting up a clamor from the river shallows and the air was heavy with smoke from the tar pots. She saddled the Choctaw pony and rode off in a mad gallop, following the trail to Tolchi's cabin. She called several times, but he was not there. Letting the sweated pony walk slowly back to the village, she tried to think of a plan to thwart the land-thieves in Savannah. Only Menewa could advise her, and he had deserted her. She could understand now why he had departed so abruptly. Menewa never compromised. He would never share food and drink with the Savannah land-thieves, and he must have surely been offended because she had done so. She must find Menewa, and try to explain why she had acted as she had.

As she rode into the village, she could hear raucous singing coming from the chunkey yard in front of the council house. A drum began throbbing. They were starting to dance. She could tell from the sounds that they had got rum from Kingsley—which meant that some of them were a step further into debt. Tolchi would be there and some of the older warriors, but they would be of no use to her now. She turned the Choctaw away, in the direction of the trading post, noting that all the windows were dark there.

She had once loved John Kingsley with all the passion of her heart. After they were married in an English ceremony in Savannah and he brought her back to the trading post, she had taught her people to look upon him as a benefactor. The vision of a mingling of the races had appealed to her then. She had dreamed of a paradise in which the best of the two cultures would take the ascendancy, the natural world of her people combined with the wares and comforts and knowledge of the whites. She waited impatiently for the birth of her first child, the tawny-skinned little boy that she at once named Opothle after her favorite uncle. Kingsley wanted him to be called Edward, and they had their first quarrel.

Through the busy months that followed they gradually grew apart. Kingsley was constantly critical of what he called her people's childlike ways, their disregard for the future. In his efforts to satisfy his needs and ambition he became anxious and unhappy. She accused him of wanting to be rich enough to buy other human beings, of making the Creeks so poor they would be obliged to sell themselves to him. Yet she knew that at heart he was not a bad man. He tried again and again to accept her as a child of nature, yielding often to her whims. But he was tainted with the greed of his race, the urge to set men against men, an enemy of the natural world.

She held tight to the bridle, looking at the dark trading post for several minutes, trying to decide what she must do. Then instead of corralling and unsaddling the pony, she fastened it to a veranda post, and slipped quietly through the unlocked front door. Without making a sound she walked back into the living quarters. The bedroom door was open, and Kingsley was sprawled on the bed, snoring, and she caught the scent of rum on the dead air. For a moment she yearned to go to him, wake him, and comfort him. But instead she picked up a blanket, an extra pair of moccasins and her pistol, and returned with them to the storeroom. There in the darkness she found a saddlepack and began filling it with biscuits, cheese, and dried meat. From the shelves she took some gunpowder and lead, a small hand-mirror, and a knife. After she had fastened the pack to the Choctaw's saddle, she returned to the bedroom and carefully lifted Opothle from his pallet. The child stirred, and she held one hand close to his face to shut off any sudden outcry, but he made only a few sucking noises with his lips.

Returning to the storeroom, she slid Opothle gently into a carrying cradle and fastened it to her back. Then she took one last look around; she could think of nothing else she might need. By this time the moon had risen, and light shining through a window slit made the jewel sparkle in the ring that General Oglethorpe had given her. She slipped the ring from her finger and took it into the office room, placing it on the top of Kingsley's desk.

Then she went out into the silvery light of the summer night, mounted the pony, and started north along the river trail. Off to the left she could hear the drums and chanting of the revelers in the chunkey yard. She wanted to weep for them, but Opothle began whimpering and she had to turn her head and try to soothe the child with her voice. Somewhere up the river was a westward-running trail that would lead her to Menewa.

3

"Distances are deceptive," Dane said, and swung his chair to point toward the range off to the northwest. "If you rode to the base of that nearest butte on horseback, you might make a fairly accurate guess as to how far it was from this cabin. But let us say you had gone there as a child of ten, and now twelve years later you start out again, it will seem a much shorter distance, don't you know. That was what happened to Grandmother Mary. She first made the journey to Menewa's village when she was ten—an age when distances and time are long. A dozen years later, they were shortened for her.

"Not until the third day of her journey did she start looking in earnest for the old Creek Path to the west. She should have reached it on the second day, but missed it somehow. Probably turned off for shade and water, and missed it." He laughed.

"Lucky for me, she did miss it, or I would not be here to tell you about her. Maybe she was just riding along with her face to the sun, so gladdened by her new freedom that she would not have seen the trail if it had been as wide as the Yellowstone at flood time."

About midmorning of the third day, Creek Mary was surprised to see a small cluster of buildings across the river. It was not an Indian village, but a white man's outpost, a crude fortification built there by the Carolinians for trade and defense. She turned off the trail at once, keeping behind a meadow of high canes so that she would not be seen. Since the second day she had been alert for strangers, but had met no one, and only once had sighted what appeared to be a trader's pack train moving far ahead of her.

After an hour or so she turned the Choctaw pony back to the trail and was surprised to see rapids running in the river. By the time she reached a roaring waterfall she suspected that she might have passed the trail. She was not certain of this, however. She thought that perhaps the fort might not have been there when she had made that childhood journey and perhaps she had forgotten the waterfall. She had no compass, of course, but she knew that if she turned west she would eventually come to either a Lower or Upper Creek village and could then find her way to Menewa. And so she urged the pony on up the rocky winding path, but by sundown she had found no sign of any diverging trail.

She slept that night in high country, hidden among a thicket of scrub cedars. A strong wind blew incessantly, making musical sounds in the needlelike foliage, but chilling her under the single blanket. Opothle was awake at first dawnlight, crying from cold and hunger. Fog hung over the earth thick as water, forming droplets on her deerskin cape. She chewed some dried venison and a piece of biscuit, tonguing the masticated food into the child's willing mouth. She still had enough food left for three or four days, but she could find no water on the rocky height and both she and the boy were thirsty.

By the time she got the pony saddled, the mists were lifting. A pale red sun appeared and the clouds took on the shape of an enormous winged creature outspread above her, black and menacing. She shivered. The day was not starting well.

The trail twisted, growing narrower and rockier as it seemed to climb to the sky. During the morning there were two more bad signs. A coachwhip snake came flying along the trail, its black and shiny head held upright as though to stop her passage. At the last moment, it turned aside and vanished into the brush. Soon after that a black turkey buzzard began gliding in circles just above her, dropping lower and lower so that she could see its reddish eyes fixed upon the horse, the woman, and the child.

As the sun rose in a metallic sky the three grew thirstier, the child crying, the pony snuffling and reaching for green shoots of shrubbery at every opportunity. By midday the heat and humidity were almost unbearable. Suddenly the pony halted, its ears quivering. It tried to lunge into the undergrowth against the pull of the bridle. She held the animal steady. Off to the right she could hear water running over stones. She let the pony go then, through the brush and a narrow stand of tall pines, and there a spring gushed from a ledge of rock to form a pool before foaming off the side of a hill. Around the edge of the pool were recent moccasin tracks.

While the pony drank she used her hand as a cup, dribbling water into Opothle's mouth and over his face until he began laughing joyously. From the ledge she could see across a series of timbered ridges that turned from green to purple in the farthest distance. Along the western horizon thunderheads were piling up and lightning was playing across the blackest of the storm clouds.

Although the water was like ice, she bathed Opothle quickly and then undressed and plunged in, forcing herself to stay under until she could feel the cold penetrate her flesh. Then she and the child lay naked in the sun, nibbling at their dry rations and listening to the trickling water and the hum of insects until they felt warm and sleepy.

A roll of thunder brought her wide awake. As she dressed the child and herself, she watched the storm clouds moving toward them, a white scud racing out in front. The only shelter was the ledge, a few feet beneath the slant of rock. She led the horse there and tied him to a hickory sapling, and then turned with Opothle in her arms to watch the wind tearing at treetops on the nearest ridge. The sun was darkened abruptly. Close around her everything turned suddenly still, birds and insects falling silent, and then a burst of wind swept across the hillside, thrashing the great pines. For the first time since leaving Bluff Village she felt fear, and when lightning crashed upon the rocks to create thunder that shook the earth, her imagination fed upon this fear to create terror. She wanted to run, run, but a sheet of rain struck her with the force of an ocean wave, drenching her completely. She turned her back and tried to calm her frightened son and warm his wet body. The pony, beset by its own fears, struggled madly to break away from the rawhide that held it to the hickory sapling.

It seemed to Mary that the ordeal would never end, the hissing of the chill rain against the gray rocks, the shrieking of wind in tortured pines, the sheets of water cascading upon her back. But at last it ended, and she felt the exultation of survival. For a while, rain dripped from thinning clouds and then suddenly the sun was out again, scorching hot, raising curls of steam from the wet rocks. Again she undressed Opothle and herself to dry their clothing before the sun was gone. She also cleaned the child's cradleboard, and dried some moss and grass to reline it.

Next morning she was awakened by a cheerful mockingbird, which she considered a good sign until she discovered that the tender parts of her body were covered with insect bites. She ignored the itching and was in the saddle by sunrise. An hour or so later she found a branching trail, heading straight away from the rising sun. It was very narrow, and did not appear to be much used, but when she dismounted and studied the hooftracks and half-dry dung she guessed that four horses had passed along it

the previous day. As she settled back into her saddle, a dark blue
hawk appeared suddenly above her, circling and darting,
screaming a piercing call. "Go back, go back!" it seemed to be
crying. Her skin quivered and she felt that same terror of the
imagination that had gripped her during the storm.

"But where can I go back to?" she asked aloud, and Opothle
tried to reply to her question, using the four or five words that
he had learned from her. She started the pony forward, and the
hawk became more agitated, diving and screeching until at last
it sped away in a straight course toward the highest of the distant hills thrusting up beyond the thick forest below.

She soon forgot the hawk; she was entranced by the wild
grandeur of the country through which she was passing. In open
meadows she sighted large flocks of turkeys and herds of deer.
She wanted fresh meat, but her only weapon—the pistol—was
useless for hunting.

By late afternoon the trail had shrunk to little more than a
pathway covered with green moss, showing no signs of recent
passage. It brought her to a wide stream swollen by recent rains,
but she could see the pebbled bottom and forced the reluctant
pony into the swift waters. About halfway across, its front feet
plunged downward, almost throwing her from the saddle, and
then the pony was afloat. She had to swim three or four yards
with Opothle in the cradle on her back. As soon as she reached
the bank, she rushed downstream to catch the frightened pony's
bridle and lead it ashore. She was dismayed to discover that the
saddlepack was gone. She searched along the bank but found
only the sodden blanket which contained her pistol, extra moccasins, mirror, and knife. Her food supply was gone. Worst of all,
the trail she had been following seemed to have ended at the
stream.

She found a pine log, recently downed by a windstorm, and
used it as a drying place for wet clothing and the blanket and its
contents. The child was fretful, being afflicted with numerous insect bites also, and the drying effect of the sun made the red
spots itch like fire. She sat on the log with the half-dried blanket
around her hips, disconsolate because she no longer had a trail

to follow and acutely feeling pangs of hunger. She knew she had nothing to eat and would soon have to search for berries and roots. She was scratching at insect bites under her knees and watching a dragonfly skimming across a pool of water when she heard the snapping of a twig behind her.

Before she could turn, a strong arm encircled her breasts and held her tight. At the same instant a hand covered her nose and mouth. Her first thought was of the hawk keening to her that morning: "Go back, go back!" The next moment she feared for Opothle; the boy was in his cradle, propped against the log, crying himself to sleep.

"*Akusa?*" a deep voice breathed behind her. "Creek?"

She managed to nod her head. The arm that was crushing her breasts was encircled with a silver band bearing an eagle design.

"Where are the others?" the male voice asked in Cherokee.

She shook her head violently, pulling away as the hand released her. The man's face came into her view. "*Tsalagi,* Cherokee," she said, looking him straight in the eyes. She found no warmth there. His eyes were those of a hunter regarding a captured animal.

4

"You may wonder," Dane said, "how they understood each other, the Cherokee speaking Iroquoian, and the Creek speaking Muskogean. But the two tribes had been making war and making peace for as long as anyone could remember. In peacetimes they traded and visited and played ball games—so they learned a good amount of each other's language. Creek Mary, as you know, spoke English quite well and the Long Warrior—the Cherokee who had captured her—knew most of the English trading terms. In addition they both knew a mixture of Chickasaw-Choctaw jargon, somewhat comparable to your pidgin English, that was used all over the Southeast at that time. And so they had no trouble making themselves understood."

Except for the damp blanket around her middle and the coin gorget hanging between her breasts, she was unclothed. "Release me," she commanded angrily, and to her surprise he obeyed her. She quickly draped the blanket around her shoulders.

"Where are the others?" the Long Warrior repeated. "Your people."

She knew there was no point in pretending there were others. "My son and I travel alone," she replied. "We are going to Menewa's village."

He laughed scornfully. "Menewa, that sore-arsed old bear of the *Akusas*?"

"More times than once Menewa and his warriors have sent the Cherokees running like frightened old women," she retorted.

"He told you that?" The Long Warrior was standing with hands on hips looking down at her with his piercing eyes. He wore a dark red turban with an eagle feather in it over lustrous black hair that was longer than she was accustomed to seeing on male Creeks. She knew he was a Cherokee chief because of the eagle feather and the eagles on his armband. He also wore a sleeveless buckskin waistcoat, English traders' trousers, and muddy leggings. He was taller than most Creek males. "When I was a boy," he said casually, "we drove Menewa's warriors from these hills and built new towns here. I will take you to my town."

"I am going to Menewa's village," she said defiantly.

He turned and whistled, and another Cherokee appeared from

behind a screen of brush and vines. He was leading four horses, two of them laden with trade goods—cloth, blankets, axes, and gunpowder. "*Akusa*," the Long Warrior told him. "Alone as we thought."

The other man smiled at her, one corner of his mouth twisting oddly. He had a scar running from his mouth to his left ear. Never taking his eyes from her, he leisurely fastened the four horses to a tree and then walked over to her pony. "Choctaw," he said. "Good. I like." Then he came to the pine log, methodically examining the flintlock pistol, the knife, and the mirror. "I like," he said.

"The woman is mine, Qualla," the Long Warrior declared.

"And whose is this?" Qualla asked, picking up Opothle's cradle. The sleeping child awoke and began screaming at the sight of Qualla's unfamiliar face. "Look, look at this *Unega*, this paleskin." Qualla held the cradle up so that the Long Warrior could see. "How ugly it is."

"We'll leave the paleskin here," the Long Warrior said.

Mary pulled the cradle away from Qualla and took Opothle from it. The boy squirmed and kicked. The insect bites on his naked body had swollen into red blisters.

"The little jaybird is spotted," said the Long Warrior, coming closer. "Not smallpox. Chigoes. He screams because one is in his ear." For the first time his eyes softened. "We'll go and see the *adawehi*, the old healer priest, Bear Killer." He noticed the same bites on the tender flesh between Mary's breast and arm. "You also."

His fingers reached for the gorget. "What is this?" He gave it a jerk, but the silver chain held. With her free hand, she slapped him hard in the face. He did not flinch, but his eyes showed anger. She hated him at that moment because he held power over her, yet as she looked into his face, the olive skin barely scarred with old smallpox marks, she felt drawn to this stranger.

"You are a headman, a chief," she said.

"The Long Warrior of Okelogee." He smiled. "A moment ago

I wanted to strike you with a war club. But when you are without anger your speech is like the singing of birds."

"And yours is as guttural as a bad-tempered bear's."

"Who are you?"

"Amayi, the Beloved Woman of the Creeks."

"Your name is known to us. But you are still my captive. You know what that means."

"That depends upon the women of your town. They will decide."

Opothle broke into loud cries again. "Let's go," said the Long Warrior in a tone of disgust. "Your mewling paleskin, like his *Unega* father, wants something of ours."

Dane stopped his story to refill our coffee mugs. "When Grandmother Mary would tell me these things about Uncle Opothle," he said, "it was difficult for me to imagine him as a helpless child. When I first became aware of Opothle's existence, he was a sturdy man of about fifty, with a short beard turning gray, a man who valued his light skin so highly that when he went outside he avoided the sunlight whenever possible, wrapping his neck and lower face in kerchiefs and wearing a broad-brimmed hat. Being my only uncle, Cherokee clan law required him to look after me, but he rarely had anything to do with me. He may have been embarrassed that I had Cherokee blood while he did not—yet he considered himself to be of the Cherokee Nation. Very much so."

Dane tested the coffee and squinted off across the brightening Montana landscape. "Someone out there, looking for something," he said. His eyes were sixty years older than mine, yet it was all I could do to see the distant figure on horseback.

"But the first things she told me about her first view of Okelogee, the Long Warrior's town, seemed very real, because that is where I was born and grew up. The place changed very little, I suppose, during the half century between Grandmother Mary's arrival and my coming into the world. Except that it was burned by the Carolina militia after the War of the Revolution and had to be rebuilt, long before my time.

"To Mary the town itself was not much different from a Creek village, the windowless houses were solid, and all the families had an *asi*, a small winter house—I've heard white men call them oasts—they're quite like the sweat lodges of the Cheyennes. I think what most impressed her was the setting of the town, along the Little Singing Stream, and the mountain beyond that they called the Sleeping Woman. It was the first thing that everyone saw when they stepped from their doors in the mornings —that long low mountain shaped like a woman's body at rest, rounded head at the north end, a hollow for the neck, the swelling breasts and flat belly, and a narrow pinnacle at the south end shaped like a moccasined foot pointing to the sky. The sun always came up late in Okelogee, over the Sleeping Woman. There were bawdy tales about the Sun, the Moon, and the Sleeping Woman." His voice trailed off, as though he were jogging his memory.

"What did Mary mean when she told the Long Warrior that the women of his town would decide?" I asked. "Decide what?"

"Oh, yes. I've been getting ahead of myself. Old man's wanderings. It was customary then for the women of the Nation to decide what should be done with captives, especially female captives. They might be put to death, sold, ransomed, set free, or adopted into one of the clans. Females were usually sold or adopted. As she rode into Okelogee, Mary expected that the Cherokees would try to ransom her and Opothle to Menewa.

"The first thing the Long Warrior and Qualla did was take her to Bear Killer, the old *adawehi* who very gently smeared the insect bites with some kind of smelly grease that eased the itching immediately. He then blew herbal smoke into Opothle's ailing ear and soon had the child laughing instead of crying. By this time it was dark and she was taken to a house for the night.

"She soon learned that the Long Warrior's wife had died some months before in one of the smallpox epidemics that periodically swept through the villages, usually following a visit by white traders from Carolina. After his wife's death, ownership of the house was in dispute—Cherokee wives always owned the dwelling houses. The Long Warrior's sister-in-law moved in, claiming it and perhaps expecting the chief to make her his wife, but instead he brought in his two sisters. There were hard feelings between these women, and Mary took it as a bad sign that all of them resented her presence there. The first night she forced herself to stay awake, and after everyone was asleep she took Opothle and slipped outside to run away. But her Choctaw pony was gone from the hitching post, and she could see someone sitting in the shadows of the house across the way, evidently watching her. So she went back to her bed.

"She slept soundly until dawn, felt much better, and went outside into a beautiful cool morning to bathe in the stream and watch the sun coming up over the Sleeping Woman. She often said that she had a feeling then that she had lived in this place, long before, and had come home after an absence of many years.

"That day the business of deciding what to do about the Long Warrior's captive woman began to occupy the time and thoughts of all the adults in Okelogee. The women met in the council house, the men met in the council house, the women and men met together in the council house. Mary had no idea what they were talking about, but she was beginning to find out that among the Cherokees everyone was equal, women as well as men, and that no one could force anyone else to take action. Not even the headman. All that the Long Warrior could do was try to persuade, but Mary was not sure what he wanted to persuade them to do. They simply had to keep talking until they reached an agreement, and the debates went on evening after evening, leaving her free to wander around the place, but if she tried to walk outside the town, Qualla was always there, usually mounted on her Choctaw pony, smiling his crooked smile.

"One evening the Long Warrior came to the house, bringing a large watermelon and inviting her to join him under a brush arbor outside. He broke the melon open and handed her a juicy piece of the heart. It was the sweetest watermelon she had ever tasted. He told her then that the people of Okelogee had made a decision. His jealous sister-in-law (who at that moment was peering out at them from inside the door of the house) had wanted to sell her to the Catawbas so that she would be taken far out of the country. But the sister-in-law had been overruled. The Cherokees had agreed to give the Beloved Woman of the Creeks her liberty. At dawn of the next day, she and her child were free to go wherever she chose.

"The Long Warrior suggested that she stay in Okelogee, pointing out that she would have more freedom as a Cherokee woman than as a Creek queen. Mary replied that she was content with the freedom of the Cherokees, but she was Creek and must go back to her people. He was disappointed, he said, and if this was to be her last night in Okelogee he would consider it as a gift of remembrance to sleep with her and keep her warm against the chill of the night air. The summer nights in Okelogee, she replied, were warm enough already. He then rudely accused her of being afraid the barbarous Creeks would cut her ears off for being an adulteress. They were soon quarreling, she accusing the Cherokees of selling Creek lands to the Georgia colonists, and he boasting that the Cherokees were more clever than the Creeks because they knew how to fool the Georgians. It ended when he tried again to take the Danish coin from around her neck. She fought him fiercely, both rolling on the ground in close embrace until she scratched blood from his face. He strode away, angrily cursing the stubbornness of all Creek women."

5

Before dark Qualla appeared with her Choctaw pony, saying nothing, but smiling that sideways smirk of his. He presented her with her pistol, knife, and mirror, and a saddlepack filled with dried corn bread and *gahawisita*, parched corn ground into a meal which when mixed with water made an instant gruel. She slept little that night and was up before daylight, saddling the pony and preparing to depart. She had just fastened Opothle's cradle to her back when a horseman rode slowly out of the gray light.

"*Siyu,*" the Long Warrior greeted her. "Hello."

"You did not sleep well?" she said with a bite of sarcasm in her voice.

"I brought you fresh *anuh,*" he said. "Strawberries." He dismounted and offered her a wild strawberry from a basket. She opened her mouth and he put the berry between her teeth. It was light enough now so that she could see his smile and the dried marks of her fingernails on his coppery cheek.

He helped her into the saddle. "I will go with you to the main trail," he said, "so that you do not become lost again."

"*Astu.*" She used the Cherokee word. "Very good."

He led the way out of the town. When they topped the first ridge west, she turned to take a last look at the Sleeping Woman, silhouetted against the brightening dawn sky. She felt as though she were losing something forever.

It was early afternoon when they reached the Flint Path turning southward toward Creek country. He pulled his horse to one side and motioned down the broad trail. As she passed him, he bowed to her and she returned the gesture, urging the pony to a faster pace and never looking back.

During the afternoon, whenever she halted, she sometimes thought she heard hoofbeats, but when she looked back she saw no sign of a horseman. Late in the day she came to a small grassy glade beside a clear-running stream, and stopped for the night. She unsaddled and tied up the pony and was feeding Opothle when she heard the hoofbeats again. This time she saw the horseman. The Long Warrior was approaching slowly.

"*Siyu*," he greeted her. "It will be cold tonight under the stars. I meant to give you this bearskin." He dismounted, unfastening a bundle. "A farewell present."

He spread an enormous black bearskin across the grass. "You will need a fire." He gathered dry sticks and started a fire with flint and steel. He added wood slowly, building up a bed of coals until twilight darkened the glade. She came and lay on the bearskin, looking into the fire.

"Time for me to go back," he said, and removed his moccasins, passing them back and forth over the low flames.

"You believe that will keep snakes from biting you?" she asked.

"It has always done so for me." When he stood up, she pulled half the bearskin over her. "*Egasinu*," he said. "Go to sleep, Amayi. The fire will keep you warm."

"There is a fire in my loins," she said.

He kneeled beside her and rolled the bearskin back. She was naked. "*Agiya*, my beloved," he whispered.

"*Asgaya, asgaya*." She used the Cherokee. "Man, man." Then she raised herself, looking him hard in the face. "I will not be your property, but a friend and companion."

"*Astu*," he said, and took the Danish coin in his fingers. "*Asehi*, surely—"

She reached behind her neck, unfastened the silver chain and took the gorget off so that there was nothing between them. Then she rubbed her cheek against the dried scratches on his face and rolled with him into the bearskin.

6

"Well, the next day they returned to Okelogee," Dane said, "and began the long slow process of getting Mary fully accepted into the Cherokee Nation through adoption by one of the clans. The first thing the Long Warrior did was move his sister-in-law and two sisters out of the house so that it would belong to Mary as his wife. I use the word *wife* although there were no Cherokee words then for *husband* and *wife*. A man and woman simply decided to cohabit and the union was as strong as a marriage, with unwritten rights and duties of sharing. But if one or the other decided the union was unsuitable, he or she dissolved it by moving out, by taking 'half of the blanket.' That was the way Mary dissolved her marriage with John Kingsley. She moved out, taking her blanket, and although by the laws of Georgia she was still wedded to Kingsley, by the laws of the Creeks and Cherokees she was not."

"Whatever happened to Kingsley?" I asked.

"She never learned for certain. Some months after becoming a Cherokee she heard that her people had been moved from Bluff Village up to the Double Branch, but another trader replaced Kingsley. She heard rumors that he had fallen into disfavor with the Georgia Trustees and had been returned to England. What happened to him after that she never knew. Although she considered him a traitor to the Creeks, I think no one ever heard her speak ill of John Kingsley after leaving him. And her people did not remain for long at the Double Branch. The soil was poor there and they moved of their own will to one of the villages in

Menewa's Creek confederacy. She was to see them again there on two momentous visits."

"What did Mary have to do to become accepted by the Cherokees?"

"Most of the doing was on the Long Warrior's part. He had to persuade one of the seven clans to adopt her so that she would have Cherokee rights, and this was not easy. He was *Anikawi*, the Deer clan, with considerable influence among them, but blood law forbade marriage to a member of his own clan even though they might not be related. His first wife had been *Aniwadi*, the Paint clan, but his sister-in-law blocked efforts to have the Paints adopt Mary. Finally Qualla, of the Wolf clan, used his sly skills as a diplomat and Mary was adopted and became a Wolf."

"And so you must be a Wolf."

"No, no indeed. My father was a Wolf, of course, being Mary's son. But he married a girl of the Bird clan and so I am a Bird." He laughed. "The Cherokees believe in the power of women. We know who our mothers are but are never certain about our fathers."

"You said that the Long Warrior's sister-in-law opposed Mary's becoming a Paint. Did she cause Mary trouble in other ways?"

"For a time. She was jealous because she had wanted the Long Warrior for herself. She spoke ill of Mary and tried to make her an outcast, but her efforts created disharmony in the community and Cherokees cherish harmony above all things. After a while the sister-in-law found that she herself was becoming an outcast, and so she changed her attitude immediately. Cherokees can't abide being outcasts. After a few weeks the sister-in-law and Mary became friends.

"Another thing that the Long Warrior had to do was find a 'brother' for Mary so that she would have someone to protect her and look after her children. Cherokee fathers had no rights over their children and usually left their guidance in the hands of an uncle, one of the mother's brothers. Qualla was my grandfather's closest friend, and so naturally it was he who was pressed into this duty, and he must have served well. My father, Talasi the Runner, often told me that while he was growing up Qualla was his truest adult friend.

"Not until the Runner was born was Mary accepted by everybody in Okelogee. But she said that what put the crown on her head as a Cherokee was a visit paid by Ghigua, the Beloved Woman of the Cherokees. The War of the Revolution was just beginning about that time. Ghigua journeyed down from the Hiwassee country, visiting the Georgia Cherokees to persuade them to join the colonists in their war against the British soldiers. She happened to be of the Wolf clan, and had heard about Mary, the Beloved Woman of the Creeks. She went to see her first, before going to the council house to make her speech. The two women were of about the same age, and got along like old friends. Ghigua welcomed Mary into the Cherokee Nation and insisted that they smoke together from her long pipe sheathed in speckled snakeskin.

"But when Ghigua tried to enlist Mary on the side of the colonists, she would have no part of that. She hated British soldiers well enough, she said, but she had no love for the Anglo-Americans either. They were all the same, she said, land-thieves and cheaters and murderers of Creeks and Cherokees and the other tribes. Let them destroy each other. Ghigua must have been disappointed in Mary, but she had no better luck with the Okelogee council. At that time the fighting was too far away for the Georgia Cherokees to be concerned with it.

"What brought it closer was a company of Scots soldiers that a British commander sent over into the mountains and then must have forgotten about. The Scotsmen built a permanent camp with strong fortifications somewhere east of the Sleeping Woman, but from time to time their supply lines would be cut by the Carolina militia and they had no way of obtaining food except to hunt wild game—which was becoming scarce—and to barter with the Cherokees. Every so often a party of Scots dressed in their splendid uniforms would come over to Okelogee to trade for corn and squash and beans or whatever food the Cherokees could spare. As the soldiers had no coffee or tea,

Mary showed them how to make black drink from holly leaves—the Cherokees kept a few bushes transplanted from Carolina for that purpose—the leaves contain caffeine stronger than in this coffee we are drinking.

"One day about a dozen of those foraging Scots came running into the town, their faces red from exertion. They had barely escaped ambush by the Carolina militia, who were in hot pursuit. Almost all the Cherokee men were out hunting that day, but Mary and some of the other women concealed the soldiers in their winter houses, root cellars, corncribs, and lofts. The militiamen surrounded the town, but they found not a trace of those Scotsmen.

"When the Long Warrior heard about this, he became very angry. The border militia would destroy Okelogee if they found out the women had protected British soldiers, he said. At the council meeting that evening he proposed that no more food be traded to the British soldiers, but the women hooted him down. Since the outbreak of the Revolution, white traders seldom came as far as Okelogee and the women needed the pots and pans and knives and other things they could obtain from the soldiers.

"North of the Hiwassee River, the Upper Cherokees were having a very hard time of it. Some of the chiefs had been armed by the British and they led their warriors out to fight the Anglo-Americans. Most of the others were neutral. A few like Ghigua were sympathetic toward the colonists.

"In that time there was no single leader of the Cherokees. Oh, some headmen of a few neighboring towns would band together, one of them acting as leader. Old Tassel was one, but the Cherokees were so opposed to any interference with their personal liberties that they distrusted any strong leader. Consequently the separate towns were unable to defend themselves. When raiding parties of militia would storm out of the white border settlements, they would burn the first Cherokee town they came to, not caring whether the inhabitants were for the British, neutral, or sympathetic toward the colonists. The war, in fact, gave these Anglo-Americans an opportunity to drive all the Cherokees out of lands they coveted for settlement.

"Only once during the war was Okelogee threatened with destruction. One day a force of mounted border ruffians came
dashing into the town, their fur-capped leader brandishing a
burning pine torch. He shouted out a warning that if a single
British soldier was found concealed in the town he would set fire
to every house and outbuilding. Mary had a hard time holding
her tongue while the invaders were ransacking her house. They
found nothing, and rode off. Not long afterward the Long Warrior came in and admitted that he had helped the Scots soldiers
save a pack train of supplies from being captured by the border
militia. He had led the Redcoats and their train down a creek
bed and into the safety of a cave. The frustrated border raiders,
suspecting that Cherokees had been involved, had given up pursuit and tried to find them in Okelogee.

"Although the town escaped destruction during the Revolution, it was not so fortunate a few years later. For the Cherokees,
the war did not end with the surrender of Cornwallis and the
colonists' victorious treaty of peace. With an end to their
fighting, the Anglo-Americans claimed all the land to the Mississippi River. They accused the Cherokees of helping the British—
although most did not—and forced them to cede great tracts of
land. But even this was not enough. The whites kept pushing
their settlements westward, crowding upon the Cherokee towns.
If the Cherokees made any resistance at all, the border militia
would use this as an excuse to burn the nearest town.

"Those north of Okelogee, along the Hiwassee and the Tennessee, were the first to suffer. Old Tassel was murdered by
raiders who approached him under a truce flag. His half-blood
nephew, John Watts, who chose the name Young Tassel, tried to
organize all the Cherokee towns into one defensive force. He
sent the people of Okelogee a bundle of bloody arrows and a
scalping knife with a message for them to 'take up the hatchet'
and join him in a war against the border settlers.

"The Long Warrior and the Okelogee council were still debat-
ing what to do about this when a mob of raiders came riding
into the town early one morning. Mary recognized their leader
as the same fur-capped ruffian who had threatened them with a

pine torch during the war. This time several of the riders were carrying torches and without any warning they began setting fire to the houses.

"Taken by surprise, there was no way the people could defend themselves. Flight was the only way to escape being killed. About all that Mary saved from the house was that big black bearskin given her by the Long Warrior. He had to force her to leave, dragging her along by one arm while Opothle was carrying Talisi the Runner. They crossed the Little Singing Stream, leaving Okelogee in flames behind them. The raiders took all the horses, including Mary's beloved Choctaw pony.

"The Long Warrior led his numbed and dispirited people westward to the Chickamauga country where they found friends in a little town known as Cedar Tree. Other refugee Cherokees had come there from the northeast, and everybody had to work hard to build temporary shelters of poles and bark and to find enough food to keep from starving. Luckily for them, this all happened during the warm months of the year.

"All the time that the people from Okelogee were struggling to feed, shelter, and clothe themselves, they were planning revenge against the border raiders. Mary's fury against the whites was so keen that she announced she was going south to seek help from the Creeks. To keep her from leaving her children, the Long Warrior sent a messenger to Menewa. Two weeks later, to his great surprise, more than a hundred Creek warriors arrived at Cedar Tree. Menewa sent his regrets to Mary that he could not come himself. He was too busy fighting off the white settlers. The Creek towns were suffering the same ruthless attacks that the Cherokees were—raiders galloping in to burn houses, trample crops, steal horses, and then dashing away.

"With the Creek warriors on hand, the Okelogee Cherokees could no longer delay action. They knew that somewhere north along the Tennessee, Young Tassel and his war chief, Taltsuska, had united five towns and were making preparations to retaliate by carrying the war into the white settlements. The Long Warrior and his Cherokees and Creeks packed what food they could find and started north. Mary wanted to go with them, but there was no one to look after Opothle and Talasi the Runner. Her children were of more import to her than following the men to war, and so she remained at Cedar Tree. She watched them depart, the Creeks mounted, most of the Cherokees on foot, shouting and singing their war songs."

7

Of the events that occurred during the Long Warrior's military undertaking against the border invaders, Dane was not too assured as to details and chronology. He had heard fragments of incidents told by his grandmother and by others, and he cautioned me that not only were the stories vague by the time they were told to him, but that much more time had passed since he had heard them.

In the early years of his manhood, the Long Warrior had fought a number of little skirmishes with Catawbas and Creeks, but his big war, the adventure of his life, was the war that he participated in against the border settlements. After it was over, at the Cherokees' annual Green Corn ceremonies he would join with the other survivors of that ordeal in relating deeds of bravery and superhuman exploits until the incidents became a mythical saga in his memory. This was the part of the Long Warrior's life that Creek Mary most envied, because she experienced the events only vicariously, resenting the enforced tediousness of her own existence at Cedar Tree with two young sons while he traveled on a path of glory and excitement.

In truth, as she was to learn eventually, the Long Warrior

loathed most of the episodes of that violent undertaking while they were actually occurring. It was only in retrospect that a luster of grandeur grew around them, glowing into legend with the telling and retelling through the passage of time.

Years afterward, when she would tell Dane of his grandfather's great adventure, she would laugh while relating his confessed dislike for going into battle naked except for a loin flap. Red and black war paint did not keep off the cold, he said. The fighting began in the Big Chestnut Moon in the chilly foothills of the Smoky Mountains and lasted until the next spring, a time of year that no sensible Cherokee would choose to fight a war. More than once he took the coat off a dead militiaman to stop his shivering, always discarding it before the next battle. He knew that fighting naked decreased the danger from wounds. A bit of clothing driven into a wound by a bullet or an arrow made healing difficult, was often fatal. He resigned himself to fighting naked in the bitter cold, but he hated it.

When they left Cedar Tree early in the Moon of Black Butterflies and went up the Tennessee Valley, the Long Warrior and his followers found Young Tassel, or John Watts, camped along a small tributary of the river. A thousand Cherokees were gathered there, almost all victims of border raids, and they were burning for revenge. Young Tassel's war leader was Taltsuska, who proudly used the name Bullhead, which had been given him by his white enemies. Although only slightly older than Young Tassel, Bullhead was the latter's uncle, the brother of the murdered Old Tassel. Another of Bullhead's brothers, Pumpkin Boy, had recently been killed while fighting a raiding party from the Knoxville settlement, and on the day that the Long Warrior met him Bullhead was in a fierce and sullen mood.

The war leader's head was shaved except for a narrow frizzed crest beginning at the crown and widening to the back of his head and ending in a long plait ornamented with silver quills. He wore a tiny brass cross affixed to the lobe of his left ear, and carried a pair of silver-mounted pistols that he had taken from a luckless British officer in the War of the Revolution. During the next few days the Long Warrior heard rumors that after slaying the British officer, Bullhead had chopped the man's body into small pieces and eaten some of them in a savage blood ceremony.

Bullhead and Young Tassel had decided to prepare for war in the same way their enemies did, by drilling the men to fire by command, and for several days the warriors who had come there from Cedar Tree had to march in formations up and down a rough drill field alongside a creek. It all seemed very foolish to the Long Warrior, but he had committed himself to the war and in council with the leading chiefs he reluctantly agreed to this new way of fighting. Qualla and another veteran warrior from Okelogee, the Stalking Turkey, made strong protests, but they were overruled. The object of war, the Stalking Turkey declared, was to gain honors through individual exploits, and this would be difficult if not impossible to accomplish if the Cherokees marched upon their enemies as the white men did, standing and firing by commands. Bullhead angrily replied that the object of this war was to terrorize the white settlers and drive them out of the Cherokee lands, and this could best be accomplished by attacking them in strong formations.

Early in the Big Chestnut Moon, Young Tassel named the day they would march out on the old military trace that led toward Knoxville, giving the warriors three days to make their preparations. All the women who had accompanied their men to camp were ordered to leave during the purification ceremonies, and supplies of *gahawisita*, dried corn bread, and moccasins and sinew were rolled into blankets. The men stripped to their breechcloths and painted themselves red and black. The *adawehi* packed live coals in a clay container to ensure good luck on the march.

On the morning of departure, Bullhead circled the drill field three times alone, beating slowly on a drum, and the thousand warriors then assembled in ranks facing Young Tassel, who addressed them. "My fighting brothers: Our enemies the *Unegas*, the border settlers, have made the Path bloody between us. Let us leave this place with great courage. Have strong hearts, never shut your ears, have no fear of the cold. Never show fear to the *Unegas,* our enemies, but let them see that you are men and true warriors. Use all your powder and lead, all your arrows, and then strike and kill until your war clubs are drunk with the blood of the *Unegas.* Then, if it is necessary to escape, do not hesitate to throw yourselves into the water to conceal your retreat well."

Young Tassel raised his right arm and Bullhead began beating again on his drum. They marched out single file, armed with their old trade guns, bows, tomahawks, and war clubs, their supplies rolled in the blankets slung across their naked backs. When they reached the military trace that led eastward toward Knoxville—their main objective—Bullhead shouted them into formations and they marched along like British Redcoats on parade.

The next morning scouts were sent forward, and when they came hurrying back to report a force of mounted border raiders approaching on the trace, Bullhead sent his warriors wheeling off into the woods to form semicircles on each side of the road. The *Unegas,* dressed in fur caps and hunting shirts, well armed with long rifles, came riding recklessly along. Hidden behind a clump of sumac bushes, the Long Warrior put his rifle sights on a big bearded man and thought how stupid the raiders were to be riding so close together in the open.

A moment later the shrill call of a bobwhite sounded from across the road, and Bullhead's deep voice responded with a quick command to fire. The volley cut into the raiders, lead and arrows hitting riders and horses, the animals rearing and screaming. Bullhead led his warriors out with their war clubs. Less than half of the border men got their mounts turned around and started back down the trace, and for a hundred yards they had to run a gauntlet of fire that took a dozen of them from their saddles.

Even so, Bullhead considered the ambush a failure because enough of the enemy escaped to race back to the nearest blockhouse and give warning of their approach. When the Long Warrior came out on the road, Bullhead was scalping one of the dead raiders. The war chief's morose face looked evil under its smear of paint. Although Qualla and the Stalking Turkey joined in the scalping, the Long Warrior had no taste for it that day, and he waited impatiently for the march to resume.

Late in the afternoon the scouts warned of a formidable blockhouse in the next valley. The chiefs held council and decided to approach it from a forested ridgetop. Filing off into the woods, the warriors resumed their old way of stalking the enemy, keeping well apart, and moving as quietly as possible.

When they were all assembled on the ridgetop, the Long Warrior and Qualla volunteered to scout the blockhouse below. By the time they worked their way down the rocky hillside, twilight was deepening over the valley, and the white families who lived in the blockhouse were gathering their cattle in from the meadows. Women and children were running nervously about, unlocking and locking gates and shouting at the animals, while the men carried rifles and kept an alert watch all around.

The Long Warrior counted only twenty men before the gates were closed on the stockade. "They are mostly women and children down there," he said.

"Yes," Qualla replied. "Their men paid today for stealing Cherokee ground."

"All the ground is Cherokee to the Knoxville station. But I do not kill women and children even though they be *Unegas*."

"Have you forgotten what they did to us at Okelogee?"

"Their women and children did not burn our houses," the Long Warrior said. "And their men did not kill us."

"They would have killed us had we not run. They have killed many of our people in the Tennessee country."

The Long Warrior shook his head. "At the council I shall speak for passing by this blockhouse station and throwing all our force upon the garrison at Knoxville. Without the goods that come from the Knoxville storehouses, these little stations will wither and die like gourds on a cut vine."

During the council, however, only a few of the chiefs supported the Long Warrior's proposal. Bullhead and Young Tassel both spoke for attacking the blockhouse and burning it to ashes.

These *Unegas* had been too bold, they said, penetrating so far into Cherokee country.

After collecting several pine knots for torches, they waited until it was late enough for the people in the blockhouse to be asleep and then they crept down the slope, surrounding the stockade. The cattle inside the gates must have sensed their presence, for they began moving restlessly around. A few moments later the quick flash of a gunlock showed in one of the portholes and a warning shot broke the silence. At Bullhead's command the warriors who carried torches lighted them and rushed the stockade, some trying to set fire to the heavy logs, others throwing their firebrands upon the roof of the blockhouse.

The Long Warrior was in the second wave of attackers. He ran to a porthole and fired blindly inside. He ducked low, and through a tiny crack between the logs he could see a white man lunging toward the porthole out of the smoke and flames of the burning pine knots. There was no time to reload. The Long Warrior reached for his war club, and as soon as he saw the rifle muzzle thrusting out, he struck the end of it with all his power. He heard the crunch of gunstock against flesh and bone, and then a muffled voice cried out in pain. Kneeling, the Long Warrior began reloading his rifle.

Down the farthest end of the stockade, one of the Creeks had climbed to the top and was shooting arrows into the defenders below. Rifle fire from inside the blockhouse knocked the Creek to the ground. A volley from the loft of the blockhouse rained bullets into one of Bullhead's formations, felling half a dozen warriors. The defenders were first-rate marksmen, and they had far better weapons than the Cherokees and Creeks. After another volley from the loft, Young Tassel gave the signal for withdrawal to the wooded ridge. The chief's arm was bleeding from a flesh wound, and while the *adawehi* was dressing it and chanting a healing song, the other leaders gathered around him and a fire that someone had started. The casualties had been counted. One Creek and three Cherokees were dead. Several had been wounded.

"The Long Warrior spoke wisely," Young Tassel said. "If we

fight against all the garrisoned stations between here and Knoxville, we will lose much blood for nothing. I speak now for passing around the blockhouses until we are ready to strike at the
Knoxville settlement." He looked at Bullhead, who was sitting
with his long chin pressed against his chest, watching the Long
Warrior across the firelight.

"If this chief who comes to us from Okelogee is so wise
a man," Bullhead said in his deep voice, "then he should lead us
to Knoxville."

The Long Warrior spoke up. "I am not a war chief. Bullhead
has made his name known across the Cherokee land as a leader
of warriors. I say that Bullhead is our war chief who will show
us the way to Knoxville."

Bullhead's heavy lips parted in a grimace. "I know what they
say of me—that I have eaten a great quantity of white men's
flesh, that I have had so much of it I am tired of it, and think it
too salty." He laughed, but the others remained silent.

Young Tassel, the half-blood, waited a moment. "It is agreed,
then? We march around the stations until we reach Knoxville?"

"So be it," Bullhead said, his heavy-lidded eyes still fixed on
the Long Warrior.

As soon as the dead were buried under piles of marked stones
—so that their relatives could come and find them after the flesh
was gone and the bones had dried—the war party left the ridge
and filed off toward the rising sun. All through that day they
kept to the forests, avoiding roads and stations.

At dusk Bullhead held council and it was decided to bivouac
until midnight and then move up quietly in the darkness to the
Knoxville storehouses, set them afire, and attack the surprised
garrison. But Bullhead either misjudged the distance or the rate
of movement of his large force. The eastern sky was brightening
when the advance sighted a small blockhouse a few miles outside of the Knoxville settlement.

At about the same time, three white men came out of the
blockhouse and saw the approaching warriors. One of them hurriedly began saddling a horse, but Bullhead sent several of the
mounted Creeks racing ahead and they killed the man before he

had galloped a hundred yards toward Knoxville. The other two *Unegas* retreated within the blockhouse and closed the portal.

The Long Warrior went forward to consult with Young Tassel. Almost the entire force was now gathered in a field of corn stubble facing the blockhouse. "That is Cavett's Station," Young Tassel said. "Before we can strike Knoxville, full daylight will be upon us."

"Then we must conceal ourselves in the woods for another day," the Long Warrior said.

Bullhead, who had come striding back, overheard his suggestion. "First we will kill all the *Unegas* in this station," he growled. "Or they will warn their Knoxville brothers." As he finished speaking the sound of a cannon reverberated across the hills from Knoxville. Bullhead grunted angrily. "They have already been warned," he said.

"That was only the garrison's sunrise gun," said Young Tassel. He glanced at the Long Warrior. "But we must silence the Cavetts."

"Should there be heavy firing," said the Long Warrior, "the Knoxville militia will be warned of our presence. Perhaps if we take cover—"

Bullhead's interrupting voice was harsh: "We attack the Cavetts now." He did not wait for any further discussion. He signaled the warriors to surround the small blockhouse and begin the attack.

Although the defenders kept up a steady fire from their loopholes for several minutes, killing five Cherokees, they were so far outnumbered that they soon showed a white flag and asked for a parley. Young Tassel, Bullhead, and the Long Warrior approached the stockade.

"Who are your chiefs?" a voice demanded from inside.

Young Tassel named the leaders and called on the defenders to surrender.

"You are John Watts, then?"

"My white father gave me that name," Young Tassel replied.

"I am Alexander Cavett. We will cease resistance if you will allow us to go unharmed to the Knoxville station."

"You will be held as prisoners until we have destroyed Knox-ville," Young Tassel declared.

There was a long silence, and then Cavett answered: "Should you fail in your purpose, will you guarantee the safety of our women and children?"

"We will not fail in our purpose," Young Tassel cried. "If you want to live, leave your arms in the blockhouse and come out and surrender to us."

A minute passed and then the portal was opened. Two men, three women, and seven children filed out into the morning sun-shine. They were without weapons of any kind.

"These are all?" Young Tassel asked.

Cavett nodded his head.

Bullhead frowned, and beckoning to three of his warriors, led them into the blockhouse for a search. They all carried war clubs with sharp metal spikes. When they came back outside, each man brought several long rifles. At a low command from Bull-head they dropped the captured rifles on the ground and rushed upon the backs of the unsuspecting prisoners, using their spiked war clubs to crush their victims' skulls. The Long Warrior after-ward said that he could not believe he was witnessing so foul a deed. He was so sickened by Bullhead's attack upon the defense-less women and children that for a moment he was unable to move. Then he leaped forward and seized the youngest boy in his arms, saving him from Bullhead's war club.

"You are a child killer, a savage!" he shouted into Bullhead's contorted face.

Bullhead snarled: "Is not that what the *Unegas* call us? Is it not better that we savages kill *Unegas* than let them live to kill us? You are a softhearted old woman, you who ran away from them at Okelogee."

The Long Warrior reached for his war club, but Young Tassel caught his arm. "We *Tsalagi* must not kill each other!" he cried, and there was disgust on his face when he looked at Bullhead. "The lookouts have warned us that militia from Knoxville are marching to fight us. Go and make your warriors ready."

Except for the young boy that the Long Warrior had rescued,

the surrendered prisoners were all dead, their skulls smashed by the war clubs of Bullhead and his three warriors.

During that morning there was heavy fighting between the Knoxville soldiers and the combined force of Cherokees and Creeks. At times, the opponents battled at close range, and the Long Warrior tried to find a way to let his young captive escape safely to the militia, but he finally had to conceal the boy in a brush-filled gully, warning him to stay there until the fighting ended. After the soldiers withdrew to Knoxville, the Long Warrior went back to the place of concealment. He found the boy lying there with his arms spread wide, his small hands clenched, his face split open by a tomahawk.

That night the Long Warrior thought a long time about the meaning of savagery. Once he had argued with Creek Mary about the meaning of savagery. He had believed in the purity of being savage, but she had said that savagery was neither pure nor impure. "We are all savages," she had said, "down beneath the skin, no matter the color of the skin, down there we are all fierce, cruel, bloodthirsty as the beasts. It is a part of the balance of nature." Perhaps she was speaking the truth, he thought.

There was much savagery through the remainder of that autumn and on into the Windy and Duck-Killing moons. Out of the valleys of the Clinch, the Holston, and the French Broad rivers came hundreds of border men led by Nolichucky Jack Sevier, who hated all Indians. When the Cherokees and Creeks set ambushes, they found that their old smoothbore trade guns were no match for the frontiersmen's longer-ranged and more-accurate rifled guns.

Driven south to the Hiwassee Valley, Bullhead and Young Tassel divided their forces in a try for entrapment, but Sevier's militia cut them entirely apart and they never united again. The Long Warrior's men and the Creeks tried to stay with Young Tassel across the Lower Blue Ridge, but again the border men scattered them. Many a warrior's bones were left to dry in those high hills. In a close encounter, Qualla received a bad leg wound that would not heal, and the Stalking Turkey's right eye was blinded. They later became separated from the other Okelogee men and although the Long Warrior led a search for them, he could find no trace of either one.

The loss of his two good friends darkened his spirits, and he began brooding over the defeats suffered by the Cherokees and their Creek allies. Was this a warning of worse evils to come in the future? Were the tribes doomed by the mighty power of the white men?

With the coming of springtime the shrinking remnant of mounted Creeks decided to go home. In the Cherokees' last fight with the border men, a small skirmish along the Etowah, they had no weapons left but bows and arrows. They were badly routed. "We did not run," the Long Warrior always said of this fight, "we only walked very fast."

In the first days of the Strawberry Moon, the Long Warrior decided they could fight no more. They had no food other than what they could find in the forests, and their last moccasins were worn out. And so they started back for Cedar Tree, dreading what they might find there. They had been driven far south of their old home country, and on the way north the Long Warrior suggested that they follow the Flint Trace and see what was left of Okelogee.

As they came over the last ridge and faced the Sleeping Woman, for the first time since his childhood the Long Warrior felt tears in his eyes. He held his breath, looking down into that beautiful valley, and then he heard strange sounds coming from the direction of Okelogee—the blows of axes, the crashing of trees, and the shouts of men and women. With his warriors close behind, he ran down the last section of trail, and there all along the Little Singing Stream, log houses were being built on the sites of burned-out homes. He looked toward the place where he and Mary had lived, and to his astonishment saw the new frame of a house—sturdy logs at the corners and crosspieces connecting them. He hurried along the pathway beside the stream. A red-bearded white man in linsey-woolsey trousers was using an ax to bevel a log end.

"Who are you?" the Long Warrior demanded in English.

The man looked up at him and was startled by this apparition of a long-haired wild man in a dirty tattered deerskin mantle. "I am Hugh Crawford," the man replied in a thick Scottish accent.

"And why did you come here to Okelogee?"

"I am here to assist in taming this wilderness," the man answered boldly.

"What wilderness?" demanded the Long Warrior with rising anger. "This is no wilderness. By what right do you build a cabin on this place?"

The red-bearded man drew himself erect, balancing his ax as a weapon. "By the rights of that woman yonder," he said, pointing down the Little Singing Stream.

The Long Warrior turned and as he did so he heard Creek Mary's rich laughter. Her back was toward him and she was laughing at Opothle and Talasi the Runner, who were wrestling in the water. As he strode across the pebbles, he felt his whole body aching for her. She heard the crunch of his footsteps on the gravel, and turned to face him. Her mouth opened slightly, one hand flying up to cover it, her eyes brightening with recognition.

"They told me you were dead!" she cried.

"You could not wait until my bones were recovered before bedding with another man?" he shouted accusingly. "And he one of the *Unegas*. While I fight them you find one to build a house for you!"

"Four hands are needed to build a house, Long Warrior, and he is a kind man. Could I rebuild my house alone, a woman with two children and no man?"

8

Dane was watching the horseman, still far away across the Montana plain, but closer than before. "He's looking for something, all right. He could be that young Crow. If so, he's looking for my granddaughter Amayi, although he would deny it if asked."

He turned back to face me. "I don't want you to get the idea," he said, "that the old Cherokees were not good fighters. They were as good as Mr. Roosevelt's Rough Riders, but I doubt if men like my grandfather and Qualla and the Stalking Turkey would have gone charging up that San Juan Hill in rank formation. It was not the nature of those old woods fighters to battle that way. Bullhead and Young Tassel–John Watts soon found that out. They should have known better."

"When all the fighting was over, none of them believed they had lost their war to keep settlers out of Cherokee country. Scattered though the Cherokees were, they had drawn blood from the border militia, punished them so severely they did not bother them again for a long time. Settlement did not stop, of course. The white intruders kept on 'winning the West' by moving into lands of less stubborn tribes. Not until about the time I came into the world did the trouble start all over again for the Cherokees." He stopped for a minute, his face turning somber, the wrinkles deepening around his mouth into a painful sadness.

"Yes, every Cherokee and Creek warrior was his own commander, to fight or not to fight as he pleased, to leave the war when he pleased. Qualla and the Stalking Turkey were not so badly wounded they could not have continued fighting, but they chose to go home. My grandfather found them at Okelogee."

He saw them right after he walked angrily away from Creek Mary and went on to the council house. The pillars and rafters of that building were so heavy they had not burned, and only the roof and seats had been damaged. Several men were busily working on the repairs, and both Qualla and the Stalking Turkey were among them.

Qualla saw the Long Warrior first. *"Unginili!"* he shouted. "My elder brother! Returned from the Land of the Dead!"

They had indeed believed him dead. Someone had seen him fall in battle while crossing a mountain stream, had watched his body floating away in the rapids. "I was only fooling the *Unegas,"* the Long Warrior declared. "They were thick as quails along the banks of that stream."

"But I saw it all in a dream," said the Stalking Turkey. "You were dead in the water."

"Your dream was not of the past," replied the Long Warrior. "Perhaps of the future."

For the Long Warrior the reunion was not a joyous one. The men wanted to celebrate the return of their chief and his warriors with feasting and dancing, but he refused the honor. He would be spending some hours with Bear Killer, the *adawehi,* searching for a chant formula that might bring Creek Mary to her senses and rid them both of that red-bearded Scotsman, Hugh Crawford.

After Bear Killer gave him two chants, the Long Warrior left Okelogee and walked the long distance to the Sleeping Woman, climbing to its highest point, the rounded head at the mountain's north end. Facing in the direction of Okelogee, he sang the formulas four times.

There was no moon that night and the town was quiet and very dark when he returned to spread his blanket in one corner of the unfinished council house. The council fire had not yet been started and frost was in the night air. He lay there begging sleep to come, but it would not. In the silence he could hear Mary's life-filled laughter resounding in his head, and he thought that if he had to lose her, he could bear losing everything but that vibrant laughter.

At last his eyes closed, but as sleep drifted down upon him, he heard a rustling sound at the entrance, the sound of a ghost dragging its burial robe across the hard-packed earthen floor. In the pitch blackness he could see nothing, but then he heard breathing and he knew that it was not a ghost. Someone else seeking shelter against the night air, he thought, and then a whisper came close and sharp to his ear: "Where are you, you old fool? I can smell you."

He flung out an arm, his fingers gripping a bearskin. Mary laughed softly, and then she and the bearskin were all around him. "I had no blanket to take my leave of the man Crawford," she said. "Only this bearskin gift from the Long Warrior, my friend and companion."

"*Sge!*" he said. "Listen!" He remembered the chant formula given him by Bear Killer, and he repeated it four times:

> Your spittle, I take it, I eat it.
> Your body, I take it, I eat it.
> Your flesh, I take it, I eat it.
> Your heart, I take it, I eat it.

Her long clean hair covered his face. "My spirit has come to rest at the edge of your body," she whispered. "You are never to let go your hold upon it."

9

"The next morning Hugh Crawford was gone from Okelogee," Dane said, "so there was no need for the Long Warrior to use

Bear Killer's curse formula to send the Scotsman to the Darkening Land. Later they heard that he had crossed the Sleeping Woman to join a community of Scots immigrants who had settled around the old stockade built during the War of the Revolution. Some of these men stayed there after the war ended, marrying Cherokee girls from a village north of their encampment. Others went back to Scotland and then returned, bringing wives and families. A few bachelors like Hugh Crawford were on the lookout for Cherokee wives, and after losing Mary he found one over at Coosawatie. The later generations of Crawfords became an important family among the Cherokees, as did other half-blood descendants of the Scots—the McDonalds, Campbells, Rosses, Taylors, McIntoshes, Rogers, McBees, and many others whose names I have forgotten.

"Although they built their cabins and cleared farms on Cherokee land, the Scots were never looked upon as intruders. The two races had a good deal in common, both being fierce and independent, loyal to clans, and suspicious of leaders claiming too much power. In the second generation their blood was mingled, and those half-bloods and quarter-bloods became the most Cherokee of all the Cherokees. My Uncle Opothle married one of the half-bloods, Suna-lee Rogers.

"Grandmother Mary often said that the time between the return of my grandfather from his war and the wedding of Opothle passed more swiftly than all the other years of her life. She had her hands full with two growing boys, each completely different from the other. My father, Talasi the Runner, was given guidance by his 'Uncle' Qualla, who taught him how to hunt and fish, how to live wild in the woods. Like Qualla, my father was of the Wolf clan and he soon became a leader in clan games and ceremonies.

"Opothle, on the other hand, was a puzzle to Qualla. Being Mary's son, Opothle was also a Wolf, but he cared nothing for ballplay or hunting and fishing. For a while Qualla tried to train him to be an orator so that he might be Okelogee's speaker at important councils, but Opothle was not interested in oratory either.

"After one of the Rogers families settled a farm nearby Okelo-gee, Mr. John Rogers took a fancy to Opothle because he could read and write English well. Mary had taught him English, tell-ing him that since the Cherokees were surrounded by the *Unegas,* they could better defend themselves if they knew the language of their enemies. However, she had never learned to do sums, and so Mr. Rogers decided to enlarge Opothle's knowledge by showing him how to add and subtract and multiply numbers.

"For the remainder of his life, I think, Opothle loved numbers. As I've said, I did not know him until he was gray-bearded, but the thing I recollect best about Uncle Opothle was how he was always figuring on bits of paper. If there was no paper handy, he would use a slate or a smooth piece of wood, filling the surface with columns of numbers. Before he was twenty, he was in the trading business. With Mr. Rogers's help, he started buying up deerskins and furs from Okelogee hunters who did not want to wait until the traders came over from Carolina, trading for less than the traders would later trade him, of course. In a short time Opothle was acting as local agent for the traders. Then he started stocking things to trade to the Cherokees—blankets and stroud cloth, ribbons and calico—and after the Cherokees began keeping milk cows like their Scots neighbors, he laid in a supply of cowbells. My father said that whenever he wanted to infuriate his older brother he would crawl through a hole in Mary's corn-crib—where Opothle kept his stores—and ring all the cowbells.

"Yes, there was a great rivalry between the two brothers that lasted through their descendants. One of Opothle's grandsons is living over at Pine Ridge now with the Sioux, a Christian preacher man he is, and when we exchange visits once a year we always have strong arguments about the differences between his God and my Maker of Breath. He was greatly disappointed when Amayi chose to be a medicine woman instead of a Chris-tian missionary." Dane laughed as he moved his chair so that he would stay in the slant of sunlight coming through the east window.

"That rivalry perhaps was good for my father, Talasi the Runner. At first he resisted all of Mary's efforts to teach him to

read and write English. He had no time for such indoor non-
sense; he was going to be a Cherokee hunter and warrior like his
father; he was always traveling to Coosawatie or Oostanaula or
some other town for ballplay. But when he began complaining
that Opothle had a fine horse and he had none, Mary told him
that if he wanted power equal to his brother he would have to
learn to read and write. And so the Runner learned to read and
write English.

"One of my grandmother's favorite stories was about
Opothle's courtship of Suna-lee Rogers. She said it was the
longest courtship in all the history of the Cherokees and Creeks.
'They could have given me ten grandchildren in all the years
they spent courting,' she would say. 'Why could not Opothle find
himself a Cherokee girl who would let him get her pregnant instead of that God-fearing half-blood Rogers girl? Why, all she
wanted them to do was hold hands and whisper in each other's
ears when they could have been pleasuring themselves in bed
and bringing me grandbabies.'

"Of course the delay may have been Opothle's will as much as
Aunt Suna-lee's. He wanted to be a man of property before starting a family, and he was. The wedding was a grand affair, the
first Christian wedding in Okelogee.

"Mary was willing to go halfway with the wedding plans, half
Christian and half Cherokee, that is, but when she heard that the
Rogers family was opposed to any 'pagan' ceremonies in the
wedding of their daughter, she secretly rounded up about a
dozen of her young women friends and planned a surprise wedding dance. She also kept prodding at Opothle to go out and kill
a deer to bring to the wedding feast as proof of his ability to
feed his forthcoming family, but Opothle pointed to his new
house and his cribful of deerskins and trade goods and told her
that if he needed venison he was rich enough to send someone
else out to do the hunting. Mary finally did persuade Suna-lee to
bring a fresh ear of corn to present to Opothle as evidence of her
skill as a food raiser.

"Much to Mary's displeasure, the ceremony was held in the
Rogers house, in a room so small that only the family members

and closest friends of Opothle and Suna-lee could be present. A considerable number of the Rogers relatives and friends came over from the Scots community, bringing hams and beef and two fiddlers for their kind of dancing. As it was early summer, the Rogers family agreed to have the feasting on the ballplay yard adjoining the council house so that all the Cherokees might attend.

"My father once told me that the most frightening time in all his young life was that wedding day. At the last moment, Opothle sought out the Runner and told him that the Presbyterian minister wanted him to be a member of the wedding party. 'What do I have to do?' the Runner asked. 'The preacher says I must have a brother to wait on me,' Opothle answered. 'Wait on you!' the Runner yelled out. 'Can't Suna-lee wait on you?' All the Runner had to do, of course, was stand beside his brother while the preacher read from his Bible and joined Opothle to Suna-lee in holy matrimony. My father told me that all the time the ceremony was going on his legs trembled so, that he feared he might fall down in front of everybody.

"He was frightened again by his own mother, Mary, during the feasting in the ballplay yard. Mary had been very quiet during the solemn occasion of the Presbyterian knot-tying, and by the time they all adjourned to the feasting place she was ready to celebrate. Alongside the brush arbor where the older people always sat to watch the ball games, the men had built rough tables, and they were piled high with boiled ears of fresh corn, venison, and the ham and beef brought by the Rogerses' friends. Mary, the Long Warrior, Opothle, and the Runner sat with the Rogers family at a table of honor under the brush arbor. Mrs. Rogers had brought a large pot of tea which they offered to share, but Mary preferred black drink, made from dried holly leaves, as you know. Every once in a while she would reach in her deerskin bag and take out a bottle of rum, flavoring her black drink with it. She would always pass the bottle around the table, but none of the Rogers family members would take any. Pretty soon Mary was laughing and singing and offering to teach the Rogerses a Creek song. They tried, but the only one who could get the rhythm right was Mrs. Rogers, who was Cherokee.

"About this time the two fiddlers who had come over from the other side of the Sleeping Woman were getting tuned up beside a leveled square of smooth hard ground in front of the arbor. Suddenly the older Rogers boy jumped up from the table, grabbed Opothle and Suna-lee, and pulled them out to the dancing place. Somebody handed Opothle a leather cushion, and the Rogerses and their friends formed a circle around him. It was called the Cushion Dance. They hopped and skipped to the fiddle music, and Opothle was supposed to stop the moving circle by dropping the cushion in front of his favored girl, who was Suna-lee, of course, and then some other boy would get the cushion and the dance would begin all over again.

"Mary watched the fiddle-dancing for a while, and then reached across the table and caught one of the Runner's wrists, squeezing it so hard that he almost cried out. 'You, Talasi,' she said in a rough voice, 'have you set your eyes on a girl yet?' He was tongue-tied. There was something in her questioning that truly frightened him. 'Well, tell me, my little Talasi, who is she?' He protested that he had not chosen a girl. 'When you choose one,' she said, looking as grim as a witch, 'make certain she is full-blood. The blood of Creek Mary, the Beloved Woman, runs thin in Opothle and will run thinner in his paleskin children.' She gripped his arm tighter. 'When you choose a girl to make children for you, if she is not full-blood I will kill you!' She saw him trembling then, and burst into laughter. Always after that he was a little bit afraid of his mother, and he never dared look twice at a half-blood girl.

"If Mary realized that she had frightened her son she made no effort to ease his fear. After a while she yawned as though in great boredom from watching the fiddle dancers, and then excused herself from the table, leaving the Runner and the Long Warrior there by themselves.

"A few minutes later the Runner was startled to hear the loud beat of a drum, the shrilling of a wind instrument, and the clatter of rattles. Wheeling round the corner of the arbor came a procession of young Cherokee girls in white dancing dresses, some with terrapin-shell rattles strapped to their legs, and carrying fans made of red-dyed cane. They were led by Qualla playing a flageolet and Mary beating a drum. Raising himself straight up on the bench, the Long Warrior gave out a loud grunt of astonishment. The Runner was frightened to see his mother beating the drum. Cherokee women did not march around beating drums. He thought she had gone mad.

"Well, the fiddle dancers made way for the Cherokees, who formed a circle and started to dance around Qualla and his cane flageolet and Mary and her drum. Not to be outdone, the young men of the Cherokees rushed out and formed a circle around the shell-shaker girls, who pretended to hide their faces with their red fans. As this was a wedding celebration they naturally started to do the Snake Dance. The Rogerses and their white friends had never seen a Snake Dance, and it must have come as a shock to most of them. The Presbyterian preacher raised his arms and begged them to stop, but they were dancing so hard they neither saw nor heard him. The Long Warrior finally went out and stopped it.

"Now, I never saw the Snake Dance but once, but I can tell you it is quite . . . ah . . ." Dane frowned, searching for a word.

"Sensuous?" I suggested.

He put on a pair of silver-rimmed spectacles and reached for the old dictionary under the window. After carefully laying the broken bindings aside, he thumbed the leaves until he found the word he was searching for. When he looked up at me through thick lenses, his closed lips were creased in a smile that was like a deeper wrinkle in the webwork of his face. "Erotic, I think, would be the word."

He slid his spectacles back in their case. "Words, words, words," he said. "Grandmother Mary taught me the importance of words, showed me that the more words a man can form in his mouth the more complete a human being he is, the less like the savage beast he is. I have learned so many words, Cherokee, English, Creek, Cheyenne, Crow, Lakota, a little of the French, but they are all going away from me. Even for English, I must use this crutch, this old dictionary, to bring them back to me."

10

In the years after the first white men began pushing westward across the Appalachian Mountains, the Cherokees saw their wide domain shrink generation by generation. First they were driven from the rich grasslands and forests of Kentucky and western Virginia, and then by the end of the War of the Revolution they had lost the valley of the Cumberland in middle Tennessee and most of their Carolina territories.

For a decade after the Long Warrior returned from the war in which he had joined Bullhead and Young Tassel against the border settlers, the Cherokees lived in peace while the white men turned their westward march toward the lands of other tribes. But then with the coming of the century numbered nineteenth by Christians, the invasion began once more—this time not by force of arms but through the deception of agents representing the government of the United States, through the twisting of laws, and the bribery of corrupt chiefs. Like rodents nibbling at corn, the land-thieves ate away what is now eastern Tennessee in small bites, a strip between two streams here, a mountain valley there. These quiet cessions were accomplished by clever lawyers using money from the United States treasury for payment of annuities and bribes that went into the pockets of Cherokees who gave themselves the name of chief. The first warning of loss reaching Cherokees who lived within these ceded lands would

be the arrival of a government agent armed with legal papers ordering them to move out.

After the white men formed the state of Tennessee, a state en-
compassing thousands of square miles of Cherokee and Chicka-
saw lands, with Indian-hating Jack Sevier its governor, the nib-
bles increased to huge bites. For the first time in their history,
the Cherokees were forced to realize that if they meant to survive as a nation they must sacrifice their cherished individualism
for a powerful center—with one chief over all. Leaders from the
towns north and south agreed that Little Turkey, from one of the
lower towns, should serve as principal chief in dealings with the
outside world. Little Turkey, however, was soon overshadowed
by Taltsuska, the swaggering Bullhead. Not long after returning
from the wars, Bullhead became Speaker of the Nation. As Little
Turkey was no orator, Bullhead took the lead during the early
years of the new century in dealing with agents from the United
States government seeking permission to build roads through
Cherokee country, or sites for government trading factories, or
additional small cessions of land for white settlement. When a
conference was held in Nashville or Washington, Little Turkey
would relinquish the role of tribal representative to Bullhead,
who would sometimes return with slight increases in annuities,
but always report large losses of more Cherokee lands. And very
little of the annuity payments ever seemed to reach the Cherokees after entering Bullhead's hands.

Claiming to be "the mouth of the nation," Bullhead paid no
heed to protests from headmen of the Cherokee towns. The government agents named him chief of the tribe, and in rapid succession he ceded land in Carolina, Tennessee, and Georgia to
white speculators, reserving private tracts of acreage for himself
and his relatives. Soon he was living like a king in the wilderness. He became the owner of a plantation. He bought slaves
and fine horses. And when a few of the town chiefs opposed him
openly as a tyrant, they died mysteriously and violently.

Finally after he accepted bribes for some of the best hunting
grounds between the Hiwassee and Tennessee rivers, a group of
town chiefs secretly met to decide how to rid the Cherokee Na-

tion of Bullhead. They gathered at Hickory Log, and among the leaders was the Long Warrior.

The council meeting was brief. Not one chief spoke for Bullhead. He had betrayed the Cherokee Nation. He must be put to death. To choose his executioners, a piece of old yellowed cloth was cut into many small squares, one for each member of the council. An *adawehi* then marked a black X on three of the squares and put them all into an earthenware jar, stirring and shaking them. As each member passed from the council house, he took one of the squares out of the jar. The three men who drew those marked with an X were to carry out the execution as silently and quickly as possible.

When the Long Warrior looked at the tiny square of cloth in the palm of his hand and saw the black X mark, he was not surprised. He had been seeing visions of Bullhead ever since leaving Okelogee—Bullhead challenging him with his eyes across the council fire on the ridge above the blockhouse, Bullhead strutting in front of his warriors with two silver-mounted pistols hanging at his waist, Bullhead smashing the skulls of the defenseless Cavetts. The thought of taking a human life, the life of a Cherokee clansman, was repugnant to the Long Warrior, but the Blood Law had been invoked. He had been chosen; it was his duty to send Bullhead to the Darkening Land.

He was back in Okelogee the next day, arriving to find Mary preparing to bake hominy bread. She had a deep bed of coals ready in the yard and was mixing the dough in a flat-bottomed pan. After telling her that he had had a good journey from Hickory Log, he sat down cross-legged in front of the fire. Although it was midsummer his hands felt like ice and he held them over the coals, knowing that she was watching him with curiosity. When she turned toward her dough pan for a moment, he fingered from his turban the tiny square of cloth with its X mark, glanced at it briefly, and dropped it into the coals where it flared into white ash.

"What was that?" she asked.

"Death," he replied, and stood up.

"Something troubles you, Long Warrior. Let it out of your heart by telling me."

He shook his head. "Nothing."

She moved toward him, but he drew away. "If you are near menstruating," he said roughly, "don't touch me. Don't get up-wind of me."

"You're going to kill," she said.

"Don't meddle." He hurried off to the council house, hoping the men would have a pot of black drink ready there. A man had to keep some things from the women, but then, he thought, he could not tell the men about it either. He never spoke to anyone about the killing except Mary, and he did not tell her until the year of their bitter quarrel, the last year of his life. Long before that time she knew everything except the details.

He made some sort of excuse, a pretense of trading for horses in one of the northern towns, to take his leave of Mary and Okelogee. On the morning of his departure, she watched him ride splashing across the Little Singing Stream and disappear through the full-leaved sweetgum trees. Out of the gray rainy sky, a blue hawk dived, circled, and screamed "Come back! Come back!" Then it streaked off in the same direction the Long Warrior had gone. She remembered that time so long ago when she was riding north from Bluff Village in search of Menewa, and a dark blue hawk had warned her to turn back. If she had turned back, everything would have been different, and she wondered now if the Long Warrior was riding on a new trail in his life, perhaps toward an ending. She shivered, looking toward the sky for the hawk, but it did not return.

When the Long Warrior reached Hiwassee Garrison rain was falling steadily, and as nightfall was near he sought shelter in the stables. Five or six other Cherokees were there, all travelers, and as soon as he unsaddled and fed his horse, he climbed into the loft and joined them. One face was familiar—a town chief who had been present at Hickory Log. Neither man gave any sign of recognition to the other. "*Siyu,*" the Long Warrior greeted all of them, and gave his name and town. Then he spread his blanket on the hay, and through the open loft window watched the warm slanting rain until darkness made it invisible. He slept badly that night, his dreams filled with recurring visions of Bullhead.

He awoke facing a clear dawn sky. The other town chief, who had come to Hiwassee Garrison for the same reason as he, was gone.

That afternoon a crowd of Cherokees, mostly males of all ages, began gathering on the grounds nearby the old Hiwassee blockhouse for a stickball game. Some yards back from the playing field, the Long Warrior sat in the shade of an oak, with his back against the trunk, watching the arriving spectators. As he expected, a few minutes before the game began Bullhead and several of his friends arrived on horseback. Bullhead was riding one of his blooded horses, a shiny black mare richly saddled and bridled. He was dressed in white man's clothing—a tan broadcloth waistcoat, ruffled white shirt, tight trousers, and boots. He hitched his horse to a small tree and strutted into the spectators' arbor, going about from one man to another placing bets.

When play began, the Long Warrior opened his deerskin bag and drew out a flintlock pistol, priming it with gunpowder and then concealing it in his sash. He strolled over toward the arbor. Bullhead was sitting in the midst of the group he had arrived with, protected like a king by his guards. From time to time he drank from a flask, laughing, applauding the ballplay, and carrying on animated conversations. The Long Warrior decided to wait until the game ended and the crowd began milling about.

Late in the afternoon, a player sent a high ball spinning between two goalposts for the twelfth point and the game ended, with half the spectators swarming upon the field. In the commotion, the Long Warrior lost sight of his quarry, and when he found him again, Bullhead was already mounted, with his escorts close around him. Bullhead led the way upon the field, shouting congratulations to one of the players, and then suddenly out of the thinning crowd an old man appeared on foot to grab the bridle of the black mare. The Long Warrior recognized him instantly. He had been at Hickory Log. He was the third man who had drawn a black X.

"Stand out of my way!" Bullhead shouted at him.

As the Long Warrior pushed closer, he could see that the Third Man held a pistol. "You have betrayed our people!" the old man cried out. "The *Unegas* have bought you!"

He's going to do it, the Long Warrior thought, and then beyond the immobile scene of the horse, the rider, and the accuser, his eyes met those of the Second Man, the one who had slept in the stables loft, and he knew that each of them read the horror in the other's face. As though driven by some power over which he had no control, the Long Warrior's fingers closed over the pistol hidden in his sash, and his legs began to move.

He heard the snap of the Third Man's pistol, saw the dim flash of his misfire, and then Bullhead raised a tomahawk as he spurred the black mare forward, bringing the bladed weapon down against the side of the falling man's face. The pistol rattled against the ground, the man collapsing upon it with blood gushing over his outflung mass of gray-streaked hair. Before the Long Warrior could draw his own pistol, Bullhead was galloping away, his mounted cohorts closing around him.

"Who is he?" someone asked of the man dying on the ground.

"I know him," a young man answered. "He is a chief of a town to the west. Of the Deer clan."

The Long Warrior drew his sweating fingers from his sash. *That will make it easier,* he thought. *By the Blood Law it is my duty as a Deer to avenge a clansman.* He turned and went straight to the stables. After saddling his horse, he mounted and started up the road taken by Bullhead.

Before he reached McIntosh's Tavern, the sun was down and yellow candlelight glowed in the windows. A dozen horses were hitched to the railing. One of them was the glossy black mare. Pulling his turban low over his forehead, he entered, keeping to the shadows of the tavern room. A few minutes later someone else entered; it was the Second Man. He chose a seat only a few feet away, placing himself so that he could watch both the Long Warrior and Bullhead.

Bullhead and his followers were at the largest table, drinking rum, gambling with peachstone dice, filling the low-ceilinged room with bursts of raucous laughter, and occasionally breaking their mugs by hurling them into the empty fireplace. From time to time the tavernkeeper, McIntosh, would mildly admonish them, but they ignored him until he warned them that they must leave if they did not cease their loutish behavior.

Bullhead raised his long chin and glared at the tavernkeeper. He fondled the tiny brass cross dangling from his ear. "You live among us by permission, McIntosh," he said hoarsely. "Be silent and interfere no more."

"I try to keep an orderly tavern," McIntosh replied.

Bullhead laughed, that hateful laugh the Long Warrior had so often heard during the border war. "You have said enough." He snarled at the innkeeper: "Go away or I shall kill you."

The Long Warrior exchanged glances with the Second Man. He had counted four candles in the dimly lit tavern room. He arose and walked to the nearest one, extinguishing it with his fingers. The Second Man followed his example. The tavernkeeper, noticing the fading light, backed away from Bullhead. The Second Man picked up a wet towel from the counter and dropped it over the candle on Bullhead's table. At the same instant the Long Warrior knocked the last light from a barrel top and the room was suddenly dark.

Bullhead swore angrily out of the blackness, his voice a target. A pistol fired, the flash lighting the room for a second, and the doorway filled with fleeing patrons. Bullhead was moaning. Someone relighted the candle on his table, and his friends crowded around him.

The Long Warrior sat motionless. He pushed his unfired pistol farther down in his sash and waited. Other candles were lighted. The Second Man was gone.

Some of Bullhead's men ran outside, shouting at those who had fled, but only one had mounted, and the hoofbeats were fading away in the night. They helped Bullhead outside and lifted him into his saddle, one of his friends riding behind to hold him erect, and started back toward Hiwassee Garrison.

Returning to the garrison stables, the Long Warrior spent a second night there, but he did not sleep. Bedded down in the loft were several of Bullhead's companions, and throughout the night horsemen came and went below. He listened carefully to the talk, learning that Bullhead was not dead, but was wounded in the shoulder. An *adawehi* came, and then a doctor from the white settlement. Bullhead was somewhere near, but no one said in which building he was staying.

At the first gray light of dawn, the Long Warrior left the sleeping men in the loft and went outside, nibbling at the last of the hominy bread that Mary had put in his saddlepack. He walked to a well beside the old blockhouse, drew up a bucket of water, drank from a gourd dipper and washed his face, using his turban for a towel. Adjoining the blockhouse was a new trading post, and two or three Cherokees were seated on the steps waiting for the trader to open the door. A few paces beyond the trading post was a small schoolhouse, and a hundred yards past it were two dwelling houses side by side. Bullhead would be in one of these buildings.

Strolling up to the trading post, he greeted the seated Cherokees, climbed the steps, and walked casually along a wooden sidewalk past the doorway of the schoolhouse. He noticed something then on the weathered gray planking of the sidewalk, tiny brown spots no larger than a thumbnail. The line of dried blood spots turned to the right at the sidewalk's end and continued up an outdoor stairway to a loft above the schoolhouse.

The Long Warrior stopped and glanced back at the Cherokees on the steps. They were paying no attention to him. Nor was there any sign of life at the stables. He climbed the steps quickly and silently. The door at the top was open slightly, probably for ventilation; when he opened it he saw only one small window beyond a pallet on the floor where someone lay completely covered by gray sheeting.

As there was no one else in the room, and no guard posted inside or out, the Long Warrior wondered if Bullhead had died during the night. He crossed the room, the loose flooring creaking under his moccasins, and pulled the sheet away. As though released by a spring, Bullhead sat erect, naked except for his drawers, his eyes opening wide, his right hand grasping for a tomahawk that lay beside him. His left shoulder was covered with torn strips of bloody cloth. "Who are you?" he demanded. "Where are my boys?"

"They've deserted you, Bullhead," the Long Warrior said quietly. "They know you are condemned."

"You!" Bullhead exclaimed. "The chicken-hearted chief from Okelogee."

"You're a hard man to kill."

"They sent *you?*" Bullhead's belly muscles tightened, and before the Long Warrior could aim his pistol, he sprang from the pallet, tomahawk raised. The Long Warrior ducked, but Bullhead's knees struck the side of his ribs, knocking the pistol from his hand and leaving him breathless for a moment. With a loud grunt of pain, Bullhead fell heavily to the floor. Before he could rise, the Long Warrior leaped upon his back, fighting for the tomahawk.

When Bullhead tried to throw him off, his grip on the tomahawk loosened and the Long Warrior seized and lifted it, bringing it down with all the force he could summon into the back of Bullhead's shaven skull. The chunking sound of sharp metal tearing flesh and bone and brains apart would disturb his dreams for the remainder of his life.

Later he was puzzled as to why he felt bound to remove the tomahawk. It was so deeply embedded that he had to put one foot on the dead man's back and use both hands to pry it loose from the skull. But he did so, wiping it on the sheet. He then picked up his pistol and left the room, closing the door behind him. Halfway down the outside stairs, he dropped to the ground and circled behind the buildings until he came to the well. For the first time he noticed that his hands were bloody and that he was still carrying Bullhead's tomahawk. He dropped the weapon into the well, washed his hands in the water he had left in the bucket, and then went on to the stables. Two young men, former companions of Bullhead, were saddling their horses.

"*Siyu,*" the Long Warrior said, barely glancing at them.

"Do you have tobacco?" one of them asked.

He gave the men two pipefuls. "*Wadan, wadan,*" they both said. "Thanks, thanks."

While they were smoking he finished saddling, and then mounted and rode away from Hiwassee Garrison.

11

"For months after my grandfather slew Bullhead," Dane said, "there was much uneasiness among the Cherokees. Bullhead's relatives and friends feared there would be more killings, but there were not. The reasons for his execution were known, and most Cherokees approved of it. However, when President Jefferson sent an agent to visit the Cherokee towns to persuade the people to move west of the Mississippi River, one of Bullhead's brothers-in-law, who feared for his life, decided to go, the government taking land in exchange for that given him in the West. He and his family and friends were the first Cherokees to move to the Arkansas country, but no one else of course would even listen to the agent. They did not dream that within a few years almost all of them would be dragged without their consent from their beloved country to the dark land of the setting sun.

"It must have been a stirring time, those years just before I was born. All along the frontier between the Appalachians and the Mississippi River from the Great Lakes to the Gulf of Mexico, the tribes were becoming more determined to resist any further land seizures by the whites. For many Indian people the great hero of the time was the Shooting Star—Tecumseh of the Shawnees—who worked to form a confederation of all the tribes. Without such a union, Tecumseh said, the Indians would never stop the westward march of the white men.

"His strongest ally in the South was my grandmother's old friend, Menewa of the Creeks. Late one summer a party of Shawnees and Creeks visited the Cherokee towns, inviting the chiefs to attend a great council for Tecumseh at Tallagalla, the town on the Tallapoosa that Menewa had built after being driven from Georgia by the border raiders.

"By this time the Cherokees had decided it was impossible to have one chief, and so they formed a Committee of Thirteen to deal with matters concerning the whole nation. The thirteen chiefs were sworn to cede no more land and to resist all efforts of the United States to move the tribe to the West. As the Long Warrior was one of the Committee of Thirteen, the Tecumseh delegation was especially eager to have him attend.

"When they came to Okelogee, the Long Warrior gave them a friendly welcome, but he told them he was too busy with other matters to make the five-day journey to Tallagalla. Well, Mary was outraged, of course. She was a great supporter of Tecumseh, even claiming blood kinship through his Creek mother.

" 'The council will choose someone else to go in my place,' the Long Warrior assured her that night after she gave him one of her scoldings.

" 'This would be an insult to the greatest leader of our people,' she shouted at him. 'You must go yourself.'

" 'They say in Nashville,' the Long Warrior answered, 'that the Shooting Star is a spy, an agent for the British who are preparing to fight another war against the Americans.'

" 'Who says that? The *Unegas?* Those horse-trading white friends of yours that you complain about for lying, cheating, and stealing?'

"The Long Warrior did spend a lot of time those days horse trading. Grandmother Mary told me that it took the place of gambling for him, and at the time set for the Tallagalla council for Tecumseh, he had arranged to accompany several horse dealers, white men, all the way to Natchez to trade for Texas mustangs. She partially forgave him after he presented her with a gentle little arch-nosed pony that reminded her of the Choctaw she had ridden from Bluff Village.

"But they had another quarrel when Mary decided that she was the one who should represent Okelogee at the Tecumseh council. Because of her status as a Beloved Woman, she was highly respected by the Okelogee men. Also by this time she had passed the menopause, which gave her the right to take part in councils and ceremonies forbidden to menstruating women. The Long Warrior, however, protested that both the Creeks and Tecumseh might take offense at a woman delegate.

"'Menewa would welcome me,' Mary declared, 'with his arms opened in friendship.'

"That may have been the real reason why the Long Warrior was so opposed to her going to Tallagalla. He had always been jealous of Menewa's place in Mary's memories. But in the end Mary got her way, as she usually did. With her younger son, Talasi the Runner, as her escort she set out joyously for the Creek country.

"All through my boyhood I was to hear much about this event from both my father, the Runner, and from Grandmother Mary. She memorized the speeches made by Tecumseh, wrote down the words, and often would quote from them at council meetings. Even after all the years that have passed, I can remember some of the words of Tecumseh as if I had been there."

12

Creek Mary and the Runner left Okelogee in the Little Chestnut Moon, traveling in ideal weather—the days warm and sunny under blue skies, the nights just crisp enough for a blanket. When they rode into Tallagalla, she was amazed at the size of the assemblage gathered there to welcome Tecumseh—more than five thousand Creeks, Choctaws, Chickasaws, and Cherokees. She was also astonished to find that Menewa had become a man of wealth, living in a fine house set on high pillars, with large cleared fields behind it filled with herds of cattle and horses. He boasted to her of his trade with the Spaniards, sometimes loading as many as a hundred horses at a time with deerskins and furs to drive to Pensacola. British agents were active along the coast, he said, making arrangements for a military base to be used in a new war against the Americans. If the war came, he would join in fighting the Georgians out of revenge for what they had done to his people.

Menewa had grown much heavier since the days of their youth. His face was fleshy, but his eyes still held their old fire, and she could tell that he was the idol of the Creek women when he walked about the town in his brilliantly striped jackets and red-feathered caps. He welcomed Mary and her son as though they were blood relatives, insisting that they stay in his already overcrowded house during the week of festivities.

In the day that remained before the arrival of Tecumseh, Mary renewed acquaintanceship with those of her people from Bluff Village who had fled to Tallagalla. Among them was Tolchi, with a wife whom Mary remembered as a little girl, and now they had four children, one as old as her younger son. She wanted to weep at this reminder of the rapid passage of her life, but instead she laughed and praised Tolchi for fathering such fine children.

Late the next day, the arrival of Tecumseh and his entourage of twenty-four Shawnees, Kickapoos, and Sioux created tremendous excitement. After formal greetings at the council house, Menewa received the great leader in his home. When Mary was introduced, she embraced him, calling him cousin. The Runner was embarrassed by his mother's adoring attitude toward this man from the North, who was not nearly the imposing figure that he had imagined him to be. Tecumseh was not as tall as the Long Warrior, his body was thin, his skin more sallow than coppery, and he limped on a slightly twisted leg. Much more ap-

pealing to the Runner were the six Sioux warriors, tall, handsome
young men with their luxurious hair gathered in full plaits. They
had a wild, free look about them, spoke to no one, and kept to
themselves.

At last came the evening of the main event, Tecumseh's oration to the Creeks. That afternoon the ballplay field was raked
clean and the dancing square enlarged by scraping away the
grass. A high pole was erected in the center, and a fire started
close to its base. At sundown the spectators began gathering, and
by the time darkness fell, masses of men, women, and children
were thickly packed around the field. Menewa had built a platform for himself, his guests, and old heroes and heroines of the
Creeks. From this vantage point, seated between his mother and
Menewa, the Runner could see and hear everything that happened on that field lighted by orange flames of pitch pine.

Out of the council house and down a corridor formed by two
facing lines of Creek warriors, Tecumseh led his twenty-four followers. Wearing only their breechflaps and deerskin pouches at
their waists, their naked bodies painted black, they shook their
red war clubs as they danced to the pole at the center of the
square. There they turned and danced single file all around the
edges of the pressing crowd. Three times they danced around,
and at each turn Tecumseh took a handful of tobacco from his
pouch, scattering it to purify the ground. Circling back to the
pole, they all emptied their pouches into the fire, and then Tecumseh uttered a piercing Shawnee war whoop that was echoed
by all the dancers in unison, a cry that reverberated through the
valley. As the sound died away, they broke into a war dance, beginning slowly as though they were setting an ambush, creeping
stealthily, then leaping upon an invisible enemy, dancing faster
and faster, beating their hands against their screaming mouths.
It was the most fearsome sound the Runner had ever heard in
his life, but Mary was enraptured, clapping her hands together,
her feet drumming on the log flooring of the platform in rhythm
with the dance.

Suddenly the dancers broke away, fading off to the edge of
the crowd, leaving Tecumseh standing alone in the center of the

square with the firelight full upon his face. He spoke in Muskogean, his mother's tongue, Creek Mary's tongue, in a voice so res-
onant and hypnotic, his body so charged with emotion, that not
one of the thousands gathered there moved or made a sound.

"Once our people were many. Once we owned the land from
the sunrise to the sunset. Once our campfires twinkled at night
like the stars of a fallen sky. Then the white man came. Our
campfires dwindled.

"Everywhere our people have passed away, as the snows of
the mountains melt in the Mulberry Moon. We no longer rule
the forests. The wild game have gone with our hunting grounds.
Even our lands are nearly all gone. Yes, my brothers, my sisters,
our campfires are few. Those that still burn we must draw together.

"Behold what the white man has done to our people! Gone are
the Pequot, the Narraganset, the Powhatan, the Tuscarora, and
the Mohican. The white man has put his hand upon them and
they are no more. We can no longer trust the white man. We
gave him our tobacco and our corn. What happened? Now there
is hardly land for us to grow these holy plants.

"They have driven us from the Great Salt Water, forced us
over the mountains, and would push us beyond the Great River—
but we will go no farther. The only way to stop this evil is for all
to unite and claim a common right to the land as it was at first,
and should be now—for it never was divided but belongs to all.
No tribe has a right to sell the land. Why not sell the air, the
clouds, and the great sea, as well as the land? Did the One
Above not make them all for the use of his children?"

He paused, holding one hand high, his body trembling, and
then he spoke again, his voice soft at first, then rising and hurling his words out as though they were flying arrows.

"The Muskogees, the Creeks, were once a mighty people. The
Georgians trembled at their war whoop, but now your blood is
white, your tomahawks have no edge, your bows and arrows are
buried with your fathers. Awake, Muskogee brothers of my
mother, brush away the sleep of bondage from your eyes, and let
the white race perish!

"They seize your land, they corrupt your women, they trample on the graves of your dead. They must be driven back whence they came upon a trail of blood. We own this country and the paleskins must never enjoy it.

"All the tribes of the North are dancing the war dance. Soon the time will come to strike, and we will all strike together from the North to the South. Shake your war clubs, shake yourselves, and you will frighten the Americans. Their arms will drop from their hands. Lift up your war clubs, be strong, and when the time comes to fight, you will hear my war cry as I fight beside you, my Muskogee kinsmen!"

He spoke on into the night until his painted body was shiny with sweat, until his voice became a whisper. When he stopped, the crowd—released from the spell of his words—roared out its own pent-up emotions. Several minutes passed before Menewa, standing on his platform, could make himself heard in a short speech of approval. Menewa spoke of how the Creeks had been driven from their rich lands in Georgia, but boasted of the punishment his warriors had given the border militia, bloodying them so badly that they now kept a respectful distance from the towns of the Creeks. "Let them come again," said Menewa, "and we will bleed them to their bones. This time our enemies will fight not one tribe, but all tribes united in one common cause against a common foe." He glanced down at Mary, whose attention was still fixed upon Tecumseh, a silhouette now against the dimming fire. "Before we go to our beds this night," Menewa continued, "let us look upon and hear the words of the Beloved Woman of our Creek people."

Mary was not expecting this; Menewa had given her no warning. Brushing her hair back nervously, she stood erect. "What words can I add to the magic of Tecumseh and the wisdom of Menewa?" she cried. "Tecumseh has told us that we must draw our campfires together. I am a *miko* of the Muskogees who for many years has shared her campfire with a chief of the Cherokees." She reached down and caught the Runner's hair in her fingers, pulling him painfully to his feet. "Look! Here is a symbol of the union of old enemies—my son, Talasi, Creek blood mingled with Cherokee blood. Our nations must and will remain as one. But let us not boast, as Menewa has done, as so many other Creeks and Cherokees have done, of how we bled the *Unegas* when last they drove us from our homes and stole our lands. They leave us alone now, yes, because they have not yet filled our stolen lands with their towns and farms, nor destroyed all the animals and cut all the trees from our stolen forests. When they have done these things they will come again. Let us remember that. Let us be as one tribe and never again shall we be driven from our homes like fallen leaves before the winds."

13

Mary insisted that Tecumseh return with her to Okelogee to spread his message among the Cherokees, but the Shawnee politely declined. He was like a migrating bird, he told her. His pathway was set; he must follow it back through the country of the Chickasaws and on to the Prophet's Town on Tippecanoe River. At some later time, he promised, he would visit the Beloved Woman's town.

The Runner was relieved that Tecumseh and his party did not return with his mother and him to Okelogee. He knew that the Shooting Star was a great and eloquent man, but he was uneasy over the effect he had upon Mary. In the presence of the Shawnee orator, her behavior was out of character. She became like a silly young girl, making sweet eyes at Tecumseh and caressing him with her hands.

One evening on the return journey to Okelogee, after Mary

sighed loudly and remarked for the twentieth time that she was unhappy because Tecumseh was not traveling with them, the Runner told her bluntly that he was happy that the Shawnee had taken a different path from theirs.

"So my son is jealous of the great Tecumseh?" she said in surprise.

"When you are near him you behave like my sweetheart, Sehoya."

Mary stared at him for a moment, and then she broke into laughter. "And what is so wrong with Sehoya's behavior? You've told us you are going to take her for your wife."

"She is barely seventeen. She is supposed to be coy and flirtatious in my presence."

"And am I an old woman, not young enough for such things?" Anger showed in her eyes. "I have never felt younger in my life, Talasi the Runner. Being with Tecumseh made me feel young. Menewa made me feel young. They both regard me as though I am young and so I feel young with them. You and Opothle and your father, the Long Warrior, do not think of me as being young. You are all very dispiriting."

The Runner knew he had distressed her. "I think of you as being beautiful," he said. "But you are my mother. I do not expect you to behave like Sehoya."

When beset by unwelcome emotions Mary could always laugh. She laughed now, and went over and embraced her son. "When will you wed Sehoya?" she asked.

"As soon as the Long Warrior and Qualla help me build a house."

"You do not need a house now. My house is big enough for you to start a family. We'll have the wedding as soon as we can make all the arrangements."

If the Runner had wanted to change his mind about Sehoya, or even if he had wished to postpone the event, his chances of doing so were slight once Mary took charge of the proceedings. Sehoya was the daughter of the headman at Oostanaula, and the Runner had wanted her when he first saw her there on one of his frequent visits with the Okelogee ballplay team. Following their first meeting, Sehoya often accompanied her father to Okelogee when the Oostanaula players came for a game. As her father was a chief, they were always guests of the Long Warrior and Mary. After it was understood that the Runner and Sehoya were to be wed, they had spent several nights together in the corncribs of each other's parents.

Mary saw to it that they had a proper Cherokee-Creek wedding. The Runner went into the deep forest beyond the Sleeping Woman and killed a bear, bringing the meat as his contribution to the feast. Sehoya baked bread made from corn she had raised and from chestnuts she had gathered.

Not for years had Okelogee experienced such merriment as on the wedding day, with vocal and instrumental music, dancing, and feasting that lasted far into the night. The ceremony itself was quite simple, Mary borrowing it from her Creek heritage. Sehoya and the Runner, each carrying a small pole and accompanied by a circle of dancers wearing white, met each other in the dancing square. There they drove the poles into the ground side by side, and then Opothle and Sehoya's oldest brother brought a long tendril from a vine and twined it around the two poles.

Mary was the first to embrace them. "Make me many grandchildren!" she cried, brushing tears from her eyes and shaking with her usual hearty laughter. Everyone brought gifts. Opothle presented them with fine blankets from his storehouse, and the Long Warrior gave them a pair of matching riding horses. The only damper on the celebration was the departure of the Long Warrior immediately after the noon feast. He had to journey up to Nashville to arrange some important business with an important gentleman—a part-time horse and slave trader, lawyer, land dealer, and major general of the Tennessee militia. He was in the market for horses to be used for mounting his militiamen. His name was Andrew Jackson.

In the springtime following the wedding of the Runner and Sehoya, Okelogee received the startling news that the British were at war again with the Americans. All around them the border settlers were arming, and the Cherokee chiefs gathered hastily to debate what course their nation should follow. For some time the Cherokee council had been considering the advantage of adopting a government similar to that of the United States. As long as they could remember, friendly white men had been advising them to become like the *Unegas*—choose their leaders through elections, invite missionaries to teach them to be Christians, build schools so their children could learn to read and write English. Although the Long Warrior was too busy to take part in many of these discussions, both his sons became involved in the Okelogee councils, and for once the brothers laid aside their old differences and volunteered to assist in organizing a new government. Opothle went so far as to draft a proposed constitution modeled on that of the United States.

The coming of the War of 1812 brought an urgency to these aims, but there were bitter disagreements over what action the Cherokees should take. Should they remain neutral, or offer aid to either the British or the Americans in hopes of being recognized as an independent nation by the victors when the war came to a close?

14

"It is always difficult," Dane said, "for two Cherokees to agree about anything for very long. When Mary heard that both Tecumseh in the North and Menewa in the South had allied themselves with the British against the Americans, she began urging the Cherokees to follow the two leaders. She visited several towns, speaking in the councils for a British alliance. The Long

Warrior, influenced by Andrew Jackson, took the opposite view. General Jackson, he said, was raising an army of thousands, and wanted the Cherokees and Creeks to send their warriors to fight under his command. With such a leader and such a force, the Americans were certain to defeat the British, and the Long Warrior was sure that when the war was over, the Cherokees would be recognized as a nation equal to the United States and would no longer have to worry about any more land seizures or intruding settlers.

"The Runner and Opothle, however, both distrusted Andrew Jackson. Opothle had continued to prosper, building up a large trading business. In partnership with his father-in-law, John Rogers, he also operated a large farm, planted a thousand peach trees, obtained several plows and mules to pull them, and began raising corn and cattle and hogs to sell. To get the work done, he went up to Nashville and bought a few black slaves. He and the Runner had many quarrels about those slaves. The Runner wanted Opothle to set them free; he detested slavery and never forgave Opothle for bringing them to Okelogee. About the only thing the brothers agreed on was absolute neutrality for the Cherokees in the War of 1812.

"So you see, the family was divided, bitterly divided for a time. Opothle visited Nashville often enough to learn a good deal about Andrew Jackson, and whenever the Long Warrior would praise the man and urge Cherokee warriors to join his American army, Opothle would say that Andrew Jackson was responsible for more stolen Indian lands than any man in Tennessee, and that the Cherokees should have nothing to do with him and his war.

"During this time Opothle built a big new house out near his farm—eight or ten rooms it was, with a front veranda and whitewashed walls. The day it was finished he invited Mary and the Long Warrior to come and see it. The Long Warrior wandered around through the empty rooms, climbed the winding staircase, peered out the windows of glass, and asked Opothle if he had not become so much like a white man that he thought he was going to live forever.

"'I know I will be dust someday,' Opothle replied in his dignified manner, 'but I want this house to prove to white men that Cherokees can live as well as they do. If they see that we are as civilized as they are, they will stop telling us to move west across the Mississippi.'

"Mary shook her head. 'You will only make them jealous,' she said. 'The *Unegas* will want to take this house away from you. By God, Opothle, this house is big enough for twenty children and you have only three. You and Suna-lee work so hard at getting *things*, you never have time to make me more grandchildren.'

"She was always quarreling with Opothle about the English names he gave his children—William, Priscilla, and Jotham. Mary gave them all Creek names, but I have forgotten what they were except Priscilla's. Telassie, Mary called her, and for a time Priscilla seemed to prefer that to Prissie."

"They were your cousins," I said. "Much older than you?"

"William and Prissie always seemed like grown-ups to me, although they could not have been more than eight or ten years older. But Jotham was only a year older. Jotham and I became close friends, even though we were always rivals."

Dane chuckled quietly, and I thought he was recalling some amusing incident from that long-ago time, but he was watching the horseman outside, who had come within a hundred yards of the cabin and was beginning to circle it. "That young Crow boy out there—he knows I have a visitor and he's looking for the horse, but there is no horse." He sat rocking back and forth, continuing to smile until he heard his name called.

"Come to the door with me," he said, getting out of his chair and stamping the stiffness from his legs. "Seeing a stranger who might be a rival will give him something to think about."

A rather handsome young Indian sat astride a spotted pony. "You seen anything of my old man's Hereford bull around here?" he asked Dane, but his eyes studied me.

"No bull been around here," Dane replied.

"Must've gone off some other direction."

Dane nodded.

"He come over this way, you corral him?"

Dane said he would.

The young man touched the brim of his high-crowned hat. "See you." He gave me one more hard look, and rode off down the dirt road toward Dundee.

Dane closed the door against the cold morning air, and then laughed gleefully, like a mischievous child. "He wasn't looking for a bull. He was hoping to find Mary Amayi here. We'll see if he's smart enough to find her, that young man of visions." He went over to the fireplace and took a long-stemmed Indian pipe from the mantel and tamped tobacco into the slanted bowl. "Visions," he said. "We Indians live on visions." He plucked a small orange coal from the hearth with his bare fingers and deftly dropped it into the pipe bowl.

"Illusions, I suppose you would call them. Grandmother Mary began having visions one day after a blue hawk came crying from the north and told her Tecumseh had been killed in a battle with the Americans. A few days later the event was confirmed by a messenger from Tennessee. She was not one to spend much time grieving for those she loved or admired. The Maker of Breath had claimed Tecumseh and no one could bring him back. She turned her thoughts to the living, to Menewa, whom she thought would take Tecumseh's place.

"The Long Warrior, of course, would not listen to her pleas for an alliance with Menewa, especially after they heard from the Creek country that Menewa had raised the Red Sticks of war in several Creek towns, and was fighting those of his own people who would not follow him in his war to the death against the Americans. Nor would Opothle give her any support. Finally she went to the Runner and told him that she wanted him to go south with her to find Menewa and bring him back to the Cherokee country. She was sure that she and Menewa together could make the Cherokees understand that they were in great danger unless they united with the Creeks in their fight for survival.

"When the Runner realized that he could not persuade his mother to abandon her vision, he offered to accompany her if she would delay the journey until Sehoya gave birth to their first child. Sehoya was having a difficult time.

"Mary was sympathetic but she feared delay would be fatal to her plan. One night after everyone had gone to sleep, she slipped out of the house and rode off alone on her arch-nosed pony to find Menewa—just as she had ridden away many years before, except this time she was not burdened by a young child and was no longer a youthful woman. She must then have been close to sixty years. Afterward of course she knew it was all a vision, an illusion as you would say, but Grandmother Mary never cared much for a sensible and safe life. Without visions—or illusions—life had no flavor in it for her.

"Next morning they all knew where she had gone. The Long Warrior held a mild discussion with Qualla about riding after her, but Qualla advised against it. She would return only when her vision told her to return. Opothle offered the opinion that she must have been struck by senility, but the others only laughed at him for so foolish an observation. The Runner worried about her safety, and promised to go and bring her home as soon as Sehoya gave birth.

"A day or so later, Mary's departure faded into the background with the arrival in Okelogee of General Andrew Jackson and a company of militia. Jackson was desperate for more soldiers. He had been down the Coosa River butchering Creeks on the pretension that all Creeks were fighting for his British enemies. Most of his militiamen, however, had marched home to Tennessee at the end of their term of voluntary enlistments, some of his cavalrymen were deserting, and the Regular soldiers promised him by the United States Army were late in arriving.

"At that time, my father later told me, Jackson looked like Death himself, taller than six feet but thin and bony, one arm in a sling from an old wound, his cheeks hollow, his eyes glassy and feverish. 'We are all brothers fighting in one cause,' he told the Okelogee people, 'against the Red Stick Creeks armed by our British enemies. If the Red Sticks prevail, they will burn your Cherokee towns as they have burned peaceful Creek towns. Join with me in destroying them and you will gain the gratitude of your American brothers. The time will come when you will need powerful friends. Win the friendship of your American brothers now by your bravery.'

"He promised the Long Warrior he would give him the rank of a major of volunteers if he would raise companies of Cherokees from four towns and bring them to a stockade near the Ten Islands on the Coosa. As soon as Jackson rode off to the south, Opothle and the Runner confronted the Long Warrior and begged him not to help Jackson, but the Long Warrior had made up his mind. After securing the promises of most of the young men in Okelogee to follow him as warriors, he went off to recruit in three other towns.

"If Mary had been there, most likely she would have got out her old flintlock pistol and shot General Jackson out of his saddle, and a blessing it would have been for the Cherokees in the end. God knows what she would have done to the Long Warrior."

15

After leaving Okelogee, Mary rode long and hard each day so that she reached Tallagalla late on the fourth day. The nights were cold, the year being in the Little Spring Moon before the swelling of buds. As she approached the town through the last grove of bare trees, she wondered at the quietness. No barking dogs, no laughing children, no sounds of activity announced the presence of life in Tallagalla. When the trail brought her out upon a level bench of gravel, she saw only devastation where the town had stood only a few moons ago.

Instead of houses there were heaps of ashes, blackened skeletons of buildings, ruined fences. She rode on to where Menewa's great house had stood. Only the broken half of a mud chimney remained. His herds of cattle and horses had vanished. In a temporary shelter she found an old man and two old women. They told her that a great number of white soldiers and half-blood Creeks had come without warning while the town was undefended, and they destroyed everything. Menewa, his warriors, and the survivors of Tallagalla were said to be fortifying themselves at the Great Bend, a day's journey up the Tallapoosa.

Near sundown of the next day Mary found Menewa, a thousand warriors, and as many women and children, all hard at work building breastworks of logs across the neck of a peninsula surrounded on three sides by the Great Bend of the river. They had named the place Tohopeka, the fenced fort.

If Menewa was surprised to see Mary there he gave no sign. "Where are your sons, where is the Cherokee chief of Okelogee?" he demanded. "We need fighting warriors, not more women."

"My men are blinded," she answered. "Come back with me to Okelogee and help me open their eyes."

He shook his head. "There is no time for washing stupor from the eyes of the Cherokees. Tohopeka is the last stronghold of the Red Stick Creeks. We have been driven from Tallagalla, from Hillabee, from Artussee, from all the towns that would resist the march of the white conquerors. Here we can gather strength to carry the fighting once more to our enemies. Go back to the land of the Cherokees, Beloved Woman, and tell them of Tohopeka where there are men and warriors who are not afraid to die."

"Not until I have worked beside you in building this fort. When it is finished I will go, and bring you Cherokee warriors to help defend it."

At the Great Bend with Menewa was Red Eagle, a half-blood Creek known to his white enemies as William Weatherford, and it was he who was directing construction of the stockade. Pine logs had to be floated across the river and rolled into place, ends fitted, and portholes cut. For several days Mary worked with an ax until her hands were blistered and her muscles and bones ached. At last the barricade extended across the isthmus from water's edge to water's edge. It was taller than any man, with upper and lower ranges of portholes, and it curved to the center so that a frontal attacking force would meet fire from two sides and two levels.

On the day before Mary planned to start back to Okelogee, Creek runners came in from the west to warn Menewa of an approaching force of soldiers led by the Sharp Knife, Andrew Jackson. Their line of march was longer than the eye could reach, hundreds of walking soldiers, some in blue uniforms, and hundreds of mounted riflemen. Most disheartening of all were the many Cherokee auxiliaries led by chiefs who had once claimed friendship with the Creeks.

"They have been bought with Sharp Knife's false promises," Menewa said, his voice bitter as he turned to Mary. "What will you do now, Beloved Woman of the Creeks?"

"My place is here," she told him. "I will live or die at To-hopeka."

But the next morning she was provoked to anger when Menewa ordered her to accompany the women and children to a place of safety across the river. "I can shoot as well as any warrior," she protested.

"Go with the women and children," Menewa said sternly. "The seed of this tribe must be preserved."

"At my age," she replied, "seed lie sterile within me."

"Go. They have need of you. You are their Beloved Woman."

And so she went with the other women, crossing the river in canoes, and then wading through a muddy swamp to a mound of high ground concealed by thick brush. They had to wait there in silence, without fires to dry their moccasins and leggings.

Before midday she heard the first rattle of musket fire, followed by the continual crashing of small cannons. Although Mary saw none of the terrible scenes at the Battle of Horseshoe Bend, two members of her family were there, and one lived to tell her of what he saw.

Two days after Sehoya gave birth to a son, the Runner left Okelogee to journey into the Creek country in search of his mother. As she had done, he followed the old trail that led to Tallagalla, but on the third day somewhere along Chockelocko Creek he found a broad track left by a passing army, Andrew Jackson's army. He knew that the Long Warrior and his Cherokees were with these marching men. Reasoning that Jackson would be in pursuit of Menewa's Red Sticks, and that Mary would be wherever Menewa was, the Runner decided to follow the army—which he judged to be no more than a day or two ahead of him.

The Runner did not overtake Jackson's army, but he was close enough to hear the same clamor of opening battle that Mary heard. Crossing a narrow stream, he came out upon an open slope and was astonished to see masses of men drawn up in ranks before him. Two cannons, placed on a knoll facing the Red Sticks' formidable rampart, were firing alternately but the balls sank harmlessly into the soft pine logs. From portholes in the stockade, Creek sharpshooters occasionally scored a hit on the gunners or on the blue-uniformed Regulars who were trying to furnish protective fire.

After a few minutes of this futile exercise a bugle sounded and drums began to beat. Three horsemen came cantering to a halt on the Runner's right, and he recognized the center man as Andrew Jackson. The general wore a sour expression upon his long emaciated face, and he held his unhealed arm against his chest. Shouted commands echoed across the field, and several formations of foot soldiers began moving toward the log barricade. Frontiersmen in coonskin caps and deerskin jackets joined the Regulars in blue to make a sudden charge upon the stockade. Before they could reach it, the Creeks opened fire from the portholes, and the attackers quickly withdrew with their casualties. The cannons also were being pulled back up the slope.

Jackson was cursing and shouting. He sent one aide galloping down to his left, the other to his right. The Runner watched him as he painfully dismounted, holding to his bridle with his crippled arm while he urinated beside his horse.

In the brush behind Jackson, the Runner saw a sudden blur of movement, and then a Creek warrior came racing out with uplifted tomahawk. Reacting instantly with a shout of warning, the Runner turned his horse toward Jackson, who had spun around and was fumbling for his sword. It fell to the ground. A second later the Runner was out of his saddle, catching up the weapon. When he swung its point toward the crouching warrior, the Red Stick jerked to a stop. A pistol fired then, so close to the Runner's head that it made his ears ring. The Red Stick fell. Jackson strode forward, pistol in hand, and with the toe of his boot turned the body over. "Goddamned skulker," he said, and stared hard at the Runner, who was handing him his sword.

"Who are you? You have no deer tail on your head."

"Talasi the Runner. The Long Warrior's son."

Jackson frowned. "Your people are over there across the river." As he pointed to the bend of the Tallapoosa, his aides came galloping back, and Jackson turned toward them with a burst of profanity, not bothering to thank the Runner for saving his life.

By the time the Runner got his horse across the muddy river, the staccato of musket fire was increasing in intensity behind him, and when he came up onto high ground, he saw that the cannons were firing over the stockade into the Creeks' stronghold. He saw that the Red Sticks were completely surrounded. All around the bend of the river facing the peninsula were Cherokees wearing deer tails to distinguish them from the Red Sticks. And scattered along in the trees at their rear were mounted riflemen from Jackson's Tennessee militia.

Holding his nervous horse with a tight rein, the Runner scanned the long line of Cherokees, searching for the Long Warrior. A sudden outburst of yelling drew his attention back to the stockade. Through clouds of powder smoke he saw Jackson's soldiers scaling the barricade. A few minutes later as fleeing Red Sticks gathered on the river rim of the peninsula, the Cherokees and mounted riflemen opened a heavy fire upon them. Afterward the Runner learned that the Creeks had fastened canoes along their side of the river, but the Cherokees had swum underwater and pulled most of them away. Now the only means of escape for the Creeks was to leap into the river, where they became easy targets with no means of defending themselves.

For a few moments the Runner felt light-headed, intoxicated by the crackle of musket fire, the shouts of exultation and pain, the smell of acrid smoke that hung over the earth and river, the swift flow of men killing and dying. For that brief spell of time he wanted to be a part of the madness; he felt that he must lend himself to the fury of bloodletting; he must risk his life as the others were risking theirs.

And then he saw his father in the river, water reaching to his barrel chest, his white hair like silver under turban and deer tail. He was urging his warriors to follow. He seemed intent upon reaching the peninsula itself, for what reason the Runner could not guess. Jackson's blue-coated Regulars were already there, killing what few Red Sticks remained in the gullies and potholes.

Relaxing his reins, the Runner set his horse in motion through a thicket of budding willows. When he glanced at the river again he saw the Long Warrior floating in the water. At first the Runner thought his father was swimming, but he was moving too swiftly, his body tumbling in a narrow current. The Runner slapped his horse into a lope, grazing tree trunks as he splashed along the muddy bank, watching his father's white hair bobbing until it swirled into a shore eddy. There it joined a dozen dead men turning in a circle of bloody foam, their naked limbs intermingled. All around the bend many other bodies were lodged against logs and brush. If any Creek warriors had survived that deadly fire of the Cherokees and mounted riflemen, they were nowhere in view.

The Long Warrior was dead, a musket ball in his brain. From somewhere, Qualla suddenly appeared to help pull the body ashore. "A long time ago," Qualla said, "the Stalking Turkey saw this in a dream. It was foretold." The Runner had always thought of his father as the tallest of men, a giant image from childhood, but now in death he seemed shrunken and unshielded. Qualla built a fire and they sat beside the dead man through the night, saying nothing.

At dawn Jackson's army began moving out toward the south to pursue what remnants were left of Menewa's Red Sticks. As the mounted frontiersmen departed, some of them halted long enough to drag dead Creeks from the river, taking long strips of skin from the bodies to be dried and used for belts and bridles.

As soon as there was enough light, the Runner swam across to the peninsula and found an ax. He then searched for a cedar tree, chopped it down, and hewed out the center. After placing the Long Warrior in the cedar log and covering him with his blanket, he and Qualla held a ceremony over the fire, praying to the Maker of Breath and then extinguishing the fire with water to symbolize death. As no rocks were nearby to cover the log, they dug a hole in the sand and buried the Long Warrior on the high bank of the river.

Because there had been no women or children inside the Creek fortifications, the Runner guessed that they must have been in concealment somewhere near, but he did not know whether or not they had followed the fleeing Red Sticks. Nor was he certain that his mother was with them. Taking opposite directions, he and Qualla started circling outside the area of battle. He had not ridden a hundred yards through the late-morning mist when he saw several women struggling in swamp mud below a dome of high ground. They showed fright at his approach, and he called out: "Amayi, the Beloved Woman. Have you seen her?" One of them pointed toward the high ground.

He found two women beside a badly wounded man and he was about to ask where his mother was when he suddenly recognized her as one of the women in disheveled mud-spattered clothing. Her hair was matted and tangled. "Talasi!" she cried, and ran toward him, repeating his name over and over, embracing him as he dismounted.

The wounded man was Menewa, the other woman his wife. Menewa had been knocked down by a sword when the soldiers overran the stockade. Although his arm bled badly, he had lain still, hoping to be passed by as dead, but a soldier shot him in the head, the bullet passing through his mouth, tearing away several teeth. When he recovered consciousness it was dark. He crawled to the river, floated downstream, and then dragged himself across the mud to the high ground.

While Mary was telling the Runner about this, she saw something in his face that made her stop. "What is it, Talasi?" she demanded.

"The Long Warrior," he said. "Qualla and I buried him by the river."

He read the pain in her eyes before they closed. "He took the wrong pathway," she whispered. "But he was a warrior and did all the good he could as he saw it. He taught me how to laugh at the world no matter how hard things may be."

She sat down on a hummock of grass, breathing deeply. "You have come for me, have you not, my little Runner? But now there is no reason for me to go. Soon there will be no place for any of us. The Creeks will lose their homeland first, and then it will be the turn of the Cherokees. The most unyielding of the warriors are all dead now, or so torn in flesh like Menewa here they may never fight again." She looked up at the sun showing itself like a pale moon through the lifting fog. "Perhaps the Long Warrior is luckier than we. He is in the Country of the Spirits. They say it is always fair weather there, that one is never hungry. May he live in a warm and pleasant country of pure waters and every species of wild game. No, Talasi, there is no reason for me to go back with you. I shall stay here with the bones of the Long Warrior until the Maker of Breath claims me also."

The Runner kneeled in front of her, putting his hands on her shoulders. He was still slightly afraid of her, disturbed because he had seldom seen tears in her eyes before. "Creek Mary's blood is not here," he said. "It is in Okelogee. You have a new grandson."

Her eyes brightened at once. "Sehoya's child? My first full-blood grandson!"

"You must see him," he said.

"Yes, I must see him. I will go back with you, Talasi, if you will let me name this boy."

He nodded.

"Oh, Talasi, you do not know how my bones ache. I have

grown old and foolish. I want to see my full-blood grandson and I am lonesome for the Sleeping Woman."

16

"Horseshoe Bend," Dane said, "was the American Indians' Waterloo." He smiled one of his quick sardonic smiles. "I was told that by Mr. Teddy Roosevelt, your President. More Indians fought and were killed at Horseshoe Bend than in any other battle in the long history of warfare between your people and my people."

I confessed that I had never heard of Horseshoe Bend.

"No," he said, "the schoolbooks don't tell about Indian history. For us it was the turning point, the beginning of the end. Mr. Roosevelt and I, we talked about that one time when he was out here on a hunting trip. If Andrew Jackson had not destroyed the Red Stick Creeks at Horseshoe Bend, Mr. Roosevelt said, then he would have been ordered back to Nashville by the Governor of Tennessee and ended up as a forgotten frontiersman, and his name would not be in the schoolbooks either. But with the help of his Cherokee allies he destroyed the Red Sticks and that was *his* turning point. He became a great hero to the border settlers, went on to the Battle of New Orleans to become a greater hero, and because he promised the settlers he would drive *all* the Indians west of the Mississippi River and open our lands for them, they made him their President.

"Without his Cherokees there on the riverbank at Horseshoe Bend, Andrew Jackson would have won no victory. Most of the Red Stick Creeks would have got away to fight another day."

"So the Cherokees created their own engine of destruction by making General Jackson a hero?"

"Of course they thought then that they were gaining his undying friendship, making sure that the Cherokee Nation would endure as an ally of the United States. The best of the young Cherokee warriors were there at Horseshoe Bend. The Ridge, who was a major like my grandfather, and ever afterward called himself Major Ridge, was there, and Junaluska and Going Snake, and so was the great John Ross and several other Scots halfbloods. After Andrew Jackson betrayed them, turned upon them, they bitterly regretted what they had done. Old Junaluska said if he had known that Jackson would drive the Cherokees from their homes he would have killed him that day at the Horseshoe. And at least a hundred times in my youth I heard my own father, the Runner, curse himself as a blockhead for saving Jackson's life that day. If he had let that stalking Creek put a tomahawk in Andrew Jackson's skull the Indian people would have been rid of their most powerful enemy.

"Only Grandmother Mary saw the truth at the time, and what was to come in the future. She knew the meaning of Horseshoe Bend and was resigned to dying there, but after the Runner brought her back to Okelogee she was soon full of fight again. She always gave me credit for reviving her spirits."

"You were the Runner's and Sehoya's firstborn child, then?"

"And their only child. Sehoya died of the 'great chill' soon after Mary and the Runner came back to Okelogee, and Mary had to take care of me. As you know, she named me for that young Danish sea captain who brought his ship up the Savannah River before she met John Kingsley. Until I was four or five years old I thought Creek Mary was my mother. After my father took a new wife, Walina, I was told to call her 'mother,' and Mary became 'alisi' or 'grandmother.' But I was always closer to Mary than to Walina. We all lived in the house that had been Mary's and the Long Warrior's, although Mary gave its ownership to Walina. Opothle wanted Mary to come and live with his family in his richly furnished house with its black servants, but she would not leave the Little Singing Stream and the wonderful view of the Sleeping Woman.

"It's strange how old memories of people get mixed up with little things. The first object that I remember was Mary's neckpiece, that Danish coin. On warm summer days she wore only a skirt, leaving her breasts bare as all Creek women did before the white men came and shamed them into covering their bodies. Her breasts were round and firm as a young woman's until quite late in her life. She would sit with me in the shade of the arbor, holding me on her lap, singing or talking, sometimes laughing in that deep-toned way of hers until I would join in. And I remember that Danish coin always there between her naked breasts. She also had an hourglass that the Long Warrior had brought her from Nashville. She would let me hold it, watching the white sand drop grain by grain until I went to sleep.

"And to this day when I smell dried fruit—peaches or apples— or hear the sound of buzzing wasps, Grandmother Mary's face is always there before me. Every summer from the Little Ripening Moon to the Big Ripening Moon she would get peaches and apples from Opothle's orchard, slice them up and put them to dry on the roof, where they drew great swarms of lazy wasps.

"As soon as I began to talk Cherokee, she taught me Creek words and English words, every day a few new words, telling me over and over again that words are what give us power, that without words we are nothing, we do not exist. She also never let me forget that I had the blood of Creek Mary in my veins, that I was her only full-blood descendant. 'Sogonisi,' she would say, 'child of my son, someday you must take as your mate another full-blood. Never look upon the daughters of the Unegas, not even the half-bloods. Keep Creek Mary's blood always red.'

"But like most of us, her thoughts were not always in harmony. One day she told me the story of the Lady of Cofitachequi, a Georgia Creek who welcomed the Spanish explorer De Soto. 'She was a Beloved Woman of my people,' Mary said, 'and her warriors carried her in a chair decorated in many colors to meet the Aniskwani, the Spaniards. She took a necklace of pearls from her neck and gave it to De Soto, and like the evil white man that he was he repaid her by raiding Cofitachequi and taking all the pearls he could find in the town. And then he seized the Lady and carried her off with him on his marches. Not until many days afterward did she escape to return home and later bear De Soto's child. From the Lady of Cofitachequi my father was descended, and so you see I have the blood of the *Aniskwani* in my veins.' Well, the next time Grandmother Mary warned me that I must keep her blood red by taking a full-blood for my wife, I reminded her about that Spanish blood she carried. Oh, but she was angry at me, so angry that she emptied a cup of water on my head. 'You little whiddler,' she shouted. 'That was just a story. Don't you know truth from story?'

"No matter how bad I was, she never punished me by caning as the Scots people did their children. Instead she would try to make me look ridiculous in the eyes of others for whatever it was I had done. Her keenest punishment of all was to refuse to touch me, or talk to me, so that I would fear she had lost her affection for me. That pained me much more than a switch or a cane ever could have.

"In some ways she also had to take the place of my Uncle Opothle. Being my only uncle, Opothle was duty bound to teach me to hunt, but he seldom had the time for such instructions. He tried to teach me how to play *anetsa* and other games of ball, but he was awkward and my father took over. I played with the Bird clan boys, but was never good enough for the Okelogee teams. After my father brought Walina to live with us as his second wife, Grandmother Mary found time to teach me to hunt. As she often boasted, Mary could shoot as well as any of the men, with a muzzle-loader or her old flintlock pistol. She was fair with the bow and arrow, but after she taught me what she knew about shooting arrows, I soon surpassed her in distance and aim and seldom missed a deer after I'd got it in my sight. This seemed to please her. 'The old ways of deer hunting are the best,' she said. 'Gunpowder is the white man's curse upon us.' She taught me never to kill an animal without begging its forgiveness, and never to kill if we did not need the meat.

"Those were the happiest times of my life until I met Sweet

Medicine Woman, but that was a long time afterward and many long miles from Okelogee." He stretched his arms, stood up, and stamped his feet. "Old bones." He squinted out the window. "Sun's high and I'm hungry. Time to eat."

"Perhaps I should go back into Dundee," I said.

"Nothing to eat there. And your train east won't be coming till about dark. I got plenty beef stew and some smoked buffalo tongue."

"Buffalo tongue? I thought the buffalo were all gone."

"They're coming back. Cheyennes keep a secret herd down on the Lame Deer. Only white man ever killed one of our buffalo was Mr. Teddy Roosevelt. All he wanted was the head."

"I'd like some buffalo tongue and a bowl of your stew," I said. "And I want to hear the rest of Creek Mary's story."

He brushed a red-flowered calico curtain aside and went into a little pantry, returning with a big pot and an ancient rawhide parfleche that contained the buffalo tongue. After he had worked over the coals in the fireplace, he put the stew to going and sat cross-legged with his back to the heat.

"I said I was happy growing up in Okelogee, but I knew that the older people often were not. They talked over the heads of us youngsters much of the time about Andrew Jackson's betrayals, about agents trying to bribe Cherokee leaders in their unending greed for our lands, about white settlers getting thicker and thicker around us. But their greatest fear was of the government, which never stopped trying to persuade the Cherokees that they should move beyond the Mississippi River. The same things were happening to the Creeks, and helped bring the two tribes together again after the old wounds of Horseshoe Bend.

"The Cherokees were so fearful of being forced out of their homelands that they decided to become as much like the white people as they could. The chiefs kept working away to form a government with written laws, but they could not agree on whether they wanted to continue as a separate nation or become a state like Georgia or Tennessee. They invited missionaries to come in and start churches, and some of the more prosperous began to send their children north to New England schools.

"One of the liveliest memories of my youth was going on horseback with Grandmother Mary over to Oothcaloga Town to welcome the first students home from New England. Almost a thousand Cherokees gathered to see them arrive and hail them as heroes. All I could talk about on the way home to Okelogee was going to school in New England as soon as I was old enough.

"I never went, however. You see, two of the students fell in love with white daughters of the New Englanders, married them, and brought them back to the Cherokee Nation. They were Major Ridge's son, John, and Buck Watie, who later changed his name to Elias Boudinot to please an old gentleman of that name who befriended him. Now, it was perfectly all right for white male missionaries to take Cherokee girls for wives, but it did not set well with those New England church people for dark-skinned male Cherokees to mate with their pure-blooded lily-white daughters. No sir, they were mortified. After John and Buck made off with those Yankee girls, the New England churchmen closed their schools to Cherokees and opened little mission schools in the Cherokee country. This kept their daughters safe from the rest of us Cherokee boys who had set our hearts on going north to school."

With a laugh that was almost a cackle, Dane turned to stir the stew. "Well," he said, "I suppose they were like Creek Mary, they wanted to keep their blue blood pure. But in those times Mary was a good deal more concerned with saving the Cherokee Nation than her blood. She went around to all the neighboring towns, making speeches in the councils and talking to any who would listen. She ended every speech by shouting: 'Not one more foot of land to the whites!' And her listeners would usually repeat the words after her in a kind of chorus, several times. It became the Cherokee slogan.

"She always took me along on these journeys, to carry things for her and look after the horses. She wanted the Cherokees to put into writing their unwritten Blood Law which condemned to death anyone who sold Cherokee land or accepted bribes for ceding land. She also wanted them to hold elections the way the whites did, and let everybody vote for a single tribal chief. Her choice was 'Little John' Ross. 'He may have *Unega* blood,' she would say, 'but his heart is all Cherokee.'

"On one of her speaking journeys she met Sequoyah, and gave him no rest until he agreed to come along with us to Okelogee. You may have heard of Sequoyah. Not long ago the whites over in California named a certain kind of tree for him. He invented a Cherokee syllabary, so that for the first time our people could write and read in their own language. He was about Mary's age, and had a badly crippled leg. She told me that the way he dressed reminded her of the Long Warrior—an old-fashioned turban, a checked matchcoat, beaded belt, jeans, and buckskin leggings. Every time we stopped on the way home he would light up a long-stemmed pipe, puffing with such spirit that he surrounded himself in a cloud of smoke. I took a great liking to Sequoyah. He smiled often, talked in a soft voice, and before we reached Okelogee he taught me how to write and read sentences in Cherokee. He somehow discovered that the Cherokee spoken language had eighty-six different sounds, or syllables, and so he made eighty-six written characters, one for each sound. Sequoyah's syllabary was easier for me to learn than written English because as soon as I knew the eighty-six characters I could start writing and reading in Cherokee. I heard him tell Mary that he had left his wife. She had burned all his papers because she thought he was practicing witchcraft. In a way, I suppose he was."

17

While Dane was entering the first painful years of adolescence, a time when he and most of his friends began abandoning breechflaps to wear the white man's trousers, the Cherokees at last adopted a written constitution modeled after that of the United States. To further prove that they were as advanced as their troublesome neighbor nation, they established an elected legislature which began passing laws for the collection of taxes, issuing of licenses, building of roads, regulation of liquor sales, support of schools, and all the other things that the white men did through their governments. They elected Creek Mary's choice, John Ross, their principal chief. By special decree they declared that any individual Cherokee negotiating the sale of land to the whites without consent of the elected council would be guilty of treason and suffer death.

In Okelogee there were also swift and radical changes. After the Long Warrior was killed at Horseshoe Bend, the council chose Qualla to be their headman, but Qualla died in his sleep one night and the people turned to Talasi the Runner to guide them. Perhaps they knew that he would be well advised by his mother, Creek Mary.

It was she who was most insistent that Okelogee have a school for its young people who could no longer attend the white men's schools in New England. A log schoolhouse and an adjoining dwelling were built a short distance up the Little Singing Stream from the town, and with the assistance of John Ross they found a willing teacher who called himself a Methodist missionary.

Early in the Moon of Black Butterflies, the Runner and Dane drove over to Ross's Landing on the Tennessee River in one of Opothle's farm wagons to meet missionary Isaac McAlpin and his wife Harriet. With the McAlpins was an unexpected third person, Isaac's young sister Jerusha. The missionary explained that his sister was an orphan and had no home other than with him and his wife. Although Jerusha and her additional baggage crowded the wagon, Dane was secretly pleased by her presence. He had never seen so fair a young girl in his life. Most of the Scots girls were dark-haired and dark-eyed, but Jerusha was blonde, her skin like porcelain, her eyes light blue. Her hair, the color of ripened wheat, was cut short and parted severely in the middle, leaving her delicate translucent ears exposed to view. Three or four curls hung over her forehead.

Two seats had been fitted into the wagon, Isaac McAlpin riding up front with the Runner, and Harriet McAlpin and Jerusha occupying the second seat. Dane had to adjust himself as best he could among the trunks and boxes in the rear. He could not keep his eyes off Jerusha and she, becoming aware of this, often turned her head, flirting with bold looks and smiling lips and making occasional trivial remarks in her high soprano voice about the fine weather and the landscape.

Not until the next day, after the new arrivals were installed in their log dwelling adjoining the schoolhouse, could Dane have given any description at all of the other two McAlpins, whom he had scarcely glanced at during the wagon journey. Isaac was a gaunt man, with a long bony nose through which he seemed to talk. His face was spotted with enormous overlapping freckles; his hair was a faded red. His wife Harriet was short and plump, with bright little penetrating eyes that looked everywhere at once. She was spare of speech, making her opinions felt mainly by slight clearings of the throat, barely audible sighs, and movements of her shoulders.

A few days before the mission school was to open, the McAlpins were invited to the council house one evening to meet the Cherokees of Okelogee and answer any questions that might be raised about the school. Dane accompanied his grandmother, and as soon as she was seated in her usual place on one of the benches near the council fire, he climbed to the highest of the slab seats to join his cousin Jotham and other boys of his age group. In the council house they were not allowed to talk loudly, laugh, or engage in any sort of rowdiness. He sat there in silence, watching the single narrow entrance, hoping that Jerusha would come with her brother and sister-in-law.

Jerusha did come with the McAlpins, and Dane watched her moving behind them in a long white dress, seeming to float like a summer cloud. The Runner seated Isaac and Harriet on the council bench, motioning Jerusha to the upper seats. She climbed slowly, her eyes searching the unfamiliar faces, and then through the gloom and smoke she saw Dane and smiled. He shifted uneasily, not knowing whether to smile in acknowledgment. He stood up when she reached the top row. "May I sit here?" she asked in her soft musical voice. He nodded, giving Jotham a shove with one leg to make more room on the slab.

She sat on the end of the slab, so close that he could feel her breath against his cheek. "You are the only young person I know in Okelogee," she said. She smelled of some kind of strange spice. Not knowing what to say, Dane introduced Jotham to her.

"Do you have white blood?" she asked Jotham directly.

"My father and mother both have white blood," Jotham replied in a tone that he felt was grave enough for conversation in the council house.

"But Dane is full-blood Cherokee," she said, touching Dane's forearm with her fingers and drawing them along his coppery skin.

"Cherokee and Creek," he corrected her.

"I would not know the difference," she said, and coughed slightly. "The smoke is dreadful up here. Why are there no windows in this old building? But you have no windows in your houses, either, do you?"

Dane had never thought about the absence of windows in the Okelogee houses, but while he was trying to offer some explanation, Jotham remarked with pride that his family had windows in their house, and that his father had given the frames for the windows in the McAlpin house and school. Below them, faces were turning in their direction. Their voices had grown too loud, and down by the council fire the Runner had risen to his feet and was speaking in Cherokee about the McAlpins and the mission school.

When Isaac McAlpin began talking in English, Mary acted as interpreter, translating his phrases into Cherokee. After he finished, she announced that anyone in the council house could ask questions about the school. The immobile audience sat silent.

"Hear, now," she declared cheerfully. "Then I will start. Isaac McAlpin, you come to us as a Methodist to teach our children. We know nothing of Methodists, but we know of Presbyterians who have a church beyond the Sleeping Woman, and they talk much about their God. Will you teach our children of your Methodist God?"

"There is but one God," McAlpin replied.

"Our God is Esaugetuh Emissee, the Maker of Breath," Mary said.

McAlpin's freckled face reddened as he groped for words. "Whatever you may call God," he said seriously, "he is the same God. The Maker of Breath is God. In our school, we shall read daily from the Scriptures, the Holy Bible. We shall teach Christian morals to your children."

"Our children do not lie or steal, and they respect their elders," Mary responded in her huskiest voice. "We want you to teach them how to do sums so they will not be cheated when they must deal with the white people. We want you to teach them how to read and write. We want you to teach them of the great world around us. We want you to teach them of what has happened before they came into this world. We want you to teach them to be proud they are Cherokee. When you have done these things, you may teach them Christian morals and read from your Scriptures." She made a little bow to McAlpin, and turned her gaze around the crowded tiers of seats to see if anyone else wished to speak.

From the council bench the Stalking Turkey arose. His blind eye seemed fixed in a fierce stare upon McAlpin. His hair was streaked with gray, but he stood erect as a young warrior. "Does the *Unega*, McAlpin, come to us from heaven?" he asked.

McAlpin replied that he did not come from heaven, but was born on earth as were the Cherokees. He had come to Okelogee from the north, he said, from Pennsylvania.

"If he does not come from heaven," the Stalking Turkey continued, "how can he tell us what God would have us do?"

With a sigh, McAlpin replied that he had studied the word of God in the Bible, a copy of which he held up for all to see.

"The Maker of Breath gave books to the *Unegas*," the Stalking Turkey said. "He gave the Cherokees the bow and arrow. We should be satisfied to hunt for a living. We have taken the white man's clothes and trinkets. We have beds and tables like him. Some of us have books—and cats. All this is bad for us. The Maker of Breath is angry, and the wild game is leaving our country."

Some of the older Cherokees made soft sounds of agreement, but the Stalking Turkey knew he was expressing the opinion of only a few. No one spoke in his support, and no one in the crowd had other remarks to make or questions to ask.

Mary sat down, and the Runner took her place before the council fire. "Our hearts are good and straight," he said, and made a sign that the council was ended.

For Dane and Jotham, attending the mission school was a new and exciting adventure, and the presence of Jerusha McAlpin added allurement to an unaccustomed discipline that otherwise might have quickly become tedious. About thirty pupils were enrolled, their ages ranging from six to seventeen. For the first time in their young lives, most of the boys wore trousers instead of breechflaps. As Dane and Jotham were among the older group and were the only Cherokees who already knew how to read and write English, Isaac McAlpin placed the two boys with Jerusha in the rather complicated instruction schedule that he had to maintain in his one-room school. The three were therefore thrown together much of the time, Jerusha flirting first with one and then the other whenever she was sure that she was not being observed by the watchful eyes of her older brother.

At the midmorning recess periods, when the pupils were released for a few minutes to run and shout in the schoolyard, the three fell into the habit of seating themselves against the trunk of a large beech tree. From there they would disdainfully observe the childish actions of the younger pupils, and Jerusha would tantalize first Dane and then Jotham with remarks meant to make each think that he was favored above the other.

One day Jotham was absent from school because he had to assist his older brother, William, in rounding up a herd of cattle that had strayed, and for the first time Dane was alone with Jerusha at the recess period. He was uneasy because of this intimacy, and was made even more so by her first remark. "What are your feelings toward me, Dane?" she asked in the voice that seemed always to surround him with enchantment.

He was unable to find words to respond to such a direct question, and she went on: "You think I like Jotham more than I like you, but I do not. When we are older, I am going to be your wife."

He was stunned because he had never allowed his dreams to go beyond fantasies of holding this ethereal female creature in his arms, of mating with her as men did with women, an act that as yet he knew little about. In his elation he risked looking into her pale blue eyes, and then suddenly the face of Creek Mary rose up between them, and he could hear his grandmother's throaty voice denouncing him for his faithlessness: *Child of my son, never look upon the daughters of the Unegas. Keep Creek Mary's blood always red.*

"I cannot marry you," he said, the words seeming to force themselves painfully from his mouth. "I can marry only a full-blood of my people."

He feared that she would take offense, but she only laughed gaily, reaching out with one hand to tousle his thick hair. "You'll see," she said. "Our children will have glossy black hair like yours and cornflower eyes like mine."

After school was out that day, and on into the evening until he went to bed, he could not escape the persistent image of Jerusha McAlpin. She haunted his dreams, and the next morning he avoided his grandmother out of some strange dread that she would read what was in his thoughts.

When Jotham came by on the way to school, everything was quickly changed. Jotham walked in an uncharacteristic strut, and he had much to tell in loud conspiratorial whispers. The previous day after he and his brother William had recovered their strayed cattle, they had ridden their horses back by Moonherrin's Mill. Old Jack Moonherrin was not at home, but his four daughters were, and they had invited the brothers to stop. In the course of the visit, the two older daughters had taken Jotham and William into the mill loft. William had been there before, but it was the first time for Jotham, and he described the adventure in graphic detail to Dane. "I'm going back again right after school," Jotham said, "and you are going with me."

Less than a year past, Jack Moonherrin had hauled his mill wheel and grinding machinery over the mountains from somewhere in Carolina, setting up on a swift-running descent of the Little Singing Stream about a mile beyond where the new schoolhouse was later built. He had brought with him four half-blood daughters, but no wife, and the girls assisted in husking corn ears and shelling the grain which he ground into meal. Moonherrin had expected most of his trade to come from the Scots and their half-blood descendants, but the Cherokees also found it convenient to bring their corn to the mill, giving the miller a share of their grain in exchange for the quickly ground meal.

In the meantime a considerable number of rumors about Moonherrin had spread around Okelogee. It was said that he had killed his Cherokee wife and was asked to leave Carolina. It was also said that he secretly made a kind of *tafia* from corn that was much stronger than rum, and that sometimes he and his daughters got drunk and sang and laughed and danced all through the night. From time to time, Moonherrin would load his wagon with bags and casks and drive away to trade in the villages east of the Sleeping Woman. He never took his daughters along on these journeys, which lasted for several days. It was during these times that the older boys of Okelogee discovered the availability of the Moonherrin daughters, visiting them usually under cover of darkness.

And so it was that Dane on that one day in late autumn expunged the persistent image of Jerusha McAlpin from his mind, replacing it with the tawny vision of one of the Moonherrin girls. In reality he found Ellen Moonherrin to be ill shaped, and coarser than any of the Cherokee girls that he knew. But she was patient, jolly, and instructive, and he was grateful to her for initiating him into the secret pleasures of conjoining males and females.

Next day, to Dane's dismay, Jerusha returned to his inner vision, this time with more urgency than ever before. When he glanced secretly at her in the schoolroom, he wondered if she had the fleshly passion of Ellen Moonherrin. How soft were her thighs, how thick was her bush? Unlike the wiry black tuft of Ellen Moonherrin, her golden hairs there surely would be as fine as the down on a young eagle's breast.

A wooden ruler rapped sharply against the top of his head, and the nasal voice of Isaac McAlpin ripped his vision apart. "Come to attention, young man! I shall repeat the question only once again."

18

Old Dane's beef stew was balanced with exactly the right amounts of tender cubes of meat and juices and herbal flavors, surpassing anything in that line the renowned chef at Willard's Hotel in Washington ever offered his admiring public. On the other hand, the buffalo tongue was a bit tangy for my over-civilized palate, and my wise host somehow knew that. "Tongue is better eaten raw, fresh after the kill," he said almost apologetically as I nibbled at what was meant to be a rare epicurean treat. "I can barely remember now how my Cherokee stomach revolted at raw tongue and liver when I joined the Cheyennes for my first buffalo feast."

We dined at a folding table that extended ingeniously from beneath the cabin's east window, giving us a splendid view of the enormous landscape, the distant flat-topped butte, and the high blue sky. "It's strange what a person remembers from days long gone by. Little snatches of words said by others, sudden expressions on people's faces, scenes in the mind like frozen pieces of time. In those days when I was more sensitive to blooming life, I was aware of great events taking place around me, but I did not think of them as affecting me. They were things to be dealt with by my elders, leaving me free to roam the woods, compete at ballplay, learn the secrets of the flesh.

"There was much talk about the building of a capital for the Cherokee Nation. New Echota, it was called, and the Cherokee leaders saw it as their Washington City. The new town was only a day's journey from Okelogee, and I remember my father's enthusiasm for its future, how he described its broad streets and predicted a day when New Echota's crude log buildings would be changed into the permanence of brick and stone. I remember Grandmother Mary's keen excitement when my father brought home from New Echota a first copy of the *Cherokee Phoenix*. Buck Watie, or Elias Boudinot as he called himself then, was the editor, and the newspaper was printed in both English and Cherokee, from type especially made to use Sequoyah's syllabary. This was the first newspaper published by any Indians in America, and it contained news of our nation, texts of new laws passed by our legislature, and occasional pieces meant to whet our interest in learning, civilization, and politics. We all were very proud of the *Cherokee Phoenix* because it symbolized more than anything else the success of our efforts to become so much like the Anglo-Americans that they would stop thinking of us as being savages. We thought they would want us to stay where we were on our ancestral lands, a good-neighbor nation exactly like them, and that there would be no more talk about moving the Cherokees west of the Mississippi River.

"Many full-blood Cherokees began changing their names, so as to have first and last names like the Anglo-Americans. Uncle Opothle started using Kingsley for his last name—Kingsley was his father's name as you know—and my cousin made me envious at school when he signed his name as Jotham Kingsley. For a while I called myself Dane Warrior, but Grandmother Mary always laughed uproariously at me for such false show and I soon dropped it.

"It was at about this time that Andrew Jackson became President of the United States, and if the Cherokees had been allowed to vote, almost all would have voted for him. As you may recall, many of our leaders helped him win that battle at Horseshoe Bend, and they believed that as President he would now show his gratitude by protecting the Cherokees from ever increasing intrusions on our land by Georgia settlers.

"To encourage President Jackson's support, Chief John Ross led a delegation to Washington, and my father was one of those chosen for the journey. I found out afterward that Ross had first asked Grandmother Mary to go, but she had formed such a dislike in her heart for Andrew Jackson because of what he had done to the Creeks at Horseshoe Bend that she feared she would not be able to hold her tongue and thus do harm to the Cherokee cause. And so the Runner, my father, went in her place. At the time, I was so busy hunting after deer in the forest and girls in the town that I don't even recall my father's leavetaking, but I well remember the sullen anger that hung about him for days after he returned.

"Grandmother Mary tried to get him to talk but he would say little more than that President Andrew Jackson was a betrayer of the Cherokees. In strong words Jackson had told the Cherokee delegation to move their people west before the whites of Georgia overran their towns and caused bloodshed. I think that what annoyed my father most was Jackson's manner toward the Cherokee delegates, most of whom had been so loyal to him during the war. He called them 'my children,' as though they were unworthy of being treated as equals. And then when they went to seek help from congressmen, they met with the same patronizing talk. 'The Congress has always aimed to own the Indian tribes,' the Runner said to Mary, 'and if they get away with that, someday they will think they own all the whites, too.'

"But the most crushing blow of all came soon after my father returned from Washington. I could sense from the words and faces of the adults in Okelogee that we were under some great danger after the government of the state of Georgia declared there was no longer any Cherokee Nation. All lands claimed by Cherokees were now a part of the state of Georgia, soon to be opened for settlement by whites. In other words, the Cherokees no longer had any title to the land on which they lived. Furthermore, all our own Cherokee laws were wiped out. Whites no longer had to honor contracts made with Cherokees, and Cherokees could no longer testify against whites in any court, no matter the grievance. And what seemed harshest of all, we were forbidden to hold meetings.

"I remember Grandmother Mary saying that the Georgia politicians were trying to frighten us into fleeing our country, but that we should refuse to be frightened. Every town in the Cherokee Nation held a forbidden meeting as soon as they heard about the Georgia law, and Chief John Ross was soon on his way to Washington to use the white man's courts to challenge the law.

"As you must know, it has never been easy for our people to be heard in your courts, and John Ross was not surprised to find doors being closed in his face everywhere he turned. The chief of the Supreme Court, a man named Marshall, claimed to be sympathetic toward the Cherokees, but he said his court could not hear our case against the state of Georgia because we were a foreign nation! It was as if we had no right to be in America. Ross and his delegation came home, believing that the United States recognized us as a nation, and hoping maybe that would keep the Georgia whites from invading our lands.

"A few months later, however, all hope of aid from the United States was crushed when the Congress passed the Indian Removal Law. It was late spring, I believe in the Moon of Violets, with leaves full green on the trees, the air filled with blossom fragrance, birdsong, and insect buzzings, the Little Singing Stream running over its banks, when the news came to Okelogee.

"Grandmother Mary had foretold this black day when all the tribes east of the Mississippi would be banished from their homelands. This was something that land-greedy old Andrew Jackson had wanted for a long time, and now he had used his power to get it written into law.

"At the Okelogee council that my father as headman called immediately, Mary scolded the warriors unmercifully. I can remember some of her words, coming strong like a chant: 'You refused to listen to Tecumseh. Instead you turned upon the very people who could have saved us. Now the sun has gone down on all that. We will not look behind us. Now we must face the *Unegas* who would drive us from the lands of our ancestors. I leave it to our leaders to tell us what we must do. If they tell us to fight and die here, Creek Mary will fight and die. My own feet will never willingly take me from these hills and waters that I have learned to love as I love my children.'

"For several days the councils continued, and then one afternoon a runner came to our house from New Echota with a mes-

sage for my father from Chief John Ross. President Andrew
Jackson had summoned the leaders of Indian tribes east of the
Mississippi to gather at Nashville. Jackson wanted to meet them
there to discuss conditions for immediate removal of their people
to lands west of the Great River.

"I could tell from my father's face as he read the message that
he was both angered and pleased. He called Mary to come and
see it. 'Little John Ross is going to defy the Sharp Knife Jackson,'
he shouted. 'Not one Cherokee will attend the President in Nashville. Instead our nation will gather at New Echota to make our
own decisions.'

"For the first time in many days, Mary's deep laughter came
booming out in the house. 'A national council in defiance of
Georgia law,' she said. 'Hear, now, only the Maker of Breath can
keep Creek Mary from speaking at that council in New Echota.'"

19

During the last weeks of that summer of 1830, only a few sprin-
kles of rain fell, and on a certain day in early autumn an observer standing on the highest point of the Sleeping Woman
could have marked the location of all trails to New Echota by
lazy streamers of red dust lifting into the windless air above the
trees. It seemed that every living soul in the Cherokee Nation
was bound for the capital to learn what their leaders could tell
them of their future. They came in wagons, in buggies, on horseback, and on foot across many miles of mountains and valleys.

Some may have feared but none could accept the dreaded

probability that this great gathering in defiance of the laws of Georgia and the demands of the President of the United States might be the last time they would ever see their elected council assemble in the roughhewn capital of this doomed democracy of the American Indians.

At sunrise two of Opothle's wagons left Okelogee loaded with nine passengers, blankets, bedding, tenting cloth, and foodstuffs to last three or four days. They started with Opothle and his wife Suna-lee, his daughter Priscilla, and Jotham in the first wagon, and the Runner, Mary, Dane, Isaac and Jerusha McAlpin in the second. At every stop, some of the young people would exchange places in the wagons, and when the going was slow on upgrades, they would get out and walk.

Before that morning of departure the families held long discussions about who was to stay in Okelogee and who was to go to New Echota. The Runner's wife, Walina, being shy and not caring for crowds, begged to remain at home to harvest her late summer garden. William wanted to go, but Opothle asked him to stay behind to look after the house, the livestock, and their black slaves. Of late, Opothle had been worried about reports of white riders from the south who called themselves Georgia Pony Guards. Pretending to be official keepers of the peace, the Pony Guards raided prosperous Cherokees and stole cattle, horses, and slaves. They had never come as far north as Okelogee, but Opothle warned William to keep a sharp lookout for strangers, and to make certain the slaves brought the livestock into the barns every night.

"Would that you could go to New Echota," Opothle told him. "John Ross asked that we bring our sons and daughters so that they may hear and remember what is decided, and can then tell it to their sons and daughters. The fate of our nation may be decided at this council. Each of us will try to remember what is said and tell you what we have heard."

Because the mission school was closed for the New Echota council, the Runner invited Isaac McAlpin to attend as an observer. Soon afterward, with Dane's willing assistance, Jerusha managed to join the pilgrimage. If Harriet McAlpin desired to go or resented being left alone, she gave no clear indication of either. On the morning of departure, Harriet gave Isaac a quick farewell kiss on his cheek, but her bright penetrating eyes were fixed entirely upon Jerusha, who lifted her skirt to climb boldly into the wagon and place herself close beside Dane among the piles of bedding. Harriet cleared her throat loudly and sighed with exasperation as she watched the wagon roll away.

The two wagons reached New Echota shortly before sundown, and by the time they found a camping place in a pine grove, built a cooking fire, and brought water from the ever flowing spring around which the new capital had been located, darkness was upon them.

During the early evening, friendly visits were made back and forth among the families whose wagons and campfires ringed the broad level area from which they hoped would rise one day a capital worthy of the Cherokee Nation. There was no dancing or music; the occasion was too solemn for celebration. Yet all were dressed in their best clothing, the women and girls in bright-colored calicos, many of the men wearing Anglo-American shirts and trousers and an occasional beaver hat, but most still favored moccasins over the stiff uncomfortable trading-post shoes. Here and there was an old man in a deerskin or blanket tunic with a red sash around his waist and a blue cotton handkerchief fashioned into a turban, as in the old days.

After suppers were finished and chores completed, hundreds of young people walked around the entire circle of campfires. Dane and Jerusha and Jotham and his sister Priscilla were soon joined by Griffa McBee, one of the half-blood Scots girls who had recently begun attending Isaac McAlpin's school. Their progress was like a slow circling dance, and the firelight reflected on the moving figures lent a romantic air to the autumn night. Jerusha walked very close beside Dane, her body touching his in secret little caresses.

"How handsome the Cherokees are tonight," she whispered. "Especially you, Dane. When will we be married? So we can be together like this always!"

Before he could say a word, Mary's accusing face materialized out of the dim light, fading away when Jerusha's quivering mouth touched his ear: "I would like to sleep on the ground with you this night, instead of in the wagon with your grandmother," she said.

That was always the arrangement when the Cherokees traveled by wagon; the women and girls slept on the wooden beds of the vehicles, with tent cloth draped across the sideboards to shield them from dew or rain and give them some privacy. The men and boys slept where they chose, sometimes under the wagons or sheltered by tent canvas beneath the trees.

Next morning a yellow sun in a smoky sky promised another cool day. For the first time, they could see clearly the beginnings of New Echota—a huge log council house, a courthouse, four stores and trading posts, the printing shop of the *Cherokee Phoenix*, and six dwellings, some with brick chimneys and clapboard sides.

Everyone was expected to attend the speeches, which began soon after breakfasts were finished, although the crowd—formed in a wide semicircle facing the council house—was so immense that not half the listeners could hear what was said. Around the fringes of the assembly, two companies of Cherokee Light Horse, wearing blue blanket-cloth tunics, kept a lookout for stragglers and strangers. This cavalry guard had been organized by Major Ridge to keep the peace, and its strength was increased for the council.

Old Going Snake was chosen speaker for this council. Dressed in a frock coat and wearing the cockaded hat given him by Andrew Jackson at Horseshoe Bend, he used his voice like a trumpet: "The *Unegas* in their greed for our land are like the cougars we see in the forests, with slain deer all around them, so filled with meat they can scarcely drag their bellies across the ground, yet never satisfied, always wanting more. We hold this country from our ancestors. We have a blood right to it. We call on the Maker of Breath, of Earth, Sky and Weather to witness what we do here and help us choose what is best for our people."

The speeches continued through the morning. Many great

leaders of the Cherokees made statements, including Major Ridge, his son John who had been educated in New England, editor Elias Boudinot, and his younger brother Stand Watie. Opothle spoke in favor of another appeal through the white men's courts, but he also advised that the people of each town organize a local Light Horse company to defend themselves from marauding Georgians who under the new state law could no longer be brought to court by Cherokees for assaults on their persons or theft of their property. When it came Mary's turn to speak, the listeners rose to their feet, crowding closer to hear her words.

"I speak for the women of our people," she cried, "for those who endured pain to bring all of you into this world, the women who cultivate our land, who grow the food that sates your hunger. Who, more than we women, knows the value of our lands? I speak to the men: Your mothers, your wives, your sisters, your daughters beg of you not to part with any more of our land, but keep it for our children. The Maker of Breath placed us here to live in peace, but we women have borne and raised up warriors to defend us in our villages. Do not behave like a craven dog that carries its tail on its back but when frightened drops it between its legs and runs. Our lives are in the hands of the Maker of Breath. He gave to our ancestors the lands we live upon. We are determined to defend them, and if it is His will, our bones shall whiten on them, but we will never give them up. Not one more foot of land to the *Unegas!*" *Not one more foot of land to the whites!* the crowd began chanting. *Not one more foot of land to the whites!* The sound rolled across New Echota like the low thunder of a summer storm.

After the noon rest, Dane and his companions would have preferred wandering off into the surrounding woodland, but except for Jerusha McAlpin none would have dared being caught leaving the council grounds. When the crowd was reassembling in the afternoon, Jotham and Griffa McBee somehow became separated from Dane, Jerusha, and Priscilla. Long before the last oration was finished, Jerusha was asleep, her head resting against Dane's shoulder with Prissie looking on disapprovingly.

When they all met again at their camping place, the sun was still an hour high. While Suna-lee and the girls began preparations for supper, Jotham touched Dane's shoulder and motioned for him to move away from the wagons. "Do you think you could persuade Jerusha to slip out of the wagon tonight?" he asked in a cautious whisper.

Dane felt a sudden dryness in his mouth. "I will ask her." He was eager for a night adventure, yet he feared that what might happen would draw him into a permanent commitment to Jerusha.

"Griffa says she'll come out if Jerusha will," Jotham said.

The arrangement was made while they were eating dinner in the twilight, Jerusha becoming so animated that Dane feared she would arouse everyone's suspicions. At bedtime, which came soon after the campfire died to coals, the two boys took their blankets a few yards back in the pines from where their fathers and Isaac McAlpin bedded under a wide tent cloth slung over a tree limb. Wide awake with expectancy, the boys waited until the sounds of deep and regular breathing came from the tent. Then they left their blankets and crept deeper into the woods, to their prearranged rendezvous—a large chestnut tree with low-hanging branches.

"Suppose the girls don't come?" Dane said, half hoping they would and half hoping they would not.

"Griffa will. Jerusha may be afraid."

A rustle in the dry undergrowth and a snapping of twigs announced the approach of someone. Although there was no moon, the starlight revealed a feminine form moving uncertainly toward them.

"Griffa!" Jotham called out in a loud whisper.

"No, it's me, Jerusha." She laughed with sudden delight at finding them so easily.

"Keep your voice low," Dane warned her. She was still wearing the red dress with the neat white collar she had worn that afternoon. She seemed to float right out of the starlight to fling her arms around his neck and kiss him on the lips. "Your dear grandmother," she said. "I think she may have seen me slip my nightgown over my clothes, but she went right to sleep, breathing a soft little snore. All I had to do was slide out of the wagon."

A few minutes later Griffa was there, almost startling them with her sudden appearance. Jotham pushed the low limbs of the chestnut aside. It was like entering a tent, the dancing leaves dimming the starlight and making the distant campfires flicker like fireflies.

With unspoken understanding, Jotham and Griffa vanished to the farther side of the great tree trunk. After brushing away dead leaves and chestnut burrs to clear a place on the sandy ground, Jerusha seated herself cross-legged and removed her morocco shoes. In the faint glow of light she was a smiling enigmatic ghost. "I love you, Dane," she whispered, leaning forward to touch her forehead to his.

The words he meant to say stopped in his mouth. Instead of telling her that she was in his heart, too, but that he could never marry any *Unega*, he circled her with his arms and they lay on the sand. First he sought her lips and then their bodies pressed close together. For a moment he wished that she were Ellen Moonherrin, who needed no instruction, and then she caught his roving hand. "I've never—I'm only seventeen, Dane." She drew away and sat up, frowning at him, but her fingers loosened their grip on his wrist and began caressing the back of his hand. She leaned forward and kissed him, her lips warm and yielding against his. He could feel her breasts against his chest.

A flare of light and sudden sound—the crashing of underbrush —struck their senses. Someone carrying a pine torch was prowling very close. Through the chestnut leaves Dane could see the light moving directly toward the tree. "It's brother Isaac," Jerusha whispered. "Looking for me!"

Without a word they scurried around the trunk. Although still locked in an embrace, Jotham and Griffa were watching the light. They stood up, and all four pressed against the chestnut trunk. When Isaac thrust his torch through the overhanging limbs on the opposite side, Jerusha moaned in Dane's ear: "My shoes, my shoes!" But evidently her brother did not see the shoes among the leaves and chestnut burrs. He went on, stumbling through thick brush, leaving the tar scent of burning pitch pine behind.

"I must run!" Jerusha gasped. "I'll beat him back to the wagon. If he caught me here, he'd make my flesh smart with a whipping." Dane followed her around the tree trunk and helped get the morocco shoes back on her feet.

"Isaac knows you were gone from the wagon," he said.

She sniffed petulantly. "If he dares say anything I'll scold him for thinking females don't have to answer a call of nature same as men and boys."

At that remark Griffa started to giggle, but Jotham put his hand over her mouth. "Shut up! He'll hear you."

Jerusha had already ducked through the branches, and was running toward the pines. After a moment, Dane followed, walking slowly at first. Then he saw Isaac's torch moving far to the left, and he risked trying to catch up with her. But by the time he reached his and Jotham's blankets he knew she must already be back in the wagon with his grandmother.

The next day there was some excitement when the speechmaking was interrupted by the unexpected arrival of a well-dressed white man, a government agent from Washington. The Light Horse guard escorted him and his mount in to the council bench where he presented his credentials to Going Snake. "I seek Chief John Ross," the man said. "I was told he would be here."

From across the table, Ross nodded to him. "What is your business, sir?"

Before the agent could reply, Creek Mary was on her feet. "Let him speak to all of us," she said. "Let him say why he has come here, so that all may hear."

Ross smiled. "Agreed," he said, and motioned to the visitor to speak to the assembly.

"I am Colonel John Lowrey," the agent said in a loud voice as he turned to face the crowd. "I thank you for granting me leave to present the views of the American government toward promoting the future peace and happiness of all our people."

Major Ridge rapped his knuckles against the tabletop. "For whom do you speak, Colonel Lowrey?"

"For the American government, sir," Lowrey replied, his face flushing.

"The American government is made of men, as ours is made of men and women. What man sent you?"

Hesitating a moment, Lowrey answered: "I am a personal agent for the Secretary of War."

"Ah!" This time Elias Boudinot rose to his feet. "So you speak for Secretary John Eaton, whose mouth speaks the words of Andrew Jackson." Boudinot's handsome face showed anger and his voice had a cutting edge to it. "We have a report from Washington that Eaton stated publicly that it is his belief the Cherokees can no more be educated in the ways of white men than can wild turkeys. Look around you, Colonel Lowrey. Do we look to you like a flock of wild turkeys roosting in the forest?"

Loud hoots and laughter drowned out Lowrey's response. Although now quite ill at ease, he continued: "I will put plainly to you the message I was ordered to bring your principal chief, John Ross. It is now the law of this land that all Indian tribes east of the Mississippi River must remove to the west of that river. For those tribes that go in peace, the American government will pay fair recompense for personal property that must be left behind, will pay the costs of removal, and will guarantee tribal lands equal in extent to the lands abandoned. But for those tribes that resist peaceful removal, those who must be removed by force of arms, there will be no payment of any kind."

Before Lowrey could say more, a spontaneous chant began at the front of the crowd and spread quickly to a thunderous reply: "Not one more foot of land to the *Unegas!* Not one more foot of land to the *Unegas!*"

And no sooner had the emissary from Washington mounted his horse and started away than Creek Mary was on her feet demanding that the council draw up a statement to the American government protesting the removal order. During that afternoon the papers were passed through the crowd and before nightfall more than three thousand Cherokees signed their names to the petition. It would be taken to Washington at the earliest possible date and presented to the Congress by Chief John Ross.

At their late supper in the pines that evening, Mary was in a jolly mood. She joked with Dane and somehow managed to draw him aside from the others for a moment. He never ceased being amazed at how much she knew about him. "That yellow-haired girl," Mary said in a husky whisper. "She has the sweetness of honey. Taste the honey if you must, but remember your promise to me, Dane. Creek Mary's blood." Her eyes widened as she looked into his. He was not sure whether she was laughing at him or not, but he was sure she meant what she said.

That night he had no problem in deciding what he was to do about the sweet honey of Jerusha McAlpin. At bedtime her brother Isaac slept under the wagon, with his long legs thrust out below the tailgate.

Most of the Cherokees began leaving New Echota early on the morning of the last day of the council. Chief John Ross had his buggy brought up beside the council house, and the remaining company of Light Horse lounged beside their mounts, waiting to escort him home. Being a headman, the Runner remained for the last black-drink ceremony, and Opothle was busy helping with the final written draft of protest against removal that Ross and his delegation would soon be taking to Washington.

In the pine grove Suna-lee and the girls prepared a hasty noon meal while Dane and Jotham hitched the horses to the wagons. Isaac McAlpin was loading the last of the bedding when Opothle and the Runner came out of the council house and started directly toward the wagons across one of the weed-grown squares of New Echota.

Suddenly from an opening in the trees across the way, a file of six horsemen appeared, moving in a slow trot. They were white men, bearded and roughly dressed, some wearing leather dragoon caps, others wide-brimmed hats. All carried heavy-barreled flintlock rifles slung against their legs; some were also armed with pistols, long knives, and belt axes. The riders headed directly toward the wagons, their rhythm marked by the faint sound of tinkling bells. Just about the time that Opothle and the Runner reached the wagons, the horsemen halted only a few yards away.

The leader of these riders had an empty socket where his left eye should have been; the healed flesh was a corrugated rubescent scar. A piece of one nostril had been bitten away in the same eye-gouging fight that had lost him his organ of sight. Long unkempt hair the color of dirty sedge grass sprayed from beneath his black hat brim, which drooped under the weight of several tiny bells that were braided to the leather. Wreathed in a band around the crown was the withered skin of a rattlesnake.

"You-uns live hereabouts?" he asked. As he spoke, tobacco juice ran from the corners of his mouth. He spat, exposing gaps between yellow teeth, and then wiped his lips on his sleeve.

The Runner glanced at Opothle, who answered: "We all live at Okelogee."

"What you doin' so far from home?"

Opothle looked him straight in the eye. "We had business to attend here."

"Business?" The man laughed, making the hat bells jingle, and some of his companions joined in the mirthless laughter. "What do you iggerent redskins know about business? Dressin' up in white men's clothes don't make you white men. You half-breed, ain't you?"

Opothle could not keep the disgust from his eyes, but he managed a dignified affirmative. "My father was an Englishman."

"All dressed up like you was a gentleman, ain't you? Well, we got word you Cherokees havin' a meetin' up here. If you havin' a meetin', it's agin' the law of Georgia, and we come to break it up. I reckon you heard about the Pony Guard. That's us."

The man turned his head, the sun glistening off the rattlesnake scales on his hat. He fixed his one eye on Jerusha. "Who's that white gal?"

"She's my sister," Isaac McAlpin answered. "I'm schoolteacher at the Okelogee mission."

The man nodded. "I reckon you knowed you got to have a

permit from the Governor of Georgia to live among these God-
less red niggers. You got that permit on you?"

Isaac shook his head.

The Pony Guard leader took a twist of tobacco from his
pocket and bit into it. He grinned at a pimply-faced rider with a
wispy chin-beard, who was on his left. "Cyrus, you reckon we
oughta take this here schoolteacher back to Milledgeville?"

Cyrus jerked a thumb toward the council house. "Looky
there."

The Cherokee Light Horse in their blue tunics were formed
into a rank facing the wagons, obviously concerned by the presence of the Georgia Pony Guard.

"Goddamned red rantallions," the one-eyed man growled.

"Let's give 'em a chase," the pimply-faced Cyrus said.

"Hellfire, they's two of them to one of us. When it's t'other
way around, we'll take 'em." He looked at Isaac McAlpin. "Next
time I see you, schoolteacher, you better have that permit. I ain't
got no use for a white man let his little sister mess around redskins. Let's go!" He wheeled his horse, his five companions following quickly, and they filed off in the same slow trot toward
the woods from which they had come.

"Rabble!" Mary shouted after them. "The scum cods should
all be hanged from the nearest tree."

Chief John Ross's buggy, with the Light Horse following
smartly behind, left the road and angled toward them across the
open ground. Ross pulled his team to a halt and stood up. "They
made threats, I suppose?"

"The threats were addressed mainly to me," McAlpin replied.

"The leader of that gang is a murderer and a thief," Ross said.
"Name of Suggins. His men call him One-Eye Jack. With the
laws of Georgia behind him and no law on our side, he's a dangerous threat to us. We must show him a wide berth until we
can secure some protection from the American government."

"We must prepare to defend ourselves from such marauders,"
Opothle declared.

"He may have marked you," Ross said, "and you'll be travel-

ing much of the way by night. Six men of the Light Horse will
escort you home to Okelogee."

20

"We returned to Okelogee without any trouble," Dane said,
"but Uncle Opothle did not waste any time organizing a local
Light Horse to protect us from such as One-Eye Jack Suggins
and his Pony Guard. Maybe those Georgia bullies heard about
Okelogee's Light Horse and stayed away, but more likely it was
our remote location, maybe it was the nearby presence of Moonherrin's Mill and the Scots families that saved us for a while.
Anyway, every day or so we would hear about trouble in other
Cherokee towns, no longer just stolen horses and cattle but barn-
and fence-burnings, and then when people began to fight back
they were beaten and taken off under arrest for resisting the
Georgia laws. One day we heard they had arrested Elias Boudinot for publishing reports about these raids in the *Cherokee
Phoenix.*

"Not long after that, One-Eye Jack Suggins and his marauders
came back into our lives. They didn't ride in on the main trail
from the south, where our Light Horse kept a regular watch.
They slipped in from the west, following the Little Singing
Stream down out of the hills, and surrounded the schoolhouse,
about twenty of them this time. It was Friday afternoon, and
Isaac McAlpin had the younger pupils lined up for their spelling
bee while we older ones were busy studying words for our turn.
I heard hoofbeats outside, but paid no attention until the door

flew open at our backs and the jingle of little bells sounded behind me. I knew it was Suggins before I turned around, dreading to look upon his monstrous face. He had a big trace chain slung over one shoulder and was grinning like some wild beast of the forest. Five or six men came in with him, their pounding boots making the floor shake as they marched down on poor pale-faced Isaac.

"'You're under arrest, schoolteacher,' Suggins said. He looped the trace chain around Isaac's neck and clipped it fast like a dog collar.

"'I have a teaching permit from the Governor of Georgia,' Isaac protested.

"'That don't matter no more,' Suggins replied. 'The law says no more teachin' by whites to these red niggers.' He jerked on the chain and pulled Isaac after him across the schoolroom and out the door. We all sat or stood where we were, dumb and terrified. Out a window I saw Harriet McAlpin almost flying across the schoolyard, but before she could reach Isaac, one of the big bearded Pony Guardsmen cut her across the shoulder with his whip and she fell to the ground. Off went the whole bunch then at a trot right through Okelogee, Suggins dragging Isaac running and stumbling along by the trace chain. The two Cherokee Light Horse on watch south of the town had no time to give an alarm. All they could do was get out of the way of those bully boys when they came riding by with Isaac on the chain.

"My father called a council at once and sent messengers off to New Echota and Ross's Landing, but we all knew there was little we could do for Isaac McAlpin. Before the council ended late that night we heard that white schoolteachers and missionaries and even some blacksmiths were being arrested in Cherokee towns all around us. Next morning we learned that Pony Guards had ambushed Chief John Ross and tried to kill him, but Ross managed to escape.

"Suggins and his men made Isaac McAlpin walk all the way to Lawrenceville settlement, where there was a Georgia courthouse. His neck was rubbed raw and his feet bleeding when they locked him in a jail with several other teachers and mis- sionaries. One of those frontier Georgia courts sentenced them all to four years at hard labor in a prison camp for consorting with us Cherokees, which showed how slow-witted those whites were. They didn't have the sense to know that every one of the missionaries was backed up by churches through the North and East and even in Georgia itself. As Grandmother Mary said, the Pony Guards were so thickheaded they'd have lost their arses if they'd been loose. When the churches heard about the treatment of their missionaries they stirred up a storm and sent lawyers by the dozens into Georgia. Even the American government took notice because these were white men, not Indians, being oppressed. They rushed cases through the courts and pretty soon that Supreme Court chief named Marshall declared that Georgia had no right to imprison the missionaries, and that the whole set of laws against the Cherokees was null and void. He said that Georgians had no rights in the Cherokee Nation without our consent.

"I can tell you there was much celebrating in the Cherokee towns when we heard the good news. But of course it did not last. As I have said, Indians never had much luck with your courts of law. And we forgot about our powerful enemy, Sharp Knife Andrew Jackson. It was Elias Boudinot who brought us the bad news from Washington. President Jackson had let it be known that he would never enforce the decision of the Supreme Court. If the Cherokees wanted to live peaceably, old Sharp Knife said for the hundredth time, we'd have to move west of the Mississippi River.

"Of course when the Governor of Georgia found out about that he kept the missionaries in jail a while longer and turned the Pony Guard loose on us again. And on top of that his legisla- ture passed some new laws against us. They sent surveyors out to mark off the Cherokee lands into one-hundred-and-sixty-acre plots, which were to be given out to white settlers through a kind of lottery. They would draw numbers, you see, and if the number of the plot they drew had a Cherokee house on it, they got the house too.

"For a while that summer, the woods and meadows around Okelogee were filled with surveyors with their axes and chains, blazing trees and marking numbers on the blazes with black paint. They left the Rogers family and Moonherrin's Mill alone, but they marked off Opothle's farm and the little place where my father, the Runner, dug up the ground every spring for Walina to grow the finest corn and melons. Even the schoolhouse and the McAlpin house where Harriet and Jerusha continued to live after Isaac was arrested were included in the survey.

"I suppose the lottery survey was the last blow to the hopes of many Cherokee leaders. Some of those who had fought the hardest to keep our lands now gave up completely. The Ridge family, Elias Boudinot, and his brother Stand Watie, they all said if the President of the United States was so vile a man that he would not enforce the laws of the country he governed then we would be better off living as far away from such a lawless country as we could get. Chief John Ross, however, stood fast, believing that time was all we needed, that if we could hold out until Sharp Knife Jackson was no longer President, then the Cherokee Nation would survive. 'If Jackson will give us no protection in Georgia,' he told us again and again, 'how can we expect him to keep his word and protect us in the West?'

"To Grandmother Mary's great distress, Opothle went over to the side of the Ridge-Boudinot people. Not long after the Georgia surveyors marked off his farm, he began trying to convince everybody in Okelogee that they should move across the Mississippi River. 'The sooner the better,' he said. 'Let us not stay here and be driven out by offal such as Suggins and his Pony Guard. Only by moving the Cherokee Nation can we save the Cherokee Nation.'

"'That is John Kingsley's blood talking!' Mary would shout back at him. 'Not Creek Mary's!' She and my father, the Runner, had sworn to each other they would never leave Okelogee. Because of these different viewpoints, the family split apart again. For a long time Mary would not acknowledge the presence of Opothle at councils, would not speak to him when he visited her, and the two half brothers became silent enemies. The same thing was happening in many other Cherokee families. A great rift divided the Cherokees just at a time when they needed unity to survive.

"If Opothle had not supported the American government's removal law, however, we all would have been driven out of Okelogee much sooner than we were. Because neither my grandmother nor my father would listen or talk to Opothle, they did not know that he had been given permission to remain in his house until the American government set a date for all the Cherokees to be moved to the West. Not until long afterward did we learn that Opothle had persuaded the government agents to delay claims of Georgia lottery winners upon Okelogee land plots so we could all move west together.

"Some lottery demands were allowed on plots nearby Okelogee, and one of the first to be claimed was the McAlpin house and the land around it. The holder of the lottery ticket was a red-haired lout that Jack Moonherrin brought home with him after one of his trips to the settlements. This red-haired fellow married the oldest Moonherrin daughter, and the fact that he somehow obtained a lottery claim on the nearby McAlpin house showed us how dishonest was that whole Georgia scheme to take our lands away from us. Moonherrin's red-haired son-in-law and his ruttish bride moved into the McAlpin house in midwinter, and, being too lazy to cut wood, he broke up all the benches in the schoolhouse and burned them in his fireplace.

"The McAlpins? Well, Harriet and Jerusha had no place to go, so Mary convinced Walina and my father to make room for them in our house until the state of Georgia let Isaac out of jail. It's strange, is it not, how a single happening like that can change the course of entire lives—Jerusha's life and my life, I'm thinking of."

21

When Isaac McAlpin returned to Okelogee—after the missionaries were at last released from Georgia imprisonment—he found his house in the possession of a "lottery winner," his schoolhouse plundered of its benches, windows, and doors, and his wife and young sister refugees in the home of Creek Mary's family. He reluctantly accepted the invitation of Walina and Mary to share their crowded quarters, promising that it would be for only a short time.

"I shall inform my missionary board at once of the state of affairs here," he assured Mary. "I am certain that funds will be forthcoming to repurchase the house and repair the schoolhouse. In the meantime I shall hear the children's lessons out of doors in good weather, and if Chief Talasi will permit, in the council house during bad weather."

Isaac's bitterness over losing his house was somewhat allayed when he heard that Chief John Ross not only had lost his home to a Georgia lottery winner but had been forced to flee to safety across the Tennessee line. He repeatedly apologized to Walina and Mary for his family's intrusion upon them, and when he found that Dane had given up his bed to him and was sleeping out in the *asi*, the winter house, he offered to use the winter house himself.

Dane, however, preferred the privacy of the *asi* to the overcrowded main house. He was accustomed to sleeping without clothing of any kind, but after Harriet and Jerusha had moved in with them, Walina made him wear a long shirt for sleeping and he detested it. Although the nights were beginning to chill with frost, the round conical-roofed *asi* with its thick plastering of clay was so cozy that he needed only a thin blanket. The Long Warrior had built the structure well, but no one had slept in it since his death, and Walina used it for storing pumpkins and squash.

On the day that Isaac joined the crowded household and it became necessary for Dane to sleep in the *asi*, Mary built a fire in its center pit to smoke out the insects and then brought in a cane mat from the main house to cover the oak-splint couch upon which she and the Long Warrior had spent many a winter night rolled up in the old bearskin he had given her.

As Mary was coming out of the four-foot-high entrance of the *asi*, her head bent low, she heard a hawk crying. She raised up quickly, her eyes searching the sky, and was not surprised to see a blue hawk circling overhead. Its cry was exceedingly mournful, like the wailing of a grieving human being. "What are you telling me? What do you warn me of, blue hawk?" she called to the bird.

At the sound of her voice, Walina stepped out of the main house. "What is it, Mother Amayi?"

"That blue hawk. It is warning us of some bad thing."

Walina looked at the circling bird of prey. "It is hungry, perhaps," she said, and went back into the house.

Late that afternoon a party of Creeks dressed in little more than rags, and led by an old man, appeared suddenly in Okelogee. The old man was none other than Tolchi, Creek Mary's childhood friend when they had lived at Bluff Village, and those with him were his children and grandchildren. They were fleeing from the turmoil and starvation that had overcome their people, and were hoping to escape being transported to the West by seeking a haven among the Cherokees.

For a long time Mary had heard nothing of her Creek relatives, and she was saddened by what Tolchi and his sons now told her. Twenty moons or more ago, they said, at the urging of agents of the American government, Menewa and the other Creek chiefs had given up most of their remaining land to the state of Alabama for white settlement, on the promise that they

could live as a free and independent people on what land was
left to them. In this treaty the American government promised to
protect the lives and property of the Creeks and keep out white
intruders.

None of these promises had been kept. As soon as the government agents departed with their signed treaty, the *Unegas* began
preying upon the Creeks, stealing their livestock, burning their
homes, raping the women, and killing the men. To find enough
food to stay alive, Tolchi and his family had to leave their town
and go into the white settlements, begging for scraps to eat. The
whites treated them like wild dogs, hurling stones and curses at
them. In desperation, they had turned north hoping to survive
among the Cherokees.

That evening the Runner opened the Okelogee council house
to Tolchi and his relatives, and every family in town brought
food and clothing for them. This was during the Falling-Leaf
Moon, a clear and crisply cold night, a night that Dane would
forever remember. He was leaving the council house with his
grandmother, supporting her with his arm, when the entire sky
seemed to explode into a million fragments of fire.

"All the stars of heaven are falling!" Mary cried out. "The
blue hawk tried to tell me that a bad thing was going to happen.
Now the Maker of Breath is throwing his stars upon us to warn
us of disaster."

For a minute or so the meteor shower diminished, then renewed itself in continuous streaks of light. All the people coming
from the council house stopped, and stood watching the fiery
skies in awe.

Old Stalking Turkey gripped one of Dane's shoulders with a
clawlike hand. He no longer cut his white hair, and it fell like a
drift of snow over his bent neck. "I saw the stars spin like that
when I was a young man," he said in a feeble voice. "We were
traveling from Charles Town, where we went to trade deerskins
with the *Unegas* for the first time. The fall of stars was a warning to us, but we were young like you, boy, and paid no heed.
When I was a young man we had no iron hatchets, pots, knives,
or guns. We made use of our stone axes, clay pots, flint knives,

bows and arrows. We had no fear in that time. The first trade goods I carried on my back from Charles Town, a distance the *Unegas* measure as four hundred miles from Okelogee, all the way on foot, for then we had no horses amongst us. But neither did we have fear in that time. The *Unegas* gave us many things, the worst of them being fear."

"Yes," said Mary in a husky voice, "for the first time in my life I have fear of what is to come. First the blue hawk, then poor Tolchi and his family, and now the falling stars. My bones ache, *sogonisi,* child of my son. Take your old *alisi* home to her bed."

Dane guided her along the wide pathway beside the Little Singing Stream, keeping a watchful eye on the sky, but now only an occasional meteor skimmed across the star-sprinkled expanse of blackness. As they came up the gravel bank into their yard, he saw Jerusha rise from the bench under the arbor. "Thank goodness, you've come," she called to them. Although she was wearing a heavy coat, her teeth were chattering. "I was so afraid of the falling stars!"

"Where are Harriet and Isaac?" he asked.

"Asleep. I was frightened by noises in the woods behind the house and could not sleep. When I looked out to see if you were coming home from council, I saw the stars falling." She extended a hand tentatively as if to touch Dane for reassurance, but was restrained by the presence of Mary. "I wanted to run I was so frightened."

"Go on to bed now," Mary said. "The stars were only a warning."

"A warning of what?" Jerusha asked.

"I cannot tell, but we will know soon enough." Mary waited at the doorway until Jerusha went inside. Then she whispered to Dane: "Watch out for that yellow-haired girl, *sogonisi.* Her eyes glitter like a raccoon's when she looks at you."

"Sleep well, Grandmother." He turned and went straight across the yard to the *asi,* ducking his head for the low entrance and twisting his body adroitly through the L-shaped passageway that the Long Warrior had built to keep out cold winds. He welcomed the solid darkness where he could be alone with his thoughts. Jerusha was too often in his thoughts, he knew. Since she and Harriet had come to live with them, she was always near, her eyes always watching him in the evenings although he deliberately avoided speaking with her. She and Harriet spent much of their daytime hours now at the Rogers place helping with the chores, and bringing back milk and rich butter and cornmeal which they gave to Walina. If only Jerusha were an Indian. How often had he thought of that! He stripped off his clothes, placing them carefully at the foot of the oak-splint couch, and rolled himself into his blanket. The aroma of Walina's pumpkins stored beneath the bed drifted around him as he fell asleep.

How long he had been asleep he did not know, but he was suddenly wide awake, aware at once of a spicy body scent now mixed with the fragrance of pumpkin. Someone else was in the *asi*. Close by in the blackness he heard a soft exhalation of breath. "Dane." His name was a whisper but he knew Jerusha's presence.

He sat up, freeing his hands from the blanket roll. "Jerusha! What troubles you?"

"I'm scared of the popping sounds in the woods. Could they be the Georgia Pony Guards?"

One of her hands touched the blanket over his chest. She sat on the edge of the couch, and he could feel the round curve of her buttocks against his thigh.

"The Pony Guards would not stay in the woods," he said.

She was shivering, and her words were half formed through clenched teeth: "It's so dark in here. Don't you have a candle?"

"No."

"Why don't you go and see if the Pony Guards are out there?"

He gently touched the back of her neck. She was wearing only a thin nightdress. "The *Anisgaya Tsundi*, the thunder boys, have come out of their rock caves in the hills," he said, treating her now like a frightened child. "They come out on clear cold nights and dance to warm themselves. They would be angry if I disturbed them."

"I've never heard you speak of these thunder boys before."

"We don't talk about them. If they heard me now they might put a curse upon me."

"Have you seen them? Are they horrible like the Pony Guards?"

"They're little people, no higher than your knees, with long hair reaching to the ground."

"You're teasing me." He could feel her flesh quivering. "You have no heart, teasing me while I freeze to an icicle." She pulled at his blanket. "Let me have some covering around me, and walk me back to the house, please, Dane." She was shuddering so violently that he flung half his blanket over her shoulders. "Warm me, you are so warm, warm me," she said through chattering teeth, and lay with her back against his naked flesh. Her feet were icy against his shins.

They lay there for a long time until she was warm again, breathing like a sleeping child. He pulled slowly away from her, and she rolled to face him, her thin nightslip opening with the turning of her body. She was not asleep and she was not a child. As they came together he remembered that she was a year older than he.

On other nights that autumn Jerusha came to the *asi*, and if several nights passed without a visit from her, Dane would find a way to beg her to come so that they could renew their lovemaking. On black nights she would ask him to walk back with her to the main house, and once they came out of the *asi* to face a thin crescent of a moon that seemed as close as the treetops. "The moon is almost dark," she whispered, clinging to him, unwilling to leave him.

"Grandmother Mary always says that a moon like that is hiding her face because she is ashamed. After sleeping with the sun two or three nights, she is ashamed to show her face."

Jerusha drew away from him, looking him straight in the eyes. "Do you think I am ashamed of sleeping with you?"

"No."

"I should be because we are not married. When will you marry me, Dane?"

He shook his head slowly. She put her arms around him, holding her body tight against his. "I don't care. Even if you marry up with one of your full-blood girls, I'll keep loving you until the day I die."

Sometime late that winter she told him she was carrying his child. "Now you must marry me, Dane."

22

Seventy years later in a Montana cabin, Dane was yawning and stretching his arms. He picked up our dirty dishes and carried them into the calico-curtained pantry. "I once met a Blackfoot song-singer over at Miles City," he said, coming back to the window seat and suppressing another yawn. "You might call him a poet. He would sit on a bench at the livery stable and recite songs out of his head. One of them caused me to think of Jerusha. It was about a young girl who went beyond the limits of the heart, so far beyond the limits of the heart in her feelings for a young man that she sickened and died. Going beyond the limits of the heart is perilous for a woman, or a man. Maybe Jerusha McAlpin went beyond the limits of her heart."

"You did not marry her after she told you she was going to bear your child?"

He sighed. "I had given my word to Creek Mary that I would not." He closed his eyes. "Pride of one's race is a foolish thing—although my people had an excuse for it then, as they have an excuse for it now. Your people are still trying to make us feel that we are of a lower order than you. The human heart constantly wounded grows scars of pride. Creek Mary made me believe we were better than the *Unegas*. But I have grown wiser now. This pride of race is without meaning. What is a full-blood? Look at me. Some people say I look like an old China-man." His laughter was broken by a wide yawn. He leaned his head against the windowpane, searching the sky for the place-ment of the sun, and I realized that he had no timepiece on his person or in his cabin. "An old man must have a short daytime sleep." He bowed mockingly and went into his bedroom. "Make yourself at home," he said, and closed the door.

I walked to the front door, opened it, and stepped out into the Montana landscape. In the early afternoon it was a washed wa-tercolor of grays and yellows and browns smeared in wide brush strokes under a blinding sun in a blue dome of sky. Over the dis-tant range a dark smudge of clouds had formed, and I wondered if it was raining over there.

How was it that Dane had come to this place, so alien and so far from the gentle green-wooded hills of Georgia? He had not yet told me. I knew that the government of our people had driven out his people in a diaspora more cruel than the Babylo-nian exile of the Israelites. But here—a Cherokee-Creek here among the wild Cheyenne? And what had happened to Jerusha, to his unborn child? How long had Creek Mary endured?

We were dealing with human survivals while somewhere to the west my evening passenger train was rushing toward that lit-tle brown-stained depot at Dundee. Time was flying and my ora-cle chose to spend it in sleep. Impatient and somewhat resentful, I left the landscape with its bone-chilling wind and went back inside to warm myself in one of the big rocking chairs before the fireplace. I started to set down a few notes, but was dozing off when Dane popped out of his bedroom as spry as a young colt.

He took a tin pitcher from the mantel. "Sleep," he said briskly, "and a long drink of melted snow-water renew the spirit." He was outside the door and down to the racing stream and back before I was fully awake. He handed me a glass of water so cold it made my teeth ache.

"Have I told you more than you want to hear about Amayi and her children?" he asked, turning his head to one side and half closing his bright eyes.

"No, no. While you were asleep I was wondering what Jerusha's brother, Isaac, had to say to you when he found out about you and his sister."

Before he replied, his thin lips twisted as though he were in pain. "Isaac never knew about us, I think, although Harriet must have suspected something. You see, they got their house back about that time, a fatal thing it was for them. I don't know exactly how it was done—I recall some talk about the Georgia Methodists. Anyway, Moonherrin's daughter and the red-haired son-in-law were forced out of the house against their will. A sheriff's man came up from Lawrenceville and put them out. Then we all went over and helped clean their filth from the house.

"Jerusha and I continued to see each other secretly. Some nights we would meet in the *asi*, and some nights in the schoolhouse. Her condition did not show, but she would make me put my hands over the rounding of her belly where our child was growing. We could not stay away from each other. We could not breathe for long without each other. We prayed for time to stand still.

"One night we were in the *asi*, half asleep in each other's arms, when we heard shouts and the pounding of running feet. The sounds went on and on. Jerusha was sure the Pony Guards were raiding Okelogee. I went to the entrance of the *asi* and looked out. I could see a dim glow of firelight far up the Little Singing Stream, and the smell of smoke was on the wind. The sounds of loud voices came from the direction of the light. A hundred paces down the pathway I could see the silhouettes of Mary and Walina.

"I went back inside and dressed and told Jerusha to stay there while I went to see what was happening. She was trembling with fear, still certain that the Pony Guards had come again.

"I soon found out what had happened. Someone had set fire to the McAlpin house. Turpentine had been doused and pitch pine piled along one side, still burning when I got there, but most of the house was gone. The nearest neighbors had come in time to pull Isaac and Harriet out. Their bed was afire. They were not badly burned but they were both dead. It was later decided they had died from breathing smoke in their sleep before the flames reached them. Everyone was sure that Jerusha had been burned up in the fire. My father told me that. I did not know what to say. I stammered out that she had escaped and was safe at our house. He gave me a strange look, but said nothing.

"At the first chance I slipped back to the *asi*. I had to tell Jerusha what had happened, and then dragged her across the yard to the house screaming and sobbing. Walina and Mary met us at the door, and I told them what had happened. They tried to comfort Jerusha, but she was out of her mind by that time, I think.

"During the next few days she spent most of the time in bed weeping. Whenever I found a chance to be alone with her she would tell me that her sins had caused the deaths of her brother and Harriet. Her God had punished her by killing them, she said. It did no good for me to tell her that someone had set the fire, that everybody in Okelogee was sure that Moonherrin's son-in-law had done it. I kept telling her that if she had not been 'sinning' with me in the *asi*, that she would be dead, too, but that did no good either. I was sure she was going to die, but she did not.

"While she was recovering, either Walina or Mary discovered that she was soon to have a child. Jerusha did not tell them I was the father, but Mary knew well enough. I was frightened nearly out of my wits when my grandmother began scolding me for not heeding her warnings about Jerusha, but before she was finished with me she was laughing. She knew I would not dare make Jerusha my wife.

"But when my father learned of the situation he said that I was now responsible for Jerusha and her child, doubly so because she was *Unega* and had no clan. If she were Cherokee, he said, that would be a different matter because a clan family would take care of her if I did not choose to marry. I told him I had sworn to Grandmother Mary that I would never wed a *Unega*, and could not do so. 'If the family tries to force me to marry her,' I said, 'I will run away to the West rather than do so.'

Well, you remember the old Cherokee way; it is the uncle, not the father, who has power over the son. As angry as the Runner was at Opothle for favoring removal of our nation to the West, he went to see him, and Uncle Opothle soon sought me out to give his advice.

"'The girl must have a man to protect her,' he said, stroking his gray beard and giving me an occasional darting glance.

"I told him why I could not be Jerusha's husband. I also made it clear that Jerusha knew from the beginning that I could not marry her.

"'Yet you swived with her,' he said accusingly.

"'She came to my bed first,' I answered.

"He shook his head, sighed, and shook his head again. 'We'll see, we'll see what can be done.' I knew that he was as afraid of Grandmother Mary as my father and I were.

"In the midst of all these family trials, a letter came down to Jerusha from the Cherokee agency at Hiwassee. The missionary society that had supported Isaac McAlpin offered to transport Jerusha to a Methodist orphanage in Pennsylvania.

"The only person in our family who was pleased by that letter was my father. For him it offered an end to all our obligations. Neither Mary nor Walina made any immediate comment, but I could see they were both disturbed by the letter. As for Jerusha she took to her bed again, weeping as though all hope of life had ended. And I? That all happened a long, long time ago, but I can still feel the wrench at my heart when I faced the realization that Jerusha might vanish from my life forever. What a prideful young fool I was not to take her then for my wife!

"After a fit of crying, Jerusha begged Mary to let her continue to live with us, and to my surprise both Mary and Walina agreed that she could do so if she wished. Soon afterward my father got Grandmother Mary out in the yard and faced up to her. Why on earth did she want that yellow-haired *Unega*, heavy with child, staying on with us? 'Because,' my grandmother answered sharply, 'her child will have my blood.'

"So that was that. The only problem left was the way Jerusha followed me around whenever I was in or near the house. She began imitating the way I moved, the way I talked. She went beyond the limits of the heart.

"It was my cousin Jotham who solved that problem, probably at the suggestion of Uncle Opothle. With the closing of the school after Isaac McAlpin died in the fire, Opothle arranged for Jotham to become an apprentice blacksmith with the nephew of his father-in-law. Mr. John Rogers's nephew, Timothy, had set up a smithy near the Rogers farm, and Jotham was fast becoming skillful at shoeing horses.

"When Jotham invited me to learn blacksmithing with him, and share his room in Uncle Opothle's big house, I jumped at the chance to get away from Jerusha. At first I felt like a traitor to her, and especially to my family, because of their feelings toward Opothle and his pro-emigration friends. I not only deserted the young woman who was going to become the mother of my child, but I joined the camp of the enemy. Not very admirable, was it?

"At the time, however, I could see no other way out, and I was soon busy enough learning how to use a bellows and tongs, how to hold a horse's foot steady, how to clean and pare a hoof with a knife and file, and char it with a red-hot iron shoe that I had shaped to make a smooth fit.

"Mr. Tim Rogers's speciality was wagonmaking, and both Jotham and I favored that sort of work over shoeing horses. In building the wagons we made everything except the wheels, which were brought down from a wheelwright's place at Hiwassee Garrison. I was mightily pleased one day when Mr. Rogers told Jotham and me that he was sending us up to Hiwassee on a wagon to bring back a load of wheels. Neither of us had ever been that far from Okelogee before, and it was a great adventure. We were gone about three weeks, waiting for the wheels to be made ready. When we got back to Okelogee one day about dark and drove into Uncle Opothle's place, Priscilla came running out to meet us. 'Dane, you better hurry over to Grandmother Mary's,' she called to me.

" 'What's the matter?' I asked.

" 'Jerusha's had her baby.'

"Now, I could not exactly describe to you my feelings—scared, happy, outlandish. All I wanted was to be where Jerusha was. I ran all the way—it was like I had dreamed myself from one world into another, dancing maybe all the way to the house and through the doorway. Grandmother Mary, the Runner, and Walina were sitting by the fire, their heads raised up facing me in surprise. Mary was holding a naked baby that looked no bigger than a skinned squirrel, spooning something into its mouth. All around the fire were cracked hickory nuts; she was feeding the baby hickory milk.

" 'Where's Jerusha?' I demanded.

" 'In bed where she should be,' Mary replied. 'Look, *sogonisi*, here is the first great-grandchild in which flows the blood of Creek Mary.'

" 'Is she all right?'

" 'This is a man child, not a she.'

" 'I mean Jerusha.'

" 'She is well. Except that her milk flows poorly.' She offered me the light-skinned child, my son, but the little creature began spitting hickory milk, crying and squirming, and I handed it back to her.

" 'Has she given a name for it?' I asked.

"Mary made a face. 'I wanted to give him a Creek name, but Jerusha calls him Pleasant.'

" 'Pleasant *McAlpin*,' my father said, giving me a cold look.

" 'Ah, well,' said Mary, caressing the pale skin of her great-grandchild, 'it is a better name than John Ridge gave his new-born son.'

" 'Andrew Jackson Ridge.' My father spat the names out angrily. 'The Ridges are traitors truly, seeking favors now from old Sharp Knife—who would drive us from our homes—by giving his hated name to one of their young.'

"I went on into the back room to see Jerusha."

23

In 1835, the year that Dane became twenty-one, the Congress of the United States—which viewed the inhabitants of the Cherokee Nation as vassals subject to the whims of that majestic body—appropriated funds for a head count. The number was needed by bureaucrats employed by the War Department's Office of Indian Affairs so that estimates could be made of the costs of removing the tribe from its eastern homeland to a distant tract somewhere beyond the Mississippi River. The census takers reported that within the states of Georgia, North Carolina, Alabama, and Tennessee 16,542 Cherokees resided, although undoubtedly there were considerably more than that.

In an effort to cloak with legitimacy this enforced removal of an entire nation, the War Department appointed a special commissioner, the Reverend John F. Schermerhorn, to arrange a special treaty in which the Cherokees themselves would voluntarily agree to abandon their homeland. Schermerhorn was a bombastic man, capable of considerable deceit in his dealings with those who held less power than he. Because of his booming voice as well as for other reasons, the Cherokees named him the Devil's Horn.

The Devil's Horn let it be known that those who supported the removal treaty would be well paid for their property, and that the American government would also provide funds for transporting their goods and persons to the Cherokee Nation West. Dealing only with the Ridge-Boudinot pro-removal group, the Devil's Horn announced a treaty council at New Echota on the third Monday of the Big Winter Moon. Using typefaces designed for Sequoyah's syllabary that were purloined from the office of the *Phoenix,* he arranged for broadsides to be printed and distributed throughout all the Cherokee towns. The Devil's Horn promised that each Cherokee attending his council would be given a mackinaw blanket of the finest quality of wool, and would be issued funds to cover subsistence costs. Furthermore, his broadside decreed, those Cherokees of voting age who failed to attend the council would be counted as giving their consent to whatever was decided at New Echota.

A few weeks before the date set for the convening of the council, Georgia authorities banned any further publication of the *Cherokee Phoenix.* A unit of the Georgia Pony Guards crossed the Tennessee line, made an unlawful arrest of the Nation's principal chief, John Ross, and carried him off to a Georgia jail. He was charged with plotting an insurrection among black slaves, a completely false accusation but one that would prevent Ross from interfering with Commissioner Schermerhorn's plans during these crucial days.

Not long afterward at New Echota, the Ridge-Boudinot group and a few of their friends and followers gathered in response to the call of the Devil's Horn. They totaled scarcely three hundred, only eighty of them being eligible to vote, or less than two percent of the official population of the Cherokee Nation. The council itself had no tribal legality; it had been called by a representative of the American government, not by the Cherokee chiefs. Yet most of the Cherokee leaders who were there believed themselves to be patriots, their aim being to save their Nation. Among them was Opothle Kingsley, but no other member of Creek Mary's family was represented.

None of the usual good-natured banter and familiar reminiscing accompanied the proceedings. Old Major Ridge, his once curly dark hair now faded to a flaxen yellow, set the solemn tone with his oration: "This land came to us from the Maker of Breath, but the *Unegas* are now stronger than we. We cannot remain here in peace and comfort. If we stay here, we will lose everything, the eternal land, our lives, and the lives of our children. We must give up this land and go over beyond the Great River."

One by one most of the council members rose to speak. "I have spent more than sixty summers and winters in the Cherokee Nation," Opothle said. "Although my blood is Creek, I have lived as a Cherokee from infancy. I love the hills, the valleys, the forests and waters of this sweet country in which I have prospered well. Yet it is with the people, the Nation, that we must be concerned. To save the Nation we must move the Nation. Our lives have been threatened by our own people if we sign this treaty. My own blood kin, my mother, my brother, have turned against me. We can die, but the great Cherokee Nation will be saved. Who is there here not willing to die if the great Nation can be saved?"

The signing of the Reverend Schermerhorn's treaty was an even more solemn occasion than the speechmaking. The Devil's Horn read the treaty to them one more time, and a committee of twenty signed their names to it. "I may be signing my death warrant," Major Ridge said. Opothle, one of the last to sign, had tears in his eyes. "I may die for this, but I see it as the only way to save our Nation."

Next morning the Devil's Horn gave them the promised subsistence money and the blankets, and they started back to their different homes.

In the meantime Chief John Ross, having been released from jail, was already spurring his followers to gather signatures to a document denouncing the Schermerhorn treaty and declaring it null and void. Ignoring her aching bones, Creek Mary rode off on her pony to nearby towns to persuade those who had not done so to add their names to the John Ross declaration. The Runner rode even farther into the hills only to find dozens of others engaged in the same task. Within a few weeks the chief was in Washington with the names of twelve thousand Cherokees, two-thirds of the Nation, almost all the eligible voters, protesting the illegal Treaty of New Echota. Many members of the United States Senate—that arm of Congress empowered to determine the fate of all the native Indian peoples through treaties—

were impressed by this display of democratic unity from a people who had placed their faith in the white man's courts and laws.

In the Moon When the Mayhaws Were Ripening in the hills of Georgia, the all-knowing senators, reflecting their constituents' greed for land, ratified the Treaty of New Echota by a margin of one vote. The Cherokee Nation East no longer existed. With what it considered unusual generosity toward these dispossessed people who had tried to live in the culture of their oppressors, the American government allowed them two years to abandon their homeland to the hordes of land-hungry border settlers who were already invading their country.

While the Cherokees were still stunned by the shock of realization, news came from the south that soldiers were herding thousands of their former friends and enemies, the Creeks, toward the Indian Territory beyond the Mississippi. Those who resisted were driven off in manacles and chains.

Mary wept when she heard of these things, but when she learned that the Chickasaws and Choctaws were suffering the same fate, she began preparing herself and her family for the inevitable. But even before she foresaw their coming, a company of blue-uniformed United States dragoons armed with sabers and carbines rode suddenly into Okelogee and began a methodical search of homes for weapons. She had time enough to conceal her old flintlock pistol in a basket of Pleasant's dirty baby-clothing, but the family's two rifles were in plain view on their wall pegs when four dragoons stormed inside without a word of explanation or apology. They took the rifles from the wall, turned all the beds inside out, searched the root cellar, opened Jerusha's trunk, lifted Pleasant from his cradle, dumped the dirty clothing from the basket and found Mary's pistol. Similar searches and confiscations were in progress in every town in the Nation, and within a short time the Cherokees were left with only a few old bows and arrows with which to hunt wild game or defend themselves.

One day early in that spring of 1837, Opothle visited his mother and half brother in a final effort to persuade them to travel west with him. Although the Runner would neither talk with Opothle nor look upon his face, he sat on the bench beneath the brush arbor listening politely. "If you go now, Talasi," Opothle said, "you will be well paid. If you wait until the soldiers force you to go, and that will be sooner than you think, you and your family will have nothing but what you wear upon your backs when you reach Indian Territory."

Mary looked hard at her oldest son. "Talasi the Runner cannot be bought by the *Unegas,* Opothle. His flesh and his bones are of this land, this Cherokee Nation. His heart cannot betray the earth of which he is a part."

With his fist, Opothle struck one of the arbor posts with such force that it set the covering of branches to trembling. "Can't you see that the only way we can save the Cherokee Nation is to go to the new land? Land is land. What does it matter if my flesh and bones turn to dust here or in the Indian Territory? But I wish to live yet a good while. I wish to live on account of my children. That is why I am going."

"If my Creek blood was stronger in you than your *Unega* blood," she said, "you would stay here beside us, Opothle."

He reached for her, but she drew away from his hand. When he spoke, she refused to look at him. "Mother Amayi, it pains me to leave you and Talasi. But I must follow my course."

"Go on, son of John Kingsley," she said with bitterness in her throaty voice. "If we see you again in this world, the soldiers will have to bring us to you."

In the Strawberry Moon, Opothle and his family left Okelogee in a light carriage and three wagons loaded with clothing, bedding, cooking utensils, tools, and one plow. In addition to Sunalee, William, and Priscilla, there were also four black slaves in Opothle's party. For the remaining slaves and his house and farm, the United States government paid him a handsome sum in treasury warrants. Opothle Kingsley was the fourth richest man among the Cherokees who had signed the Treaty of New Echota, and the signers were emigrating together to the Cherokee Nation West in Indian Territory. Opothle's son, Jotham, and his nephew, Dane, accompanied the caravan only as far as Ross's

Landing, from which place they drove two of the wagons back to Okelogee after unloading the goods aboard a river steamboat.

Because blacksmith Timothy Rogers had secured a contract from the U.S. War Department to supply a considerable number of wagons for use in transporting some of the remaining thousands of Cherokees to the West, Opothle gave Jotham permission to remain at Okelogee until Creek Mary's family was forced to emigrate. Jotham and Dane moved into a shed adjoining the smithy, and boarded with the Rogers family.

Several moons, almost a year, went by before Jotham received any news of his family, and then a long letter came from the Indian Territory, some of it written by his father, some by his sister Priscilla. He read it aloud to both Dane and Tim Rogers. *Tell Tim to pack up and move his blacksmith shop to Park Hill in the Cherokee Nation West,* Opothle wrote. *We have only one blacksmith among us now, and he can by no means meet the needs of our people. A new capital for our Nation will soon be built near here, offering opportunities for all who are willing to work. William and I have finished roofing our trading post, and as soon as the rainy weather ends we will be going to Independence in Missouri to buy goods to stock it with.* In her schoolgirl script, Priscilla wrote that their cabin was very rough and small and that she very much missed her younger brother and wanted him to come on to Indian Territory. *Give our love to Dane and Grandmother Mary and Uncle Talasi and do write me about Jerusha and little Pleasant. Has Dane made her his wife yet?*

"I'd like to show this letter to Grandmother Mary," Dane said.

"Do you think she'd care?" Jotham asked.

"Oh, she might pretend not to care. But they're her blood, you know."

Before leaving the smithy that evening, Dane picked up a scrawny flop-eared puppy that a few days earlier had wandered in from somewhere wanting to be fed. As the springtime air was warm, he found Mary and Jerusha sitting on the bench under the arbor.

"I brought Pleasant a dog," he said. "He's old enough now to have his own dog."

"You remembered his birthday," Jerusha cried, smiling up at him with sudden pleasure.

The three-year-old appeared in the doorway, wearing only a long-tailed gray shirt. His hair was the same ripe-wheat color as Jerusha's, his skin light olive. "Come here, Pleasant," Dane called. "I've brought you a dog."

Pleasant padded to the arbor, but when Dane reached for him, the boy swerved toward Mary, burying his face in her lap. She tousled his hair playfully.

Dane set the puppy down at Mary's feet, and it turned on its back.

"What's its name?" Pleasant asked, looking down at the animal.

"Whatever you wish to call it," Dane replied.

Mary sniffed. "It smells like a skunk," she said. "We'll call it Dila."

"Dila," Pleasant repeated, and squatted to stare intently at the puppy's pink belly.

Words, words, words, Dane thought. *Grandmother Mary is teaching that sprout more words than it can hold in its head. She looks so old now, with wrinkles deep in her face, and pouches forming under her eyes.*

"Jotham heard from his family," he said.

"Are they all well?" she asked quickly. He offered her the letter. "Read it to me," she said. "Even by a bright candle my old eyes can't make out writing, and in this dim light . . ." Her voice grown thin trailed off.

He read the letter slowly, skipping only Priscilla's inquiry as to whether he had made Jerusha his wife.

"Poor Opothle," Mary said. "Past sixty winters he is, too old to be working so hard. Roofing a house at his age? He never did like to work with his hands. Took that from his *Unega* father." She yawned and rubbed her sleepy eyes with her fingers. "Have you and Jotham built enough wagons yet to haul us all to Indian Territory?"

24

Dane was gazing out the window, remembering green Georgia hills as he faced the brown sweep of Montana. "To the very last day my father stubbornly refused to believe that we would be driven from our home. Such a thing was against all the laws of nature, he thought, too dreadful to imagine, not even the Christian *Unegas* could be that savage.

"But early in May—Grandmother Mary always called that time of year the Mulberry Moon—General Winfield Scott brought seven thousand soldiers into the Cherokee Nation. That was about two soldiers for each of us unarmed Cherokees. He headquartered at New Echota and sent companies of men out to build several stockades to pen us up in until they could start us west by boats and wagons. Yet the Runner still paid no attention to warnings and rumors. Every morning he and Walina would go out to their farm plot, he digging the ground and she planting seeds, as if they were going to be there forever.

"One morning Walina came by the blacksmith shop and invited Mr. Tim Rogers and Jotham and me to a noontime meal to share their first little corn ears. You can be sure we all went. My mouth waters now just thinking about those sweet juicy little ears of boiled Cherokee corn we always had in late spring.

"Walina had plates fixed for everybody in the yard, but a rain shower came on just as we arrived from the smithy, and we all moved inside the house. We had hardly got started eating when we heard the sounds of horses, many horses' hooves pounding on the gravel somewhere up the Little Singing Stream.

"'What is that noise?' Jerusha asked. She was still fearful of the Georgia Pony Boys although they had not been around Okelogee for a long time.

"'I saw a blue hawk today,' Grandmother Mary said. 'Circling way high and crying a warning.'

"'What kind of warning?' somebody asked her.

"I remember she had one of the little corn ears in her fingers, waving it back and forth in front of her. 'Maybe it was not a warning,' she said. 'More likely the blue hawk was telling us good-bye.'

"The sound of horses' hooves kept growing louder. I got up and went to the door. A long file of mounted soldiers was winding down the pathway, and at every house they passed, four men would drop off the end of the file and ride up in the yard and dismount.

"'Who is it, Dane?' Mr. Rogers called to me.

"'Soldiers,' I told him.

"Four were already in our yard, dismounting quickly and taking their carbines from the slings. Jotham came up to my side just as the leader, a sergeant, pushed us away with the barrel of his weapon and strode inside. 'Everybody out of the house!' he ordered in a loud voice, motioning toward the door with his carbine. The first to obey was the flop-eared hound, Dila. He scurried from under the table and streaked through the door. Pleasant slid off the bench and scampered after his dog.

"Mr. Rogers was the first to speak. 'What is the meaning of this intrusion?' he demanded.

"'Outside!' the sergeant repeated. 'If you refuse, we have orders to use force.'

"We all walked out in the yard, facing the other three soldiers, who stood in a half circle with carbines at the ready. We stood there while the sergeant searched the house. When he came out he told us we must wait in the yard for wagons that would take us to a stockade. 'You can go back in the house one at a time,' he said, 'and each get one blanket and any personal belongings you can carry. Nothing more.'

"Mr. Rogers explained to the sergeant that he was a visitor and asked to be released to go to his own home. 'Your wife a redskin?' the sergeant asked. Mr. Rogers said that his wife was Cherokee. 'Then she'll be taken,' the sergeant said. 'But you're white. You don't have to go to the stockade.' Mr. Rogers said he would go wherever his wife went, but that he needed to return to his house to pick up a few belongings. The sergeant told him to leave. 'Go straight to your house,' he said. 'If you fool about or try to interfere, you'll be shot the same as a redskin would be.'

"Jotham spoke up then and said he lived with Mr. Rogers and wanted to go with him. The sergeant shook his head. 'No. You're redskin. You stay here for the wagons.' He turned and beckoned to two of the other soldiers, leaving one to guard us while they mounted and rode on down to the next house. Up the pathway along the Little Singing Stream we could see our neighbors suffering the same treatment that had befallen us.

"We went back into the house one by one, bringing out a blanket, extra moccasins, clothing, and a few little keepsakes. My father brought out an ax that he valued highly, but the soldier made him put it back in the house. Walina timidly asked if she could take her spinning wheel in the wagon. 'You could not walk and carry a spinning wheel,' the soldier said. Walina had traded deerskins for that spinning wheel, and many of the warm clothes we wore were made from yarn she had spun from wool obtained from the Scots. The Runner took one look at my stepmother's tortured face and went in the house and brought out the spinning wheel. He gave the wheel to Walina and lifted the frame to show the soldier that they could carry it.

"While all this was going on, Jerusha was pacing back and forth, anxiously looking up the pathway. 'May I go and find my little boy?' she asked. She was wearing an apron and had knotted it up in her nervous hands.

"'No, ma'am,' the soldier answered. 'My orders are to keep you all here.' I could see he was puzzled by Jerusha's presence among us. 'You live here, don't you?' he asked.

"'Please, sir, let me go look for him,' she begged.

"'I can't do that, ma'am.' He was a tall narrow-faced mountain settler, hardbitten against all Indians, unsettled in his mind because he had to treat one of his own kind like he was treating us.

"About this time a dozen wagons came rattling into view, some stopping along the way, others rolling on until one pulled into our yard. The driver of it wore a greasy leather dragoon cap. His face was marked with pus-pimples and he had a wispy chin-beard. He was the Georgia Pony Boy, Cyrus, who had been at New Echota that day with One-Eye Jack Suggins. Jotham and Jerusha recognized him, too, and I was sure Jerusha was going to faint from fear. I moved close to her and held her by the arm.

"'Load 'em up!' Cyrus yelled at the soldier, who went over and let down the tailgate. The soldier then fixed a bayonet to his carbine and ordered us to get in the wagon. My father helped Mary and Walina up, and then I lifted Jerusha. Her frightened blue eyes filled with tears. 'Dane,' she whispered, 'we can't go without Pleasant.' I told her that Pleasant was sure to be in one of the other wagons and that we could find him when we reached the place where they were taking us.

"Except for the driver's, there were no seats in the wagon, and we had to sit on the hard bed with our legs straight out and our backs against the low sideboards. About the time we were all in, a soldier on foot came splashing across the Little Singing Stream, pulling Stalking Turkey after him with a rope tied around the old man's waist. 'Got room for another one?' he called to the driver. 'Found him hiding in a corn patch.'

"'Pile him in,' Cyrus said.

"We made room for the Stalking Turkey. His long white hair was tangled with dead leaves, mud oozed from his moccasins, and his breath whistled in his throat after the hard run. Mary began combing the trash from his hair.

"'We should have killed them all, Amayi, when they first came to our land,' he said, separating each phrase with a gasp for air.

"'I know, old Turkey,' she answered him. 'Instead we welcomed them as friends.'

"'We lost because we tried to be like them,' he whispered. 'It is not the nature of the *Tsalagi* to be like the *Unegas*.'

"'We lost because we would not listen to Tecumseh,' Mary said. 'We lost at Tohopeka, at the Horseshoe Bend.'

"The driver cracked his whip and we began jolting over the graveled pathway. 'Look,' Mary said, her eyes opening wide as she pointed to a rain shower that shrouded the green head of the Sleeping Woman. 'She is weeping for us.' We had moved only a few yards when a band of horsemen trotted across our front, halting the wagon. The riders all wore leather dragoon caps like the driver's so that I did not at once recognize One-Eye Jack Suggins without his belled hat.

"'Look who we got here,' Suggins snickered as he pulled his horse right against the wagon, his ugly eye fixed on Jerusha. 'The li'l yellow-hair sister. You want to go with me, li'l sister, git y'rself away from these stinkin' red niggers?'

"She wouldn't look at him, just kept her head down. I gripped her trembling hand tight, not daring to do more.

"Suggins noticed the spinning wheel that Walina held between her knees. He reached for the wheel, lifted it over the wagon board, and flung it toward the Little Singing Stream. I looked at my father, saw the hatred in his eyes, and feared what he might try to do. 'Give me the wheel frame,' Suggins said to him. The Runner sat motionless. 'You know you ain't suppose to take things like that to stockade,' Suggins whined. He kicked his horse into motion and circled to the other side of the wagon, reached in and jerked the frame from my father's hands, dashing it to the ground.

"While this was happening, some of his men had entered our house and were bringing out chairs, blankets, whatever they might want. 'Find anything worth takin'?' Suggins called to them.

"'Candlestick and a good ax,' one replied.

"'They must have the good stuff on 'em.' Suggins's head turned slowly, his eye searching us for ornaments that might have silver in them. When he saw the coin gorget on the chain around Mary's neck, he eased his horse in close and his dirty hand reached out like a claw for it. Before his fingers could touch it, I was on my feet, bringing my fist down hard against his wrist. He swore, jerking his arm back in pain. The driver, Cyrus, was on me then, his heavy body pinning me to the wagon bed. Jotham, however, leaped quickly to my assistance, both hands gripping Cyrus by the ears and making him scream for mercy.

"By this time Suggins had his rifle out, the muzzle cracking hard against my cheekbone. 'I'll blow y'r head off, redskin!' Then he yelled at Cyrus: 'Git the rope off that old man and tie both them boys up!' Cyrus took the rope from around the Stalking Turkey. Then while Suggins held his rifle on Jotham and me, Cyrus tied our hands tight behind our backs and shoved us down as hard as he could, kicking each of us in the ribs with such savagery that it took our breaths away.

"When I looked up through a mist that covered my eyes, Suggins was grinning, showing his yellow teeth in pure enjoyment. 'Now let me see that purty little thing the old squaw woman got round her neck,' he said. This time my father tried to stop him, lunging for Suggins's shoulders in an effort to unseat him from his saddle. But the Runner must have lost his balance. Suggins, who'd been a gouge fighter all his life, pulled his knife out in a flash, stabbing it into my father's arm and hurling him down against the steel-rimmed wagon wheel. My father's head must have struck the rim or axle, or else Suggins did the worst of it with the butt of his rifle after he jumped out of his saddle. He would have killed the Runner right there, except the soldier left to guard us had called for his sergeant, who came riding up and shouted at Suggins to stop. Suggins claimed that the Runner attacked him, but Grandmother Mary was up on her feet telling how the Georgia Guards had robbed our house and tried to rob our persons. I'd heard her use the King's profane English before when she was angry, but this time I think she used every oath she'd ever learned in her life. A tiny little smile formed on that sergeant's hard face. He turned to Suggins and told him to get himself and his Pony Boys out of Okelogee.

" 'We're wagon drivers,' Suggins objected.

" 'Well, go drive your damned wagons,' the sergeant cried, 'and quit robbing these people.'

"While the Georgia Guards were riding off, the sergeant and one of his men eased the Runner into the wagon. My father's sleeve was soaked red with blood and he had a bad cut on his head. Walina held his head in her lap while Mary and Jerusha tried to clean the wounds and stop the flow of blood. A soldier climbed into the wagon and cut the ropes from Jotham's and my wrists. One side of my face was numb and swollen, and my ribs ached from Cyrus's kick, but I was too worried about my father to bother with such things then.

"Nobody said anything until we reached the trail fork where we passed the Okelogee burying ground. One-Eye Jack Suggins and his men were out there digging up the graves of our people, laughing and throwing bones around whenever they found any little relic that had been buried with the dead.

"'Savages!' Mary screamed at them, but if they heard her they paid no mind. We soon joined other wagons heading slowly west toward Ross's Landing. Jerusha tried to stand on her feet, bracing herself with one hand against my shoulder while she shaded her eyes with the other, straining to see if Pleasant might be in one of the wagons behind or ahead of us.

"After we topped the last rise, Mary turned and watched the Sleeping Woman slowly sink from our view. For the first time in my life I saw tears in her eyes, and then she bent to look closely at the Runner's face. He was breathing hoarsely with great effort, his eyeballs rolling back so that only the whites showed, and little bubbles of blood formed on his lips. I had always thought of my father as an immortal shield, but now the center of my universe was gone, my world was coming to an end. The last thing any of us saw of Okelogee was smoke rising from our burning schoolhouse. At last the Pony Boys were rid of that hated symbol of Indian equality.

"And, oh yes, the wagon we were riding in was one that Jotham and I had helped Mr. Rogers make for the United States Army."

25

It was midafternoon in Montana. "Would you like to take a walk?" Dane asked. "This is the best time of the day for it."

I said that I would indeed.

"You'll need your coat." He slipped on a blanket-wool vest, a wide-collared mackinaw, and a tall-crowned black hat. When we left the house he led the way along a narrow pathway the cattle had made beside the stream, his booted legs bowing as he walked. We passed a small pole-fenced corral and a sheet-iron shed and then came to a stretch of hard-packed sand where we could walk side by side. "See the green in the willows," he said with excitement in his voice. The willows were a hundred yards away, leafless, but there was a faint tinge of green mist in the line of trees along the stream.

"The quickest way to kill an Indian," he said, "is to pen him up. Freedom is in our blood. I think it must have always been there. You people talk a lot about freedom, but you don't know what it is. When you people have freedom you throw it away, you imprison yourselves." His eyes, squinting out of the network of wrinkles in his face, sparkled with old mischief.

"Freedom for the individual is the basis of our American credo," I protested.

"Freedom for individuals of your own kind is what you mean," he replied. "You people have always wanted to shunt my people aside, confine us on some faraway barren where you cannot see us. At Ross's Landing and other places along the Tennessee River you penned us behind log stockades higher than our heads so that you could not see us and we could not see you. It has been that way, in a manner of speaking, since that time, except now most of us are on reservations with the ghosts of stockades still between us.

"At Ross's Landing my family and a thousand other Cherokees struggled to stay alive for weeks under pine-pole sheds that soaked up the heat of the sun or leaked streams of rain upon us. Inside the stockade every tree had been cut so there was no shade. Most of us survived somehow on tasteless gruel given us twice each day, on foul water hauled from the river, in dirty clothing we had no way to clean, our bodies unwashed. Talasi the Runner, my father, died there unattended except by an old *adanowski*, medicine man, who had no curative herbs or any way of obtaining them, and could offer nothing but sacred prayers to the Maker of Breath. And Grandmother Mary grieved for her only full-blood son, barely enduring, her body growing frailer day by day. And Jerusha, half-mad because we could find no trace of our little son Pleasant; none of the soldiers would listen to our pleas for help in finding him.

"One night Jotham lifted me to the top of his shoulders so that I could pull myself over the sharp-pointed poles, and drop to the ground below. I had some crazy idea that I might go to other stockades and find Pleasant before Jerusha lost her mind completely. But the soldiers had cut all the trees around the stockade, and I had crawled only halfway through the stumps toward the river when they opened fire on me. I stood up facing them in the half darkness, waiting for them to kill me. Instead they took me back inside and locked me in a pine-slab privy too small to lie down and where I was surrounded by the stench of excrement for I don't know how many days.

"For what crime were you freedom-loving Americans punishing us? The crime of blocking your path toward some mythical destiny, of refusing to take your money for our homeland and exiling ourselves to where you could no longer see us, for forcing you to force us to the Darkening Land?

"One hot summer morning the soldiers opened the big stockade gate and passed the word to us that we should prepare ourselves to move out. Long lines of wagons were waiting, and we were packed into them like cattle into loading pens. For miles we bumped along over a road so deep in dust that our clothing, our faces, and our hair were powdered with it, our noses and eyes so filled with dust that we could barely see or breathe. We came to the river, and with soldiers still holding their guns on us we left the wagons and walked single file down to a strange sort of flotilla—four flatboats moored around a steamboat. We were marched aboard one of the flatboats, our family clinging to one another so as not to become separated. We sat in a little circle, Grandmother Mary insisting upon wiping the dust from our faces with the hem of her skirt. The sun was broiling down, our sweat turning the dust to mud on our skins and in our hair.

"I was sitting there beside Jerusha, both of us too miserable to speak, when a yellow flop-eared hound came slinking along the side of the flatboat. 'Dila!' we both shouted. At the sound of our voices, the hound raised its head and turned away from us, its tail between its legs. I scrambled to my feet, watching the dog sneaking toward the end of the flatboat. And there was Griffa McBee, a red bandana around her head, and in her lap was Pleasant.

"Grabbing Jerusha's hand, I pulled her after me, stumbling along over outstretched feet, ignoring the angry grunts of those we stepped upon. I thought Jerusha would squeeze Pleasant to death when she bent down and put her arms around that delighted little boy.

"We learned that the soldiers had found Pleasant and his dog on the road, fortunately placing him in the same wagon with the McBees, and they had been taken to a stockade not ten miles from where we were. The army officers could easily have found him for us, but they made no effort to do so.

"Anyway, the recovery of Pleasant made the heat of that torrid day bearable for us. Many people on our flatboat fainted under the burning sun, others became very ill. Although the steamboat and flatboats were filled with Cherokees, the flotilla remained motionless all through the afternoon. Rumors passed back and forth, but no one knew the reason why we did not leave the landing. As the sun sank low in the sky, soldiers began lining up on the bank and we were ordered to file off the boats and get back into the wagons. All through the night the wagons kept rolling between the river and the stockade, returning us to the imprisonment we had thought was behind us forever.

"Not until some days passed did we learn the reason for this. Because of the long summer drought the water in the river had fallen so low that boats could no longer descend. We would have to wait until enough rain fell to raise the water level. We also learned that other parties of Cherokees, as many as three thousand, had been taken on ahead of us down the Tennessee to the Ohio and Mississippi, and up the Arkansas to Indian Territory.

"By this time Chief John Ross had somehow brought the scattered members of his council together, and when they received reports that hundreds of our people had died on the crowded boats, Ross petitioned General Winfield Scott to grant the Cherokee council permission to manage the passage of our people to the West. The council proposed that we travel overland in wagons, in this way shortening the distance by many miles. Although General Scott agreed to the plan, his soldiers kept us penned in the stockades for several more weeks.

"The weather continued hot and dry. Our drinking water was filled with river slime. Swarms of blueflies bit us by day and mosquitoes attacked us by night. Most of us fell ill of dysentery and fevers. Poor Walina! She was the gentlest of us all, grieving in her blanket every night for the Runner, but never complaining. She was the next of our little family to die, perhaps from a broken heart, perhaps from the sickness that afflicted us all. Some soldiers followed us out to the burying ground, where Jotham and I dug a hole beside my father's grave. We wrapped Walina in her blanket and covered her with earth. Fifty graves were there before we left that stockade, most of them children and old people. Grandmother Mary could not understand why the Maker of Breath chose Walina and the Runner while she and old Stalking Turkey were left to burden the young. There were only five of us left—Mary, Jotham, Jerusha, Pleasant, and I—six, if we counted the Stalking Turkey, who had attached himself to us."

We had climbed a low sandhill, and Dane stood there looking back at his cabin with a strong cold wind blowing the plaits of his hair. "I have not thought of those things for many a moon," he said. "It was a bad time, but we learned there how to endure all the other bad times that were to come. But there were some good times, too, some good times. I was then only twenty-four years old."

Book Two

THE WESTERNERS

26

Late in the Moon of Black Butterflies (September 1838) the first detachment of a thousand Cherokees left a stockade on the Hiwassee River and began moving westward. A small unit of soldiers accompanied the wagon train, but only as observers. Chief John Ross and his council had organized this forced migration of a nation into parties of about one thousand, each to leave four days behind the other. With the approval of the War Department, General Scott granted an allowance of sixty-five dollars per person, a bargain for the American government, for from this fund the Cherokee council had to purchase cooking utensils, rations, clothing, blankets, wagons, and horses needed for the journey.

One wagon and team and six riding horses were allotted to each fifteen persons, and each wagon train was headed by a conductor, who was usually a Cherokee town chief. To assist him, he had a wagonmaster, a blacksmith, a commissary to manage the food supply, a medicine man to care for the sick, and a few members of the old Cherokee Light Horse to act as police.

The stockade in which Creek Mary and her family were imprisoned was one of the last to be organized for travel. Not until the Frost Moon of early November were enough wagons and horses assembled there to begin the journey. In a chilly gray dawn they were ferried across the river and assigned their wagons, horses, and equipment. Their conductor was Chief Salali from Coosawatie, and by noontime he and his assistants had moved the wagons into line and informed the able-bodied men and women what their special duties would be on the journey. Without ceremony the train was then started on its way.

Jotham somehow managed to find the McBees, a rather large family, and persuaded them to share a wagon and riding horses with Creek Mary's people. Although the McBees had lived near Okelogee for several years, Mary had never more than exchanged greetings with old John McBee, a taciturn beetle-browed Scot. "Why do you," she asked him now, "a white man free to go anywhere you please on this earth, choose to share the miseries of the dispossessed Cherokees?"

McBee's bright eyes opened wide in surprise, and he rubbed the gray stubble of beard on his long bony jaw. "The choice had not entered my mind, madam," he replied.

"You could have gone with the others, taken money from the *Unegas* as my half-blood son did. You could go separately now as a white man with your family. Could it be that you are a dull-witted man, John McBee?"

"Aye, that I could be. Also it might be a matter of loyalty, madam. Loyalty to my children mothered by my Cherokee wife, to my wife's people who have accepted me as one of them."

She stepped forward and gripped the thick muscle of his upper arm. "I am glad you are the captain of our wagon, John McBee."

For the first time he smiled, and then he bowed his thanks to her.

Griffa was of course the McBee that Jotham was interested in, but he was not to see as much of her as he had hoped for on this journey. He and Dane, being among the few blacksmiths in the train, were assigned to the farrier detail and spent many of their daytime hours riding up and down the line of march to assist the wagonmaster. After the first few days of travel, they often worked until bedtime over a portable forge purchased from the army—shoeing horses, mending harness, and repairing damaged wagons.

John McBee drove their wagon, with his Cherokee wife seated beside him, while Mary, Jerusha, Pleasant and his hound, and Griffa and the younger McBee children made themselves as comfortable as they could among the blankets in the rear. The older McBee boys and the Stalking Turkey used the riding horses. The

first two days were warm and sunny, and relief from long imprisonment eased the sadness of leaving their homeland. But when
they reached the Cumberland Mountains, a steady autumn rain
began falling. Canvas had to be fastened over the bows, giving
those inside the wagons a feeling of confinement again.

After a few hours in the cold drenching rain, the Stalking Turkey hitched his horse to the rear of their wagon and climbed inside. Mary made him remove all his wet clothing and wrap himself in two blankets, but the old man's toothless jaws continued
trembling for a long time.

The mountain roads were rough and difficult. Singletrees
snapped frequently on the hard pulls, and sometimes teams had
to be unhitched from the rear wagons and brought to the front
to aid in pulling the forward wagons over the steepest passages.
They had been told that the distance to Indian Territory was
eight hundred miles and that the train must travel fifteen miles
each day if they hoped to reach there before the Ice Moon of
January. In the Cumberlands they averaged only four or five
miles between sunrise and sunset.

At last they struggled out of the mountains to find that heavy
rains and the passage of a preceding detachment of Cherokees
had turned the road to Nashville into a quagmire. When they
reached the broad Cumberland River at Nashville, the ferryman
not only refused to accept Chief Salali's treasury notes, he demanded to be paid in gold and doubled the usual rates for each
wagon crossed. The train was delayed half a day while Salali
and his aides searched out a Nashville banker, who made a
handsome profit for himself by heavily discounting the paper
notes. The Cherokees suspected that the ferryman and the
banker were in league with each other, but they were not surprised at being fleeced in the hometown of their archenemy,
President Andrew Jackson, and they knew it would be a waste of
breath to protest.

Throughout the following day the train was trailed by a band
of Tennessee ruffians. Having been warned to beware of land pi-
rates when they reached the Ohio River, Chief Salali assigned a
double guard over the night camp. The horse thieves knew,

however, that Cherokees were forbidden to carry arms, and soon
after dark they raided several corrals, firing on the defenseless
guards and racing away with about thirty of the best animals.
One Cherokee guard was killed, several others suffered wounds.

The following morning the train could not move for lack of
horses, losing another precious day while Chief Salali and his
wagonmaster rode through the countryside to seek replacement
horses from farmers who might have animals to sell. After a long
search they found only one horse dealer in the area. His prices
were exorbitant because he knew the Cherokees would have to
pay what he asked in order to move their wagons. Although
most of the horses that Salali bought were the same animals that
had been stolen from them the previous night, he and his wagonmaster confined their bitter comments to the Cherokee language.
Aliens in a land that once belonged to their grandfathers, they
were growing accustomed to being exploited. But their allotted
funds were vanishing rapidly, and they had six hundred miles
yet to travel.

In Kentucky they met the tollgaters, wolfish white riffraff who
placed chained logs across the narrow road in front of their
cabins. These cabin dwellers called the obstacles "tollgates," refusing to lift the logs by their chains until each wagon paid a
toll.

Near Hopkinsville came the first threat of early winter, a bleak
rainstorm that changed to sleet and froze to the wagon canvases.
During the night a wet snow fell over the encampment. When
Mary awoke at first light and looked out the rear of the wagon,
she cried aloud at the sight of the sleeping men snow-shrouded
under their blankets. The camp resembled a ghostly burying
ground of white mounds. By the time the wagons began rolling,
the snow was melting, the roads becoming so deep in mud that
wheels sank to their axles.

For several nights after that the muddy ruts froze into stone-
hard furrows. Morning travel was so rough that many of the old
people and children preferred to walk in the shivering cold
rather than endure the rough shaking of the wagon beds. By
noontime the mud usually thawed into a morass again. But after

they crossed the Ohio River into Illinois the thawing stopped, the temperature never rising above freezing.

The night the train halted near the town of Jonesboro, Illinois, the commissary informed the conductor that all their beef was gone and that the salt pork and cornmeal rations would have to be cut in half if they were to last another week. Thirty miles away at Cape Girardeau, Missouri, additional supplies were supposed to be waiting for them, but delays had thrown the train two weeks behind its planned schedule, and no one could be certain how much food would be there.

Taking one of the empty commissary wagons, Chief Salali and his aides drove into the town and found a merchant who saw an opportunity to rid himself of a consignment of wormy bacon by selling it to the Indians for a good profit.

At breakfast the next morning, Pleasant refused to eat the slice of bacon given him because of its bad smell, but the others forced themselves to chew and swallow the meat. Their meal was interrupted by two white strangers, one claiming to be a sheriff who said that a gray riding horse assigned to their wagon belonged to his companion.

"This is certainly a mistake," John McBee cried indignantly. "We have brought these horses from Tennessee, from beyond the Cumberland Mountains."

"He's lying, sheriff," said the other white man. "That gray one is my horse."

Mary added her usual colorful expletives to the objections, and she sent Dane and Jotham riding off in opposite directions to find Chief Salali, but before the boys returned the two white men had taken away the horse. McBee knew that in their eyes he was as much a Cherokee as his wife, and he also knew that the white men were quite aware that for dispossessed Cherokees there was no recourse to the law in Illinois or any other state. He counted himself lucky that they had claimed only one horse; for the remainder of the journey one of his older boys would have to walk or ride in the crowded wagon.

Three days later, traveling in the bitterest weather yet encountered, they reached the bank of the Mississippi River. About a hundred Cherokees, the tag end of the train that had preceded them, were camped there with a dozen wagons. Instead of a mighty flowing stream the river was choked with tumbling fragments and sheets of ice. Across on the Cape Girardeau bank a ferryboat was locked in the frozen mass. They learned from the encamped Cherokees that two days earlier their detachment's passage across the Mississippi had been halted by darkness, and during that night the ice had come down from the north, trapping the ferryboat.

For the new arrivals nothing else could be done but go into camp. Afterward, no one could remember how many days they stayed there, praying for the ice to clear from the river. Food for themselves and fodder for their horses ran low and had to be severely rationed. "Every day I seemed to be hungrier than the day before," Dane recalled. "Jotham and I would go down into the river bottoms to strip bark from trees for the horses to eat, and we would dig up any kind of roots we could find for our family. A thousand others were doing the same thing, so that each day we would have to go farther. We were always cold, our feet aching from the cold, because our moccasins had worn to holes."

Then the sickness began, first among the children. Measles and whooping cough spread rapidly through the wagons. And then pneumonia struck the old people. All through the bitter nights from almost every wagon came the sounds of sickness—constant hacking coughs, the cries of children, rasping struggles for breath, the moaning of old men and women.

One morning Pleasant's hound was missing. Dane searched everywhere for the dog, but he was certain that someone had killed and eaten it. Chief Salali had given the commissary permission to kill one horse each day, but there was never enough meat for the thousand suffering campers, and the dogs disappeared one by one.

Pleasant must have sensed what had happened, perhaps had heard someone speak of the missing dogs and the reasons why. He cried through the morning, and in the afternoon was coughing almost continuously, his body burning with fever. The train's medicine man, old Jukias, who was exhausted and ailing himself, finally came and dosed the little boy with extracts of snakeroot and chinquapin leaves. The fever went down but the rattling cough continued.

The next morning the Stalking Turkey was unable to rise from his blankets under the wagon, and the young men had to lift him inside. Two of the smaller McBee children were crying fitfully; the mottled rash of measles covered their faces and necks. The wagon had become an overcrowded hospital, with Griffa and Jerusha devoting most of their time to nursing the sick.

That night, without saying anything, Mary took her two blankets and joined the men and boys under the wagon. "You'll freeze here, Grandmother," Dane said. "We'll find room for you in another wagon."

"No," she answered, "they're all the same. Everybody has thrown out kettles and cooking things to make room for the sick." She refused to be taken elsewhere, but when the cold began creeping from the frozen ground, Dane and Jotham made her lie between them, their bodies close to hers to share their youthful warmth.

"I am old and good for nothing," she grumbled. "I am but a burthen to my grandchildren."

"You keep us warm, Grandmother," Dane said.

"I have lived long enough," she answered sleepily. "My children have loved me and I have loved them. I have laughed my way through this fine world since the Long Warrior found me, but there is no time for laughter now. The time has come to let my spirit go. I want to see the friends of my youth in the Land of Spirits."

"No," Jotham protested. "We need you with us in our new land."

"To show us the way," Dane added. He could not imagine a world in which there was no Grandmother Mary. Yet her body was frailer than he had ever known it. He could feel her bones through the blanket. Always he had thought of her as robust, indomitable, forever enduring. As sleep came on he remembered the long summer days under the arbor when she held him in her lap, her breasts naked, telling him stories of her youth while the Little Singing Stream burbled musically along.

At daylight they were awakened by the hoarse whistle of the ferryboat. The ice had left the Mississippi! Recommending haste, the ferryman warned his passengers that more ice might come down the river, and all day the wagons rolled steadily aboard for the monotonous crossings, the bony half-starved horses barely able to pull the loads.

In Cape Girardeau they found the expected supplies of fodder and cornmeal, but there was no meat of any kind. Chief John Ross's representatives waiting there told them they would have to live off what wild game they could find across Missouri. They were advised to follow a northern route because so many wagons had already moved over the southern road that most of the deer had been killed or frightened away. From the Cherokees at Cape Girardeau they also heard the sad news that John Ross's wife, Quatie, had died in Arkansas on the way west.

Led by a guide who had already traversed the upper trail, they started northward, and now the dying began. Instead of two or three each day, five or six had to be hastily buried at every stop for night camp. The Stalking Turkey was one of the first of the old warriors to die. They found him one morning frozen in his blanket, and buried him beside the trail. Mary did not weep for her old friend, but she refused to let the wagons move out until her grandsons had cut and trimmed a pole to mark his grave.

Not until after they passed the town of Farmington and turned westward into thick forests did the hunters, using only bows and arrows, find deer enough to supply everyone with venison. Yet the deaths continued among those weakened by exposure and illnesses. Pleasant recovered slowly, but two of the younger McBees died on successive days and were buried near the town of Springfield.

Each day of travel became an ordeal, a struggle to survive the endless miles. Somewhere after they left Washburn's Prairie and entered Arkansas, so many were afflicted with a violent dysentery that one morning there were scarcely enough men able to

harness the teams. Neither John McBee nor his wife had the
strength to sit erect, and after Dane and Jotham hitched the
horses to the wagon, Griffa and Jerusha took turns handling the
reins. So many horses had gone lame and so many wagons were
at the point of total disintegration that the two young men were
in constant demand along the length of the slow-moving train.
Fifteen died that day, and there were barely that many left who
were strong enough to dig graves in which to bury them. Jukias,
the medicine man, had exhausted his supply of astringent remedies and could offer the sick nothing more than prayer songs.
During that night Jotham fell ill with griping pains in his abdo-
men, and at dawn they discovered so many others had been
similarly afflicted that it would be impossible to move the
wagons.

Griffa got the morning fire going until water was boiling in the
pot, and then Mary showed her how to soak an old cloth to press
against Jotham's belly, keeping hot water dripping upon it from
a pan. "Black drink would ease the hurting," Mary said. "But we
have none, nor any coffee. All I can offer my grandson to stop his
misery is hot water."

Jerusha brought Pleasant to the fire to warm him while she
sifted part of their wagon's daily ration of cornmeal into a pot
and poured hot water over it. This would be their breakfast.
Dane rolled out from under the wagon and began saddling his
horse.

About this time Chief Salali and the Cherokee guide came riding up to the fire. "What are we to do, Salali?" Mary asked. "If
we must stay here we shall all die."

"I do not know, Amayi," he replied. "The guide tells me we
are very near the Cherokee Nation, that in three or four days of
travel we can reach Park Hill, where there will be medicine and
better food and shelter."

"There are not able drivers for half the wagons," she said.

"Yes, but I have been thinking that those who are able should
go on," the chief said, uncertainty in his tone.

She frowned at him. "We cannot leave any of our people here
without food, no one to hunt venison for them."

"Jukias has nothing to give them."

"Last night through the trees I saw lights." Mary pointed toward the west. "There is a settlement not far from here."

"Cane Hill, they call it," the guide said. "The *Unegas* there could do nothing for us if they would."

"Most settlements have a *Unega* doctor," she went on. "He would have medicine for running bowels."

The chief shook his head. "He would sooner give us poison."

"Dane!" she called to her grandson. "I want you to ride to that town and bring a *Unega* doctor back to me. Not one wheel of this wagon train will turn until you come back."

"Amayi, Amayi," Salali muttered. Dane glanced at the chief, who shrugged and motioned for him to do what his grandmother wanted.

"Wait!" Jerusha cried. "I'm going with you."

"Why?" Dane turned and stared at her in surprise.

"Look at you. With your dirty hands and face, your bushy greasy hair and filthy clothes, you would frighten a catamount. No doctor would come with you." Jerusha ran a comb quickly through her hair, pulled a faded red ribbon from the pocket of her apron and banded it around her head.

"She is right, *sogonisi*," Mary said. "Saddle Jotham's horse for her."

Jerusha had to ride astraddle on Jotham's saddle, and when she and Dane came trotting into Cane Hill's single street, half the inhabitants stopped what they were doing to watch the strange pair ride into their town. At the end of the street was a small shed built of slabs, with a crudely lettered sign on the front: BLACKSMITH. Scattered around the building were several wagons in various stages of disrepair.

"Look!" Dane pointed at a man who was pounding away at a wheel spoke.

"Mr. Tim Rogers!" Jerusha exclaimed, as amazed as he was.

Hearing his name called, Rogers looked up and recognized them at once. When they rode up to the blacksmith, Dane dismounted and grabbed Rogers's offered hand. Both began talking at once, each trying to explain to the other how chance had brought them together in Cane Hill.

"Is there a doctor in this town?" Jerusha interrupted. She was still in the saddle.

"There is a doctor of sorts." Rogers looked up at her, a faint smile forming on his lips when he noticed the way her black dress billowed to the stirrups. "You want to trade for a sidesaddle, Miss Jerusha?"

"No," she replied impatiently. "This is Jotham's horse. Where is the doctor?"

"See that barbershop down the street? Most likely you'll find a female herb doctor, name of Saviah Manning, in there or upstairs over it."

"A woman doctor? Is there no other?" Disappointment showed on her face, but she turned the horse and looked back over her shoulder. "You coming, Dane?"

"Go on. I'll be there." He wanted to know why Rogers had opened his blacksmith shop in Arkansas instead of in the new Cherokee Nation.

"Things are bad over there, Dane. Soon there's bound to be real trouble between the Cherokees who supported the treaty and came out here first—the Ridge-Boudinot people—and John Ross's followers like you and me who were forced to come. So many of our people have died on the long march—"

"Don't tell me about dying, Mr. Rogers. We've buried over two hundred. I didn't know the other trains had lost many people, too."

"It's been terrible. My wife and I came with one of the first removal parties, traveling crowded on boats most of the way, sickness and death day after day. Measles took the children and bilious fever took the old. Some of the strong went, too. We lost a third of our party, buried along the riverbanks from Tennessee through Arkansas."

"We were told about that," Dane said. "For us, it's been no better in the wagons."

They exchanged more information, and Rogers again warned Dane that conditions were bad in the Cherokee Nation. "They're

starting to build the new capital. Tahlequah, they'll call it. I
thought some of putting my smithy there, but I don't like the
looks of things. The new arrivals have nothing, they could give
me nothing for my work. And the treaty people, although they'll
soon be far outnumbered, have the upper hand right now because they came out here with plenty of government money."

"Like my Uncle Opothle," Dane said.

"Opothle's doing well for himself, indeed. His trading post is
the best around the Park Hill community. He wanted me to
blacksmith near his place, but no, I told my wife we'd move over
here in Arkansas where we'd be safe if a showdown comes.
Look, I've been rebuilding these old wagons that wore out coming from Tennessee and selling a few."

Jerusha's high thin voice was calling Dane from the front of
the barbershop. "I see she found the herb doctor," Rogers said.
"You married that girl yet, Dane?"

"No." He put his foot in the stirrup and mounted.

"Well, she acts like it for sure. Why don't you marry her and
settle down here and work with me?"

"I might do that, Mr. Rogers, after we get the wagons into the
Nation. Good-bye."

"Good luck, Dane. Give my good word to Creek Mary and tell
Jotham I wish him restored to health."

Dane trotted his horse on to the barbershop, where a tall
black-haired dark-skinned woman mounted on a black mare was
waiting with Jerusha. The woman wore men's jean trousers, a
fringed buckskin jacket, and a wide-brimmed flat-topped black
hat with a yellow-dyed feather in the band. There was something Indian about her that reassured Dane. "The doctor will go
with us," Jerusha said.

"Who is he?" the woman asked, staring briefly at Dane and
then turning her attention to the adjustment of a saddlebag that
was so badly worn Dane could see surgical instruments poking
through cracks in the leather.

"Dane's his name," Jerusha replied flatly. "Dane, this is Dr.
Saviah Manning."

"Is he your husband?" Dr. Manning asked.

"That dirty no-account Indian, most certainly not." She slapped her reins and started her horse down the muddy street. "Let's go."

The three rode abreast as they left the town on the crooked road. Dane kept glancing at Jerusha, who was gazing straight ahead with no expression on her face. She had changed somehow. She had never behaved in such a manner. Always before she had deferred to him. Now she was acting like—well, like his grandmother, ordering everybody about in a most independent manner.

When they came to a steep hill the horses slowed and Jerusha broke the silence. "Dr. Manning, may I ask you a question?"

"Ask it."

"If he," she said, indicating Dane with a scornful jerk of her elbow, "had come to you instead of I, would you have agreed to bring medicine to our wagons?"

The tall woman gave Dane a searching look. "To be honest, I probably would not," she said, and her white teeth showed in a quick smile.

"Because he's Indian?" Jerusha continued.

"I'm half Indian myself, miss. No, because looking at him I might've feared he meant to rob or rape me." This time she laughed and Jerusha joined in.

"I told you, Dane." There was a triumphant note in Jerusha's voice. Her face was turned toward him when he looked at her. For the first time in many days, their eyes met and he saw an unfamiliar radiance in the blueness. He could not tell whether it was love or hate. When the horses reached the top of the hill, Jerusha urged her mount into a quick trot, racing away from him and the doctor.

Waiting for them at the wagon with Mary and the others was Jukias. After shaking hands with Saviah Manning, the medicine man studied her face with grave interest, and then asked what manner of remedies the female doctor gave to her patients.

"You should be pleased to receive remedies of any kind from me, Cherokee," she replied quickly. "Your people are invaders of my people's lands. I am half Osage."

"Ah." Jukias's expression revealed his apprehension. "But we do not come into Osage lands of our own will."

"I know that." She kneeled to open the worn medicine bag. "My father was a white physician who lived among the Osages. My mother was Osage."

"You will help us even though we are—"

"Before he died my father made me take an oath. 'Whatsoever house I enter, there will I go for the benefit of the sick.' I have doctored Cherokees before this. I know the white man's medicine, but I also am an herb doctor as you are, Jukias. My extracts and distillations come from plants gathered in the hills around here. With one exception. My laudanum I must buy in St. Louis."

"Does that come from a plant?" Jukias asked.

"From the opium poppy. Mixed with an infusion from dried persimmons and wild cherries, it will stop the bloodiest flux, easing all pain."

Jukias bowed. "We welcome you with our hearts, Osage doctor."

For three days, Dr. Saviah Manning stayed with the wagon train, leaving only occasionally to return to Cane Hill to refill her medicine bag. On the third day the dying stopped, and most of the sick were sufficiently recovered for the wagons to resume the journey. Chief Salali offered to pay the doctor from his diminishing reserve of treasury notes, but she would take only enough to replenish her stock of laudanum. When the wagons moved out, she rode with them as far as the Cane Hill cutoff, and there Mary ordered John McBee to stop the wagon while she climbed out to give Saviah Manning a present. It was the treasured hourglass that the Long Warrior had brought her from Nashville a quarter of a century past. "I give you a Cherokee name," Mary told her. "Suyeta, the Chosen One. From this day you are one of us."

"I am also Osage and white," Saviah whispered to her. "I live in that lonely place between the light and dark races."

Next day they crossed the border into the Cherokee Nation West. Winter still held the land, but the cold had lost its bite, and for the first time in weeks the sounds of laughter and banter could be heard as the wagons creaked westward.

Before the exiles left their camp of sickness near Cane Hill, Timothy Rogers had come out to visit old friends among those from Okelogee. For Jotham he drew a rough map indicating the locations of Opothle's house and trading post. On the morning of the third day after leaving Cane Hill, the wagons reached a road fork, and Salali ordered the train halted. Creek Mary, Dane, Jotham, Jerusha, and Pleasant transferred their scanty belongings to one of the empty commissary wagons, and after tearful good-byes and promises of early reunions they set out for Opothle's house.

By Tim Rogers's map they had only about three miles left to travel, and Jotham, who was driving, cracked his whip impatiently above the backs of the weary horses. Mary sat beside him, holding Pleasant in her lap, singing snatches of songs and humming to herself. The rocky trail ran through thick leafless woods, and she began naming familiar trees in Creek, Cherokee, and English—dogwood, wild plum, walnut, mulberry, persimmon, sycamore, hickory, oak. Then they swung up over a rise in the land and there in front of them across a river bottom was a low ridge, a reduced image of the Sleeping Woman. "Look!" Mary cried, but they all had seen it at the same time. "A little Sleeping Woman!"

"Her stomach is swollen," Jerusha said.

"Yes," Mary agreed, and her laughter filled the wagon. "We'll call it the Sleeping Girl with Child."

A few minutes later they came to a ramshackle cabin set back from the road among scrubby brown-leaved blackjacks. The logs were poorly chinked, its corners were unaligned, and the roof consisted of a few strips of bark.

"Is that the house?" Dane asked.

"No," Mary said. "Opothle would not live in such a place."

A mile farther on they came to a double cabin, larger but not much better built than the first, the yard filled with stumps. On the unroofed porch a woman in a sunbonnet was shaking out a straw broom. She looked up at the sound of the wagon, and then dropped the broom, flinging her hands into the air. "Oh, Prissie, come running," Suna-lee shouted. "They're here!"

27

Returning to Dane's cabin from the sandhill, we had to face a strong chill wind as well as a blinding sun that was more than midway down the sky. Neither of us spoke until we reached the shelter of the willows.

"That was the Trail of Tears," I said.

"Yes, the naming of it came afterward," Dane answered quickly. "In Cherokee it would be the Trail Where They Cried, but long before we survivors reached the Indian Territory we had no tears left to shed. Too many died too fast. Not until after we were at the end of the trail did our dry eyes refill with tears of remembrance.

"Each of us in our detachment of wagons, our moving village of wagons, thought that what was happening to us was a torment peculiar to us only. We did not know until later that hundreds of others were dying in the same cruel way—not only Cherokees but Creeks, Choctaws, Chickasaws, and Seminoles from the South, and Shawnees, Ottawas, Delawares, Hurons, Miamis, and many more tribes from the North, thousands and thousands of people being driven from their eastern homelands to die because they were Indians.

"For the Cherokees, though, I think the suffering was the most piercing. After the chiefs made counts of people from their old towns, they found we had lost four thousand by death from the time we were herded into stockades until the last wagon reached our new Nation. The bones of one of every four of us lay scattered between the Tennessee River and Indian Territory. What made the suffering worse for us was the bitter feeling between those who were forced to come, Chief John Ross's followers, and those who had signed the treaty and taken government money, the Ridge-Boudinot people, including my Uncle Opothle.

"Yes, Mr. Tim Rogers measured matters well. He felt the hatred in the air, and being one of us only by marriage he was independent enough to get clear of the violence before it came. I don't think the Ridge family or Elias Boudinot and his brother Stand Watie, or many of the others suspected how deep was the hostility toward them, the rage in so many hearts.

"Uncle Opothle knew, however. He was very busy at his trading post, a mile up the road from his house, but I'm sure he bore a burden of guilt because he had left Grandmother Mary behind to suffer the journey on the Trail of Tears, and he feared some retribution from the Maker of Breath for the deaths of my father, the Runner, and my stepmother, Walina.

"I was with Grandmother Mary when Opothle came riding down from his trading post to greet the arrival of we survivors. He had just learned of the deaths, and he clasped Mary in his arms and begged her to forgive him.

"'Words change nothing, Opothle,' she told him. 'We go on living.'

"'The Maker of Breath made me for some purpose,' he cried out. 'I have not yet fulfilled the purpose. By coming here first, I have managed to acquire a quantity of goods. I will do what I can for the people who have but few blankets and little clothing.'

"'Your father John Kingsley had some kindness in him,' she said as if talking to herself. 'But he had no heart to feel either love for him or hatred directed toward him.'

"'I have felt the hatred,' Opothle admitted. 'I can only beg forgiveness. I fear the future, Mother Amayi.'

"He was insistent that Grandmother Mary, Jerusha, Pleasant, and I stay with his family. He had built his house larger than most, intending to use half of it for his trading post, but the opening of the crossroads led him to put his trading place there. And so we lived for a time in Uncle Opothle's house."

We were at the cabin door. Dane held it open for me, the warmth from the fireplace welcoming us. He added two logs to the coals, and sparks exploded like firecrackers.

He warmed his hands for a few minutes. "You must understand the feelings of John Ross's followers. All had suffered in the stockades and many had lost relatives and friends in the dying. They knew their misery had been brought upon them by the American government, but that was something without shape, far away beyond reach. Closer at hand they could see every day those people who had signed away our homeland by treaty and had come comfortably to the new land and were living in solid houses instead of in tents or lean-tos, or in the wagons that had brought them there. But to me, this division of our people at that hard time for us was a sad and disgusting thing.

"Yet I could not help being drawn into it. Some of the full-bloods started a secret society whose aim was to create a new independent Cherokee Nation just as it was before the white men came. No one with white blood could be a member of the secret society. A few men from Okelogee were members, and as I was the son of a headman they kept after me until I joined. The very existence of the society had to be kept secret; we could not even speak of it to our families. We held our meetings at night in a cabin down in the woods near the Illinois River.

"Most of the speakers were older men who made strong talk against the treaty signers. Some also spoke against Chief John Ross. They said he was too weak in his leadership against the treaty signers, and that we should have a full-blood chief. They began urging us to return to the old Blood Law, which they said had been broken by those who signed away the eastern Cherokee Nation.

"One night a secret council was called and I slipped away

from Uncle Opothle's house and rode down to the cabin with Turtle Catcher, a young man of my age I had known in Okelogee. Summer had come on, and bullfrogs were bellowing along the river. I suggested to my companion that we hunt bullfrogs instead of going to the council, but he said the meeting was too important. 'Tonight they are going to name the ones to be killed by the Blood Law,' Turtle Catcher told me.

"We went on to the cabin, which was dimly lit by a few candles that had attracted swarms of moths. I had just stepped inside the crowded room when one of the leaders of the secret society came and said to me in a quiet voice that I should leave before the council began. 'Ask no questions,' he said, 'but leave this place. If your father were living, he would be asked to go. So I ask you to go. And remember your oath. Say nothing of this meeting to anyone.'

"I went back outside and mounted my horse. Half the sky was filled with stars, but a low cloud bank was crawling out of the west and the smell of rain was on the air. Whippoorwills were calling down in the bottoms and the deep-voiced frogs sounded like the continuous beat of faraway drums.

"On this night the secret society was going to name the condemned, and the leaders did not want me there, nor would they have wanted Talasi the Runner. I knew then of course that my uncle, Opothle, was one of those to be named for execution under the old Blood Law.

"The back of my neck went cold as if ice had formed on the hairs. For a while I could not think. I let the horse walk slowly along, certain in my mind that I could not let Uncle Opothle die without a warning. But I had taken the oath of secrecy and I did not know how I could save him. Only one person could tell me what to do. I whipped the horse into a gallop until I came to the crossroads. Opothle's trading post was dark, but a light showed in the adjoining house where my cousin William and his recent bride, Tatsuwha, lived. I knew that sometimes when Opothle worked late he took supper with them before he went home. I could not bring myself to stop and find out if he was there. So I galloped on to the double cabin, slowing my horse so that it came up quietly to the hitching posts.

"The front door was open to the summer night, and I could see all the way into the candlelit back room where Prissie and Jerusha were clearing away the supper dishes. I went inside and there was Grandmother Mary sitting in a straight-backed chair looking straight at my shadow.

"'Dane?' She spoke my name softly.

"'Yes,' I whispered. 'Come outside, Grandmother.'

"She limped as she came to the door, and I helped her over the rough boards of the unroofed porch, walking with her to the hitching posts. A sprinkle of rain blew past us. 'Where is Uncle Opothle?' I asked her. 'At William's,' she said. 'He may come soon.'

"I put my hands on her shoulders, looking through the darkness into her beautiful aging face, and told her everything.

"'I saw a hawk today,' she said, 'circling over this house. Not a blue hawk, but a brown hawk. I have not seen a blue hawk since we came to this country.'

"'What am I to do?' I asked, shaking her gently.

"'The Creeks are south of us.' She seemed uncertain of her own words. 'That is true, is it not? The same as it was in the old Nation?'

"'The Creeks live now to our west, Grandmother,' I told her.

"'Opothle could go to the Creeks,' she began slowly, 'but they are in more misery than we.'

"'We have little time, Grandmother.' I could feel her body shuddering under my hands. 'They will do it tonight.'

"'Opothle should not have signed the treaty,' she said. 'But he is of my blood, my firstborn.' She drew a deep trembling breath. 'You are forbidden to warn him, so I must do it. Help me into your saddle.'

"'It's beginning to rain,' I said.

"She pulled away from me and went to my horse and tried to mount. I lifted her into the saddle.

"'The happiest times of my life,' she said, 'were whenever I had a good horse under me.' She turned toward the road. 'Go on in the house, *sogonisi*, and wait for me.'

"Waiting for her in the half darkness of the front room of the cabin was one of the longest times of my life. I wished Jotham was there, but he was away at the McBees. Anyway, since the beginning of the full-bloods' secret society Jotham and I had grown apart. I sat in the straight-backed chair looking out the open door at the damp night, listening to the murmur of voices— Jerusha and Prissie in the back room and Suna-lee with Pleasant in the loft room. On the night before this I had climbed quietly to that loft room to be with Jerusha, but she had refused me entrance to her bed, threatening to cry out if I forced her. Since we had come to the Indian Territory, she had spun an invisible web around herself and Pleasant, tolerating only Grandmother Mary and Priscilla, rarely speaking to anyone else. On Sunday mornings now, Jerusha and Priscilla went to one of the Christian missionary meetings. They read together every night from their Bibles and took turns offering prayers over our food. Priscilla had grown plump and was almost past a marriageable age. She did not like it when Jotham teased her for being an old maid. Everything was changing. I would go out sometimes at night with one or another of the full-blood girls at Park Hill, but when I would be with them I was always thinking of Jerusha. Most of my days I spent hunting alone in the woods for deer, turkeys, squirrels, bee trees, anything to bring food to Suna-lee's table. We were allowed to have guns again, in our own Nation, and as I sat there waiting for Grandmother Mary I could see Opothle's two new rifles resting on wooden pegs against the rough cedar-log wall, with powder horns, knives, and catamount-skin shot pouches below them. Alongside these weapons, Suna-lee had hung a dozen drinking gourds.

"After what seemed a lifetime, Grandmother Mary returned. When I heard the slow hoofbeats, I went outside and helped her from the saddle. A fine mist was falling and her dress and hair were beaded with raindrops. 'It's done,' she said. 'We'll say no more of it.' She limped into the sleeping room she shared with Prissie to change her damp clothes.

"Late that night I was awakened when Jotham slipped into the shed room where we had floor pallets. I said nothing and he lay down on his straw-filled quilt. Half awake, half asleep, I listened to his breathing until I knew he was asleep, and not long after that shrill cries and hoarse shouts and the pounding of horses' hooves broke the silence of the night.

"Shaking Jotham awake, I led the way through the house toward the front door. It was open and Grandmother Mary was standing there peering out at the shadows of milling horsemen. A faint red glow shaded the whirls of mist, and out of them came my cousin William and his young full-blood wife. They were dressed in their nightclothes. Mary's arms opened to them, and then as she stepped back to let them inside, I heard her ask: 'Is it the trading post?'

"'Yes, and our house too,' William replied. He was trembling with shock and anger.

"Jotham and I both hurried to the door. The misty sky over the crossroads was stained with the color of fire. From the crowd of horsemen somebody called for Opothle. Suna-lee came to the door, holding a candle, and told them he was not there. 'Where is he?' the voice demanded.

"Suna-lee turned toward her elder son. 'I thought he was with you, William.'

"'He went somewhere tonight,' William said. 'Rode away with Bibbs.' Bibbs was the last black slave owned by Opothle. The others had been traded off to raise money for the trading post which at that moment was burning to the ground.

"Fingers gripped at my arm, and Jerusha in her nightdress was there beside me in the doorway, her eyes wide with fright when she saw the fire reflected in the sky. Like me she was remembering another fire on a night when we were naked together in the *asi* at Okelogee, the night her brother, Isaac, and his wife, Harriet, died in that other fire of vengeance. 'Dane!' she said in a loud whisper. 'Opothle may be dead in the fire!'

"'He is not,' Mary said, just as one of the leaders of the secret society loomed out of the mist in front of us, demanding that Opothle show himself.

"'Opothle is not here,' Mary told him. She was holding one of Opothle's new rifles.

"'Where is he?' the man asked.

"'Opothle is a trader,' she said, anger rising in her voice. 'He must travel to buy goods. Now take your gaping fussocks out of our yard before I fire this gun into them!'

"'I'm coming in,' the man said.

"'You'll lie dead if you do!' Her voice was suddenly as strong and deep as it had been in my childhood.

"'Let him come,' Suna-lee broke in quickly. 'He'll soon find we are telling truth and then they'll go away.'

"The men of course found no trace of Opothle in the house or anywhere around the place, and they rode off. I realized then that Grandmother Mary and I were the only members of the family who knew the full meaning of what was happening. But neither of us could vision the bloodiness that was yet to come during that black night.

"None of us slept any more in the hours before daylight. Jotham and I went up to the crossroads, but by that time the flames were dying out and there was nothing to see but a few pots and twisted metal utensils in the embers of the trading post.

"In the early daytime our community began stirring with wild rumors of violent deeds. First we heard of the deaths of Major Ridge and his son, John. The assassins trailed the old man to the house of a friend, set an ambush, and filled his body with bullets. They then stormed into his son's house, dragging him from his bed, and out into the yard, where they stabbed him to death with knives. It was daylight before they found Elias Boudinot in Park Hill, boldly tricking him into ambush, one man stabbing him in the back with a knife while another split his skull with a tomahawk. We learned afterward that Boudinot's brother, Stand Watie, received warning of the Blood Law pact and escaped to Fort Gibson, an army post near the border of the Creek Nation.

"Meanwhile Jotham and William were desperately trying to learn where their father was so that they might warn him of the danger. At the first opportunity I asked Grandmother Mary if she knew where Uncle Opothle had gone, but she shook her head. 'He told me we would hear from him,' she said. 'Opothle always keeps his word, and Bibbs is with him to look out for him. We'll hear from Opothle.'

"I suspected that he might have gone to the Creeks, but I was wrong, and Mary was wrong, because we never heard from Uncle Opothle. Not from him directly, that is. From Bibbs we heard of the bloody way in which Opothle Kingsley died.

"About duskfall the following evening Bibbs came riding up to our doorway on a sweated gray gelding. He was in such terror that he could hardly speak, and after he managed to impart to us the dreadful truth that we would never see Opothle again, we were drawn into his state of panic and grief. You may be assured that he was grieving. Back in Georgia, Bibbs may have regarded Opothle as his master, a barrier to his freedom, but in the strange wild Indian Territory he had come to look upon Opothle as his protector, and he was beset by genuine sorrow.

"Like Bibbs we were all so shaken by the calamity that we lost our reason, the women grieving piteously, William, Jotham, and I determined to seek safety for them and ourselves, fearing some further retribution. All through the night we worked at loading three wagons saved from the fire, emptying the double cabin of its contents, and at sunrise we started eastward for the Arkansas line.

"Opothle had traveled that same way, we learned later from Bibbs, intending to seek temporary safety with his wife's kinsman, Mr. Timothy Rogers at Cane Hill. He and Bibbs had ridden hard through the night until they crossed the line into Arkansas. It was late and Opothle decided to put up at one of those shabby Arkansas inns that existed mainly for the purpose of selling whiskey to Cherokees, strong drink being outlawed in the Nation.

"Next morning when they were approaching the stables for their horses, without warning several guns fired a fusillade into Opothle. Bibbs said the murderers must have been hidden behind the hayrack, because right after the firing a bunch of riders came dashing out, galloping their horses over Opothle's bleeding body. He died there in the manure-covered straw.

"We never knew who did the killing and we never knew how the executioners of the Blood Law tracked Opothle to that inn. We questioned Bibbs about the other guests at the inn. He remembered seeing a Cherokee, a stranger to him when they first arrived, and soon afterward saw the man riding off fast toward the Nation.

"But these things we soon had to put out of our minds. Life was hard for all of us during those first months in Arkansas. Without the help of Mr. Rogers we would have come near to starvation. William told Bibbs he was free to go where he pleased, but the black man would not leave us, working harder than any of us at getting a log shelter built nearby the blacksmith shop. We hunted deer and bear and wild hogs in the Boston Mountains, and the women dried and salted the meat. Then William went up to Independence in Missouri, where his father had some kind of credit arrangement with a trader in dry goods and staple provisions. He brought back a small supply of trade goods and started peddling things around the nearby settlements.

"Another who helped us was that half-blood Osage woman, Saviah Manning, the herb doctor. Suna-lee and little Pleasant both fell desperately ill with disease of the lungs, and I think they might have died that first winter had not Saviah Manning dosed them with her medicines. She also brought us food, although we had no money to pay her or anything to give her. For some reason I was uneasy around her; maybe it was because she always wore men's trousers. But she and Jotham were always joking back and forth, and I became jealous of him after he told me privately that he was sure he was going to get into bed with her some night. It was just a matter of time, he said, she was skittish like a mare that had never been rode.

"That winter Jotham and I worked at rebuilding wagons for Mr. Rogers. Hardly anybody in that part of the country had such a thing as money, and the only way he could pay us was to give each of us one of the wagons we rebuilt for him. We tried to sell them so we would have some way to get clothes and other things we all needed, but nobody wanted our wagons.

"From someone, probably William, we got the idea of taking the wagons to Independence. I remember William telling us about the long trains of wagons he saw leaving Independence, hauling goods to a place called Santa Fe. We thought that maybe we could get a good price for our wagons if we drove them to Independence.

"And so one morning in early spring, Jotham and I took four of our six horses and hitched them to the wagons. Frost was on the grass and Bibbs was there, wearing a strange-looking coat he had made of bearskin, helping with the trace chains and harness. Grandmother Mary and Jerusha brought out baskets full of dried meat and *gahawisita,* packing them carefully under our seats. Prissie and Suna-lee had made spare pairs of moccasins for us.

"Just before I got into the wagon, Grandmother Mary tried to put her arms around me. I gave her a hard squeeze and turned to climb up to the seat. Jerusha was already there, holding the lines, a teasing smile on her face.

" 'You can't go,' I said.

" 'I would not go if you begged me,' she answered. 'I wanted to hear what you would say.'

" 'I don't understand you anymore,' I said.

" 'Someday you will. I have a hard time understanding myself, Dane. But now I know who I am.'

"When I looked at her and saw the tears in her blue eyes, she shoved the leather lines into my hands and dropped down from the wagon. 'Take care,' she said almost in a whisper. Feeling ill at ease, I shouted the horses into motion and did not look back until I heard Jotham's wagon following behind.

"After having crossed half of America, the seven-day wagon ride to Independence was nothing to us. But we had never seen anything like such a town. Independence had twice as many buildings as Hiwassee Garrison and a hundred times as many people, all crowding the streets, the blacksmith sheds, the grog-shops, and the corrals of oxen, mules, horses, and wagons. Everywhere we looked were great heaps of boxes and barrels of clothing, glassware, grain, sugar, bacon, whiskey, and many other things being loaded into wagons.

"William had given us a letter to a Mr. Louis Tessier, the trader that he and Uncle Opothle dealt with, and so we sought out this man and asked him how much a good wagon was worth in Independence and where we would likely find a buyer. Mr. Tessier was a Frenchman and neither Jotham nor I could understand much of what he said to us, but he was a very kind man. He gave us a place to sleep in the back room of his store, and that evening after he closed his doors, he took us to a fine clapboard house at the end of one of the streets. And there we met a gentleman by the name of Mr. Samuel Lykins."

Dane stopped talking, closing his eyes for a moment against a bright beam of sunlight that the setting sun poured through the west window. "Our lives are often touched by chance, are they not?" He turned and stared at me as though in wonder. "I call it magic, the crossing of our paths with the paths of others, how quickly, how completely, these magic meetings can turn us into directions we never dreamed of. So it was for me that evening in Independence when my path led me across the path of the Santa Fe trader, Samuel Lykins.

"He was not old, not young, he had a dreamer's look in his eyes, this Lykins. He favored fine clothes, always wore a big wide bright-colored cravat tied in a bow, and a waistcoat, but he was no dandy and he would not tolerate laziness. A very energetic man, Mr. Samuel Lykins.

"Well, he went and looked at our wagons, and as he examined the wheels and peered under the running gear, I could tell he was a man who knew wagons. He named a price for them, and then without wasting time, he said to Jotham and me: 'I need drivers more than I need wagons. Especially young men who can shoe horses and repair wagons. I'll pay you top price for your wagons if you'll drive them in my next train to Santa Fe.'

"These words changed everything for me, I can tell you, because I would not be here talking to you in the state of Montana had Mr. Lykins not said those words. 'You young men may think on it,' he said in that slow way he had of speaking. 'I'll come by in the morning with money for your wagons.'

"We did not sleep much that night, but by morning we'd made up our minds. One of us had to take the money and our horses back to Cane Hill, and Jotham finally said he would do it. He had it in his mind to marry Griffa McBee, anyway, and was afraid if he did not wed her soon, he would lose her to a rival. Oh, he wanted to go on that journey to Santa Fe, but not as badly as I did. Neither of us had the slightest notion how far or where Santa Fe was.

"Next morning, as Mr. Lykins promised, he came with the wagon money. He was riding a big red roan stallion, with a gray mule behind on a lead rope. When we told him what we had decided to do about his offer, he looked first from one to the other of us with those dreamer's eyes of his. 'In truth I was hoping for you, the lighter-skinned one,' he said to Jotham. Then he looked at me. 'You,' he went on, 'are as dark as a wild Pawnee, and although you speak my English tongue as well as I, my drivers do not take to Indians. I suppose I'll have to dress you and pass you off as a Mexican.' Just as he said that, the gray mule on the lead rope laid his head back and brayed. It was almost like an animal laugh. Haweeee! Haweeee! I can hear that mule now, laughing at me. Haweeee!"

Off in the distance then, as if in counterpoint, came the hoarse lonesome whistle of a steam locomotive, and through the west window I saw a passenger train no larger than a toy against the vast plain, black coal smoke streaming above it, slowing for the Dundee station.

"Is that my train?" I cried, rising quickly from the rocker.

"It is," said Dane. "And it will be gone out of sight before you can take a dozen steps past my door."

28

I believe Dane was secretly pleased that I missed my train. He told me there would be an eastbound passenger express some-time later in the night, but that train never stopped at Dundee. To calm my distress, he took me into a tiny room off the kitchen, his granddaughter Amayi's room, and showed me a comfortable couch that she used when visiting overnight. He made it quite clear that I would be a welcome guest while awaiting the passage of another twenty-four hours, and so *I* be-came secretly pleased that I had missed the train.

Before we went to bed he told me of the magic and wonder of the American West when he first came to it as a journeying In-dian from the East.

"I soon found out that Mr. Samuel Lykins meant it when he said he was going to disguise me as a Mexican. On the day before his wagon train left Independence, he took me to his storehouse and gave me a pair of ridiculous pantaloons. The outer seams of the legs were split open and lined with buttons for fastening. With these I was to wear a fancy-colored shirt and vest, a tall peaked straw hat covered with oilcloth, and a serape. Eventually I grew fond of the serape, a Mexican blanket with a hole for putting one's head through. It was made of wool so well woven and twisted that it shed water, and I have worn serapes ever since.

"Dressed in what then seemed to me an outlandish costume, I was ashamed to show myself to the other drivers until I noticed that four or five of them wore similar clothing. As a disguise for me, however, it was a failure. The real Mexicans quickly discovered that I knew no Spanish, and as soon as the white drivers heard me speak, they became suspicious. But by this time they had all accepted me as a fellow driver, and none of them gave me any trouble. Perhaps Mr. Lykins knew it would work out that way.

"Twenty wagons made up the train, most of them being considerably larger than the two that Jotham and I had sold to Mr. Lykins. Unlike some of the other Santa Fe traders, Lykins used no oxen, believing that mules were faster and more dependable, and as I was to find out, mules sold for a much greater profit than did oxen in Santa Fe. The wagon that I drove carried supplies for the journey—about fifty pounds of flour, fifty pounds of bacon, ten pounds of coffee, and twenty pounds of sugar for each man, as well as a few bags of grain for the mules. Each of us was also provided with a frying pan, kettle, coffeepot, tin cup, and butcher knife. We were supposed to do our own cooking at the night camps, and we gradually formed partnerships of two to four men, taking turns at preparing supper and breakfast. What fresh meat we had was furnished by Mr. Lykins, who rode about a mile ahead of the train, but never was out of sight of it. Every day or so he would bring in choice cuts of antelope or buffalo that he killed. In the supply wagon was a barrel of onions that we used to flavor the meat.

"After nine or ten days of traveling, we left woods and hills behind us and entered the treeless plains. Having spent all my life surrounded by forests and mountains, this was a strange experience for me. At first the grass was tall and green, always waving in the constant wind, the land rolling as I have been told the waves of the salt ocean roll. After a few more days, the grass became much shorter and finer, a sort of grayish green. Mr. Lykins called it buffalo grass, and the herds of that remarkable animal that we now saw on either side of us often darkened the horizon. Sometimes far off we sighted Indians hunting on horseback. One of the drivers said they were wild Cheyennes and Arapahos, and I wished them to come nearer the train so that I might see these distant kinsmen of mine, but they never approached us.

"Soon the land became perfectly level, not even a hillock, so that the wagons seemed to grow larger and larger against the flatness. Because of the long hard days, I slept every night without dreaming, but my waking hours became dreamlike. Nothing seemed real to me, the immensity of the sky, the encircling treeless earth that seemed to be spinning around us. It was magical, and I wondered if all life was not a dream, dreamed by some Great Spirit who had formed us and the limitless land we moved across.

"From the talk of my companions I learned that we were taking the long trail to Santa Fe, by Bent's Fort, a route that was a hundred miles longer than by the Cimarron Trail. Mr. Lykins was to deliver a shipment of goods to the fort, which I soon discovered was the main trading place for tribes of the Southern Plains. I made no count of the days, but I think we must have traveled for about two moons before the fort came in view. Even at a distance, the place looked solid, unconquerable, its adobe walls six feet thick and three times as high as a tall man. Rising above the walls at opposite corners were two rounded towers called bastions.

"But not until many moons later was I to see the inside of Bent's Fort. When our wagons approached to within about half a mile of the walls, a white man waiting beside the trail in front of a buffalo-skin tipi stopped Mr. Lykins and informed him of an outbreak of smallpox in the fort. The white man was William Bent himself, and he had brought his Cheyenne wife and young children outside the walls in hopes of escaping the disease raging inside his fort.

"Following Mr. Lykins's directions, the drivers of the wagons containing the goods for Mr. Bent cut them out of the train while the rest of us formed our wagons into a circle nearby the trail. By the time we got our teams unharnessed, watered at the river, and fed with a little grain, it was dark. The drivers had been looking forward to a night or two of festivities inside the fort, and they tried to make up for the disappointment by playing cards by candlelight most of the night. Next morning when I awoke, I noticed three wagons about a hundred paces east of our circle. They had not been there when I went to sleep.

"Except for tending my mules, I had no duties that day. After Mr. Lykins oversaw the unloading of his Bent's Fort wagons into a corral shed outside the fort, he rode off with William Bent, leaving the train in charge of one of the older drivers, a tall red-haired Kentuckian named George Gant. While we were drinking coffee, Gant remarked that Mr. Lykins had gone out to a nearby Arapaho camp, hoping to arrange a trade for buffalo hides so that he could fill the wagons emptied at the fort. 'The goin' price for buffaler hides here is three dollars,' Gant said. 'In Santa Fe they'll bring six or more. And by tradin' gunpowder and sugar and tobacco instead of coin, there's still more profit to be made.'

"That afternoon, while I was lying in the shade under my wagon, I saw a streamer of dust far out on the plain. After a few minutes I knew they were mounted Indians, six of them, each with a led pony loaded down with what at first sight I thought to be deerskins. They were buffalo hides of course, and the Indians were heading straight for the three wagons that had arrived during the night.

"Being most curious, as I have said, to see my wild kinsmen close up, I wasted no time walking over to the other wagons, arriving only a minute or so after the Cheyennes—for that was their tribe. Instead of seeing a band of fierce-faced savages, as I had been led to believe, I saw six young men of about my age, laughing and chattering gaily in a tongue that I then did not understand. Some wore long red breechcloths, others buckskin trousers; some wore bright-colored cloth trade shirts, others nothing more than rawhide bands around their chests. They looked much healthier, more muscular and vigorous than my own half-starved people back in Indian Territory. Their skins were also darker because so much of their lives was spent under the sun.

"Their leader appeared to be no more than a year or so older than I. He was the first to dismount, dropping easily off his spotted pony and approaching the nearest of the wagons, his hand-

some face thrown back, showing large white teeth in a wide
smile. He wore two feathers in his curly unplaited hair and a
shiny silver band around one arm. He pointed to the fort and
then pecked at his face with the tip of a finger. The white man
at the wagon said: 'Smallpox, yes. Fort closed. Trade here.'

"'*Ese-von*,' the young Cheyenne said, making rapid signs toward the ponies loaded with buffalo hides. '*Na-ox-to-va.*' Although I did not know it then, he had told the white man he
wanted to trade buffalo skins for goods. For the first time I took
a good look at the white trader, and I did not like what I saw.
He was a giant in size, big-chested, big-paunched, scraggly-
bearded, and balding with tufts of pinkish hair growing out
above his ears. His eyes squinted to tiny points of light, greedy
like the eyes of a thieving carrion animal. He had already slung
a steelyard on a pole, and with his huge fat hands motioned the
Cheyennes to bring up their buffalo skins.

"First he would count out ten skins for one of his drivers to
load in a wagon, and then he would make a great pretense of
weighing on the steelyard whatever goods were wanted in trade.
I soon saw that he was giving the Cheyennes about a dollar
value for skins worth three dollars and then cheating them on
the weights of the sugar and flour and other trade goods. I
remembered Grandmother Mary's bitter anger over the way her
people had been tricked by traders for deerskins, and right in
front of my eyes the same thing was happening to the
Cheyennes for their buffalo skins. Well, I could not stand there
and watch the young men being swindled without doing something about it. But what was I to do, not knowing a word of
their language?

"I simply walked over to the young Cheyenne, pointed to the
cheating trader, and held up one finger. Then I pointed across
the way to our wagon circle and held up three fingers. He did
not understand at first. His constant smile turned to a frown. He
pointed his finger at me. 'Mex-i-can?' he asked. I shook my head.
'*Tsalagi*, Cherokee,' I said. '*Ya!*' he cried, turning to his companions. '*Sanaki.*' That's the Cheyenne word for Cherokee, I learned
later. I was making progress, so I held up one finger again,

pointing to the big trader, whose mean little eyes were now fixed on me. '*No-ka*,' the Cheyenne said, holding up one of his fingers. Again I indicated our wagons and held up three fingers, motioning to the buffalo skins that had not yet been traded. '*Na-a*,' he said, showing three fingers. He nodded. Now he understood, and his smile quickly returned. He spoke rapidly to his companions as he mounted his spotted pony.

"The big trader roared out at me: 'You son of a bitch Mex, or whatever you are! You can't steal away my buffalo skins!'

"'You've been doing the stealing,' I said, and I think my unexpected use of clear English unsettled him for a moment. Anyway the young Cheyenne on the spotted horse reached a hand down for me. I leaped up behind him and we filed off toward Mr. Lykins's wagons, all the Cheyennes turning to laugh at the big trader, who was shaking his fist and threatening me with a violent death.

"What I had failed to take into account was that George Gant had no authority to trade. He also told me that I had made a dangerous enemy. 'That's Flattery Jack Belcourt over there, one of the meanest bastards in the Santa Fe trade,' he said. 'A scoundrel and a horse thief. As soon shoot you in the back as spit. He won't rest easy till he evens the score with you, amigo.'

"Gant looked at the buffalo hides and said they were of good quality, but we would have to wait for Mr. Lykins to return. This was a great embarrassment to me. I had some difficulty in explaining the situation to the Cheyennes, but I think they finally understood. Gant made some coffee for them, sweetening it thickly with sugar, and while we waited I had an opportunity to get better acquainted with the Cheyennes. The young leader told me that his name was E-o-ve-a-no, repeating it several times and then surprising me by saying it in English: Yellow Hawk. Then I repeated my name for him until he could say it quite plainly. He knew very few English words, however, and we were still struggling to understand each other when Mr. Lykins and William Bent returned.

"Bent knew the young Cheyennes, and when he found out that I had stopped them from being cheated by Flattery Jack, he came over and thanked me. He also warned me to be careful. 'A malicious man, that Flattery Jack,' he said. 'I don't allow him to trade in my fort.'

"Mr. Lykins traded for the remaining buffalo hides, giving Yellow Hawk and his friends four or five times more goods than they would have got from Belcourt. When they rode off with their led ponies loaded with bags, Yellow Hawk turned in my direction, coming so close that he was able to lean down and give me a stinging slap on the back. 'Damn plenty rascal,' he said, pointing toward Belcourt's wagons. He turned then, raised his hand in farewell, and cried out: 'Dane!'

"'E-o-ve-a-no!' I yelled back at him.

"Well, the next morning we spent overhauling the wagons, tightening braces, setting the iron tires, greasing axles, whatever needed to be done. That afternoon the Arapahos came in with their buffalo skins, and after the trading was finished, Mr. Lykins informed us that we would be starting for Santa Fe at daylight.

"When we moved out, my wagon was about midway of the train, and at our first road halt, the drivers in the rear passed up the word that Flattery Jack Belcourt's wagons were following behind us. Mr. Lykins, being out ahead on his horse, did not learn of this until our nooning stop, and I could see then that he was more than annoyed at having the rascally trader close on our rear.

"That night when we formed our circle for camp, he cautioned all of us to sleep with one eye open in case Belcourt and his hirelings tried to steal some of our merchandise. At most night stops, however, Belcourt camped his three wagons some distance from us, and it was George Gant's opinion that Flattery Jack was keeping close to our train because he was afraid of Apaches. 'Soon's we get through the Ratons,' Gant said, 'we'll be in Apache country, and Apaches ain't afraid to take on as few as three wagons. Old Flattery Jack wants our protection.'

"I'd never heard of the Apaches, but I was as curious about them as I had been about Cheyennes and Arapahos. When I asked Gant what Apaches were like, he said they were the fiercest of all the tribes. Looking my Mexican clothes up and down, he added: 'Ain't nothin' Apaches like better'n roastin' a Mex over a bed of coals, amigo.' Gant was always talking like that. I've known Apaches in my time, and found them to be like all people, some good, some bad.

"In the Ratons the trail became very rough and steep, much worse than the passage we Cherokees made over the Cumberlands in Tennessee. For the heavier wagons we sometimes had to use ropes, every driver pulling along with the mules. After we crossed through the pass, I thought surely we had left Belcourt far behind, but one night when we camped alongside a stream called the Ocate, his three wagons appeared out of the dusk, halting not far from us.

"Next day they followed us very closely, Belcourt riding out in front on his gray horse. Once he ventured alongside our train. I was made suddenly aware of his presence when he called out to me: 'Smart Mex-Indian, how'd you like your cods cut out?' His eyes looked at me with the bad blood of a mean snake, and then he wheeled his horse, waiting for his wagons to come up to him.

"Three or four days after that we camped beside the stone and adobe ruins of what had once been a large town. George Gant said the people who had lived there were Pueblos who revolted against the rule of the Spaniards, and so many were killed that the few survivors fled to join another town. For the first time that evening I learned that we were no longer in the United States but were in a foreign land ruled by Mexicans.

"Before we bedded down that night, Mr. Lykins came to each driver and warned us he would wake us before daybreak and that we must eat cold rations for breakfast. He wanted an early start so that we might bring the wagons into Santa Fe before sundown the next day. No one grumbled about that, each of us being eager for the end of the journey. I especially wished to see, at last, our destination, the city of Santa Fe that I had heard so much about during my long dreamlike passage toward the sun.

"Next day we kept the mules moving steadily, shortening our rest stops and nooning for only a few minutes. The trail was the easiest we had traveled since leaving Bent's Fort and we had no trouble with wagons or teams until late in the afternoon. As fate willed it, the bad luck was mine. The rear wheel on the right side of my wagon began whining, and after the many days I'd spent driving I knew the axle would soon wear the hub into a wobble if I did not get some grease into it. I yelled out the signal for a halt, and the wagons began slowing for a stop.

"As usual my wagon was about midway of the train, and before I could get the wagon jack and lever into place, Mr. Lykins came riding back at a trot. He dismounted and satisfied himself from the smell of heat in the hub that it needed grease. 'Pull off here to the side of the trail before you raise that wheel,' he said. 'That'll let the wagons behind you keep rolling. I want to beat sundown into Santa Fe. You'll have to catch up as best you can.'

"I did as he said, working the jack and then slapping on grease, and some tar for good measure, all as fast as I could. I made certain the linchpin was tight, and then lowered the jack down. By this time the last wagon in line had passed me and was almost out of sight.

"I had just got into the seat and was hawing the mules back into the trail when Belcourt's lead wagon came rattling alongside, blocking my way. As I pulled back on the lines to avoid a collision, Belcourt appeared on his horse from around the other side of his wagon. He waved his driver to a stop, and yelled across at me: 'Get your damn mule team out of my way, Mex-Indian!'

"I didn't say anything. The mules were excited by the presence of the other team, and it was all I could do to hold them steady. Belcourt eased his horse around between the wagons so that there was little more than the width of my seat between us. 'Sam Lykins run his train off and left you, eh?' he said, peering under the canvas. 'Nothing of account left in your wagon, I see. You wasn't worth waiting for.'

"That thought had already occurred to me. Mine was the supply wagon, and we had used up almost everything in it. If the wagon had been full of necklaces, mirrors, whiskey, leather, tools, nails, guns, and ammunition like the others, I knew Lykins would not have moved the train without it. I was beginning to lose my good opinion of him, but right at that moment my attention was on Flattery Jack Belcourt, who had a score to settle with me.

"He was rubbing his bearded chin with one of his gauntlets; they had big white stars on the flaring cuffs. His eyes squinted to those yellow specks of light that made him look like an animal searching for prey. Suddenly, his eyes opened wide, not looking at me, but beyond me, just as I heard the clatter of hooves against rock. 'Apaches!' he shouted. I saw them then, on three wiry mustangs trotting out of a cleft concealed by gnarled and stunted pines. 'Get the wagons moving!' Belcourt screamed, but he was too late. The Apaches were already in the trail, their ponies spread out across it, facing us, four riders on three ponies. One of them was a young woman. Her moccasined feet were bound to each other with a rawhide lariat beneath the pony's belly. Her wrists, resting on the pommel of a crude Spanish saddle, were also bound. She was wearing a tan buckskin vest tight around her breasts and a short buckskin skirt. Her eyes had fear in them. The man behind her on the mustang wore a faded red turban quite similar to those I had seen old Cherokees wear. The other two men had forehead bands of purple around their long dusty hair. All three were naked except for dirty breechclouts, and boot moccasins that reached almost to their knees. They were thin-bodied and sinewy like their mounts.

"Belcourt had jerked his rifle into position and I heard the click of a hammer from the right side of my wagon. One of his drivers had come up from the rear and was using my wagon for cover, leaving me a fine target in case there was any shooting. I had no arms of any kind. However, the Apache with the faded turban was clasping his hands in front of him in a peace sign.

"'We could kill 'em all,' Belcourt muttered, and moved his horse forward a few paces. The Apache was making other signs; it was plain to me that he wanted to trade.

"'Show me what you have,' Belcourt called out. 'Show me.'

"The Apache held up some kind of jewelry, turquoise I think, but Belcourt shook his head, motioning then toward the young woman. Balancing his rifle across his saddle, Belcourt made a quick sign for copulating. The Apache nodded his head, laughing, and started his horse forward. 'Hold up!' Belcourt shouted at him, bringing his rifle back to the ready. The young woman's fingers were trembling against the saddle pommel.

"'He wants tobacco,' Belcourt said to the driver crouching on the right side of my wagon. 'Bring me five twists, but stay ready, I don't put any trust in that son of a bitch.'

"After the driver brought the tobacco, Belcourt held up three twists. The Apache shook his head and made the sign for drinking. Belcourt held up four twists. No, the Apache wanted whiskey.

"'Give me the bottle under the seat,' Belcourt said to the driver in the forward wagon. 'It's half-full.' He showed the bottle to the Apache, who nodded, but held up four fingers for the four twists of tobacco. He slid off his pony, unfastened the rawhide lariat from around the young woman's legs, and helped her to the ground. He started to tie the lariat to his saddle, but Belcourt called to him: 'I need the riata. Five tobacco twists and the bottle for the female Indian and the riata.'

"Belcourt dismounted, keeping his rifle steady, tossed the tobacco twists out in the trail and rolled the bottle after them. The Apache looped the lariat around the young woman's neck, led her up to the objects he had traded her for, and shoved her in the direction of Belcourt. Then without wasted motion he collected his tobacco and whiskey, and as quickly as they had come the Apaches rode away to the south, vanishing almost at once in that wasteland of sage and scrub cedars.

"By this time Belcourt had seized the young woman, making her sit while he tied her ankles tightly together. The driver on the right side of my wagon went out to help him. The two men whispered together for a moment, laughing as they lifted the young woman and carried her to the rear of the first wagon. I could hear the thump of her body striking the wagon bed; they had thrown her inside. Both men laughed again. I thought they were laughing about the young woman, but I soon found out they were not, at least not entirely.

"'Move it out!' Belcourt shouted to the driver of the first wagon. 'Sun's going down and it's a far piece to Santa Fe.' To my surprise and relief he trotted his horse off in the lead. I wondered if the excitement of trading for the young Indian woman had put me out of his mind.

"As soon as his last wagon passed, I cracked my whip over the mules and started the wagon into the trail. It had not rolled ten paces when the rear right end collapsed with a crash, frightening the mules so that I had to put all my weight on the lines to keep them from dragging the axle. I tied the lines and leaped out; the wheel lay on the ground still spinning. I could not find the linchpin, and I knew that this had something to do with what Belcourt and his driver were whispering and laughing about. The driver must have removed the linchpin while my attention was fixed upon the Apaches.

"Luckily there was a spare pin among the supplies. I soon had the axle jacked up and the wheel fastened back in place. Just as I finished, I heard hoofbeats coming down the trail ahead. Certain that it must be Belcourt returning, and being unarmed, I was on the point of making a dash for that crevice in the rocks where the Apaches had appeared from. But then I saw the horseman was Mr. Lykins.

"He wanted to know the reason for my delay, and I told him what had happened. 'You're lucky Flattery Jack did no worse to you than that,' he said. He slid his carbine out of its bucket and handed it to me, remarking that with Belcourt's wagons between me and the train I might need a weapon before I reached Santa Fe. My faith in Mr. Lykins was immediately restored. After giving me directions for reaching the wagon yard at Santa Fe, he wished me good luck and went loping back along the trail.

"Maybe Belcourt decided he'd settled accounts with me, or maybe he was in a hurry to get to Santa Fe with his pretty young woman. Anyway he gave me no more trouble that day. The sun was setting as I rolled down a long hill past a cornfield and over a bridge into the squares of Santa Fe. When I entered the plaza a soft gray light was falling over the town, and I could hear many voices everywhere speaking words I did not understand. A church bell began ringing, the clear sound startling me with its music. At the end of the plaza I turned left as Mr. Lykins had instructed me, and then I saw the wagon yard, twice as large as any I had seen in Independence.

"I had no trouble finding the train. The other drivers were still tending their mules, and Mr. Lykins was waiting for me. When I handed him his carbine he gave me a coin. 'This is against your pay, which you will receive after I've completed my business tomorrow,' he said. 'Now find George Gant and see about guard duty.'

"We had to stand guard on the wagons through the night, half of us until midnight, the other half from midnight until next daylight. Gant told me I was to start at midnight. 'The first guards are around the corner getting some food in a cantina,' Gant said. 'Soon as they come back the rest of you go eat. That Mexican money Mr. Lykins gave you is for food, not drink. Soon as you eat, come back and bed down under your wagon. If you're not there when I come for you at midnight you'll receive no pay tomorrow, amigo.'

"By the time I unharnessed, watered, and picketed my mules, the first guards were back. I was hungry all right, but I had something else pressing on my thoughts. I slipped away in the dark, circling around the big yard searching for three wagons. I found them in deep shadows lined up end to end alongside the stone wall of a stable. Not a sound came from them. I crouched low, my nostrils filled with the scent of hay and horse manure. Then I saw a faint flare of light under the forward wagon. One of the drivers was smoking. As there was no talking, I guessed he was the only guard. I moved across to the end wagon, rose up, and pulled back the canvas. It was packed solid with barrels. With all the stealth that Grandmother Mary had taught me in stalking a deer, I crept to the next wagon. The canvas hung loose; it was partly empty. I swung up like a cat. The darkness inside was almost solid. I heard a faint whimper, the sound of a cornered animal, and I knew she was there.

"At that moment I had the feeling that I could accomplish anything. Nothing could stop me or harm me because I had powers greater than those of other human beings. You have felt that way, have you not? More recently than I, I'm certain, you being much younger, although maybe age has nothing to do with the losing of it. We lose that feeling of power when we become shields for other human beings and start fearing risks.

"On that night I was willing to chance anything. Not wanting her to cry out, I whispered all the words I knew for 'friend,' including the Spanish *amigo* I'd learned from George Gant. She did not respond, and it was too dark for her to see any signs I might make. The only word I could think of was *Sanaki*, the Cheyenne word for Cherokee, and to my astonishment she repeated it. Then I touched her very gently, took out my knife, and cut the rawhide from her ankles and wrists. Because I wanted Belcourt to believe she had escaped by herself, I stuffed the cut lariat inside my shirt. While I was doing this, she tried to stand, but she was very unsteady on her feet.

"I led her back to the tailgate and helped her out as noiselessly as possible. We crawled on hands and knees until we were almost to my wagon at the end of the row. One of our guards was pacing back and forth. When he made his turn away from us, I lifted her inside. There was enough light from the starry sky for her to see me bring my closed right hand down in a sign for her to stay there. Then I put my fingers to my mouth and pointed toward the plaza, and she must have understood that I would try to bring her food. Anyway she smiled for the first time.

"In the cantina round the corner, the Mexican coin that Mr. Lykins had given me bought hardly enough food for one strong man—six very thin corn cakes that they called tortillas, and two large bites of chopped meat mixed with hot peppers that had been cooked inside a covering of thick mush. With the help of a Mexican who understood English—and who was puzzled that I wore the clothing of his country but could not speak its language—I explained to the cook that I must take the food and some water to a sick friend. He wrapped the food in a napkin and gave me a jug of water, but only after making me swear to his *Dios* that I would return the jug and napkin within the hour.

"When I went back to my wagon the guard challenged me. I called out my name and told him I would soon be going to bed under the wagon. I climbed inside, but the young woman was not there. I looked out, sick at heart because I thought she had run away. A few paces off in the shadows of some weeds growing along the rail fence of an empty corral, I heard a slight rustling. A moment later she appeared, moving like a silent spirit toward me. I reached out my hands and lifted her inside. She had gone to relieve herself.

"She drank the water as though it was the most delicious liquid on earth, sighing after each long swallow. Then we sat far back in the wagon, treasuring every morsel of the shared food. After we had eaten, she put a hand against my cheek very lightly, but when I tried to embrace her, she drew quickly away from me.

"How I wished that I could make her understand my thoughts with words! I was thinking of this, of the importance of words, when the sounds of an angry voice broke the stillness. It came from across the wagon yard, and most certainly was Flattery Jack Belcourt's drunk and angry bellow. There was no doubt in my mind as to the cause of his outburst.

"Indicating to the young woman that she should make no sound or movement, I unrolled a piece of canvas and threw it over her. Then I took my serape, jumped out of the wagon, and rolled up on the straw beneath, pretending to be asleep. The footsteps of the nearest guard clumped back and forth, and then, as I expected, came the solid tread of Belcourt, his slurred voice calling out: 'Seen anything of a runaway Injun gal?'

" 'Seen nobody,' the guard replied.

" 'I'll have a look around your wagons,' Belcourt said. He squatted, and through my half-closed eyes I could see him rocking drunkenly on his bootheels as he peered at me. 'Who's that under there?' he asked.

" 'One of the drivers,' the guard said. 'I told you no strangers been around here. Every wagon's guarded.'

"Belcourt wanted to look inside the wagons, but the guard refused him. 'Where's Lykins?' Belcourt demanded.

"'Not here,' the guard said. 'Most likely gone to bed. You know every wagon is sealed till tradin' time tomorrow. You come back then.'

"Belcourt swore, but he turned his back and marched off, swaying, and talking to himself. I lay there wide awake, wondering what I was going to do about that young woman just above me in the wagon. If she remained there until daylight, Belcourt or somebody else was certain to see her. I thought of going to George Gant and asking his help, but I knew he would do nothing without Mr. Lykins's approval. I had to find Mr. Lykins, and find him before sunup.

"So there was nothing to be done but go in search of him. On one side of the plaza I had noticed a large adobe inn, and there I went through the thinning crowds of the late evening. The clerk at the desk frowned at me. I guess I did look out of place in that fine inn, my hair uncut for many days, my Mexican clothes greasy from wear and travel. 'I'm one of Mr. Lykins's drivers,' I said, and was relieved to hear the clerk reply in English: 'Mr. Samuel Lykins?'

"I nodded, and told him some urgent business had come up. The clerk scratched at his ear. 'Mr. Lykins dined here this evening,' he offered, frowning at me again. Suddenly he turned and trotted over to a gray-haired man seated in a big chair. They both looked at me, whispering together, and I wondered if they were going to order me out of their fine inn. But the clerk returned to inform me that Mr. Lykins was occupying the house of another trader, Mr. Felix Aubry's house, only a few steps from the corner of the plaza.

"Thanking the clerk, off I went and found the house, and was glad to see candlelight in one of the curtained windows. At the doorstep, however, my courage almost failed me. I hesitated, fearing that Lykins would turn me away, order me to return the young woman to Belcourt, and bother him no more. I rapped on the door panel.

"When he opened the door, Mr. Lykins was holding a candle, and he was quite surprised to see me there. 'Something wrong at the wagons?' he asked quickly.

"'Not with your wagons, sir,' I answered, 'but I do need your help badly.'

"'You have got yourself into trouble in Santa Fe so quickly?' He was plainly annoyed with me. 'Couldn't Gant help you?' His hand was on the door as if he meant to close it, but he must have seen the despair in my face. 'Oh, come on in,' he said.

"The room he led me into was very small and simply furnished, one small table, two high-backed leather chairs, a painting of a horse on the wall. Scattered over the table were long sheets of paper covered with numbers, reminding me of Uncle Opothle and Okelogee. Mr. Lykins motioned me to a chair, but I remained standing until I told him everything I had done that evening. Seated by the table, he listened without the slightest change of expression.

"'I want nothing to do with wild Indians,' he said then, 'and I'm beginning to wonder about you civilized Cherokees. Wild Indians are much trouble. And their females are more trouble.' His fingers tapped softly on the tabletop. That dreamer's look came into his eyes, and he went on as though he was thinking out loud: 'Yet there would be some satisfaction for me in confounding Flattery Jack Belcourt. He'll undersell me tomorrow, force me to trade some of my merchandise at less than cost, because half his stuff is stolen. We honest traders know Belcourt's ways, but there's little we've been able to do about him.' His lips twisted in a faint smile. 'Can you get that Indian woman here, to this house, without being noticed?'

"I assured him that I could.

"'Bring her here, then,' he said. 'By God, what a story this will be for me to tell Felix Aubry when next I see him. I, sharing his house with a wild Indian woman!'

"Well, I brought the young woman to the house, and Mr. Lykins discovered right away that she was Cheyenne. In his years of trading he had acquired a few words of Plains Indian languages and he knew more of their signs than I did. Her name was Mae-ve-kse-a. 'That's Red Bird Woman,' Mr. Lykins said, with a glance at me. 'Not Red Bird. She's a married *woman.*'

"The Apaches had captured Red Bird Woman somewhere

along a little stream called the Nako southeast of Bent's Fort. With several other young women of their buffalo camp, she had gone out to pick wild berries. The Apaches had surprised them, but while they were capturing Red Bird Woman the others managed to escape. Mr. Lykins asked her a number of questions in which the word *Nako* was used several times. He seemed quite interested in her replies, but not until he showed Red Bird Woman to her room for the night and then was bidding me good night did he tell me what he learned from her.

"We were standing in his doorway and I was thanking him for helping me out of my difficulty. 'What do you propose that we do with your Cheyenne beauty?' he asked me.

"'I'd like to take her back to her people,' I replied.

"He smiled, shaking his head. 'You might spend a lifetime doing that. Her people are Southern Cheyennes, of which there are dozens of separate small bands. They move constantly, following the buffalo herds.'

"'She would know where they travel.' I was in no mood to be denied my dreams.

"'You are a romantic,' he said. I did not know the meaning of the word then, but I suppose he was right. On that night, as I have said, I felt that nothing was impossible, that I could achieve whatever I desired, with Red Bird Woman riding at my side. What did I care if she had another man? What did it matter? I already knew from the gleam in her eyes when she looked at me that she recognized me as a man of magical powers. Or so I imagined.

"'She could be useful to me,' Mr. Lykins said. 'We traders have heard of a trail the Apaches use on their horse raids against the Comanches. Some say three days shorter than the Cimarron route. I tried to scout it years ago, alone. Failed to find a single water source. Had I not been fortunate enough to kill an antelope and drink its blood, I should have died of thirst. This Red Bird Woman was brought out on that trail, stopping at springs and water holes. She could be a useful guide if I decide to return that way. Good night.'

"He had said nothing about me accompanying him and Red

Bird Woman, and during the next two or three days I found myself growing jealous of Mr. Samuel Lykins. She had to remain in his house day and night. Even though Flattery Jack Belcourt apparently gave up the search for her after the second day, he was always watchful around the wagon yard, and whenever he saw me he gave me a hateful scowl, knowing that I was the only one outside his own men who might have helped her escape.

"Every evening after dark at the time of the ringing of the church bells, I visited her and Mr. Lykins, and on each visit it seemed that more and more of the admiration for me that I had seen in her face that first night was being divided between me and the trader who had provided her with a refuge. After he paid me, I spent a good part of the money on clothing, discarding all my shabby Mexican garb except the serape for a leather hunting shirt, leather-seated jean trousers, and a pair of fancy boots. She silently approved of my new costume, but I was disappointed that she said nothing, even though I would not then have understood her Cheyenne words. You can see what a young fool I was, as full of myself as a mating prairie cock.

"One evening I went there to dinner, at Mr Lykins's invitation, and after he gave me a cigar he told me quietly that we would be leaving Santa Fe before daylight the following morning. He had sold half his wagons and mules, and George Gant and the other drivers would be returning to Independence with the remainder. I was to accompany him and Red Bird Woman over the Apache trail to the Nako, that is, if I was willing to risk the dangers. If I had wanted to conceal my joy I could not have done so. I fairly leaped out of my chair, shaking the dishes on the table, and offered him my hand in thanks.

"We were out of Santa Fe, traveling on the trail toward the deserted town of the Pueblos when the sun rose in our faces. Each of us had a good horse, and in addition Mr. Lykins brought along two led mules loaded with supplies that included several leather-covered water jars. My main duty was to keep the mules moving as fast as the horses, not an easy task by any means. When we reached the place in the trail where I had stopped my wagon and the Apaches had appeared, Red Bird Woman led us through the pine-screened rock cleft and down a winding passage so narrow in places that I was forced to dismount and lead my mules single file. For a while, then, we followed the level floor of a dry stream, the sand hard-packed, so that we could move at a more rapid gait. Yet during most of the afternoon we wound slowly up and down through wastelands of rock.

"That evening when we camped, Mr. Lykins remarked that we had been skirting the wagon trail most of the day and could have traveled considerably farther on it in a day, but he wanted Red Bird Woman to follow the landmarks by which she had been brought south. Early the next day she turned us toward the east, following a small stream until we crossed the wagon trail at a place where our train had camped one night.

"Each day after that we continued toward the rising sun, and each day the Apache trail became easier, the land flattening. The sparse vegetation had a gray look, the earth was dry, and the sun burned with the strength of fire. I thought to myself that the year would be in the Drying-Up Moon if we were back in the old Cherokee Nation. From Red Bird Woman I was learning Cheyenne words and signs so that we could make ourselves understood to one another. When I asked her what moon it was, she looked puzzled, then laughed and said that in her country it must be the Moon When the Plums Turn Red and that she would be happier if she were there. I told her that I was homesick for my country, too, but that I could never return because the land had been taken from my people. She could not understand this. How could land be taken away? Did the white men take away the sky, also?

"She constantly surprised me with her ability to follow the trail over stones or through thick grass where I could see no sign of passage. One afternoon while we were crossing an immense plain, emptier and more level than any I had seen on the way to Fort Bent, the sky suddenly darkened behind us. I thought the wind was bringing rain. Instead we were struck by a wall of sand that stung my face, the fine dust penetrating eyes and nostrils. After the wind passed, the trail we had been following was no longer there, and with the sun still high in the sky I was uncertain of the four directions. Red Bird Woman reined in her horse, turning slowly in her saddle, and then pointed toward the horizon. There I saw the faintest outline of a reddish rock. Had she not directed our eyes toward the rounded knob, I am certain that neither Mr. Lykins nor I would have noticed it on that vast expanse.

"'That's north,' Mr. Lykins said. 'If you came from there.' She bowed her head and indicated by signs that she had come from that direction. Mr. Lykins dismounted, took a stick from one of the mule packs, and drove it into the ground. Then he scribbled something on a piece of notepaper, thrust it inside an empty bottle, and placed the bottle upside-down on the top of the stick. 'Direction marker,' he said. 'In case I pass the word to my trader friends that I've found a better route. The Cimarron Trail is not far to our south. This may be the shortcut I've been looking for.'

"Well, as it turned out, the almost invisible trail that Red Bird Woman led us over soon afterward came to be known as the Lykins Cutoff. Two or three times a day Mr. Lykins stopped and posted a stick-and-bottle marker. As hot and dry as it was, we never needed any of the water in those leather-covered jars the mules had hauled all the way from Santa Fe. It seemed that whenever we and our animals grew thirsty, Red Bird Woman always brought us to a spring or a little hidden creek. Mr. Lykins constantly expressed his surprise and gratification. 'There's more water, more wood, and more grass on this trail,' he said, 'than on the Cimarron route.'

"About noon one day she sighted the Nako, crying out with joy, and whipping her horse into a fast run. We followed her to a low ridge covered with briers above the stream bank. It was the place where the passing Apaches had captured her. With one hand she shaded her eyes, gazing far across the shallow Nako to an abandoned campsite.

"'They've gone, yes,' Mr. Lykins said. 'Her people have moved on, following the buffalo herds. North, south, east, or west? What do you propose to do with her now, my romantic young friend?'

"'Help her find her people,' I replied.

"'And her man. He may try to kill you if you find him.'

"'For bringing her back to him?'

"'If he thinks you've slept with her. Wild Indians. They're unpredictable. I don't understand them.' He looked at Red Bird Woman. She had dismounted and was standing beside the horse, her shoulders drooping, a figure of despondency.

"'Well,' he said, 'if we follow along the Nako we can reach the Arkansas before dark, ford it there, and take the trail east for Independence.'

"'I'm staying with her,' I said.

"'All right.' He dismounted and walked over to the mules, unfastened two of the water jars, a pack of foodstuffs, and his spare carbine, and brought them over to me. He pushed a handful of paper cartridges and balls into one of my shirt pockets. 'You'll need my two horses,' he said as he climbed back into his saddle. 'But I'm taking my mules with me. Good luck.' He started off without another word, but as he swung around a bend in the Nako he turned and shouted back to me: 'If you find what you're looking for, remember those horses are mine. You'd damn well better bring them on to me at Independence. My carbine, too.' That was Mr. Samuel Lykins. He was more like a wild Indian at heart than any white man I ever knew."

Dane stood up and stretched his arms. "By God, I am sleepy." He stamped his feet and went over to the fireplace to warm his backside. "The Old West, it was a place of wondrous happenings, a place of magic. Sometimes what seemed real was not real. Maybe it was all a dream." He scratched his buttocks and yawned. "I'd best get to bed before the coyotes come and start telling me about their dreams."

"Wait a minute," I protested. "Did Red Bird Woman find her people?"

29

They splashed across the shallow Nako to the abandoned Cheyenne camp, where circles of yellowed grass ringed by stones marked the recent presence of tipis. Red Bird Woman said that her people had been gone for almost a moon, but there were still faint marks of travois poles heading toward the northwest. She followed these tracks until they reached a crossing of the Arkansas River, but so many travelers had come there in recent days, leaving a dozen or more trails pointing in different directions, that she confessed she could not distinguish one from the other.

"The buffalo herds have turned back north," she said, "for better grass and water." Dane recalled that they had seen only occasional small herds since leaving the Cimarron country, all so far distant that Sam Lykins had not taken the time to venture in pursuit. "My people have gone to the Hotoa, or maybe as far as the Smoking Land," she guessed, and led off toward the north.

Late in the afternoon they sighted several antelopes feeding in a bowl of land between two low cedar-covered ridges. They exchanged glances; after several days of eating Lykins's dried beef, both were hungry for fresh meat. Swinging to the right, they circled until they reached the base of the ridge. There they dismounted and picketed their horses. Taking Lykins's carbine, Dane led the way up through the cedars. When they reached the top, most of the antelopes had moved out of range. There were hundreds of them, the same color as the brown grass. He loaded the weapon, took careful aim, and fired at the nearest animal. The bullet pinged off a rock inches to the left of his target. Leaping high in the air, the antelope spun around as though seeking the source of the sudden explosion. The others moved farther away.

Red Bird Woman laughed softly. "Antelopes don't hear like we do," she said. "That one does not know where the sound came from."

After Dane reloaded, she took the carbine, aiming high so that the bullet struck dry ground beyond the antelope, kicking up a spurt of dust. Frightened by the dust, the antelope sprang forward, bounding for several yards before stopping at the base of the ridge, in easy range. She handed the carbine back to Dane. He brought the animal down with the next shot.

Before nightfall they were roasting antelope steaks on hot coals alongside a trickling stream. Dane ate until he felt the pressure of food against his belly muscles, and then lay with his head on his saddle to watch the first stars appear in the darkening sky. He felt well content, yet restless. Red Bird Woman was across the dying fire, her blanket thrown loosely over her legs. Except for the chirr of insects and the sound of their horses nibbling at grass, the land was heavy with silence. It was as if they were the only people on the earth.

He remembered what Mr. Lykins had said about taking her back to her man. *He may kill you if he thinks you've slept with her.* Tonight for the first time he was alone with Red Bird Woman. He had yearned for her on other nights, and he had seen Lykins look at her in that way, too. He had not been with a woman for many moons. She had not been with a man for many sleeps. Perhaps they would never find her people. Would they go on forever searching, sleeping apart like brother and sister? He sat up, looking across the fire at her, and he knew from her stirring that she was awake.

Walking without sound around the dead fire, he kneeled to look at her face and saw the flutter of her closed eyelids. But when he placed a hand on her shoulder, she struck him hard against the ear with her open palm, almost unbalancing him. "I am Lean Bear's woman," she said without anger.

"I wanted only to touch you," he whispered. "I am lonely."

"I also am lonely," she said, "but I am Lean Bear's woman." She turned her back to him as though settling the matter.

Next morning he was not sure whether that brief encounter had actually occurred or he had only dreamed it. All that day he kept seeing visions in the sky, phantasmal shapes that might have been clouds or only fancies from his mind. He felt lost upon the limitless grass without a tree to break the monotony of earth and sky. He longed for the green hills of Okelogee, the Sleeping Woman, and the Little Singing Stream.

Darkness overtook them on that desolate plain. While Red Bird Woman gathered buffalo chips to make a fire, he picketed their horses, using iron spikes from Lykins's saddlebags. The sky had become overcast, the wind dying to an ominous stillness, and lightning danced along the western horizon.

Throughout that day they had exchanged few words, but while they ate their scanty meal, Red Bird Woman talked almost continuously. She feared a storm, warned him to make certain the horses were securely fastened to the spikes, chattered about winds that had lifted tipis into the air, speaking so rapidly at times that he could not follow the unfamiliar Cheyenne words. He was glad when she stopped so that he could go to sleep.

A sudden gust of cold wind awakened him. Lightning filled the sky, printing grotesque figures against boiling clouds, and the rumble of thunder never ceased. In a flash of lightning he saw Red Bird Woman running to check the horses, trying to soothe them with her presence.

Great drops of water followed by hail the size of acorns struck him hard in the face, rattling against the ground. He stood up, covering his head with his serape, and heard her cry out in pain. He saw her struggling with her windblown blanket, and hurried to help her. A bolt of jagged lightning blinded him, followed by a deafening thunder blast that shook the earth. With loud whinnies the horses jerked at their picket pins, tore them loose, and ran wildly away into the storm.

"Lie down!" she shouted. "Thunderbird is angry tonight, flapping his wings and blinking his eyes. Lie down, or his arrows will strike you."

The only shields they had against the beating hail and rising wind were his serape and her blanket. They tried to make a combined shelter, clinging together and holding to the edges. The hail and wind gradually diminished, but the thunder and lightning seemed suspended above them, the firebolts striking on all sides. At each crash, she clung tighter to him, trembling, her face against his neck, whimpering with fear. Drenched by the cold rain, each sought warmth from the other, breathing the animal odors of wet buckskin and wool.

At first daylight they awoke in loose embrace. The sky was cloudless. He moved against her, but she forced him away, sitting up to search for her buckskin skirt. "*Aho-ya!*" she said. "That evil Thunderbird. If I had the right to wear the *nihpihist*, it would not have happened."

"*Nihpihist?*" he asked, not understanding the word. She was surprised that he did not know of the protective cord made of soft twisted deerskin that young women wore after their puberty ceremonies. Before traveling or sleeping, unmarried Cheyenne girls looped the cord around their waists and between their thighs, winding it around their legs almost to the knees. If a man removed this cord, or even tried to do so, he might be slain by male relatives or stoned to death by the females. Married women, she said, had no right to wear it.

"It is not a custom among the Cherokees," he told her, rubbing a sensitive place along the lower side of his neck. It prickled painfully. He remembered her biting him there.

Now they began the search for the horses, carrying the saddles and packs on their backs. Not enough rain had fallen to destroy the tracks, and even where the buffalo grass was thick he had learned from Red Bird Woman how to pick out signs, a bruised stem, a slight difference in coloration, a changed direction of the leaves. Before noon they sighted a small camp, a dozen tipis along a fringe of cottonwoods. Shading her eyes, she studied the camp for several minutes. "Arapahos," she said then, and started walking very fast.

As they came up to the camp, Dane recognized their runaway horses. They were near a large tipi, picketed with the iron spikes they had dragged across the plain. An old man, half reclining against a willow backrest, was sunning himself. Two women were scraping flesh from a buffalo skin staked to the ground. Children were playing under the cottonwoods along a shallow stream. "The young men are at the hunt," Red Bird Woman said. She saluted the old man, who stood up to welcome them, making signs toward their horses. He had thought they belonged to white men because of the metal pins on their tie ropes.

"I am Lean Bear's woman," she told him. "Have you seen the Cheyenne Dog Soldier people?"

He nodded, his eyes brightening, and pointed toward the north. Three sleeps past he had seen them, camped with Big Star's people along the Hotoa. They were awaiting a big herd moving there for water; he prayed that some of the buffalo would come near this Arapaho encampment.

From the food pack, Red Bird Woman took the last of their sugar, which was wrapped in a piece of oilcloth, and gave it to the old man. They saddled the horses then, and she led off at an easy gallop.

That afternoon the largest buffalo herd that Dane had yet seen streamed slowly off a land slope to the east, blackening the horizon as it moved northward like a wide river. "They are going to the waters of the Hotoa," she said, "but not as fast as we." Before sundown she pointed toward a camp, two circles of tipis, one much larger than the other, almost a hundred lodges all together across a clear running creek.

Red Bird Woman turned toward the smaller circle. They splashed through water to the horses' chests. A few yards down the creek bank, a white-haired man was drinking from cupped hands. He rose up quickly when he saw them, calling Red Bird Woman's name.

"Big Star! Uncle!" she cried.

"You yet live," he said, smiling until he looked at Dane. "Lean Bear grieves for you, niece. He has taken no other woman."

"He's there, in the Dog Soldier circle?" she asked.

Big Star made an affirmative sign, and she lashed her horse up the bank. Dane followed, but at that moment he wanted to be somewhere else, regretted that he had not gone on to Independence with Sam Lykins. As they came into the small circle, an old woman beside one of the tipis looked at Red Bird Woman and uttered a high cry, *Aie-eee*, and threw a cloth over her face, rocking her body back and forth.

A man came outside, blinking against the sunlight, a big man with black hair parted in the middle and reaching to his shoulders. He wore only a bright red breechflap and a beaded choker. Red Bird Woman dropped from her saddle, rushing toward him, but he held a hand out to stop her, his eyes still narrowed, his full-lipped mouth under his aquiline nose fixed in a hard line. His glance shifted back and forth several times from Red Bird Woman to Dane, always hesitating when he looked at Dane's Mexican boots as if there were some hidden meaning to be understood from them. Dane dismounted to hold both the horses.

Somewhat roughly Lean Bear reached out and grasped his wife's arm, leading her inside the tipi. Dane could hear their voices rising and falling, but indistinct, and then the old woman got up and came closer, turning her head like some curious bird to peer at him. She was examining the teeth marks on his neck. He turned away from her and fastened the top loops of his hunting shirt.

When Lean Bear came outside the tipi alone, he did not look at Dane, but walked stiffly around to the back of the tipi, returning in a moment with a pinto pony. He led the pony up to Dane and offered him the rawhide tie. "I have two horses," Lean Bear said. "One of them is yours."

"No, I . . ." Dane was about to say that he had no need of another horse, but he saw Red Bird Woman at the open flap of the tipi, bowing her head and making frantic signs for him to accept the gift.

"This is a fine animal," Dane said quietly, taking the tie rope.

"A small thing for what you have brought to me." Lean Bear clasped his hands together and smiled for the first time.

That evening Big Star gave a feast in his large tipi to celebrate

the return of Red Bird Woman, with Dane as the honored guest.
As the evening progressed, Dane learned a little about the
Cheyenne soldier societies, which were quite unlike the clans of
his own people, having nothing to do with birth or family rela-
tionships. Big Star, the chief, was also a leader of the Red Shield
society. His nephew Lean Bear led the Dog Soldiers, who were
so renowned as warriors that a number of Sioux had left their
tribe to become members. Whenever the Dog Soldiers camped
with their people, they always made their own circle of tipis.

For Dane, the surprise of the evening occurred just before the
feast began. The bottom of Big Star's tipi had been rolled up to
admit the breeze, and a large fire was burning in the center, with
a circle of Cheyennes, mostly older men, seated around it. Big
Star sat with Dane on one side and Red Bird Woman and Lean
Bear on the other. Dane watched the chief's wife and daughter
tending the kettles and other utensils over the fire. With the
firelight playing upon her face, the young girl seemed so beautiful to him that he could not stop staring at her. She reminded
him of someone, not Red Bird Woman, who was quite pretty,
but someone else. This girl had a shyness about her, but from
time to time she would look sideways at him. If her eyes met his,
she would glance quickly away. Big Star lighted a pipe and was
showing Dane how to smoke to the Spirit Above when a sudden
drumming of hooves sounded from the camp entrance. The
riders, six or seven young men, scattered in different directions,
one of them trotting up to the chief's tipi.

Big Star laid his pipe down. "The buffalo scouts," he said.
"Let us hear what my son has to tell us."

The chief's daughter moved in front of Dane, her face turned
toward the rider, and when she smiled he knew whom she reminded him of—Yellow Hawk, the young Cheyenne he had met
at Bent's Fort. And it was Yellow Hawk who dismounted, stoop-
ing to enter the lodge.

"Big hunt tomorrow," he announced. "The herd is resting
along the Little Fork of the Hotoa."

Big Star nodded approvingly. "After our feast, the criers will
announce it. We'll go at daylight."

Yellow Hawk turned his head, surprised at the size of the circle. "What's this, a feast—" He saw Dane and Red Bird Woman then, and shouted his amazement. After a great deal of handshaking and laughter and explaining, Yellow Hawk brought his sister to Dane. "Many times I have told Sweet Medicine Girl of my friend, the *Sanaki*. She is timid of boys, but never tires of hearing of you."

Sweet Medicine Girl bowed her head shyly, but offered her hand. Her fingers felt small in his clasp, trembling like a captured bird.

After the feast, which Dane later learned was boiled young dog cooked in a gravy of buffalo fat and wild sweet potatoes, Big Star announced that the young people could dance the Night Dance to bring the celebration to an end. The old men wandered off to their tipis, their places being taken by young men and women who had been waiting outside. The girls gathered on one side of the fire, the boys on the other, and then a drummer took his place between them and began a slow beat.

At a cry from the drummer, the girls arose and with folded arms danced slowly across to the seated young men. "Don't look up," Yellow Hawk whispered to Dane. "Direct your gaze at your feet."

A pretty girl danced up to Yellow Hawk and kicked him on the sole of one moccasin. He jumped up, seizing her by the belt. She linked her fingers in his belt, and they started a column of couples, dancing around the fire. A moment later, Dane felt a gentle tap on one of his Mexican boots. He looked up into Sweet Medicine Girl's expectant face. Somewhat awkwardly, each held to the other's belt, and they joined the dance. He hoped it would last forever, but it was soon ended. Big Star signaled the drummer to cease beating and summoned Sweet Medicine Girl to assist her mother in lowering the sides of the tipi.

Dane slept that night in the back part of Big Star's lodge in one of the beds reserved for guests. He dreamed of Sweet Medicine Girl—her soft liquid eyes glancing shyly at him, her small hand clasped in his, her graceful movements beside him as they shuffled round the drummer and the fire. A sharp pull on his hair awakened him. "Buffalo hunt," Yellow Hawk whispered.

At Yellow Hawk's suggestion, Dane rode Lean Bear's gift pinto, which was trained to hunt buffalo. With a hundred other men, old and young, they rode off toward the Little Fork as a huge orange sun floated into view on the horizon.

They found the buffalo scattered into groups varying from a few hundred to a thousand, feeding along the Hotoa. Big Star chose a herd of about five hundred that was massed into a triangular flat between a ridge and the stream. At his signal, the riders divided into two files, one wheeling off toward the ridge, the other riding straight along the stream bank. Dane followed Yellow Hawk to the ridge, and when they reached the top he saw that the files of hunters were encircling the buffalo, which were already beginning to mill. But before the animals attempted to stampede, the circle was completed and the Cheyennes began tightening the ring, moving in for the kill.

The pinto pulled at its bridle, dancing as though impatient to begin. "Look at him," Yellow Hawk said. "Prancing as if his heart was glad." He fitted an arrow to his bow. "I think the bow is the best weapon against buffalo," he said, "although some of us prefer lances and guns."

Dane told him that he had never shot a buffalo and asked what part of the animal's body was most vulnerable.

"Aim just behind the left shoulder as it makes a forward stride. Then the ribs are spread apart so that an arrow or a bullet will go straight through to the heart." He was watching his father, who suddenly raised his arm in a signal to begin shooting. "Aim at the heart!" Yellow Hawk cried, and off he went, riding in close to a fat cow and driving an arrow through its ribs.

Dane missed with his first shots until he discovered that the pinto needed no guidance. Turning the halter loose, he let the pony take him into the herd, where he found a target at close range. He fired and the buffalo leaped and fell with thrashing legs, the pony swerving out of its way. Dane begged the animal's forgiveness, wondering if the Cheyenne hunters were doing the same for all the dying buffalo covering the ground. Here and there an animal escaped, hunters breaking away in pursuit. The unguided pinto joined in one of these chases, and to Dane's dismay, as it leaped over a grassy hummock he found himself sailing through the air to land in a shattering sprawl upon the ground. By the time he got to his feet and retrieved his carbine, the pony had circled back to him, standing still and shaking its shaggy head as though apologizing for the spill. Dane heard Yellow Hawk's merry laughter behind him.

"*Ya!*" Yellow Hawk cried. "Pinto thinks you must be *Veheo,* a white man." The Cheyenne dismounted. "We have killed enough for one day. Let's ride for the women. They'll be bringing knives for the skinning and butchering."

When that day was done, Dane was certain that he had never worked harder nor had ever been filthier with blood and dust in his life. After they brought the meat and skins back to camp, the women and girls went around a bend in the creek and the men and boys went downstream. Clothing and bodies were thoroughly washed, and then everyone came back to camp to dry beside big fires where buffalo humps and marrow bones and choice cuts of meat were roasting. While waiting for the cooked portions, they ate the tongues and liver raw.

Dancing followed the feasting, and although Dane joined one of the circles, he was so thoroughly weary from the unaccustomed excitement and industry of the day that he soon withdrew. He wandered around the camp searching for Sweet Medicine Girl, and found her dancing with several young girls in front of her parents' tipi. Big Star and his wife, Bear Woman, who were watching the dance, invited him to sit beside them.

"You have enjoyed the day?" Big Star asked.

"I am a happy man," Dane replied. "For the first time I feel that I am one of the People, those whom the white men call Indians."

"The *Sanakis,* your people, have lived much with the whites, my son tells me."

"Yes, the Cherokees have taken the white man's way."

Big Star sighed. "Someday I fear more of the *Veheos* will come to our country. I could not live like a white man."

The circle of girls grew more spirited in their dancing; they were laughing and playing tricks on one another. "The young never tire," Bear Woman said. "But when I think of tomorrow with all the meat to be dried and hides to be dressed I long for my bed."

"Yes, I too must sleep," Big Star said. "The men will hunt again tomorrow."

Dane expressed his surprise that they would kill more buffalo so soon.

"Buffalo are like the wild plums," Big Star told him. "They don't stay around very long. We ask each animal to forgive us for taking life from it, and we use everything we kill, meat and hides and bones. The herds will leave us soon and then we will start for the Ghost Timbers to winter with our cousins from the north."

From out of the shadows Yellow Hawk appeared, shouting teasing remarks at the dancing girls. "My body is like a stone," he said to Dane. "Why are we not resting ourselves for tomorrow's hunt?" They followed Yellow Hawk's parents into the tipi, and in a minute Dane was stretched under a light blanket on the comfortable willow-and-sinew bed. He watched the tiny flickerings of the low fire as his tired muscles relaxed. Bear Woman called her daughter to come to bed. The laughter and dancing stopped, followed by soft girlish voices and subdued giggles near the tipi flap.

He saw a crouching shadow beyond the fire, gliding noiselessly across the tipi floor, not toward one of the family beds but circling toward his. Beyond the first shadow appeared others, moving as though walking animal-like on all fours. The first shadow was soon very near him. He caught the scent of her, and then she sprang toward his bed, lifting the blanket and lying beside him, her head on his outflung arm. She seemed to be trembling, but he could tell that it was only repressed laughter. The other forms stood erect then, tittering above them in the semidarkness, as Sweet Medicine Girl tried to leave him. But he turned the prank on her, holding her tight until he felt the cords around her thighs through her thin cloth dress, the *nihpihist,* forbidden to him, and he let her go.

In a sleepy voice Bear Woman ordered all of them to bed. The other girls scurried out of the tipi, and Sweet Medicine Girl vanished into the shadows. From across the fire he could hear the rustle of clothing and then a sigh after she crawled into her bed. All around him was the aroma of sweet grass from her hair and the fading female fragrance of her clean young body.

Dane remained with the Cheyennes through the Moon of Ripening Plums, awakening each day with a feeling of exhilaration that he had rarely known before. Now and then the sensation he experienced when first coming to the Plains recurred—that life was a dream. But his senses were so keen that he knew everything was reality—the excitement of the hunts, the hard sweaty work, the joy of dancing, the happy mischievous children, the pure freedom of the Cheyenne way of life, the shyly innocent coquetries of Sweet Medicine Girl.

With the coming of the first chilly nights, Big Star announced that they would soon start for a place they called the Hinta Nagi, the Ghost Timbers, to make winter camp. Dane knew then that his happy sojourn was coming to an end. He could not remain forever a guest of the chief and his family; he had given his word to Sam Lykins to return the horses and carbine; he longed to see Creek Mary and tell her of his adventures. And his thoughts kept returning to others of his family—Pleasant, Jerusha, Jotham. It was time to start back, return to the old life.

On the morning that he left he was surprised at the number of Cheyennes who came by Big Star's tipi to wish him a safe journey, to give him little farewell presents. Lean Bear, who sometimes still looked at him in a strange way, came with the buffalo hunters. Red Bird Woman and her mother—Rainbow—the old woman who had come up to him that first day to peer at the teeth marks on his neck—brought him a pair of beaded moccasins.

He rode off on the pinto, leading Lykins's two horses. Yellow Hawk and Sweet Medicine Girl accompanied him to the top of the first ridge. There Yellow Hawk offered his hand in farewell.

And then as though on impulse, his sister dismounted and removed a horse bell from around her pony's neck. She took the
bell over to the pinto and fastened it around its neck. Dane
leaned down, reaching for her, but she backed quickly away.

"That present is truly from her heart," Yellow Hawk said.
"The bell was a gift from me and she has prized it above all
things."

"Someday I will bring the bell back to you," Dane promised
her.

She mounted. "May the spirits guard you," she said. Before
she wheeled her pony he saw tears glistening in her eyes. Then
she was gone at a fast gallop, with her brother following. Dane
started down the slope of the ridge, looking back until they
vanished behind him like shapes in a dream.

With no difficulty he found the trail to Independence. By traveling steadily from daylight to dark each day, and alternating
mounts, he reached the Missouri River in ten days.

It was evening of a dusty late summer's day when he rode up
to Sam Lykins's white clapboard house and dismounted at the
hitching rail. Lykins must have seen him from a window; he
came out waving a lighted cigar. "I would've wagered a fortune," he cried, "that I'd never set eyes on you and my horses
again! Did you get the Red Bird Woman to her folk?"

Dane told him of his adventures and spent the night, after enjoying a warm bath in Lykins's big washtub and sharing the
trader's food, which seemed too richly flavored after the simple
meals of the Cheyennes. It was in Dane's mind to leave for Arkansas early the next day, but Lykins refused to hear of such a
quick departure. Throughout the morning the trader kept inviting him to drive one of the wagons in his autumn train to Santa
Fe, but Dane kept begging off. Finally Lykins put the proposal to him as an obligation. Dane was the only driver who had
traveled the cutoff route that Red Bird Woman had guided them
over, and his presence was needed on the first wagon journey
over that poorly marked trail. "Besides," Lykins added, "I
trusted you with my horses and gun for that outlandish mission
of yours."

"I'll go," Dane finally told him, "but only if I can scout on horseback as you do. Not as a wagon driver."

"For a supposedly unenlightened Indian," Lykins replied in a tone of mock indignation, "you squeeze a man mighty hard." Then he slapped his fist against his knee. "Done! We leave within the week."

That second journey to Santa Fe was not nearly as exciting for Dane as the first. They did have one adventure with a Comanche hunting party. He and Lykins came near to being ambushed, but by putting spurs to their mounts and forcing them across a deep ravine they made it back to the safety of the wagon train. Upon arriving at Santa Fe, they found the market swamped with cheap goods. Lykins refused to sell at the prevailing low prices, and talked Dane into going on with him to El Paso.

Afterward he always remembered that journey as one of continual discomfort—a burning sun by day, freezing cold by night, of sand and thirst and recurring attacks of homesickness. With one delay after another—wrecked wagons, snowstorms, and flooded river crossings—they did not return to Independence until late spring.

On the last morning of the return journey, Dane awoke before sunrise, a strange feeling of dread oppressing him. He was in one of the empty wagons, and when he dropped silently upon the dewy grass to face the graying eastern sky he saw the black shape of a bird circling low, a hawk. Suddenly the hawk cried out, and with a quick flap of its wings sped toward the place where the sun would rise. In the faint light he could not determine the color of its feathers. It was only a sliding shadow against the slaty sky.

He thought of Creek Mary, and the dread came upon him again. He ached to see her, to touch her, tell her of his travels. Her voice sounded in his ears, and then he heard a boot scuff against sandy earth. He turned and saw Sam Lykins standing beside the wagon, yawning while he buttoned his shirt. "You in a hurry to get started?" Lykins asked.

"I'm riding on ahead," Dane said.

"You'll stay with me in Independence?"

"No, I'm going home."

He saddled the pinto and started off at a gallop for Independence. There he took the road southward into the Ozarks. Four days later, under low and threatening clouds, he turned into Cane Hill's single street and trotted past Dr. Saviah Manning's barbershop and office, seeing no sign of her presence. As he approached Timothy Rogers's smithy and the log cabin they had built after fleeing from the Cherokee Nation, he was dismayed by the dilapidated appearance of the buildings. Someone had removed the sturdy front door from the cabin and most of the shakes from the roof. The blacksmith forge and tools were gone; the weathered doors of the empty shed swung open. Weeds were beginning to grow in the yards. He did not have to dismount to know that no one had lived there for many months.

Heartsick, he turned the pony and faced down the empty street, the dark skies adding to his gloom. What could have happened to all of them?

From a narrow side road, a buggy wheeled into the street and moved away from him. Above the lowered top he could see the driver's flat-topped black hat with a faded yellow feather in the band. Dr. Saviah Manning. He overtook the buggy as it came to a stop in front of the barbershop.

"Dane!" she cried. "You look as though you'd seen a night spirit."

He motioned toward the abandoned cabin and smithy. "I have. What happened to them?"

She leaped out of the buggy, lithe as a young boy in her jeans trousers. "You don't know? Of course not, you ran off from them." Raindrops spattered from the hovering clouds. She began hurriedly unhitching the black mare.

"They went back to the Nation," she said. "Chief Ross visited them one day and told them the Cherokees had covered the bones of the dead, that it was safe for them to return."

"They're all right then?" he asked anxiously.

"I have heard nothing of them. Little news comes to us from

the Nation these days. Jotham promised to come back to see me, but he has not."

She led her horse around to a stable in the rear of her place, and he followed. "Put your pony in the stall," she said, "unless you mean to ride into a rainy night."

"The pinto needs a rest," he said. "As I do."

She invited him to share dinner in her room above the barbershop. During the meal they exchanged only a few words, he telling her briefly of where he had been, and she commenting on the differences between him and Jotham. "You have a wildness about you that repels me," she said frankly, "although you do bear some physical resemblance to your half-blood cousin. He and I are much alike, our white blood constantly struggling with the Indian in us."

The rain drumming on the roof made him sleepy. He reached for his saddlepack and stood up, thanking her for the food. "I'll go find a place to sleep," he said.

Her dark eyes studied him a moment from across the candle burning on the little table, and then she followed him down the stairway to the latched front door. When he opened it, rain swept into their faces. "Where will you go?" she asked.

He shrugged. "Up to the old cabin."

"It has no roof," she reminded him, "nor does the smithy."

"Your stable has a loft."

"Only rafters." She touched his arm lightly. "Stay here. Remember, your grandmother made me one of your tribe. Suyeta, the Chosen One." She smiled. "I will give you something that will make you dream."

After he removed his Mexican boots and rolled his serape out on the floor, she brought two cups of light-brown liquid and sat cross-legged facing him. They drank in silence, sipping the slightly bitter drink. "Lie down," she said, "and dream." She disappeared with the candle, and he drifted into a strange sleep, half-unconscious, half-awake.

Brilliant streamers of color swirled from above, encircling him. Faces and then full figures of people he had known, clothed in bright reds and greens, floated in the air. The hands of Red Bird

Woman and Jerusha and Sweet Medicine Girl reached for him until Saviah Manning, soaring like an eagle in brown nakedness, intruded upon them, pushing them away with her strong masculine hands, seizing him with a mouth that became a beak plucking at his belly. Their moans were intermingled. Her voice kept calling Jotham's name as though she were in torment. He wanted to scream but his mouth was stopped.

He awoke in her bed, saturated with sweat. She was pounding on his chest. "Get up and dress," she commanded. "I want you out of here before daylight."

"Why?" He felt listless, unable to move.

"The people in this town believe me to be a half-breed spinster who hates men. It's better for me that they keep believing that." She pushed him off the bed, and after he dressed she followed him naked to the door, lifting the latch and pushing him out into the damp darkness. "Tell Jotham he lied to me," she said, and closed the door behind him.

30

At that point in his life, Dane left me to go to bed. I had no difficulty in falling asleep, but was soon awakened by coyote harmonies, not a quartet or an octet, but what seemed to be a mighty choir of all the prairie wolves of Montana. I'm sure that I heard Dane's voice from time to time joining in the performance as interlocutor. Eventually the singers departed, the sound of their melodies gradually receding as if they were members of an opera company departing into the wings.

After that I must have fallen into a deep sleep. When I awoke, Dane was bathing in the icy stream of melted snow that ran below my window. Just as I finished dressing in the shivering chill of the Montana spring morning, he came bounding in to warm his backside at the fireplace. He had already cooked breakfast for us.

"Saviah Manning pushed you out into the wet dawn," I reminded him.

"Yes, I stopped telling you about that last night because I did not want to go to sleep with bad memories of my return to the Cherokee Nation. I suppose everyone who leaves his kin for a long time and then returns must suffer the same shock of discovering that everything changes, and that he is not the center of the world as he had thought, but only a grain of dust in other people's lives. It was especially painful and grievous to me.

"Must've been past midnight when my tired pinto brought me to the double cabin Uncle Opothle built and that we had abandoned so hastily to flee to Arkansas. The house was dark, and I did not know for certain they had returned to it. I knew that if I awakened Grandmother Mary she would never go back to bed; she would want to know everything I had done.

"And so I rolled up in my serape on the porch and went to sleep. Aunt Suna-lee awoke me to the smell of woodsmoke and frying pork. She had seen the pinto from the window, and came out to investigate. When I rose up, she rushed to embrace me, weeping so freely that I felt her warm tears on my face. I had never known her to behave in such a manner. Still sobbing, she led me into the house and back to the kitchen, where Prissie stared at me in disbelief until tears came to her eyes.

"'Where's Grandmother Mary?' I asked, knowing that she was always the first to arise, the guardian of all my childhood mornings.

"'She still sleeps,' Prissie said. 'Each day she whispers to one of us that she will not go to the Darkening Land until you return.' Prissie led the way to the open doorway of Grandmother Mary's room. I could see the shape of her frail form under the blanket. Her face was only a skull with dark withered skin stretched across it. Her eyes opened slowly and she tried to rise, her trembling bony hands reaching out to me. When she said my name her voice was like the crackling of dry corn leaves.

"I went to her and held her up by the shoulders while she placed her hands on my face. Her body began to shake and I thought she was crying, but then I heard the laughter, husky and triumphant, and I bent to see the gleam of victory in her old eyes. 'I defeated them,' she whispered. 'I knew you would come, *sogonisi,* before the dark spirits took me away.'

"'You sent the hawk for me, grandmother.'

"'Yes, I sent the hawk and it brought you back to me.' She tugged at the silver chain that held the Danish coin, lifting it from her breast and motioning for me to bow my head so that she could place it around my neck.

"'No,' I whispered.

"She shook her head angrily when I tried to give the silver piece back to her. 'You are my only full-blood left,' she said. 'You must guard it for me.'

"I stayed with her until she fell asleep again, breathing easily like a child. Afterward Prissie told me that Jotham had married Griffa McBee, and that they were living in a new cabin near the crossroads. He and William had rebuilt the trading post, and Timothy Rogers's smithy adjoined it. They were all busy and prospering.

"'Pleasant and Jerusha?' I asked. 'Where are they?'

"Prissie shook her head, clucking her tongue at me. 'You stayed away too long, Dane. Your son is no longer your son. Soon after we came back to the Nation, Jerusha married the Reverend Thomas Crookes.'

"'The Reverend Thomas Crookes,' I repeated in astonishment. 'Who is he?'

"'A true man of God,' Prissie replied. 'He knows that Pleasant was born in sin, but he has taken him as his son, and is bringing the boy up in the ways of salvation.'

"I wanted to go and see them, but I could not leave Grandmother Mary. Whenever she awoke from her fitful spells of sleep, she would call my name. That night I lay on the floor beside her bed, answering whenever she awakened to whisper my name. For a time before the dawn came she was silent, and when it was light I arose and looked at her face and knew she would never speak my name again. I could not weep because of the numbness that froze me, the desolation that surrounded me. Creek Mary had always been there, as certain as the stars she pointed out to me in the night skies, and I had thought she would always be there. Now she was gone to the Darkening Land.

"I awakened Prissie and Aunt Suna-lee and then went outside and saddled the pinto. Where the pony took me I did not care. I wanted only to be in motion across the earth, seeking something, I did not know what. Upon reaching the Illinois River bottoms, I turned into deep woods, riding and riding until darkness came. How long I stayed in the forest I don't know, two or three days maybe, grieving. Not until a heavy rain drenched me, not until I took off my shirt to dry it and saw the Danish coin against my chest did I come to my senses.

"The next morning I rode into Aunt Suna-lee's yard but found no one in the house and so went on up to the crossroads, which had become a cluster of buildings—a new church bearing a thin coat of whitewash, three or four dwellings, the trading post, and the smithy. Mr. Tim Rogers and Bibbs were working under the shed, but I was then in no mood to talk with them, and they were too busy to notice me. Gathered around the church were several mule-drawn buggies and wagons, and I could hear the high voice of a preacher man echoing from the windows.

"Beyond the church was the new burying ground, with several mounds of upturned raw earth. I dismounted and found Grand-mother Mary's grave, the marker a solid block of cedar with letters burned into it with a smith's iron: AKUSA AMAYI. I was pleased that Jotham had marked it that way instead of 'Creek Mary.' I would tell him so, I thought, trying to hold back my tears. And then from the full-leafed woods came a sweet scent of wild blossoms and such a burst of birdsong as would have made my grandmother cry out her joy in being alive. My tears flowed until I thought I could hear her laughing at me in that deep husky way of hers, and I wondered how she felt about sleeping forever in the burying ground of a *Unega* church. Noticing some yellow flowers growing in the shade of the woods, I went and picked them. When I kneeled to place them beside the marker, the Danish coin pressed cool against my chest as if she was touching me gently in farewell.

"I heard my name called then, and turned to face Jerusha. Behind her the buggies and wagons were wheeling away from the church grounds. Skipping toward us over the graves was a little boy, Pleasant, my son, taller and skinnier than I remembered him.

"Jerusha brushed loose strands of her blonde hair away from her face, waiting for me to speak, but I could say nothing.

"'Your grandmother befriended me,' Jerusha said, 'more than anyone else. But she loved you most of all.'

"'She would not have seen us wed,' I said. 'How could you not hate her?'

"'You would have wed me if you truly loved me,' she replied. 'I knew you were forever lost to me when you did not return from Independence with Jotham.' Her lips trembling, she looked away from me, and then stammered out: 'I—I had to find—a father for Pleasant.'

"The boy had moved closer to her side, standing with his thin bare legs wide apart, examining me with some faint recognition from the past. His face had changed. I could see my nose and chin and ears forming out of his immature countenance. 'Do you know the pledge?' he asked me in a grave voice that was high and thin like his mother's.

"Jerusha smiled. 'We've been to Reverend Crookes's morning temperance meeting,' she explained, 'where everyone repeats the pledge.'

"'Your husband?'

"She nodded, and Pleasant recited by rote: 'Do you solemnly pledge yourself to never use nor buy nor sell nor give nor receive as a drink any whiskey, brandy, rum, gin, wine, fermented cider, strong beer, or intoxicating liquor?'

"I could not keep from laughing, but a time would come when

I would remember those childish words with sadness. I wanted to step forward, lift my half-blood son up in my arms and praise him, but a white man in a black suit was approaching us from the church. 'Is he the Reverend Crookes?' I asked.

"'He's been good to me and Pleasant,' she said, and then her lips barely moved as she whispered: 'But I can never love him as I've loved you, Dane.'

"The Reverend Thomas Crookes looked to be a man who ate well and often, and was used to having his way. He was plump of face and figure, his mouth covered by a growth of sandy mustache badly in need of trimming. As he came nearer, his glance shifted back and forth from Pleasant to me.

"'You're the boy's father,' he declared accusingly. 'You could not deny that.' His tone was such that I knew he viewed me as an agent of his Devil, if not the Devil himself. He came no closer than Jerusha, and did not offer his hand.

"He looked at Grandmother Mary's grave. 'I preached for her funeral,' he said with a note of self-importance. 'Although she died a heathen, refusing to be baptized and cleansed of her sins.'

"'She believed in Esaugetuh Emissee, the Maker of Breath,' I said, and started toward the pinto. Crookes fell into step beside me, with Jerusha and Pleasant trailing along behind. 'I love a sinner,' he began almost cheerfully. 'Especially the heathen. By following your pagan gods you wronged this good woman who is now my wife, in the eyes of the true God.'

"What could I say to him? Words would have changed nothing. So I said nothing. But he went on with his sermon, his words pouring out in a flood. 'Full-bloods such as you,' he said, 'are the most difficult. Those hereabouts are a most degraded company of savages, but the day will come when with the help of God my hard-fought battles against sin, the world, and the Devil will bring victory. My martyrlike spirit will conquer the difficulties of bringing the Cherokees to civilization and religion.'

"'We tried your civilization and your religion in our eastern homeland,' I finally said, 'but your Christian brothers drove thousands of us from our homes to our deaths. Take care of my son, Mr. Crookes.' I turned and bowed my good-byes to Jerusha and

Pleasant, feeling sorry for them, but there was nothing I could do for them, so I mounted my pony and rode across to the trading post to see Jotham.

"Jotham had changed, too, but not as much as the others. We talked of the old days, laughing over the joyful incidents, brushing aside the sad ones. He was happy living with Griffa, who was already expecting a child, and so I did not remind him of Saviah Manning and her charge that he had lied to her.

"During the next two or three days I saw most of my old friends and acquaintances. They told me of their hopes and fears for the new Cherokee Nation, as well as giving me news from afar. Sequoyah was somewhere in Mexico, searching for a band of 'lost' Cherokees who wandered west during the War of the Revolution, and I wondered if our paths might have crossed while I was traveling with Mr. Lykins's wagon trains. I was much surprised to learn that several hundred Cherokees had escaped capture by General Scott's soldiers and were still living in strongholds in the Smoky Mountains. For a day or so I thought of going back east to join them, but they were from the upper regions of the old Nation, far more alien to me than the recent friends I had made among the Cheyennes of the Plains.

"Indeed my thoughts constantly returned to Big Star's happy wanderers, to Yellow Hawk and the buffalo hunters, to Sweet Medicine Girl. Dared I return to them? Abandon my kin and clan and tribe to become a Cheyenne? Well, I thought, if my grandmother had the courage to follow her heart away from her people to become a Cherokee, then surely I could follow her example. Creek Mary's blood would uphold me.

"When Jotham announced one day that he and Bibbs would soon be going to Independence to buy goods for the trading post, I told him I would accompany him, but that he should still take Bibbs along because I would not be returning to the Nation.

"He was distressed. 'The Nation needs you, Dane,' he said. 'Why don't you stay? You are entitled to land. You could become a farmer, live well, settle down as I have done.'

"I tried to explain my feelings, my restlessness, but I don't think he understood that whatever comes easily to us we turn away from, but that which slips away from us we will pursue to the ends of the earth.

"When we reached Independence, I used most of the money Mr. Lykins had paid me to buy a rifle and a pistol. I was disappointed to learn that he was in Mexico, but Mr. Louis Tessier, the Frenchman who supplied Jotham and William, found me a place with a wagon train going to Bent's Fort. Late in that summer, after a long search, I found Big Star's people camped far to the northeast of Bent's Fort along a stream called Sand Creek."

Dane lifted the smoke-blackened coffeepot from the fireplace and refilled my cup. "So now you've heard Creek Mary's story," he said.

"Not entirely," I answered. "You've just told me of your assuredness that her blood would sustain you in your decision to become a Cheyenne. Through you and your children and grandchildren she lived on."

A brightening of his eyes, a smile forming on his thin lips, told me that he was pleased by what I had said. He was about to reply when the rattle of wheels against ruts made him turn to glance out the window. "That Crow boy again," he said. "This time driving his old man's wagon. Wonder what he wants now?" He went to the door, opened it, and stepped outside, waiting for the wagon to turn in. "Hi, Dane," the young driver called out. "Old Red Bird Woman sent you some lodgepoles. Where you want 'em?"

"God damn," Dane said. "I thought she was only fooling me with her talk. How many poles did she send?"

"Sixteen or seventeen maybe."

"Damn! That's enough for a big tipi. Reckon you better put them in the corral shed."

"Sure." The young man started the wagon down toward the rusted sheet-iron shed, Dane following.

I went out to watch, feeling the sun combating the chill air around me until they returned. This time Dane introduced me to John Bear-in-the-Water, but the Crow youth's eyes were still suspicious of my presence there. He started the wagon, but stopped again before we were through the cabin door. "Hey, Dane," he called. "When's Amayi coming back?"

"Soon," Dane shouted back at him. "Soon, I hope."

After we were inside he dropped into his chair, shaking his head and groaning. "Red Bird Woman wants to make a tipi with buffalo hides. Says she and I must die together in a tipi."

"Red Bird Woman?" I repeated. "Is she the same—"

"Yes, she's the Red Bird from the days of my hot-blood youth. She's a coyote like me, hard to kill." He squinted at a beam of sunlight streaming through the window. "I guess you might say Red Bird Woman always has been a kind of guardian spirit for me, a luck-bringer. She was the first one who saw me coming back to join the Cheyennes in their camp on Sand Creek. I had put that horse bell given me by Sweet Medicine Girl around the pinto's neck, and she recognized the sound. By the time I crossed the shallow stream, she had Sweet Medicine Girl there to greet me. I dropped off the pony and it was all I could do to keep from putting my arms around that shy little girl. For the first time in my life I knew I was where I wanted to be.

"Well, that evening when her brother, Yellow Hawk, came in with the buffalo hunters, I took him aside and told him I wanted to be a Cheyenne and that I desired his sister for my wife. Whatever deeds I must perform, whatever ordeals I must endure, I would do so with a good heart.

"We talked for a long time, and it was soon clear to me that I must accomplish three things. First I must obtain Sweet Medicine Girl's consent to be my wife by courting her in the Cheyenne way. Then I must become a member of one of the soldier societies in order to be worthy of a chief's daughter. And then I must make a present of several horses to her father, Big Star, before he would give his daughter to me in marriage.

"Without the willing help of Yellow Hawk my road would have been even more difficult than it was. My first obstacle was Magpie Eagle, a year or two younger than I, who had set his heart on winning Sweet Medicine Girl. On buffalo hunts I had admired Magpie Eagle's skill and daring, but I resented his boldness as a courting rival. At the dances he wore colored ribbons in his hair, bright porcelain beads around his neck, and wolf tails fastened to his knees. He found ways to draw Sweet Medicine Girl away from the circles, and I would see them in the shadows with his blanket over both their heads while they stood very close together. This was not an unusual custom among the young couples, but it seemed strange to a young Cherokee, I can tell you. At first, I could not bring myself to try blanket wooing, nor was it much easier for me to pay court by playing on a bone whistle. Magpie Eagle was very good at this, and in the evenings he would stand outside Sweet Medicine Girl's tipi, playing the same notes over and over.

"Because I was a suitor for Big Star's daughter, I could no longer sleep in the chief's tipi, but used a bed in the tipi of an old man named Whistling Elk. He became interested in my courtship and presented me with a bird-bone whistle with which he said he had won his deceased wife. Whistling Elk taught me how to play the shrill little instrument. 'You must work up a tune of your own,' he advised me, 'so she will recognize your presence in the dark.' After several evenings of practice, I gathered my courage and went over to the front of her tipi about dusk and played my tune. Magpie Eagle soon joined me, playing so expertly that I felt humiliated. I could see Sweet Medicine Girl standing inside the open flap, smiling at us, and I wondered if my serenade sounded as foolish to her as it did to me.

"Not long after that, Red Bird Woman visited me one morning and said the time had come to press my courting. 'It is known to me,' she said, 'that Magpie Eagle has given Sweet Medicine Girl several rings, but she has not yet worn any of them.' She took a bracelet from her wrist, a silver band with two grizzly-bear claws mounted on it. 'Give Sweet Medicine Girl this bracelet,' she said, 'and watch to see if she wears it. If she does, you need not fear Magpie Eagle as a rival any longer.' After I thanked her, she told me that Lean Bear had given her the bracelet when he was courting her and that she had worn it for him. 'It has magic power,' she assured me.

"'What will Lean Bear say when he finds you have given me this bracelet?' I asked.

"'It was he who counseled me to bring it to you,' she replied, laughing at my misgivings. 'Lean Bear says Magpie Eagle is not good enough for his cousin Sweet Medicine Girl.'

"At the next dance I found a chance to slip the bracelet into Sweet Medicine Girl's hand. She said nothing, her eyes turning shyly away when I tried to read her feelings for me and the gift, and I feared that the bracelet's magic had failed me.

"On the following evening, when I went to her tipi to play the bird-bone whistle, she came outside, lifting her arm so that I could see the bracelet on her wrist. I stopped playing at once, my heart beating like a soaring bird's, and walked over to her, lifting my serape and boldly enclosing both of us under it. She was perfumed with the fragrance of sweet grass and white sage. 'Why did you wait so long?' she whispered. I told her I was thick-witted and had little knowledge yet of Cheyenne customs. I promised her that if she would wait for me that I would perform such superhuman deeds that all the soldier societies would invite me to join them and that I would bring a herd of the finest horses to her father's tipi.

"She promised to wait, no matter how many moons must pass before I accomplished these tasks. Her fingers found Creek Mary's Danish coin that I always wore around my neck. 'This is your power?' she asked.

"'It is great magic,' I said. 'The day you become my wife it will be yours. It is very old and has been kept for you.'

"With the coming of the Dry Grass Moon, Big Star's people started north for the Ghost Timbers to make winter camp, and Lean Bear's Dog Soldiers accompanied us as rear guard for the column. Along the way, Yellow Hawk told me that his society, the Fox Soldiers, was planning an autumn raid against the Crows or Shoshones to replenish pony herds. At one of their night meetings, Yellow Hawk proposed my name as his guest for the raid, but Magpie Eagle objected. However, the society's leader, War Shirt, overruled Magpie Eagle, and I was given permission to go on the raid. 'Watch out for Magpie Eagle,' Yellow

Hawk warned me. 'He is still jealous of you for winning my sister.'

"After camp was made at the Ghost Timbers, the Fox Soldiers spent four days preparing for the long raid north. I went through all their rituals—dancing, singing, and praying to the Great Medicine. We cleaned our guns and sharpened our knives and arrow points. In order to obtain a bow and arrows and a red breech-clout such as the others wore, I traded my pistol to old Whistling Elk. He also gave me a medicine pouch containing seven magical herbs and an eagle foot. I did not have the heart to tell him that Creek Mary's gorget provided me with all the protection I needed, so I wore the pouch anyway.

"Early one morning about thirty of us set out for Shoshone and Crow country, War Shirt leading us over a roundabout route through coulees and behind screens of willows and cottonwoods so as to keep our presence unknown to any hunting or war parties of the enemy. Every night we camped in thickets, building no fires, eating only a little of our pemmican and dried berry cakes.

"One day the forward scouts, coming upon the scene of a recent buffalo kill, found an arrow in some high grass. Because the shaft was thicker and heavier than our arrow shafts they knew the hunters had been Crows. War Shirt at once sent out his best four trackers, keeping the remainder of us hidden in a deep gulch. After a short time the trackers returned to tell us that the Crows were camped across a river ford with an unusually large horse herd. Some of the animals still had Sioux designs painted on their flanks and must have been recently stolen. The camp was a temporary one, of about sixty Crow warriors and their women and children, and from what the scouts could see of it, they appeared to be preparing to move the next day.

"About dusk we all moved closer to the river, and after War Shirt made a reconnaissance of the camp, he proposed a plan. The Crows were very careless, he said, and a good part of their horse herd was corralled along the opposite bank with no guard set. He asked for ten volunteers to cross the river downstream and make a mock attack on foot just as day was breaking so as to draw the Crow warriors away from their corral.

"Because this mock attack would be more dangerous than stampeding an unguarded horse herd, all the younger Fox Soldiers volunteered. Among them were Yellow Hawk and Magpie Eagle, and of course I asked to go because I was eager to prove my bravery. There was also a very young boy, no more than fourteen or fifteen. I had seen him on buffalo hunts but did not know his name.

"The night turned off very cold, and when we swam our horses across the river just before daylight, the water felt like ice. We fastened our ponies in a thicket close by the river and started upstream toward the Crow camp.

"When we could see sparks from their fires rising above the willows, we spread far apart and moved slowly forward, trying to avoid making any noise. One of their dogs must have smelled us. It howled a warning, and the Crows came charging on foot out of the willows. There was just enough light so that they could dimly see us, and because all of us fired at once and were spread out, the Crows were not sure of the size of our party. At Yellow Hawk's signal, we backed away a short distance, taking cover behind bushes or trees, reloading and firing our guns again. In this way we slowly drew the Crows out from their camp. As soon as we heard the cries of our mounted Fox Soldiers and the splashing of the captured herd in the river shallows we all turned and ran for our ponies. Those Crow warriors didn't know what to do next—chase after us on foot or run back to their camp and mount whatever horses they had left.

"They must have had quite a few animals picketed around their tipis, because our little party of ten was only halfway across the river when a dozen Crows came streaking after us. We lashed our ponies and headed for a coulee where War Shirt's men and the captured herd were supposed to be waiting. Suddenly my pinto stumbled in a muddy place, spinning around to regain its footing, and I saw one of my companions and his mount on the ground behind me. The other young men in our party had swept on ahead of us. The Crows were galloping fast from the riverbank, one of them far out in front on a swift pony.

"What I did next was done without thinking. The unhorsed Cheyenne was that young boy of fourteen or fifteen. His pony still lay motionless, and he was limping toward me. As I said, without thinking of bravery or danger I jabbed an arrow point into the pinto's flank and made him leap forward. I swung him around right in front of the limping boy, but the lead Crow was closing upon us, his lance drawn back ready to hurl. I had to stop him with my first shot. Whether it was Creek Mary's gorget or Whistling Elk's magical pouch, I'll never know, but my medicine was strong that day. I shot that Crow out of his saddle, reached for the boy's wrist, and lifted him up behind me. Then I heard gunfire from ahead. Yellow Hawk and the others had turned back to help, and not far behind them came War Shirt and his bunch. The outnumbered Crows scattered for the river.

"When we reached the captured horse herd, the boy behind me slid off slowly, favoring his sprained leg. Magpie Eagle came rushing up then, grabbing the boy in his arms and brushing the mud off him. 'You stole my girl,' Magpie Eagle shouted at me, 'and now my young brother's life belongs to you. What else do you want?' His scowl turned to a grin, and he reached up a hand. When I took it to shake, he pulled me out of my saddle, spilling me roughly on the ground. Everybody broke into laughter.

"That night after we made camp, Magpie Eagle proposed that I be invited to join the Fox Soldiers. He also gave me his share of the horses we had taken, and then War Shirt said that after we divided the animals evenly among us, there would be eight left over. Ordinarily these extra horses would belong to War Shirt and Yellow Hawk because they were the leaders in the raid, but both said that I must have them for my offering to Big Star.

"As soon as we returned to the Ghost Timbers, I was ready to take my horses to Big Star's tipi, but Yellow Hawk and Magpie Eagle told me that I could not do this myself. I must first find a 'mother' to adopt me, and then she would take the horses to Big Star and ask for Sweet Medicine Girl. I remembered Grandmother Mary telling me of her difficulties in finding a 'brother' so that she could become a Cherokee, but her troubles seemed slight compared to mine. Every woman I went to who was old enough to be my mother refused to adopt me as a son, some quite rudely, and as the day went on I began to suspect a tribal plot among the women to keep me from marrying Sweet Medicine Girl.

"The whole thing, however, was a trick, a kind of joke arranged by Yellow Hawk and Magpie Eagle to test my steadiness. Long before sundown I was in despair, sitting beside Whistling Elk's tipi and hating all Cheyenne women, when Red Bird Woman's old mother, Rainbow, came up to me and said she was looking for a son to adopt. As I jumped up to embrace her, Yellow Hawk and most of my Fox Soldier brothers appeared, all laughing over how they had tricked me.

"From that moment, everything went along like a dream. Rainbow led my horses one at a time over to Big Star's tipi, while I obeyed her instructions and moved my things into her tipi. There I was to wait for Big Star's answer. Across from me on the edge of the Dog Soldiers' circle, Lean Bear and Red Bird Woman sat in front of their tipi watching with great amusement. Every once in a while Lean Bear would make a teasing remark, and then suddenly he jumped to his feet and cried: 'Here they come!'

"To my great joy, Big Star had given his permission and the marriage ceremony was beginning. Wearing a fine red dress, Sweet Medicine Girl was mounted on one of the best of the captured ponies, a splendid Appaloosa. It was led by a young woman on foot, and other young women were leading several of the gift horses that Big Star was generously returning to me. Lean Bear came running with a new blanket, spreading it on the ground in front of Rainbow's tipi, and Yellow Hawk and Magpie Eagle, both wearing their best costumes, took Sweet Medicine Girl from her saddle and placed her in the center of the blanket. Lifting the blanket by its corners, they then carried her into the tipi.

"While I and all the other men taking part in the ceremony

waited outside, the women went inside to comb and rebraid
Sweet Medicine Girl's hair, paint her face, and decorate her with
gift ornaments. At the same time, my adopted mother, Rainbow,
was preparing the wedding feast. When this was ready, we
young men were invited into the tipi.

"If I were trying to choose the happiest day of my life, that
day would be the one. The last ceremony of the evening was my
presentation of Grandmother Mary's gorget to Sweet Medicine
Girl.

"When we awoke together the next morning in Rainbow's
lodge, she was no longer Sweet Medicine Girl, she was Sweet
Medicine Woman. Her *nihpihist* cord lay on the tipi floor beside
our bed, and without shyness she let me look upon the silver
Danish coin lying between her naked breasts.

"Rainbow called us to a breakfast she had prepared over coals
outside the tipi. I dressed first and went out to thank her again
for adopting me. Rainbow came up close to me, pulling my head
down so that she could examine my neck. There were no teeth
marks this time for her to see. 'Your wife is beautiful,' she said,
'but she has not the fire of my daughter.'

"'My woman's fire burns in a different way,' I told her, but she
was laughing so hard that I don't think she heard me."

31

After the last winter snows melted around the Ghost Timbers,
Big Star announced that in the Moon of Greening Grass they
would start north to spend the summer along the streams that

flowed into the Yellowstone. Lean Bear and the Dog Soldiers chose to go south for the season, however, and so the Fox Soldiers were assigned to lead the movement of march.

For Dane the slow journey northward was so pleasurable that he could not help but contrast it with the misery of the Cherokees on their exodus from the East. His duties as a Fox Soldier required him to ride back and forth along the caravan to maintain order and see that the families kept close together. Instead of traveling in wagons, however, the Cheyennes used travois. These were tipi poles fastened to each side of a horse's saddle with the lower ends trailing on the ground behind. Tipi covers tied across these poles formed litters for carrying parfleches packed with food, clothing, and household goods. Old people too feeble to ride or walk and some of the youngest children also were carried by travois. Instead of suffering from starvation, sickness, and harassment as the Cherokees had, the Cheyennes delighted in an abundance of food and the constantly changing scenery. Sometimes they stopped for three or four days along pleasant streams to hunt or laze away the warming afternoons. Occasionally they met small bands from friendly tribes, but not once did they encounter white men.

The country of forests and rich grass into which Big Star led them was a paradise of wild game. Buffalo and antelopes were everywhere, and rarely a day passed that they did not see elk and deer, beavers and bears. The skies were filled with hawks and eagles of many varieties, the waters were covered with ducks and geese, and the earth offered them wild berries, choke-cherries, and breadroots.

They camped for the summer along a stream of sweet water flowing from the Bighorns, and for the first time Dane met the northern cousins of these people he had made his own. Many of the Northern Cheyennes still disdained the clothing and blankets of white men, using buckskin and buffalo robes, and they spoke in a harsher dialect, often using Lakota words borrowed from their Sioux neighbors. He also met some of these Sioux, who were divided into subtribes—Oglalas, Brules, Minneconjous, and Uncpapas. What all these people took from that paradise to sustain themselves seemed to have no more effect upon it than a handful of water taken from a lake. He was told that no white man had ever seen this country.

That summer was the happiest of his life. He and Sweet Medicine Woman had their own tipi now, and they spent hours each day simply sitting close beside each other, sheltered by the benevolent land and the open sky. Upon waking each day, he looked upon his young wife and thanked his Maker of Breath and her Great Medicine for bringing them together upon the earth. There was about her the graceful delicacy of a flower, but he knew she was strong, as tenacious as a wild plant whose roots can split creviced granite. She told him one morning that his child was ripening within her.

Because their summer paradise turned into a winter land of snow and ice, in the Moon of Falling Leaves the tribes began moving toward their winter camps. Again Big Star led them to the Hinta Nagi, the Ghost Timbers, where walls of giant cottonwoods and red willow brush shielded them from the bitter winds of the Plains. In the Deer Rutting Moon snows began to fall there, small ones at first, and then blizzards the equal of which only the oldest of the Cheyennes remembered seeing in that place. Because of the weather they spent most of their time gathered in tipis, listening to the old storytellers vie with each other in relating tales of ghosts and monsters, of heroes and villains, of trickster animals and bawdy lovers. After bedtime the howling winds made the trees shriek and groan like the ghosts after which they were named.

Sweet Medicine Woman's belly grew heavy with the child, and she and Dane worked constantly at sealing their tipi against the frigid air. They collected wood to be used later to keep their infant warm, and bargained for bearskins to make a bed that could not be penetrated by cold. In the Moon of Popping Trees, the child was born, a bright-eyed boy with a voice louder than the painful outcries of his mother. They named him Swift Eagle.

The next day when Bear Woman came to bathe her grandchild, she held its face close to her own and began shaking her head. "He has the Frenchman's nose," Bear Woman said.

Dane, who was poking at the fire, looked up at her. "What do you mean, the Frenchman's nose?" he asked.

"Big Star can tell you more than I," Bear Woman said. "His grandfather was a French trapper. Big Star does not have the Frenchman's nose, but his dead brother had it."

Dane was outraged. "Why did you not tell me of this?" he shouted at Sweet Medicine Woman. She was lying on their bed, covered with a bearskin and smiling across at the baby.

"I thought it of no importance," she replied, surprised at his sudden outburst. "My father seldom speaks of the Frenchman."

"I swore to my grandmother that I would marry only a full-blood," he cried angrily. He walked toward her, his hands half clenched as if he meant to seize and shake her. "And now I find that my wife has the blood of the *Veheos*."

She had never seen him so infuriated. Tears formed in her eyes, and she tried to sit up. He pushed her gently back, awkwardly adjusting the bearskin around her. "It does not matter," he said quietly. "The child is what matters."

He said no more about the Frenchman, but he thought often of the irony of fate that had brought him a wife and son who were not full-bloods. He wondered how Creek Mary would accept the situation. Most likely, he thought, she would view it as a marvelous prank played upon mortals by the Maker of Breath. He could almost hear her deep laughter ringing over the Hinta Nagi. Sometimes, however, he would hold Swift Eagle in his hands, examining the tint and texture of the child's skin and the thin aristocratic nose that was a heritage from the Frenchman.

Sweet Medicine Woman once saw him doing this, and her temper flared up. "So you think your son is ugly?" she cried accusingly. She was pounding dried buffalo chips into powder.

"They say he resembles you," Dane replied teasingly.

She was in no mood for banter. She slammed the pan of buffalo-chip powder down beside the fire to warm it. "If he is uncomely," she said, "perhaps it is the Cherokee in him. Don't blame everything on the Frenchman." She came over and took Swift Eagle from him, undressing the child within the warmth of the fire. Dane saw that the little boy's buttocks were badly chafed. He watched his wife dust the buffalo-chip powder over the tender flesh and then place him gently back in his cradle.

"He is the most handsome boy in the Hinta Nagi," Dane said, reaching for her waist. "Let us make another one."

Before the winter ended great herds of buffalo, driven by the blizzards, tried to find shelter in the Hinta Nagi. They resembled ghosts themselves in their icy coats, and were such easy kills that every family had frozen meat hanging in the trees—to keep it out of reach of dogs and wolves. Dane hunted almost every day, and he soon had a great heap of buffalo skins for trading when spring arrived.

During the Moon When the Geese Lay Eggs, a half-blood Arapaho wearing white man's clothing visited the Hinta Nagi and invited the Cheyennes to bring their buffalo skins to Fort Laramie. He represented a St. Louis fur company which had stocked many trade goods at the fort and was offering top prices for hides. As Laramie was easier to reach than Bent's Fort, Big Star decided the Cheyennes should go there to trade.

Fort Laramie was a sturdy structure of adobe and timbers, with pointed-roof parapets built at opposite corners and above the entrance gate. It stood just across a shallow river also called Laramie. Some Brule Sioux were already camped in a grove nearby the walls, and so the Cheyennes set up their tipis along the grassy east bank amid a multitude of wild flowers. No soldiers had yet come to Fort Laramie, but an American flag was flying, and several white men from the fur company were there to welcome them.

Dane and Yellow Hawk crossed the stream together, carrying a few buffalo hides on their horses to test the trading market. About two years had passed since Dane had seen a white man, and they looked and smelled strange to him. He caught the friendly eye of a lean weatherbeaten man with flaxen hair falling to his shoulders, a drooping yellow mustache, and a short beard cut to a sharp point.

"Trade?" the man asked, and began talking in a sort of singsong Cheyenne-Arapaho jargon.

"Name your prices in English," Dane said.

The trader stared at him in disbelief. "Good God, man! Where'd you learn to speak the lingo?"

Dane explained, telling him he was Cherokee-born from the Cherokee Nation in the state of Georgia.

"Wa-agh! And I was born in Augusta Town on the Savannah! I reckon this calls for a drink."

The trader's name was Jim Carrothers and he had made his way to St. Louis in his teens to travel west with the American Fur Company. He had taken an Arapaho girl for his wife. "We got four young-uns," Carrothers said. "Live up on the North Platte. I never been back to St. Louis but once."

Dane traded his first hides for sugar, coffee, flour, and a length of red stroud cloth for Sweet Medicine Woman. Then he noticed some pocket notebooks covered in black leather on Carrothers's worktable. "How much for a notebook?" he asked.

"On me," Carrothers said, handing him one.

"I'll need a pen and ink," Dane added.

"Good God! You write the lingo, too? All I can do is scrawl my name and make figgers." With a shrug he gave Dane an ink bottle and a pen.

That night in their tipi, after Sweet Medicine Woman had gone to sleep, Dane took out the notebook, dipped his pen in the ink, and made a first entry: *Swift Eagle, Robert Dane, of one-half Cheyenne blood mixed with French blood, three-eighths Cherokee blood, and one-eighth Creek Mary's blood, of which there may be some Spanish, was born at the Ghost Timbers in the year 1844 in the Moon of Popping Trees.*

Although he could not record the exact day, he knew, as he wrote the words giving his son Swift Eagle an English name, that in the act of writing he had revealed to himself that he was not yet free of his ties to the white man's world.

32

"My second son, Little Cloud, was born in 1845," Dane said. "I wrote an English name for him in my book too, William Jotham Dane, but we never used it, not even when I took him to the seminary to be enrolled as a student. For a while I tried calling him Little Billy, but he would not answer to that, so I quit. Little Cloud did not have the Frenchman's nose. He looked so much like his mother while he was very young that strangers took him for a girl. He was always undersized, but a splendid little fighter. I've always wondered what he'd have been like full grown. . . ."

He turned his head away but not before I saw the shine of moisture in his eyes. "It's strange how a man views life in a different way when he discovers that his existence is necessary to other persons. I don't know why I never felt that way about Jerusha and Pleasant. Maybe I was too young. Maybe it was because they were so much a part of the white man's world that I was not necessary to them.

"You see, in those days there were always two levels in the world of the Cheyennes. We did not consider the world of hunting or hide curing or arrow and moccasin making, or any of those things as the real world. The real world was a place of magic, of dreams wherein we became spirits. I lived with the Cheyennes a long time before I learned how to cross into the real world, and all that time my wife and children could do this and they were puzzled because I could not join them there. By fasting for long periods of time and through the ceremony of the Medicine Lodge, I was finally able to find my way into the real world with my family. I discovered mysterious powers within my memory and learned that when you pray for others to become strong you become strong, too, because that connects you with everything else. You become a part of everything and that is how I knew that I was necessary to my family and they were necessary to me."

"What was the ceremony of the Medicine Lodge?" I asked.

"Oh, that was the Cheyennes' Sun Dance. The Sioux borrowed part of the ceremony from the Cheyennes and called it a Sun Dance. It's a renewal of life. When the white men penned us on the reservations they forbade the ceremonies among all the tribes. The missionaries could not stand the sight of us putting roped skewers through incisions in our breasts and then tearing the flesh loose by dancing and pulling at the ropes fastened to the Medicine Lodge pole. Maybe that was our way of baptizing. We never tried to stop the missionaries from baptizing or any of their other practices that seemed barbaric to us." He unbuttoned his shirt and showed the old yellow scars on his pectoral muscles, then rolled up his sleeve to another scar. "No more damaging to me than this smallpox vaccination mark that a dirty-fingered contract surgeon forced on me when we came back here from Canada."

"What is it like, the real world?" I asked.

He remained silent for a while and then spoke slowly. "Being a man who loves words, I've often thought about that. But some things cannot be put into words. The closest I ever came was one English word. Shimmering."

"Shimmering?"

"Yes, like swimming in moonlight." He grinned at me, and I was not certain whether he was teasing or being serious.

"The Cheyenne way of life as you've described it seems idyllic," I said. "Was it really?"

"Idyllic?" he repeated. "Pleasing, picturesque, romantic, I think the word means. I suppose it was all of those things, especially to an outsider like me. Oh, we killed and were killed. We had our quarrels, accidents, pestilences, deaths. But most of our diseases came from the whites. Mainly it was a balanced world that we lived in. We were in harmony with the animals and plants, the forests and waters. When the white men came they destroyed the balance and almost destroyed us. They are still at it. One day there will be only coyotes here."

"Did any of you foresee what was coming?"

"I thought of it more than the others, I suppose because I had seen it happen to the Cherokees. Red Cloud of the Oglala Sioux saw it coming, and later on so did Sitting Bull of the Uncpapas. But none of us dreamed how quickly the storm would sweep over us."

"Was any effort made to unite the tribes in the way that Tecumseh tried in the East?"

"Red Cloud brought all the Sioux, Cheyennes, and Arapaho together, but his world was that paradise along the Yellowstone. The Black Hills, and the valleys of the Powder, the Tongue, and the Little Bighorn. That was his vision of an Indian Nation. But as more and more white men came surging across the Plains, the tribes began to come together in a kind of natural response. Tribes that had long been enemies met in councils and made peace.

"One of the keenest memories of my early time with Big Star's people was a council we held one summer with the Kiowas and Comanches near Bent's Fort. Many years in the past the Cheyennes and Sioux drove those tribes out of the northern paradise into the Southern Plains. For a while the Kiowas and Comanches fought each other over territorial rights, but when they found there was room enough for both they became staunch allies. Now they wanted to be allies with their old enemies the Cheyennes, and so we held council with them. They were fierce, proud, and handsome people, the Kiowas and Comanches, rich in fine horses.

"When the time came for us to exchange presents, the Kiowa chief said that his people had more horses than they needed. 'We do not wish any horses as presents,' he said, 'but we shall be pleased to receive any other gifts.' And so we brought out our best blankets, making a pile on the ground higher than a man. In exchange the Kiowas and Comanches gave us horses, fast-footed little mustangs, so many that some of us received five or six.

"Because Big Star felt the exchange was too much in our favor, he invited all the Kiowas and Comanches to a big feast. I think every kettle we owned was put to use. All the food we had traded for at Bent's Fort was thrown into the kettles—cornmeal, dried apples, beans, and molasses. Our guests declared it to be the finest feast they had ever partaken of, and they must have meant it because they ate everything in the kettles. The next day, after they struck their tipis and moved off to the south, we went back to Bent's Fort and traded some of the horses they had given us for a new supply of blankets, cornmeal, dried apples, beans, and molasses." Laughing softly, Dane got up from his chair, took a long-stemmed pipe from the shelf above the fireplace, and thumbed a charge of shag tobacco into the bowl. After he lighted it with a live coal, he blew the first puff skyward and then compulsively pointed the stem toward the earth and the four directions before drawing more smoke.

"Did you ever return again to the Cherokee Nation?" I asked. "To visit your own people?"

"Oh, yes, a few times. I must tell you about Jotham and his trading post. Fort Carrothers. That changed all our lives. You remember I told you of meeting Jim Carrothers, the old fur trapper turned trader, at Fort Laramie. Well, after the U.S. Army took over the fort and made it a military station, old Jim built himself a trading post east of Laramie—between the Ghost Timbers and Laramie. He called his place Fort Carrothers. Moved his Arapaho wife and family down there and did a lot of trading with the Cheyennes and Sioux. We always stopped at Fort Carrothers going and coming from our winter camp at the Timbers.

"When the Great Medicine Road—the Oregon Trail—got busy with wagons heading for the Far West and Mormons going to Utah, old Jim had more to do than he could handle. One spring when we stopped there on our way north, he asked me if I'd like to go to Independence with him, maybe travel on to St. Louis. 'This old buffaler wants to get away from this place for a spell,' he said. 'From the all-fired figgerin' and the old woman and the young-uns. I'm gettin' on in years and I want to see what it's like back there 'fore I lose my eyesight complete. Besides I can get double money on hides I deliver instead of sellin' 'em to a wagon freighter. I got two wagons and need another driver.'

"I thought about his offer all day, and that night made arrangements to go with him. An old French trapper who worked for Carrothers was to look after the place while he was gone, and Carrothers's Arapaho wife promised me she'd take good care of my family. I helped Sweet Medicine Woman get our tipi fixed up behind the trading post, alongside a clean little stream. She did not want me to go. She cried through most of the night before Jim and I left for the East. I guess she thought I was deserting her.

"Carrothers gave me trading credit for some white man's clothes for the journey, and when Sweet Medicine Woman saw me dressed in broadcloth trousers, black boots, and a linen shirt, she turned her back on me and refused to say good-bye. After four years of wearing buckskins, I didn't feel at ease myself in those clothes for several days.

"But old Jim and I were like a pair of workhorses set free, with no cares except for the two wagonloads of hides and furs. Only thing that upset us was the constant stream of covered wagons we kept meeting on our way, long trains of wagons filled with men, women, and children. 'Good God!' Jim kept saying. 'Looks like the whole damned white race is running after the western sun. Oughta be plenty room left back East for old Mountain Men and Indians.'

"Well, there didn't seem to be any shortage of people in the towns we saw springing up along the Missouri. A whole new town had been built west of Independence. They called the place Westport Landing, and it looked to us as if all the steamboats in the world were gathered in the river waiting to unload. I soon discovered that Mr. Louis Tessier had built a new warehouse at Westport Landing, and he generously offered Carrothers and me the use of one of his rooms for our quarters. Mr. Tessier said that William and Jotham still traded with him and he was expecting one or the other of them to arrive almost any day from the Cherokee Nation to buy supplies. I felt a wave of homesickness for the old family, just thinking about them.

"One morning I was down at the landing watching the steamboats unloading when I noticed a young boy doing the same thing a few yards in front of me. Something in his stance seemed familiar. His brown-streaked sandy hair sprayed out from beneath a round-topped hat that was too small for him. I was circling around to get a better look at the boy's face when a voice came from right behind me. 'That's him all right, Dane. Except for his lighter skin and hair he could be you, back in Okelogee.'

"I whirled around. 'Jotham!' I yelled, and after we'd embraced, pounded each other, and laughed wildly, he called Pleasant over to us. The boy shook hands and studied me with considerable curiosity. I could see Jerusha in his pale blue eyes, and I felt that old sense of something treasured lost forever.

"Afterward Jotham told me that Pleasant had quarreled with his stepfather, the Reverend Crookes, and had run away from home. Jotham tracked him down and persuaded him to become an apprentice blacksmith. 'He's a good worker, and I don't blame him for not wanting to live with old Crookes. I don't know how Jerusha can endure that man.'

"Jotham and Pleasant slept in their wagons behind Mr. Tessier's warehouse, and during the next three or four days we spent a good deal of time together. Jim Carrothers and Jotham took a liking to each other, and one evening old Jim announced that he was going to sell Fort Carrothers to Jotham, and buy himself a spread of ground for a log cabin on one of the ridges above Westport Landing. 'I'll put two porches on it,' he said. 'One to set watchin' the sun go down in the west and t'other to set watchin' the steamboats in the river.'

"I could see that Jotham was excited by the idea of owning his own trading post somewhere out West. He and Jim spent hours talking about prices and credits. However, I never thought anything would come of it. Carrothers didn't seem to be the kind of man who would want to live near a crowded place like Westport Landing, and I knew Jotham did not have very much money. But the world is full of wonders, and the next spring a real surprise was waiting for me at Fort Carrothers."

33

In the spring of 1849, when Big Star's Cheyennes left their winter camp in the Ghost Timbers and started north, they noticed more than the customary activity on the Great Medicine Road. Wagons drawn by oxen and mules, and many men on horseback, moved along at a swifter pace than usual, and the Cheyennes wondered why the *Veheos* were in such a hurry.

What Dane and his friends were witnessing was the first mad rush of white easterners toward the goldfields of California. This human flood was also a signal of doom for their way of life, but on that fine spring morning in the Moon When the Ponies Shed, the Cheyennes were unaware of the ominous meaning of the dust-clouded trail.

They kept to the south side of the Platte, across from the wagon trains, until they sighted Fort Carrothers. There they crossed the river at a sandy-bottomed ford so shallow they did not have to unload the travois. Dane rode near the head of the column. Beside him was five-year-old Swift Eagle on a gentle gray pony. Little Cloud, still too young to ride horseback, was strapped on the travois behind Sweet Medicine Woman's bay mount.

As he swung around to the front of the trading post, Dane was annoyed to find a dozen Conestogas drawn up there, with white men, women, and children swarming in and out of the entrance and chattering like a flock of hungry birds. He had been looking forward to camping there for a day or so, making a few leisurely trades, and talking with old Jim Carrothers. But an overnight stop was out of the question because all the young grass for as far as he could see had been grazed to the roots by passing teams of mules and oxen.

He glanced back and saw that Big Star's face reflected the same feelings of disappointment and aversion. Dane noticed then that blacksmith equipment had been installed under an open shed beside the main building. To his amazement he recognized Bibbs, who was shoeing a horse, and Pleasant, who was assisting a big solemn-faced immigrant in resetting a wagon tire. Dane dropped off his horse in an instant, his eyes meeting those of the black man. "Holy Ghost!" Bibbs cried out. "Dane! They told me you'd turned into a wild Injun, and damn if you ain't done it." Bibbs dropped his tools on the ground and offered a sweaty hand. Pleasant quickly joined them, staring at his father's Cheyenne clothing with intense interest.

Soon they were all there, Jotham bounding excitedly about and running back inside to bring Griffa, who seemed uncertain as to whether she should embrace her old friend Dane or keep a respectful distance from what appeared to be a wild Indian in buckskins. Dane helped Sweet Medicine Woman dismount to shake hands shyly with her husband's relatives. After that the children had to be shown, Swift Eagle and Little Cloud, and then Griffa quickly rounded up her and Jotham's pair. They had named their boy Opothle after Jotham's father, but called him Young Opothle. He was a year older than Swift Eagle. Meggi, the little girl, was only four, and she broke into screams of fright when Dane reached out his arms for her. "She has Grandmother Mary's voice," he said.

"Ah, yes," Jotham agreed proudly. "She is much like Akusa Amayi."

"I wish she were with us," Dane said. "If William's family and Prissie were here, all Mary's blood would be together again."

Jotham laughed. "William and Prissie think I'm a madman for taking on this post in the wild West. I don't know which of them is the worst old woman."

Meanwhile the whites had all come outside the trading post, gathering for mutual protection around their wagons. Most of their attention was upon Big Star and the Cheyennes, who had moved off about a hundred yards with their travois. The whites were gaping and pointing and murmuring among themselves.

Jim Carrothers appeared suddenly out of the entrance. "Damn me!" he cried, "so it's Big Star's people caused all this commotion. Dane, old friend, me and Jotham been meanin' to ride over to the Timbers, but every day we get crowds of these crazy fool gold hunters. I oughta be on the trail to Westport right now, but I can't bring myself to forsake this greenhorn lad." Carrothers blew out a breath of air that fluttered the ends of his drooping yellow mustache. "Now you're here, old friend, you can take my place. Stay at Fort Carrothers and grow rich with your cousin. These daft gold hunters bound for Californ-i-a seem well supplied with money. They'll pay three dollars a horse for shoein', and if you'd largen my corral and stock it with good horses you could do right good at tradin' for their wore-out animals."

"What I need right now," Jotham broke in, "is a wagon man to bring supplies from Westport. We're out of soap and brandy, getting low on gunpowder. I need you, Dane."

While they were talking, Sweet Medicine Woman had moved in close beside Dane, and when he felt her hand on his arm, he turned and saw the distress on her face. She had learned enough English from him to get the meaning of what Carrothers and Jotham were proposing. "*E-have-se-va,*" she whispered. "It is bad. *Maka-eta,* money. It is bad. I will not stay here. If you stay, I will go with my people." He caught her hand in his, pressing it reassuringly.

"*Na-tsi-sta,*" he said to Jotham, using the Cheyenne so that Sweet Medicine Woman would understand what he was saying. "I am Cheyenne now. *Zes-tan.* Cheyenne. Cherokee only by blood. This is not my life, Jotham."

"I told you, greenhorn," Carrothers said, slapping Jotham on the back. "Your Cherokee cousin's gone pure wild Indian."

Before the Cheyennes left Fort Carrothers, Dane met one more member of the "family" that had been transplanted so quickly from the Cherokee Nation. At the last minute, while Dane was tightening saddles and travois, Bibbs brought his new wife out to the horses. "Wewoka," he said proudly. Wewoka was half Seminole, half black, a slave who had escaped from her Seminole owner and made her way across Indian Territory to the Cherokees, where Bibbs had met her. "Reverend Crookes, he married us, Dane, so we all proper and legal. Then Mr. William and Jotham made me a freedman and they say Wewoka is freedwoman, too."

Wewoka had strange luminous eyes with a violet sheen in them, but Dane could see fear in them, too, and it disturbed him when he realized that he and the Cheyennes were the objects of her fear. What tales, what lurid falsehoods had she heard of the savage tribes of the Plains that inspired her ill-concealed terror?

Later that day, he was reminded of this again when they approached another of their favorite camping stops, a willow-shaded greensward along Lodgepole Creek. A number of covered wagons were already there, arranged in a semicircle, and when the outer guards saw the Cheyennes approaching, they arose with rifles at the ready. Dane heard Big Star's exclamation of disgust as the chief raised an arm in a signal for his caravan to turn away. There was plenty of room along the creek for the Cheyennes to have camped there, too, but the white men feared them. The Cheyennes left the Oregon Trail and the Platte behind them and went into the sanctuary of the dry sandhills, camping at nightfall without water.

That was the summer they followed a great buffalo herd from the Powder River country down to the North Platte, and it was the summer that Dane met Red Cloud of the Oglala Sioux. The Oglalas followed the same herd, and they camped nearby the Cheyennes all through the Moon of Red Cherries. Both tribes ran short of ammunition, and a dozen or so young men from each camp, including Dane and Red Cloud, decided to travel to Fort Laramie for gunpowder and musket balls. They were three days on the journey and they made of it a summer pleasure outing—that is, until they reached Fort Laramie. There they were told quite firmly by the licensed trader that he was forbidden by the U.S. Army to trade either guns or ammunition to "hostile" Indians.

They were angered by such treatment. After all, they had

been dealing with traders most of their lives, giving double value for half value in most cases, and now to be suddenly denied the use of firearms they took as a gross insult. Dane at last calmed them down by suggesting that they ride on another two days to Fort Carrothers.

On this part of the journey, Dane spent most of his time with Red Cloud, learning Lakota words, and teaching English words to his companion. The future leader of the Oglalas was then in his late twenties, a few years younger than Dane, and when he learned of Dane's origins he began plying him with numerous questions about the White Nation in the East, expressing a desire to visit there sometime to see the great villages.

After they turned into the trail along the Platte, they met several long wagon trains. Red Cloud's reaction was somewhat the same as Jim Carrothers's when he and Dane were traveling to Westport Landing—that the numerous white emigrants must be leaving the East empty of people. "Count the blades of grass on these plains," Dane said to him, "and you will know the numbers of the whites."

Traveling on toward Fort Carrothers, Red Cloud was dismayed by the overgrazed prairies that were already beginning to erode, by the destruction of cottonwood groves where his people had wintered when he was a boy, and by the total absence of wild game where it had once been so plentiful. When they reached the Lodgepole Creek camping site, it was Dane's turn to express disgust. The friendly willows had all been cut away and the once pure waters of the creek were fouled by a dead oxen, a broken wagon, discarded kegs, harness, tins, boxes, and other offscourings of the passing whites.

"They are worse than summer locusts," Red Cloud said, "like maggots eating at the heart of our land."

At Fort Carrothers, Jotham and the others were delighted to see Dane again, although they seemed to be wary of his fierce and demanding companions. Jotham also had been ordered to trade no arms or ammunition to "hostile" Indians, but as Dane was a "civilized" Cherokee and therefore not "hostile," a sale of a considerable quantity was made to him. They left under the cover of night, their saddlepacks filled with powder and lead.

All the way to their camps on the North Platte, Red Cloud and Dane discussed the lengthening shadow over their way of life, agreeing that the only hope of survival for their people was to keep the whites from invading the north—the valleys of the Powder, Tongue, and Yellowstone, and the sacred Black Hills.

34

"I have met few men, Indian or white, as strong in purpose as Red Cloud was then," Dane said. "He would get a thought in his head and let it grow there. When the troubles came he knew what to do, and the other chiefs listened and followed him. Red Cloud won many victories, but in the end he had to compromise to survive and the spirit went out of him. I went to see him the last time I visited Pine Ridge. He's almost blind, hair whiter than mine, but still a man whose face is pleasing to look upon.

"He brought presents to our camp on the Powder when he heard a daughter had been born to Sweet Medicine Woman. Blankets and bear-claw necklaces and earrings. Most of the young Cheyenne women in our camp gathered around just to look at this handsome young man from the Oglalas. At that time in his life, Red Cloud was always getting into trouble over women, other men's wives, because he was so handsome and showy.

"That day on the Powder he ignored the young women, though. He had other things on his mind. After he gave Sweet Medicine Woman the presents, he asked what name she was going to call our first girl child. 'Amayi,' she told him, 'Dane wants her named for his grandmother.'

"'Amayi. That is not a Cheyenne name,' he said.

"'Muskogean,' I explained, 'Creek.'

"'It has a good sound in my ears,' he said, and then grasped my arm. 'I want to talk with you. Let's go where there are not so many gabbling girls.'

"Red Cloud wanted to talk about a great council that was to be held soon at Fort Laramie. Broken Hand Fitzpatrick, an agent for the United States, had been visiting the tribes between the Missouri River and the Arkansas, inviting them to this council, promising many valuable presents to all who would attend. Most of the Indians liked Broken Hand. He and Jim Carrothers had come west together to trap for pelts and like Carrothers he had an Indian wife and family. But our leaders were suspicious of this council.

"'What do you think they want, the *Wasicus?*' Red Cloud used the Lakota word for white men.

"'They want our land,' I said, and told him how the *Wasicus* had wormed their way into Cherokee lands by first beguiling the chiefs into letting them build roads and trading posts and forts.

"Sure enough, when we all went down to Fort Laramie, in the Drying-Grass Moon, the first thing the agents from Washington asked for was a promise from all the chiefs to protect travelers along the Oregon Trail and on any other roads that might be built through our country. That council at Laramie was the greatest gathering of Indians in our people's history, more than were on the Little Bighorn when Custer foolishly attacked us. So many came that the agents had to move us several miles down to Horse Creek so there would be enough grass for the horses that numbered in the thousands, and room for the tipis that stretched as far as the eye could reach. The remarkable thing was that half the tribes there were old enemies of the other half—Sioux and Arikara, Cheyenne and Crow, Arapaho and Shoshone, as well as Assiniboin, Hidatsa, and Mandan. For almost a moon we camped together with only a few dragoons in fancy blue uniforms to keep us apart. If we'd wanted to fight each other, those dragoons would've been run over and trampled into the ground.

"As it was, the only trouble we had was caused by a hot-tempered dragoon officer. One day, at the request of the agents, Lean Bear led his Dog Soldiers in a mock battle, using only hand signals to control the movements of his horsed warriors in fast turns and charges while they pretended to fight with their guns, lances, and bows and arrows. After the show ended, Lean Bear rode up to the big tent where the council meetings were held. He dismounted and bowed to the agents and army officers, who were clapping their hands. He was leading his horse off to make room for a parade of Oglala warriors when he passed a buggy in which a dragoon officer was sitting with his wife. This woman's hand was dangling over the side of the buggy and on one of her fingers was a ring that sparkled bright in the sunlight —a diamond, I suppose. Now, Lean Bear was always attracted to beautiful things. He had quite a collection of jewels—bracelets, rings, necklaces. Impulsively he reached for the woman's hand to examine the glittering ring, probably to compliment her, but she screamed. Her husband grabbed his buggy whip and slashed Lean Bear across the neck and shoulder. Lean Bear might've killed that officer on the spot if several dragoons had not moved in on him. Without a word then, he mounted, rode back to our Cheyenne camp, and painted his face black and white. He was riding through the tipis, summoning his Dog Soldiers to battle against the dragoons to avenge the insult, when Big Star, his uncle, came from the council tent to try to calm him down. Finally Broken Hand Fitzpatrick settled the matter by arranging for the dragoon officer to present Lean Bear with a fine blanket and offer an apology.

"As I have said, what the government agents wanted us there for was to make a treaty—which meant take some of our land— and to do this they insisted that each tribe be represented by a chief. The Cheyennes of course did not have one chief. We had many chiefs, of many small bands. Little Wolf and Dull Knife were from the Rosebud country and Black Kettle was from the Arkansas River country hundreds of miles to the south. Big Star's people moved back and forth. And there were many others. At

last we settled on old Wannesahta, keeper of the Cheyennes' sacred medicine arrows. Wannesahta was no more a chief than I
was, and did not want to be a chief, but he went to the council
meetings as our chief.

"Because I spoke English and Cheyenne, I was chosen to be
the tribe's interpreter, and so I had an inside view of how clever
the white agents were at cheating the Indians through treaties.
First they talked about the Oregon Trail being only a narrow
piece of ground no wider than two wagon wheels, but the way
they worded the treaty they were taking the whole Platte Valley
for miles across. They talked about the vast areas in which each
of the tribes would live free of white intrusion, but at the same
time they introduced provisions for more roads, with forts to protect them, wherever the whites might wish to build roads.

"Every night I talked about this with Big Star, who as a little
chief was allowed to attend the councils. 'Why would the whites
want to build a road and forts through our country?' he would
ask. 'There is no gold beyond the Yellowstone.'

" 'Someday they may find gold there, or something else they
want,' I would say. 'If they come into our country they will never
leave.'

"Red Cloud saw the treaty the way I did, but there was nothing he could do about it then. The agents named Brave Bear, a
Brule, as chief of all the Sioux, although the Oglalas far outnumbered the Brules. Red Cloud's uncle, Old Smoke, and Whirlwind and Red Water attended the council only as little chiefs of
the Oglalas. All that Red Cloud could do was fume about Brave
Bear being a trading-post loafer who would do whatever the
agents wanted him to do.

"The way they divided up the land for the different tribes
satisfied no one. The Sioux were given the Black Hills, although
that was sacred Cheyenne Territory. The Crows were given land
from the Bighorns to Powder River, although that was Sioux and
Cheyenne hunting grounds. The Cheyennes' northern boundary
was the North Platte, although most of our northern cousins
lived far above that river. The white agents solved that difficulty
by saying that any tribe could hunt where it pleased so long as

its people lived in its assigned home area. Red Cloud and I had a good laugh about that.

"For nine days the chiefs and the agents argued and harangued and then the treaty was laid out on a table, just about the way the agents had written it before the council began. The agents did agree to let us trade for arms and ammunition to be used for hunting, but we could not hunt in the Platte Valley or anywhere near where other roads might be built. After this was settled, the chiefs came up and marked their X's and we interpreters wrote their names beside the X's. Then each chief was marched into a small tent to be presented special presents. These were dragoon uniforms, light blue trousers and dark blue frock coats with gold buttons and epaulets. They were also given big medals to wear around their necks and handwritten copies of the treaty with a wax seal and scarlet ribbon. The medals had clasped hands on one side and an engraving of President Millard Fillmore on the other.

"The chiefs were told to put on the uniforms and medals and stand together outside the tent with the dragoon officers while an artist from Washington sketched their portraits. The chiefs looked very ill at ease, but most of them were proud of those uniforms. Big Star kept his for several years, wearing it only for important occasions, one of them being the day the soldiers killed him.

"After the artist finished his sketches, a dragoon fired off a little cannon that stood beside the tent, and a train of wagons loaded with bolts of calico and bags of flour, sugar, and coffee rolled into the grounds. The soldiers dumped all these presents out on the ground and the chiefs spent the rest of the day dividing them up. The treaty promised us similar presents every year for fifteen years, but in later years the government agents kept most of the goods themselves and sold them secretly to traders.

"In that time of our prosperity none of us really needed the things they gave us at Horse Creek. We could have obtained enough buffalo hides in one day's hunt in the Powder River country to trade for all those goods. Another fool thing the government agents did—they slaughtered about a hundred beef cattle they'd driven all the way from Westport Landing, and invited us to a barbecue along the creek. A few of us went down there, but the meat was stringy and tasted too sweet. We left most of the carcasses to the flies. After living on white man's food through the Drying-Grass Moon, we were ready for some buffalo tongues and beaver tails. And so in a day the thousands of tipis were struck, ending the first big land-steal in the West."

35

During the winter following the treaty council at Fort Laramie, Dane's second daughter was born while they were camped in the Ghost Timbers. Sweet Medicine Woman named her Susa, and shortly afterward Dane took his family over to Fort Carrothers for a celebration with Jotham and Griffa's family. During the several days they were all together, Sweet Medicine Woman lost much of her shyness with her husband's *Sanaki* relatives. She became especially fond of seventeen-year-old Pleasant because he spent so much time romping with his half brothers, Swift Eagle and Little Cloud, carrying them about for hours on his back. She told Pleasant that she was adopting him as a son, and he bragged about this to everybody who would listen.

One day Bibbs and his Seminole-Negro wife brought in a rocking horse they had made of strong blacksmith's iron, carved wood, and blanket cloth, as a birth present for Susa. Wewoka had painted the horse in brilliant reds and yellows, and everyone exclaimed over its beauty. Three-year-old Amayi thought the horse was meant for her, and Dane told her that she could ride it until she was old enough for a live pony, and then she must give the make-believe horse to Susa.

On the morning that Dane was preparing to return to the Timbers with his family, Pleasant sought him out in the corral. "Is it because of my pale skin that you don't like me as well as your Cheyenne sons?" he asked.

Dane was startled by the question. "I like you equally as well as my other children," he said.

"Then why do I not live with you?"

"I thought you were happier here," Dane replied, although he admitted to himself that he had never considered the matter.

"Sweet Medicine Woman told me of the good times you have every summer in the north. I think she would like me to come with you this year."

"Then by all means come," Dane said. "It is different from any life you have ever known. You may not like it, but a summer of buffalo hunting under the sun will darken that pale skin you worry about."

And so that spring, Pleasant rode north with the Cheyennes. He would not wear a breechclout because he did not want too much of his pale skin to show, but Dane found him a pair of old buckskin trousers and a long-sleeved shirt made of bighorn skin and he seemed satisfied.

Although Dane was apprehensive that Pleasant might not be accepted, the boy quickly won the approval of almost all of Big Star's Cheyennes. The girls liked his tawny hair and blue eyes, and the young men admired the reckless way in which he hunted buffalo. Then Lean Bear took him under his tutelage, helping him with Cheyenne ways and ceremonies. One day after they made a permanent camp on the North Platte, Lean Bear came to Dane and announced that the Dog Soldiers were planning a horse raid against the Shoshones. He wanted to take Pleasant along as a guest.

"We promised the treaty agents at Laramie," Dane reminded him, "that we would remain at peace with our old enemies."

"Oh, we are not going to war with the Shoshones," Lean Bear answered. "We will merely capture some of their horses. They have more than they need. Where else would we get horses if not from the Shoshones and Crows?"

Dane laughed. "All right. You may take my son along if you promise to look after him and curb his recklessness."

"I will treat him as my own son," Lean Bear promised.

Lean Bear and his Dog Soldiers found a Shoshone camp with many horses over on the Sweetwater. The raid ended up in a running fight, with each side inflicting minor wounds on the other. Lean Bear cleverly maneuvered the foray so that the choicest pair of horses, Appaloosas with beautiful symmetrical markings on their rumps, fell into Pleasant's hands. Pleasant got his ropes on them in a flash and raced off with all the coolness of a veteran raider.

The attitudes of the other Dog Soldiers toward the good fortune of their young guest varied from envy to admiration, but if any of them suspected that Pleasant's luck was largely the result of Lean Bear's maneuvering, they said nothing of it.

Soon after they broke away from the pursuing Shoshones, they came upon a temporary camp of Arapahos who had ventured up the Sweetwater for the same purpose as the Cheyennes. Lean Bear decided to spend the night with the Arapahos for added support in case the Shoshones managed to enlarge their forces for a renewal of the chase.

The captured horse herd immediately attracted the Arapahos, and Pleasant's Appaloosas became the center of attention. Several warriors were eager to trade for one or both of the mottled horses. At first Pleasant declined all their offers, and then one of the older Arapahos brought out a parfleche container, unlaced the rawhide fastenings, and removed two strange glittering objects. One was a Spanish coat of mail, the other a metal headpiece with a flap to protect the wearer's neck. The Arapaho had obtained these things from a Mexican many years before, trading ponies for them. He had kept them well, burnishing away any evidence of rust whenever it appeared. But now he was ready to exchange them for a Palouse. All his life he had wanted a Palouse. He would trade the iron shirt and headpiece for Pleasant's two Appaloosas.

Pleasant examined the coat of mail carefully. It was made of small metal rings and scales closely interwoven and then sewed upon a shirt of thick goatskin. He put it on and found that it reached to his waist, suiting his small frame as well as it fit the Spaniard who had brought it to America two centuries before. In the end, Pleasant got the coat in exchange for one of his horses. He had no use, he said, for the iron hat.

Next day when the Dog Soldiers left the Arapaho camp, Pleasant wore the coat of mail, cantering proudly along on his remaining Appaloosa. Late in the afternoon as they were approaching the place where Poison Spider Creek flows into the North Platte, not far from the Oregon Trail bridge crossing of the river, they saw a patrol of bluecoated cavalry coming toward them. The Cheyennes had heard that some soldiers were stationed at the bridge, but this was the first time they had seen any of them. Lean Bear signaled his Dog Soldiers to a halt and they waited in line for the soldiers to come up to them. While they waited, Lean Bear counted the Bluecoats. Twenty-six, or six more than the number of Dog Soldiers he had brought along for the raid. The cavalrymen would be much better armed and were not burdened with a herd of captured ponies. Lean Bear signaled his warriors to make ready their guns and bows.

The cavalrymen halted about forty yards away, a young lieutenant moving a few paces to the front of them. "We want to inspect your horses," he called out.

Lean Bear, not being certain what the lieutenant meant, glanced at Pleasant.

"We took them from the Shoshones," Pleasant replied. He remembered that three of the horses had U.S. brands on their flanks. A Dog Soldier named Sata had captured one and then traded for the other two. Sata admired the U.S. markings.

"We're coming up!" the lieutenant shouted, evidently relieved to hear English spoken, but he was also puzzled by Pleasant's coat of mail. "We've lost a dozen mounts, stolen by somebody."

The cavalrymen approached at a slow pace, circling around into the horse herd until they sighted the U.S. brands. They began cutting out the three horses from the herd. A sergeant was looping ropes over their necks when Sata danced his mount over beside him, seizing the ties. "They are my horses!" he shouted in Cheyenne. "We took them from the Shoshones."

The sergeant unslung his carbine and waved him away. Sata pulled an old pistol from his belt. "Shoot him!" the lieutenant ordered. The carbine bullet knocked Sata off his horse.

For a moment there was a confusion of movement. The frightened horse herd began to scatter. The lieutenant shouted orders in a high excited voice, and his men drew away, forming a line of defense, the sergeant leading the three army horses off to one side.

Sata was badly wounded, but he forced himself up on his knees, screaming for his horses. Lean Bear signaled his warriors into a single rank, facing the soldiers.

"I'm going to make them empty their guns," Pleasant said, reaching for Lean Bear's lance. "When they have emptied their guns, rush them and take back Sata's horses before they can reload."

"No!" Lean Bear cried. "Today I am your father and I forbid it!"

Pleasant kicked the Appaloosa into a fast run, holding the lance straight, heading for the lieutenant. "Kill him!" the lieutenant shouted. Pleasant swung the Palouse to the right, leaning out of the saddle so as to use his mount for a shield. Carbines crackled along the line, and then he heard the cries of the onrushing Dog Soldiers, the pounding of their ponies' hooves.

When the cavalrymen fled in disorder, Lean Bear killed the sergeant himself to stop him from taking Sata's horses. But the Appaloosa went down, blood gushing from its neck, and died with Pleasant sitting beside its outstretched head, crying. Not long after they rounded up their scattered herd, Sata died. They put him on a burial scaffold, led the three horses with the U.S. markings up beside it, and slew them with arrows. That night when they camped, Pleasant found two bullets enmeshed in the interlaced rings of his Spanish coat of mail.

36

"After that skirmish with the Bluecoat horse soldiers," Dane said, "the Cheyennes looked upon Pleasant as a young man of strong medicine. They called him Iron Shirt, and he became a Dog Soldier, a high honor for one so young. But he didn't seem to want to be singled out. He preferred to be alone much of the time, brooding and wondering to himself if he were an Indian or a white man. He gave the coat of mail to Sweet Medicine Woman to keep for him. Sometimes he would ask for it to clean rust specks off the metal, and then he would tell her to put it away again. Often at night in our tipi I would be awakened by moans and cries of fright from Pleasant's bed and I knew he was having terrible visions in his dreams.

"One day I was down on a sandbar with Swift Eagle and Little Cloud, telling them Cherokee ghost stories. I had taught both of them how to write their names in English, as well as a few English words, and while I was telling a story Swift Eagle took a stick and scratched his name in the sand. He then made a drawing of the wolf I was telling about and wrote *W-o-l-f* under it.

"'He can write words!' Pleasant cried out behind us. He had crept down to the riverbank so silently that I did not know he was there. Lean Bear taught him how to do that.

"'I can write my name, too,' Little Cloud boasted, pulling at his brother's stick.

"'Why is it that you never showed me how to write?' Pleasant asked in a tone of reproach.

"'Surely you can read and write,' I said.

"'Jerusha taught me how to pen my name.'

"'You never had any schooling in the Nation?'

"He shook his head. 'Reverend Crookes said words to me to put in my memory. But not to read or write.' He shrugged. 'What use has an Indian for such things!' He jumped down on the sandbar, dragging a moccasin across the letters that Swift Eagle had made, erasing them.

"'I'll teach you how to write words,' I said, but he was already running away down the riverbank.

"Another time not long after that, I found him brooding on a hilltop, facing toward the east, his face sad and dreary like an old man's.

"'How far is the Nation, how many days' travel?' he asked.

"'Are you sick for home?' I said.

"'I want to see my mother, Jerusha, again,' he replied. 'I want to be a white man instead of an Indian.'

"'You could go to the seminary at Tahlequah,' I suggested. 'They can teach you to live as a white man.'

"I was surprised at his eager response. He wanted to start that very day.

"In spite of Sweet Medicine Woman's earnest objections, Pleasant and I were on our way the next morning. During the days of the Drying-Up Moon that we spent together on trails to the Indian Territory, I came to truly know my half-blood son for the first time. The only other people we talked with while going there were our relatives at Fort Carrothers. The night we stopped at the trading post we changed to white man's clothes and I made an arrangement with Jotham so that I could use buffalo skins to pay for Pleasant's schooling in the Cherokee Nation.

"There is nothing like close travel with one companion to bring out strengths and weaknesses that may be overlooked in ordinary living. I soon discovered that Pleasant's reckless ways were only a mask for his fears. He talked once about the charge he made against the soldiers so they would empty their guns, confessing that he could never have done that without the coat of mail which was a mask over his fears. He still had terrible dreams about that, he said, feeling in his own flesh the bullets that penetrated the flesh of his shield, the Appaloosa.

"Day by day as we moved southward his spirits brightened, and when we rode into Tahlequah, he was almost singing with gladness. We soon found Mr. Ebenezer Keys's Seminary for Young Males, and I enrolled Pleasant for the coming year. Mr. Keys was a friendly little man from New England, and he promised me that Pleasant would receive the best instruction in reading, spelling, arithmetic, and geography, to be taught both in Cherokee and English.

"The next day Pleasant and I rode out to the crossroads to see Jerusha. She had no knowledge that we were in the Nation, and was almost overcome with surprise and joy. She embarrassed her eighteen-year-old son with hugs and kisses, treating him like a long-lost child. The solemn Reverend Crookes had little to say to us, and I soon left Pleasant there to spend the night while I went over to stay with William and Tatsuwha. William was beginning to show his age. He had turned fifty years and was quite reserved of manner, but he was hospitable and wanted to know everything I could tell him about Jotham and Griffa and the Fort Carrothers trading post.

"That evening in the moonlight I walked over to the burying ground to visit Creek Mary's grave. The churchyard was filled with wagons and buggies, and the high-pitched voice of Reverend Crookes rang from the open windows of the church, warning of the hand of death, the grim messenger of God, the scourge of strong drink, and the wickedness that desolated the Cherokee Nation.

"I was standing under a walnut tree that overlooked the simple cedar marker of Akusa Amayi when I was startled by a figure in white, flitting along, avoiding patches of moonlight to keep within the shadows. For a moment I thought this was a ghost, but then I knew it was Jerusha. She stopped close beside me, breathing hard. 'I saw you from the church window,' she said. 'When he kneeled to pray I slipped out. I can stay only a minute.' She sucked in a deep breath. 'I want to thank you for bringing Pleasant back to me. He is all that I can have of you.'

"I did not know what to say, so I reached out and took her hand, and then she moved against me, her arms tightening around me, her lips warm against my cheek, her whole body pressing against me so that I could feel the thinness of her legs. She shivered then and drew away quickly, running toward the church. As I have said, I believe Jerusha's feelings went beyond the limits of the heart.

"For her I felt a great tenderness, and on my lonely journey back to Fort Carrothers my thoughts were much on Jerusha and our son Pleasant. I had grown attached to the boy. There was a frailty in both of them, a constant searching for strength to draw upon. To survive, the weak must feed on the hearts of the strong.

"More than three years passed before I saw Pleasant again. After he learned to write, he would scrawl short letters to me, sending them by the stagecoach mail to Fort Carrothers. I would pick them up whenever I stopped at Jotham's place, sometimes months after they were written, and I answered every one.

"Within him seethed a pitiless conflict between his Indian and white blood, and after reading his letters I often recalled the night with Saviah Manning when she told me of how she and Jotham were much alike, their white blood contesting with the Indian in them. Yet Jotham seemed to have made peace with himself. He was more white than Indian, the passing travelers often asking him if he were Portuguese or Spanish or of some other dark-skinned race, seldom suspecting that this post trader in white man's clothing, speaking their language as well as they, was a half-blood of the native peoples they feared or despised.

"After Pleasant left the school, he worked awhile for Mr. Tim Rogers, but he found blacksmithing tiresome and tried to make his way by hunting and trapping in the Boston Mountains over in Arkansas. I remember well the last letter I received from him. 'My means are failing,' he wrote. 'My relatives are poor. I have no means of profitably employing my time. To disperse care and trouble, I have turned to drinking whiskey.'

"A few weeks after that Pleasant suddenly appeared at Fort Carrothers. He arrived on one of the Overland Mail stagecoaches that had begun making daily stops at the trading post on regular runs over the trail to California. Jotham and Bibbs begged him to stay and help with the blacksmithing, but after a day or so he joined me and my family in our tipi at the Ghost Timbers. He discarded his ill-fitting black broadcloth for buckskins, and when we started north Pleasant was with us, his mind firmly made up to follow the ways of the Cheyennes.

"That summer he married one of Magpie Eagle's nieces, a pretty girl named Rising Fawn, and his pathway might have been smooth had it not been for one thing—the craving for whiskey that had begun to afflict him while he was in the Indian Territory. In the old days he could have fought it down, would have had to fight it down, but by this time white men were bringing whiskey on the trails in wagons, setting up whiskey stores on wheels, and moving to some other place after trading to Indians who could not obtain strong drink at the licensed trading posts.

"Whenever Pleasant had buffalo skins to trade, he would seek out a whiskey wagon and come back to camp so drunk he could not stand on his feet. One evening he challenged me in front of our tipi, raging at me, blaming me because I had fathered him from a white woman so that he was neither an Indian nor a white man. The more I tried to soothe him the angrier he became, frightening Sweet Medicine Woman with his threats to kill me for creating him. At last in one of his rages he fell senseless upon the ground, and I carried him to Rising Fawn, who cried over him through the night.

"Some days afterward in that same summer, Pleasant and three of his friends, all Dog Soldiers, were hunting for blacktailed deer along the Upper Platte when they came in sight of the Oregon Trail bridge crossing. They were in territory where they were forbidden to hunt, and should not have been there, but they had drunk some whiskey, so they had more recklessness about them than good sense. From the hill where they stopped they could see the bridge and the stockade at one end in which the soldiers lived. At the other end of the bridge grazed a small herd of picketed horses, with one soldier guarding them.

"'Look,' Pleasant said, 'those soldiers down there are the ones who killed Sata after we raided the Shoshones with Lean Bear. They owe us three horses.'

"He and his companions talked about this for a while. Most likely none of the soldiers were the same ones who had been there three years before, and they probably knew nothing about Sata and the horses. Also there were two or three times as many soldiers in the stockade as those they had chased that day near Poison Spider Creek, and there were only four Dog Soldiers now. Yet they foolishly decided to rush down upon the herd, shoot the guard, and capture three U.S. horses.

"Because the soldiers were not expecting such a foolhardy raid, the four Dog Soldiers got away with three horses, leaving the scalped guard behind. However, Pleasant and his companions had hardly crossed the hills when a bunch of mounted Bluecoats came swarming after them. The first that we in our camp knew about this was the clatter of hooves and the sight of the four Dog Soldiers galloping into our midst. 'Bluecoats coming!' one of them shouted, and of course we all started helping the women and children run to cover. There was no time to dismantle tipis or pack anything. We hurried to arm ourselves with whatever we could get our hands on—guns, bows, lances, clubs, knives. While we were doing these things the soldiers set fire to some high dry grass on the slope above the camp, and a strong wind swept clouds of black smoke down upon us.

"Out of this smoke the soldiers charged us with drawn sabers, yelling furiously. Some carried burning sheaves of grass which they tossed on our tipis. Others dismounted and used our own campfires to set bedding and robes and tipis to blazing. Those who kept to their saddles struck down with their sabers anyone they came within reach of—children, women, old people.

"Because of the suddenness of their attack, we barely had time to strike back before they were gone, taking many of our horses with them. I'm sure I shot one soldier in the leg with my carbine. He was grimacing and squeezing the fleshy part of his thigh as he galloped away from me. And then I saw another dash by with an arrow deep in his shoulder. They suffered some punishment, but we suffered far more.

"Luckily for my family, we were camped at the farther end of the village from where the soldiers came in. Sweet Medicine Woman had time to get our four children into some thick brush along the river, and no damage was done to our tipi. For others it was worse. The young son of my brother-in-law, Yellow Hawk, received a bad saber cut on one arm, and we had great difficulty in stopping the flow of blood. Yellow Hawk and his wife, and several other families who were camped upstream lost their tipis and most of their buffalo robes, saddles, and parfleches to fire.

"As soon as Big Star was certain the soldiers had gone back to the bridge station, he called a council. We learned that we had lost two to death. One was a member of the Crooked Lance society who had tried to stop a soldier from setting fire to his tipi and was shot dead. The other was my dear old friend Whistling Elk, who had given me his medicine pouch for my raid against the Crows with the Fox Soldiers. Whistling Elk burned to death in his tipi, being too feeble to crawl out and escape.

"Lean Bear brought Pleasant and the three other Dog Soldiers to the council and ordered them to explain why the Bluecoats had chased them and then attacked our village so fiercely. After they told their stories, Lean Bear denounced them for being so foolish and offered them to Big Star for punishment. Big Star, however, would not punish them. 'Many moons ago my blood was hot, as theirs is hot because of their youth,' he said. 'The trouble came to us because of the soldiers. If the soldiers were not in our country, such things would not happen. We must move away from the *Veheos* and their bluecoated pony soldiers. Last winter when Black Kettle's people camped near us in the Hinta Nagi, he told me that buffalo had come back to the valley of the Smoking Land River, more than enough buffalo for all our people. That country in the south was given to the Cheyennes in the Big Treaty. Before the sun goes down, let us strike our tipis and turn our faces to the south.'

"Although the soldiers had taken many of our best horses, we also had lost much to the fires. By crowding the travois that we had horses to draw, we were able to pack almost everything we had left. We built burial scaffolds and mourned for the two men who died, and then we started southward.

"Twice along the way we were stopped by Bluecoat cavalrymen who patrolled the Plains as if we had no right to be there on land that belonged to us. They wanted to know where we came from and where we were going. But after we passed Beaver Fork of the Lower Platte we saw no more *Veheos*, and we found the valley of the Smoking Land River rich in buffalo, as Black Kettle had promised.

"Many things happened very fast after that summer we moved south. I've always blamed Jotham for some of our troubles, although they would have come later anyway. At his trading post Jotham kept hearing rumors of gold being found in the mountains of what is now Colorado. A passing stranger once showed him a pouch of gold dust he said he'd found somewhere in those mountains. Jotham wrote about that in a letter to William, and William spread the story around among his friends, some of whom had prospected for gold at Dahlonega in Georgia before the Georgians drove them away.

"A Cherokee—especially a half-blood Cherokee—can get gold fever as bad as a white man, and it wasn't long before six or seven men from the Cherokee Nation showed up at Fort Carrothers, wanting Jotham to show them the way to a second Yellow Metal, or *Dahlonega*. Jotham had no more idea where the gold was than they did, but he caught a bad case of the fever and went with them into the foothills of the Rocky Mountains. They spent most of the summer wandering from one creek to another, finding just enough traces of gold to keep them searching. Whenever Jotham found a little gold dust, he would pack it into a goose quill. After the Cherokees gave up prospecting and went home to the Indian Territory, Jotham brought several of those quills back to Fort Carrothers. There wasn't enough gold in all of them to buy a used-up saddle.

"I don't say that Jotham started that whole Pike's Peak or Bust madness that came near destroying us a year or so later, but he showed off his gold-dust quills to many a passing traveler, putting the thought of Rocky Mountain gold into their heads. And in time, so many prospectors went into the mountains that some of them made big strikes.

"When he'd show off his quills, Jotham bragged about the big strike he was going to make the next time he went into the mountains, but he never went again. Griffa wouldn't allow it. She said if he left her to run that trading post by herself for another summer she'd leave and go back to the Cherokee Nation. Jotham didn't do any more prospecting, but it seemed like every white man and boy in the East all decided at the same time to cross the Plains and dig for gold in the Rocky Mountains.

"On foot, on mules and horses, in wagons and stagecoaches, they were clogging up the Oregon Trail before we left the Timbers in the springtime to go down to the Smoking Land River again. And we'd hardly camped there before gold hunters were coming right up our valley, beating out trails in old wagons that weren't fit to travel. All of them had signs lettered on the sides, PIKE'S PEAK OR BUST. Some days they were like a ragged army on horseback, slaughtering our buffalo by the hundreds to eat only the choicest parts, leaving the carcasses to rot on the ground. The skies soon filled with carrion birds, and then the buffalo deserted us, swinging south toward the Arkansas River.

"Lean Bear was the first to turn his anger to action. He told Big Star he was going to take his Dog Soldiers down this new trail from the east and keep the crazy white men away from the Smoking Land Valley, frighten them back to the trails along the Platte, and then maybe our buffalo would return. Big Star cautioned him to beware of soldiers; he had heard of many forts being built to the east.

"Pleasant wore his coat of mail the morning he rode out with the Dog Soldiers, and I wondered if I would ever see him or any of the other warriors again. For a few days, no white men appeared in any direction, but then they began to come again. Lean Bear told me that it was like trying to stop a river with bare hands. At first he tried not to kill any white men, only to frighten them, but then the whites would shoot at the Dog Soldiers and the Dog Soldiers would shoot back. Soon the Bluecoats from the forts were chasing them, and the Dog Soldiers had to move far

off in some other direction. They went all the way to the Santa
Fe Trail, and began raiding stage stations and ranch houses.

"The Drying-Grass Moon came and went, but the Dog Soldiers did not return to the Smoking Land River, and Big Star
said that without buffalo to hunt we could stay there no longer.
We would return early to the Hinta Nagi. Perhaps the herds
would come there with the snows.

"When we first sighted the Ghost Timbers, we thought a
whirling storm must have struck our old winter shelter while we
were gone. But we soon discovered that white men wanting firewood had crossed the shallow Platte to kill our trees the way
they killed our buffalo, chopping down our windbreaks and
using only the limbs to burn. They had camped in many places
in the Timbers, fouling the earth and water with their leavings.
There, for the first time, we sensed that we were losing control of
our lives. We were outcasts, doomed to flight or entrapment. We
had no safe place to go. But we cleaned up what was left of the
old Hinta Nagi, determined to spend one more winter there.

"When I went over to Fort Carrothers to see Jotham, he
showed me a newspaper from St. Louis with an account of Indian raids along the Kansas trails. The worst of these savages,
the newspaper said, was a band of Cheyenne Dog Soldiers led
by a half-breed in Spanish armor, who attacked helpless travelers without warning, shooting and hacking and torturing their
victims without mercy. 'The man in the armor is bound to be
Pleasant,' Jotham said. 'We ought to go find him and stop him
before it's too late.'

"Well, I thought the newspaper account was like most printed
things about Indians, exaggerated lies, and besides we had no
way of finding Pleasant. As it turned out, we did not have to go
looking for him. He showed up one day at the Ghost Timbers,
worn down to nothing but bone and muscle, his skin blackened
by the sun, wearing his coat of mail and a dirty old rabbit-skin
cap. He was carrying a lance to which were attached four scalps,
none of them dark enough to be Indian. All he would say about
the Dog Soldiers, who were still on the Plains, was that he had a
quarrel with Lean Bear and he was tired of raiding and scalping.

Red Bird Woman may have learned more than that from Pleasant, but if she did she never told me. Lean Bear came in with the Dog Soldiers a few weeks later, leading many captured horses loaded with plunder, but Pleasant was gone by that time and Lean Bear never said anything to me about a quarrel, so it probably didn't amount to much.

"Pleasant tried to settle down in Rising Fawn's tipi, but he was like a burned-out spirit, too restless to loaf around the Ghost Timbers waiting for winter buffalo that never came. He kept going back and forth from the Timbers to Fort Carrothers, and he was there one day when a man arrived from Missouri to talk with Jotham about building a station for what he called the Pony Express. This man had a contract to carry mail by horseback from Leavenworth to California. When he asked if there was someone at the fort willing to be the station keeper, Jotham pointed to Pleasant. 'He's your man. Knows how to handle horses, a good blacksmith, and can read, write, and figure.'

" 'I'll hire you,' the man said to Pleasant, 'but not as a station keeper. You're young, skinny, and wiry. I want you for one of my riders.'

"And that's how my son Pleasant McAlpin became a Pony Express rider on the section between Fort Carrothers and Fort Laramie. I believe those were the happiest days of the boy's life, riding fast and free, dressed in a red shirt and blue trousers and high boots, and carrying that fancy saddlebag full of important mail. He was the envy of my second son, Swift Eagle, and of Jotham's Young Opothle, both of whom were old enough to be riders. But Swift Eagle was too Indian to suit the Pony Express men, and Young Opothle was too heavy.

"Young Opothle was so upset over being turned down that I persuaded Jotham to let him go off with us that summer to hunt for buffalo on the Little Fork of the Hotoa. Rising Fawn also went along. She had an even greater dislike for living at Fort Carrothers than did Sweet Medicine Woman."

37

Late in the summer of 1860, while Big Star's Cheyennes were camped on the Hotoa, Dane was surprised to receive a short written message from Fort Carrothers. It was brought by a half-blood Arapaho who worked as a stock tender at the Pony Express station. *I have been bad hurt in a fall,* the message read. *I need Young Opothle here, and you also, my good cousin, if you will come. Yr. obedient servant, Jotham Kingsley.*

Although the Cheyennes had found several small buffalo herds along the Hotoa, and Dane could have used more hides for winter trading, he decided to go at once to Fort Carrothers, taking his family with him. When he told Big Star of this, the chief said that he would not be bringing the Cheyennes to the Hinta Nagi that winter but would probably join Black Kettle's people on Sand Creek.

"If I can leave Fort Carrothers before the snows come," Dane said, "my family and I will come to Sand Creek. Otherwise we'll spend the winter at the fort."

"Take good care of my daughter," Big Star warned him. "She dislikes the noise and restlessness of the *Veheos* around that trading post."

Dane was not surprised that Sweet Medicine Woman objected to this early visit to Fort Carrothers, but when she saw how eager her children were to go, she made only mild protests. He invited Rising Fawn to accompany them, but she refused, saying that if Pleasant wanted her as a wife he must abandon his *Veheo* ways and live with the Cheyennes.

They traveled slowly with two travois, taking routes that kept them away from Bluecoat patrols and white travelers, and as soon as they arrived, Sweet Medicine Woman and the girls began pitching the tipi along the stream behind the trading post.

Dane found Jotham lying in bed with his leg wrapped in strips of canvas. He had broken it while racing one of the mounts that he kept for the Pony Express. The animal had stumbled in an abandoned prairie-dog hole, its full weight falling upon Jotham's leg. "The outlandishness of it," Jotham said, "is that Pleasant has ridden that same pony hundreds of miles and never had an accident. I took it out for a mile run and broke a leg."

Pleasant came in from Fort Laramie the next evening, and Dane was delighted to see how well and contented he looked. "Riding for the Pony Express seems to satisfy you," Dane said.

"I like the excitement," Pleasant replied. "But it won't last much longer." He pointed to a row of bark-stripped poles with crosspieces, which ran along the opposite side of the trail.

"I hear the *Veheos* are coming to string wires along those poles," Dane said. "Bibbs calls them talking wires."

"Telegraph. The wires are already at Fort Kearney and someday will reach the Western Ocean. When messages can be sent to California by the wires, there will be no more need for the Pony Express."

Dane shook his head. "I don't understand how this can be done. The white men have too much magic these days."

Later that evening Dane was talking with Jotham about the poles and the talking wires. "Yes, the world that you and I grew up in, Dane, is vanishing," Jotham said. "The life you have chosen to lead with the Cheyennes can't last much longer."

"I don't know. Big Star thinks we should violate the treaty and go back to the Powder River country where the Northern Cheyennes still live without hindrance. After all, the American government is not enforcing its side of the treaty."

Jotham moved uneasily in his bed. Dane noticed that gray hair was beginning to show at his cousin's temples. They were both growing older, the days flowing by. "You and your Cheyennes can run away for a time," Jotham said. "But the white world will swallow you in the end. When the buffalo are gone, you will go."

"I have thought much on these things."

"And of your family?" Jotham sighed. "Since my accident I've thought about Young Opothle and the days to come. You turned him into a wild Indian this summer. I want him to have the learning you gave Pleasant. Meggi also when she is older."

"In the seminary at Tahlequah?"

"Yes. If they are to survive in the world they must live in, they will need learning. Grandmother Amayi would agree with me, would she not?"

Dane wondered, thinking of his own sons and daughters. In the north they would be happy following Cheyenne ways if white men did not encroach. But how long would they be free of invading forces—the soldiers, the wagon trains, the gold hunters, the settlers, the talking wires?

"I've already exchanged letters with Mr. Ebenezer Keys," Jotham continued. "He invites Young Opothle 'to come and sip at the sweet waters of knowledge.' But the boy must be there in September. I was planning to take him with me to Westport for supplies and then go on to the Nation, but this leg. . . . Knowing your dislike for leaving your family, I hesitate to ask this, Dane, but will you take Young Opothle to the Nation?"

When Dane's sons, Swift Eagle and Little Cloud, learned that their father was taking Young Opothle to school in the Cherokee Nation, both immediately expressed strong desires to go also. They idolized Pleasant and were sure that they could become as dashing as their older half brother if only they could go away to the seminary as he had done. Swift Eagle was sixteen, but Little Cloud was a year younger, and Dane spent several restless nights trying to decide whether he should uproot either of them from their Cheyenne world. At dawn after a sleepless night he decided that together his sons could sustain each other in the Cherokee Nation. Alone, the strangeness of Cherokee ways might overcome Swift Eagle even with Young Opothle nearby. He would take both sons to Tahlequah.

His hardest task was trying to convince Sweet Medicine Woman of the soundness of his decision. At first she thought he was temporarily deranged, that his madness would soon leave him. But when she realized that he was serious, she stormed out at him, shouting that he was trying to make her sons like the *Veheos*. She did not want her sons to be *Veheos*. She would not listen when he spoke of his grandmother who believed that when Indians become surrounded by white men they must learn some of their ways in order to survive. It was the first bitter quarrel of their life together.

He doggedly went ahead with his plans. The night before departure the three boys dressed in their white man's clothing, but Sweet Medicine Woman refused to look at them. To himself Dane admitted that his young sons with their hair cut short and slicked down with water—wearing collars, pantaloons, and stockings—looked unnatural, like false images of themselves. For a moment he felt like tearing the clothing from them.

The next morning Sweet Medicine Woman would not leave her tipi. He had to take her sons to her to say good-bye. Trying not to look at them, she embraced them together, but her words choked in her throat. When they ran outside, Dane reached for her. She drew away, taking Creek Mary's Danish coin from around her neck and holding it out to him. "Here is the sacred power you gave me," she said. "I will wear it again when you bring my sons back to me."

38

"During the three or four days I was in the Cherokee Nation," Dane said, "getting the boys into Mr. Ebenezer Keys's seminary,

I kept hearing talk on all sides about a war between the northern and southern states of America. I could not understand why the Cherokees should be interested in this war. Indian Territory was not one of the states. But it was soon made clear to me that the fight was over the slavery of black people. The northerners wanted the southerners to free the black people, and the southerners wanted to keep their slaves.

"As a good many of the half-bloods and treaty Cherokees still had black slaves they had brought from Georgia and Tennessee, and very few of the Ross followers owned any, the treaty people sided with the South and the full-bloods with the North. I could see that old wound which had almost healed since the time of Uncle Opothle's death beginning to open up again.

"Not long after I returned to Fort Carrothers, the War Between the States began in earnest. While spring came on the next year I was waiting to hear from Big Star about his hunting plans for the summer so that Sweet Medicine Woman and the girls and I could join the Cheyennes. But the Plains were suddenly filled with Bluecoat cavalry marching in all directions. Wagonloads of white men from the mines began moving east to join one or the other of the armies. It was no time for Indians to be on the move, and so we did not hear from the Cheyennes.

"Pleasant brought us most of the news we heard about the war. He listened to all kinds of stories told by the Bluecoats at Fort Laramie, and every time he came back from there, he and Jotham argued for hours about the fighting in the East. As far as I was concerned the Unegas could shoot away at each other forever. It was nothing for either Cherokees or Cheyennes to bother about.

"Every letter that Jotham received from William told of the commotion in the Cherokee Nation. Old John Ross, who was still chief of the Cherokees, was strong for neutrality, but after the Confederate government declared Indian Territory to be a part of their new country, Ross had to give in and become an ally of the southerners. Soon after that Stand Watie was made a general in the Confederate army, and as he and William had long been friends, William's letters soon showed that his sympathies had turned toward the South. William began urging Jotham to come home and help defend the Cherokee Nation from its enemies. It all seemed senseless to me.

"Then suddenly one day Pleasant came in from Fort Laramie to tell us he had made his last ride for the Pony Express. The talking wires had reached California and all the mail would now go on the stagecoaches.

"'We can use you here at the trading post,' Jotham spoke up. 'Tending the stage horses or working with Bibbs in the smithy.'

"Pleasant shook his head. 'I signed papers for the army last night,' he said proudly.

"'The army!' Jotham cried. 'Which army?'

"'Missouri cavalry,' Pleasant replied. 'The recruits are coming through here in stagecoaches in a day or so. I'll join them here.'

"'Missouri Confederates or Missouri Union?' Jotham wanted to know.

"Pleasant grinned. 'The recruiter was wearing a blue uniform.'

"'God damn you!' Jotham cried, and began limping back and forth on his healing leg. 'You're a traitor to your people!'

"'What people?' Pleasant tried to put on a defiant look. 'Hell, I don't have any people. If the Missouri Confederates had come for me first I might've signed their papers. I just want some excitement.'

"Jotham was far more upset than I was, even though living as a Cheyenne I'd grown to hate the sight of a blue uniform. Blue or gray, to me they both meant trouble and I was sorry to see my oldest son drawn into the madness.

"A few days later two big Concord coaches rolled in from the West, rocking under the weight of the army recruits who were shouting and laughing and singing. The stagecoaches stopped only long enough for Pleasant to board one of them. He gave me a quick handshake and kissed the girls and Sweet Medicine Woman good-bye. 'When you see Rising Fawn tell her I'll be back soon,' he said and then climbed inside the coach. A recruit handed him a bottle of whiskey. He took a long swig, waving the bottle from the window as the coach rolled away. He was young enough then to think he would live forever. Sweet Medicine

Woman was crying, but all I could do was stand there in the dust and wonder if there was a curse upon Creek Mary's blood.

"The next to leave was Jotham. I think it was about the time of the Deer Rutting Moon when a stagecoach passenger left a St. Louis newspaper, some days old, and in it was an account of fighting in the Cherokee Nation. General Stand Watie's Confederate Cherokees and some Texans had battled Union Cherokees, driving them into Kansas. 'It says the fighting was at Round Mounds and Shoal Creek,' Jotham said excitedly. 'I think I'd better go to Tahlequah and bring our boys home. Mails must be cut off or we'd have heard of this from William.' He was eager to see William and his family, and talked about bringing them back to the safety of Fort Carrothers.

"Griffa and Meggi wanted to go with him on the stagecoach, but he feared the horseback journey from Westport to Tahlequah would be too dangerous because of the war. 'I'll stay no longer than necessary to get the boys and see William,' he promised. 'We'll be back here before the first snow.'

"Although Sweet Medicine Woman had been looking forward to our rejoining her people on Sand Creek for the winter, nothing on earth could have moved her from Fort Carrothers until she saw her sons return. She began counting the days.

"For the next several weeks the trading post was very quiet. The few freighting wagons going back and forth to Denver usually stopped for water and to rest horses, but there were no more immigrant wagons, and only one eastbound stagecoach in the morning and a westbound in the afternoon. For many weeks no Indians had come to trade buffalo hides. Since the ending of the Pony Express, the stock tenders and riders had left. The family, which at times had numbered more than a dozen, was now reduced to Griffa and Meggi, Sweet Medicine Woman, Amayi, Susa, and myself, and of course we counted Bibbs and Wewoka. With all the spare room in the living quarters, Griffa kept urging Sweet Medicine Woman and me to abandon our tipi for the winter and move into the trading post. It would have been much handier for me. Except when I was out hunting rabbits or game birds for meat, I spent much of my time in the trading room helping Griffa, but Sweet Medicine Woman would not give up her tipi. 'I favor my tipi,' she would say firmly, 'because it is easy to keep clean, is warmer in winter and cooler in summer. Amayi and Susa all the time have fresh air and sunshine. It would not be good for them to live inside walls like a big cave that shuts out the sun.'

"Nonetheless when I was working in the trading room, Sweet Medicine Woman often came there to sit in a rocking chair by the window, sewing beads on moccasins or quilling dresses for the girls. Whenever the stagecoach from the east came, she would go to the door and look to see if Jotham and the boys were on it.

"Weeks went by, the first snow came and then blizzards, but we received no news from Jotham. I wrote two letters to William, and we waited anxiously, hearing nothing. Then one day in spring the stagecoach driver from the east handed me a letter. The covering was streaked with rain spots and a smear of dried clay, but I recognized Jotham's scrawl and opened it at once. He was writing to me, he said, because his letter contained the saddest words he'd ever penned, and he wanted me to be the shield between the sadness and Griffa. I would have to bear my own blow and comfort Sweet Medicine Woman as best I could.

"Jotham had endured great difficulties in making his way to Tahlequah, having to pass through two armies, and was delayed for many days. When he arrived there he found the seminary closed. Most of the boys had enlisted in one of General Stand Watie's Confederate Cherokee companies, but Little Cloud was at William's place, he being too young for the army.

"After leaving William's, Jotham tried to find the company that Swift Eagle and Young Opothle joined, but no one could tell him in which regiment it was, so he had to travel from camp to camp, up the Arkansas and down the Verdigris until he learned that Stand Watie had taken all his soldiers over into Arkansas to prepare for a big battle. Jotham reached the Cherokees' baggage camp only a day after they marched north toward Fayetteville. The next day he heard cannon firing all through the afternoon, and a courier he met along the road told him a battle was raging around Elkhorn Tavern.

"Before Jotham could get there, he was stopped by thousands of Confederates—Texans, Arkansans, and Cherokees—retreating from the Union soldiers. He finally found a Cherokee officer, an old acquaintance, who took him to Stand Watie. Not until after the Cherokees reassembled at their baggage camp, and company counts were made, was Jotham told that Swift Eagle and Young Opothle were probably among the dead. Their commander, a lieutenant who had been wounded, said the Cherokees were trying to hold a hill called Pea Ridge when they came under heavy cannon fire. Many of his men had been torn to pieces, their bleeding bodies scattered over the slope. If the two missing boys were not among the wounded, they were surely dead.

"Jotham could not rest until he went to Pea Ridge and looked over the place where the cannon fire had torn up the earth, but Union soldiers had already buried the bodies and pieces of bodies of the Cherokees who died there. He then went back to William's and to Tahlequah, hoping the boys might have found their way back to the Nation, but no one had seen or heard of them.

"He closed his letter by saying that he was joining Stand Watie's army himself to avenge his son and my son, and that he hoped I would take care of his family and the trading post until he returned. He was sure the Union soldiers could be beaten by summer."

Dane stopped, laughing a bitter laugh at the remembrance of that long-ago time. "What fools we humans be!"

39

After Swift Eagle and Young Opothle enlisted in the Cherokee
Confederate company, they marched with others of their class-
mates to a camp on the Arkansas River. There a thick-bodied
Unega with long curly hair and an enormous beard, and
mounted on a white horse, addressed them. He told them he was
General Albert Pike and that he commanded all the armies of
the Indian Territory. He promised they would soon be given
horses and uniforms and better guns, but for the time being they
would have to soldier in what clothes they wore and use the old
muzzle-loaders that had been issued to them. "You are fighting
in the cause of freedom," he told them. "With your white
brothers, you will drive the Yankee oppressors from your land."

For several weeks the Cherokees drilled in formations and
fired by commands, and then they were marched off on foot to
the east with a line of baggage wagons clattering in their rear.
At a place called Cross Hollow in Arkansas they joined a camp
of Texans, and learned that the Texans had intercepted the shipment of gray uniforms that was meant for them. When a herd of
horses was driven in from Fort Smith, the Texans also took the
horses. During the next few days hundreds of Creeks, Choctaws,
Chickasaws, and Seminoles arrived at the baggage camp, some
mounted, some on foot, all wearing miscellaneous clothing that
varied from tribal dress to trading-post shoddy.

One morning all the companies were formed into ranks, and
General Albert Pike and Chief John Ross arrived in an open
buggy to lead them northward to battle an invading Union
army. General Pike was wearing a fringed jacket and wide-

brimmed hat with bright-colored feathers in its band. John Ross wore his usual black suit and black stovepipe hat, and the expression on his face was that of a man who had been captured and disarmed.

For three days Swift Eagle and Young Opothle marched through rain and melting snow, with nothing to eat but parched corn and rancid pork. Young Opothle, whose body had grown plump like his mother's, could barely keep up with his company. The shoes they had given him to replace worn-out moccasins rubbed his feet raw, and he limped first on one foot and then the other. Swift Eagle felt sorry for him, carrying his rifle and knapsack most of the way through the Boston Mountains. On the evening of the third day, the Cherokees were ordered to build fires and roll in their blankets, but at midnight they were awakened and told to leave their fires burning brightly while they marched off along a narrow road with wet flakes of snow falling in their faces.

Soon after the eastern sky paled, they heard their first sounds of the enemy off through the woods—a blaring of bugles, a furious beating of drums, and a rumble of artillery wheels. When the Cherokees came suddenly out upon the edge of a field of withered cornstalks, they saw masses of infantrymen in blue marching steadily toward them. Far behind the blue lines, puffs of white smoke formed, shrieks of hurtling metal filled the sky, and the earth shook with thunder.

Out of the woods to their right swept the Texans, screaming like wild panthers, and then from the left came the Cherokee cavalry with General Stand Watie on a glistening bay, turning to face the Cherokee infantrymen, beckoning them to follow. To Swift Eagle it was as if General Watie's piercing wide-set eyes had searched him out, and it was Swift Eagle who led the charge of his company, starting a war cry that was more Cheyenne than Cherokee, a cry of defiance out of his belly and lungs and vocal cords. Ahead of him through galloping horses and a spray of mud he saw the blue lines falter and break, the Union infantrymen fleeing in disorder.

On across the muddy field Swift Eagle ran, dashing up a slope to where Cherokee cavalry were milling around an abandoned battery of cannons. Dead Union gunners lay around the cannons in grotesque positions. No one seemed to know what to do next. The Cherokee officers shouted commands, but few obeyed. Swift Eagle joined his comrades in searching the pockets of the dead Bluecoats, but he found nothing worth keeping. Suddenly from a low ridge to their left more Union cannons began booming, sending shot whistling in their direction. The Cherokees scattered, fleeing back across the cornfield to the cover of the woods. While their officers were trying to form them into ranks again, another wave of blue-clad infantrymen came charging across the field. Their concerted rifle fire rattled like sleet popping against a tight tipi cover. The Cherokees yelled their war cry, ran forward a hundred paces, fired together, and retreated to the scrub oaks to reload.

Gradually the Cherokees became disorganized, withdrawing deeper into the woods. General Pike on his white horse kept riding back and forth, waving a sword at them, bellowing angrily, and then after a while he and Stand Watie led them off along the road they had marched over during the night. When they came to a slope, they left the road and climbed through blackjack oaks to the top. "You will hold this high ground," General Pike ordered. "Do or die!" They were on Pea Ridge.

Through the afternoon they watched the opposing cannons duel until the fields and woods below were covered with folds of smoke. Then night fell, but they were not allowed to build fires against the deepening cold. Through hours of fitful sleep they heard the voices of cursing men, the racket of moving wagons and artillery.

At dawn a cannon blast shook Swift Eagle wide awake. It was from the Confederate artillery down near Elkhorn Tavern, but the Union batteries replied with a mighty roar, one big gun after the other booming like rolling thunder. Far below the Cherokees, shattered blackjack oaks flew into the air, disintegrating into splinters. The next barrage was closer, and to Swift Eagle, who watched in frozen fascination, the advancing destruction below him was like the crushing footsteps of an invisible giant moving relentlessly closer. And then off to his left a screaming projectile burst upon the Cherokee line, throwing him to the ground. When he got to his feet he saw his companions running or crawling down the back slope. He followed Young Opothle and the others, angling to the right, stopping only long enough to peer up through the brown leaves of a blackjack at bloody legs and headless torsos of young Cherokees strewn among rocks and leaves. He fled with the others down the slope to the road, right into a platoon of Union infantrymen carrying bayoneted rifles. "Drop your arms!" a startled sergeant yelled at the Cherokees, but they had abandoned their muzzle-loaders on the slope, and had only their knives to surrender.

They were marched quickly to the rear, where a Union colonel examined their motley clothing, especially the moccasins, with distasteful curiosity. "Did you scalp our men?" he demanded.

There were eleven Cherokees, all very young, all privates, all too frightened to answer except Swift Eagle. "No, sir," he said.

The colonel ordered their wrists tied behind their backs, and for two days and two nights they marched bound that way, following a line of wagons filled with wounded and dying soldiers. Swift Eagle and Young Opothle did not know that this was the same road over which, a score of years before, their fathers had traveled from the East in wagons filled with sick and dying Cherokees.

At the edge of Springfield they were ordered to halt beneath a great oak that shaded the road. The ambulance wagons rolled on, and they waited for hours, thirsting for water, hungering for food. At last they heard a slow solemn drumbeat, and out of a dusty street came a squad of blue-uniformed horsemen. On foot behind them was a straggling formation of white Confederate prisoners, their gray uniforms soiled by dust and caked mud. As soon as the prisoners passed the oak tree, the Cherokees were shoved into line behind them.

To the monotonous drumbeat, they walked wearily into the main street of Springfield, where spectators lined the wooden sidewalks, staring with silent curiosity at the prisoners in gray, jeering and cursing the young Cherokees in their shabby clothing.

In Springfield that day was Corporal Pleasant McAlpin, dressed in a trim blue-and-yellow cavalry uniform issued to him soon after he was attached to the headquarters of General Samuel R. Curtis for special courier service. On his way from the Elkhorn Tavern battlefield, Corporal McAlpin had passed the train of wounded and the Cherokee prisoners, but he galloped past so swiftly that he saw them only as a blur of plodding humanity. Long before the Cherokees reached Springfield, Corporal McAlpin delivered his saddlebag of messages from General Curtis to the Union quartermaster and was told that replies would not be ready until early the next morning. When the parade of prisoners entered the main street, Corporal McAlpin, bored by hours of inaction, had just walked out of the Red Star Saloon, yawning.

He saw Young Opothle first, his head drooping in misery as he limped along, and just beyond him was Swift Eagle, dust-coated, taller than Pleasant remembered him, but there was no mistaking that proud Frenchman's nose he had inherited through his mother. Pleasant started to call to them, but thought better of it and followed along the sidewalk. He was surprised to see a mounted Union sergeant ride in between the white prisoners and the Cherokees, halting the Indians beside a gray stone building, the Springfield jail. The uniformed prisoners marched on to the slow drumbeat, toward a stableyard, while the sergeant dismounted to accept the jail key from a waiting civilian and then one by one he herded the eleven Cherokees into the cramped quarters of the jail, cutting the ropes on their wrists as they entered.

Pleasant stopped at the end of the wooden sidewalk, puzzled, uncertain as to what was happening. He crossed to the other side of the street and watched the sergeant lead his horse around to the rear of the jail. The civilian jailer brought out a narrow bench. The sergeant returned and said something to the jailer, who laughed and then turned and walked briskly away into the town. The sergeant sat on the bench, leaning against a rifle held between his knees.

Pleasant strolled easily toward the sergeant. "Guard duty?" he asked.

The sergeant nodded, shifting his chewing tobacco so that it made a lump in one of his cheeks. "Wild redskins," he said.

"I reckon they won't be paroled and exchanged like the white prisoners," Pleasant remarked casually.

"Nah. I heard the colonel say we'd be takin' 'em north. Goin' to parade 'em through towns to show our folks how the Rebs are usin' scalpin' savages to fight agin' us."

"Serves them right," Pleasant said, giving the sergeant a half salute. "See you in town, maybe, sergeant."

As soon as darkness fell, Pleasant took his horse from the stables and rode along the street past the jail. Two soldiers were now on duty, replacing the sergeant. Pleasant turned into a narrow alleyway down the street from them, dismounted in the shadows, and crept back to the edge of an empty storehouse, where he could hear the guards talking. He waited patiently as Lean Bear had taught him to wait when they were raiding stage stations in Kansas. Except for the voices of the guards the town was quiet. At last one of the guards stood up, stretched, and said: "I'm going up the street to the crapper." His companion mumbled something as the guard walked away. Pleasant went back to his horse and led it quietly to the rear of the jail where the guards' two horses were hitched to a rail. The animals snorted and stamped their feet while Pleasant fastened his mount beside them. He then moved along the edge of the jail wall.

The guard was no more than six feet from him, his head bent forward. Pleasant slipped out his pistol, balanced it in his hand, but then returned it to its holster and took a knife from a belt sheath. In one quick lunge he had his knife arm under the guard's chin, but the man's neck was thick and muscular. The guard struggled, sounds breaking from his squeezed vocal cords, and Pleasant knew that he must kill him. Releasing his hold, he pulled the knife blade quick and hard across the guard's throat until the man fell forward, blood gurgling as his lungs gasped for air.

Without thinking, Pleasant grasped for the dead man's hair, started to cut into the scalp. He cursed himself softly, dropped the head, and turned the body over, reaching for the big jail key on the belt. After one quick glance up the deserted street, he put the key in the lock and swung the door open. "Swift Eagle! Opothle!" he called. Out of the blackness of the crowded jail came startled grunts and sounds of moving bodies. Swift Eagle's face appeared, questioning, crying out Pleasant's name.

"Shut up!" Pleasant whispered. "Where's Young Opothle?"

Swift Eagle was dragging him by one arm.

"You two get around to the back quick. Horses there." He looked at the other nine Cherokees circling in confusion on the wooden sidewalk. "Got no horses for you," he said. "Scatter out for the woods. Go back to the Nation as fast as you can."

He turned and dashed for the horses. The two boys were already mounted. He led the way slowly along the alley into a street, gradually increasing the gait. As soon as they were away from the buildings, they broke into a gallop and did not slow until the animals were blowing froth from their bits.

When they passed through a little town, starlit and quiet except for a dog barking in the distance, Pleasant noticed clothing left out overnight to dry on a line beside a big house. He turned his mount into the unfenced yard and jerked a shirt and a pair of pants from the line. Soon afterward they came to a bridge. He dismounted, removed his uniform, and put on the shirt and pants. They were too big for him, but he rolled up the sleeves and legs. Then he wrapped his uniform around a large stone and tossed it into the creek beneath the bridge.

"You quitting the Union army?" Young Opothle asked.

"Reckon so. This war is not for us of Creek Mary's blood." He climbed back in his saddle. "It's a far piece to Fort Carrothers. Let's ride."

40

"In all my life," Dane said, "I never saw such wretched, such frazzled human beings as those three boys when they came riding into Fort Carrothers. We could not believe it was them, of course. For days we'd been mourning for Swift Eagle and Young Opothle, and heard nothing from Pleasant since he'd left us. Sweet Medicine Woman had cut her hair short and gashed blood from the calves of her legs in the Cheyenne way of mourning, but the grief in her face went quickly away after Swift Eagle returned. A few days later we celebrated again when Little Cloud surprised us by coming in on the stagecoach. We didn't do much feasting, though, as food was scarce. All of us were starving for buffalo meat.

"The night after Little Cloud came back, Sweet Medicine Woman put Creek Mary's Danish coin around her neck again, and she slept in my arms until long after the sun rose, never moaning in her sleep or rising to weep silently in the night as she had been doing.

"She was ready now to go south and join her father's people, and Pleasant was eager to see Rising Fawn. I talked to Griffa about our going, and she said that with Bibbs and Young Opothle there, she could manage the trading post without our help. As we did not know where Big Star's Cheyennes were camped for the summer, Swift Eagle and Pleasant began making long rides out to the south to see if they could find any Indians who might know where our people were, but it was as if the Plains had been swept clean of every living thing but Bluecoats. Late one day the boys came back to tell us that soldiers

were building a new fort down on the South Fork. 'They call it
Fort Starke after a general got killed back east in the war,' Pleasant said.

"'How far from here?' I asked him.

"He guessed about twenty miles.

"'Why do they want a fort there?' I wondered.

"'To watch us hostile Indians,' he said with a laugh, but we
both knew he was speaking truth.

"Before we got our bundles ready to go, we had an unexpected visitor. One night long after dark I heard a horse
snuffling just outside our tipi, and then a voice softly called
Sweet Medicine Woman. I waked her and we went to the flap
and looked out. 'Who's there?' I asked.

"'Yellow Hawk.' He dismounted and Sweet Medicine Woman
rushed to embrace the brother she had not seen for many
moons.

"Yellow Hawk had come to bring news of the Cheyennes and
to warn us not to try to cross the Plains in search of them. The
soldiers, he said, had driven most of the Southern Cheyennes
and Arapahos between Sand Creek and the Arkansas River, and
threatened to fire upon them as hostiles if they were found outside that reservation. Because there were few buffalo in that
country, Big Star and some other chiefs had gone to a new soldier fort on the Arkansas, Fort Lyon, and asked the Bluecoat
chief there if they could go to the Hotoa or Smoking Land to
hunt. The Bluecoat chief promised to obtain permission for them
to hunt, but he had not yet done so.

"'It is very hard for us,' Yellow Hawk said. 'Big Star has lost
respect for the treaty and wants to flee to our cousins in the
north, to the Powder River country, but we would have to hide
from Bluecoat patrols all the way. I traveled here only by nights
and had no trouble, but it would be difficult with travois and
women and children.'

"Yellow Hawk stayed with us only a few days. Although I
knew my family would have a hard time living at Fort Carrothers with so little to eat, after hearing his talk of the
Cheyennes' troubles I could see that they were in a much worse

plight than we. Sweet Medicine Woman and my sons were disappointed—"

Dane stopped suddenly, raising up from his chair and squinting against the bright Montana sun pouring through the window. "Damn if that Crow boy is not bringing his wagon up here again. Somebody on the seat with him. Couldn't be Mary Amayi this early." He shaded his eyes. "Red Bird Woman! What does she want?"

He strode to the door and opened it with a sigh of impatience, and I followed at a discreet distance. The young Crow, John Bear-in-the-Water, turned the wagon expertly off the road, bringing it to a stop right in front of Dane's doorway.

Red Bird Woman, her black hair only slightly streaked with gray, and braided at the sides, let herself down slowly from the seat with the aid of a long stick. She was wearing a spotted dress, full around her ample hips, and a blanket shawl. Her face was round and plump, without a wrinkle, her eyes wide open and smiling at Dane. "Where you been last two days?" she asked him.

"Watching the sun rise and set," he said.

She saw me then, behind him, and nodded as if she understood. He introduced me, pronouncing my name with emphasis. "The gentleman who wanted me to tell him about my grandmother," he explained.

"Dane talk about old grandmother a lot," Red Bird Woman said. "She must've been something."

"He told me about you, also," I said.

Entering the cabin, she shook with quick laughter as she sat in one of the rocking chairs. "Don't you believe nothing old Dane tell you." Her wide eyes searched my face, dismissed me, and turned away. "You got coffee ready, Dane?"

He was already pouring her a cup. John Bear-in-the-Water crouched by the fireplace, warming his hands.

"I was going to tell about the day Flattery Jack Belcourt came to the trading post," Dane said.

"That Belcourt was evil spirit," she declared. The smile left her face. "I hope he went to white man's hell."

"On that same day," Dane continued, "Major Easterwood also was there."

"I don't remember him," Red Bird Woman said.

"No, you never knew the major. He was a Bluecoat, but a good *Veheo*. I owe my life to him. The day I first saw him, my daughter Susa and I had been out hunting rabbits. She must've been ten or eleven then, but a damn good shot. Hunted like a boy. We crossed the stream on our horses and stopped to watch Amayi painting our tipi—"

"That was Mary Amayi's mother?" Red Bird Woman asked.

"Yes." Dane frowned at the interruption. "Amayi could draw anything, symbols she was always drawing. But she sometimes asked Wewoka to help with the colors. Together they put all our family on the tipi cover—a yellow floating cloud for Little Cloud, a great soaring eagle for Swift Eagle, a flying pony for Pleasant. Amayi drew the pony so that its tawny mane and blue eyes truly was Pleasant. He would sit on the ground and look up at the flying pony on the side of the tipi and shake his head in wonderment. For Susa she drew a prairie dog, I suppose because Susa spent so much time at a nearby prairie-dog village watching the animals and making up stories about them. And for herself, Amayi drew a *castilleja*—the whites call them Indian paint brushes—splashes of bright red, high up on the tipi so that the blossoms looked like fire coming out of the smokehole."

"What did she draw for you and Sweet Medicine Woman?" Red Bird Woman asked.

"Two sitting coyotes facing each other on opposite sides of the entrance flap." Dane's face creased in one of his tight-lipped smiles. "She knew what her parents were in the real world."

"I remember that tipi," Red Bird Woman said. "The Bluecoats burned it that winter we camped with Crazy Horse's people on Powder River."

"Yes. As I said, Amayi was painting one of her symbols on the tipi when Major Easterwood first came there from Denver. He was riding alone, saw us behind the trading post, and turned his horse toward us. His blue uniform was a warning of danger to me, and so I walked out in front of my young daughters, wondering what he wanted. He inquired politely if the trading post offered meals to travelers, and I told him we no longer did so because of the shortage of rations. He then asked if he might have a drink of fresh water.

"Major Easterwood was a tall sad-eyed man with a crooked white scar along his neck, and he limped painfully when he dismounted. I learned later that he was a professional soldier—went to West Point—had been badly shot up in some battle in Virginia and was sent out to Camp Weld at Denver for light duties while he recovered. He was such a kindly man that I invited him into the trading room, and talked Griffa out of a precious cup of coffee and some of her corn cakes for him. He was grateful and apologetic. Being an easterner, he said, he was not accustomed to the long distances on the Plains and had badly underestimated the time required to ride to Fort Starke.

"He wanted to talk, and after I told him I was Cherokee he questioned me for a time about my life. Then he sat silent, staring at the entrance door. 'I am not looking forward to joining the Colorado Volunteers at Fort Starke,' he said. I asked him why, but he just shook his head. I could see that he was very tired, and when he rested his head on the table, I asked if he would like to lie down. 'No, thank you,' he said. 'I will be all right after a moment.' However, he fell asleep. I went into the kitchen to tell Griffa to leave him be, and while I was there we heard a great clatter of horses' hooves out front and the sound of heavy boots in the entrance.

"By the time I got into the trading room there must've been a dozen Bluecoat cavalrymen crowding in, several of them poking about among our scanty trade goods. Their leader, a big beefy man with colonel's eagles on his shoulders, was standing facing Major Easterwood, who had been wakened by their noisy incoming.

"'Where are you stationed, major?' the colonel called out. At the sound of the big man's voice, I knew who he was, although I had not seen him for more than twenty years. His scraggly beard

and the tufts of once pink hair sprouting above his ears had
turned gray, but his squinty eyes still glinted with the cunning of
the evil spirit that he was.

"Major Easterwood told him he was on his way from Denver
to Fort Starke. Flattery Jack pranced over to the table, removed
a gauntlet, and offered his hand. 'I'm Colonel Belcourt, in command at Fort Starke. You must be the officer sent down to look
into our shortage of arms.' Major Easterwood bowed without
smiling.

"'A man of your abilities will soon see that we're in dire need
of better rifles to deal with the hostile tribes,' Belcourt said in
that snakelike way of his that got him the nickname of Flattery
Jack.

"'I shall give the matter my earnest attention, sir,' Major
Easterwood said.

"'I've taken on the duty of leading a patrol myself,' Belcourt
went on, 'to clean out wandering bands of hostiles that threaten
traveling civilians and Denver's supplies from the east. Would
you care to join us?'

"'Thank you, sir, but I feel the need to rest myself and my
mount,' Major Easterwood replied politely. 'I shall go directly on
to the fort.'

"'As you will, major. I look forward to your company tomorrow evening.' Belcourt turned to face me for the first time,
hatred rising in his eyes for my Indianness. 'Where's the trader?'
he demanded.

"'I'm acting for the trader,' I said.

"'Who lives in that tipi back there?'

"'My family and I,' I replied.

"'You're Cheyenne?'

"'My family is Cheyenne.'

"The little yellow points of light in his mean eyes kept studying my face. It was twenty years older than the face of the
young man who had outsmarted him at Santa Fe, but he must
have recognized something familiar in it. 'I've seen you before,'
he said, 'and I don't want to see you again. If you and your
squaw and whatever papooses you may claim, and that tipi, are

not cleared out of here by my next patrol, the tipi will be burned and all Cheyennes at this trading post put under arrest for transfer to the reservation below Sand Creek. Furthermore, if there is no white trader in charge here when I come again, the door of this trading post will be nailed shut. My authority is the Governor of this Territory, who has empowered me to drive all hostiles off these Plains. Do you understand? You speak as though you'd been schooled.'

"'I understand,' I said, trying to keep fear from my voice. It was not so much fear of Belcourt. He was a cowardly windbag, his evil akin to madness, but around him in the trading room the faces of his men, uncivilized, barely human, were all watching me, their eyes and mouths more brutish than those of carrion animals. They were the same faces I had seen as a youth in Georgia, the faces of the Pony Boys at New Echota and Okelogee empowered by another governor, a strain of human evil that has hunted my people across America and will not let us rest. No matter what barriers we may build against it, fear is always in us, especially when we stand as protectors of others. As Belcourt strode out the door, his men following, I fought against the fear in myself, remembering Creek Mary, who never ran from fear, and I promised her spirit that I would not run from it.

"No sooner had the cavalrymen gone away than Griffa, Sweet Medicine Woman, and Pleasant rushed into the trading room. They all had been in the kitchen listening, and each one began talking at the same time. Sweet Medicine Woman wanted to pack and start for Sand Creek, Griffa wondered if she could not leave the trading post in the care of Bibbs and Wewoka while she took her children back to Indian Territory, and Pleasant kept shouting that we should make a real fort of Fort Carrothers and defend ourselves.

"While we were chattering away, Major Easterwood was preparing to leave, expressing his thanks to us for our hospitality. I walked with him out the entrance.

"'What are you going to do now?' he asked.

"'I don't know,' I said.

"'Now you see why I have no taste for my assignment at Fort

Starke. Since I've been at Denver I've heard much about this Colonel Belcourt and his volunteer soldiers. They are not soldiers, but bullies, scourings of the frontier, too cowardly to fight either for or against the Union. The decent people in Denver despise Belcourt, but he has power over the territorial governor and I've been sent down here to inspect the regiment's arms and make recommendations. No matter what I recommend, Belcourt will get more arms. He has not yet many men under his command, but hundreds of riffraff in Denver will flock to Belcourt's regiment when they see that President Lincoln is in earnest about enforcing the draft laws out here on the frontier. When that happens, God have pity on you and your people.'

" 'They'll war on us?'

" 'They'll start an Indian war to keep from being ordered east to fight in a real war against the Confederates.'

"He touched my shoulder to say good-bye. 'You have a few weeks at best,' he said."

41

Not many hours after Flattery Jack Belcourt and Major Easterwood departed from Fort Carrothers, leaving everyone there in a state of alarm, Lean Bear and Red Bird Woman materialized like ghosts out of the stream behind the trading post. Lean Bear had led several Dog Soldiers and their families from Sand Creek to the Cheyennes' former winter camp at the Ghost Timbers, traveling by night as Yellow Hawk had done, using streams for pathways and avoiding soft ground so as to leave as few tracks as possible.

Other groups of Big Star's Cheyennes were following them, a day or two apart, no more than eight or ten families together, in hopes that most of them could elude the Bluecoat patrols, their plan being to rendezvous at the Ghost Timbers. From there they would go north together through the dry sandhills, moving as rapidly as they could until they reached the sanctuary of the Powder River country.

"Big Star has thought of this for a long time," Lean Bear said. "By going north we are turning against the treaty that old Wannesahta signed for the Cheyennes at Horse Creek. This troubles Big Star's heart. He does not wish to break his word even though the *Veheos* have broken their word on the treaty twenty times over. Big Star has seen in a vision that we will all die of starvation if we stay below Sand Creek. No rain has fallen there through the summer moons. Even the rabbits have fled. We must break our word to survive."

Because they had traveled without travois, the Dog Soldiers and their families at the Ghost Timbers had no shelter and very little food. "We left our tipis standing," Lean Bear said. "The others are leaving theirs. With dragging travois we could not escape the Bluecoats, and besides they will see our tipis across Sand Creek and think we are still there."

The Dog Soldiers had dug holes for concealment among the willows at the Timbers, covering them with limbs and brush, but as they dared not go out to hunt by daylight they would soon begin to hunger. "You must be very careful," Dane warned him. "The Bluecoats have built a new fort on the South Fork less than half a day's ride from the Timbers."

Lean Bear's full-lipped mouth fixed in a hard line. "We did not know of the fort," he said. "I would take the families on to the north, but Big Star will need the Dog Soldiers if the Bluecoats find him."

With Griffa's permission, Dane gave Lean Bear and Red Bird Woman a few bags of flour from the diminishing supply in the trading post. After these unexpected visitors rode away, Dane and Sweet Medicine Woman and Griffa sat with their sons in the

unlighted trading room until almost dawn, weighing the dangers
of remaining any longer at Fort Carrothers.

Griffa decided that she and Young Opothle and Meggi would
stay until Jotham came for them. She and her children, and
Pleasant, were no darker than the sun-tanned Bluecoats, and
none was Cheyenne. "I am less afraid of your Colonel Belcourt
than of the war in the Cherokee Nation," she said. "Jotham does
not want us there, with homes being burned and battles being
fought everywhere. Bibbs and Wewoka will not go back. They
are afraid of being made slaves again. So we will stay here."

Dane also thought it best for his family to remain at Fort Carrothers until all of Big Star's Cheyennes reached the Timbers.
Then he and his family would join them in the flight to Powder
River. By remaining at the trading post they could furnish some
food to the helpless Cheyennes in hiding at the Timbers; they at
least could risk hunting by daylight. But because of Belcourt's
threat to arrest any Cheyennes found there on his next patrol,
they decided to start keeping a watch from the loft room.
Through slits in the high walls they could see any movement on
the Plains for several miles. If an approaching patrol was
sighted, all the full-blood members of the family would conceal
themselves in the root cellar.

Old Jim Carrothers had built his root cellar well, its entrance
so secret and unhandy to use that Jotham and Griffa never both-
ered to store anything there. It had no trapdoor. To gain access,
a heavy kitchen table had to be moved to one side, and two full-
length floorboards, with false wooden pegs in them, lifted at the
ends. At daybreak Dane inspected the cellar and found it dry
and free of snakes, with more than enough space for his family
to conceal themselves in comfort.

Sweet Medicine Woman proposed that Griffa and her children
go north with the Cheyennes. "Never," Griffa replied with a
laugh. "In a village of tipis I would be as helpless as a fresh-
hatched bird. No, we will stay here."

And so they began their new daily routines, each member of
the family taking turns as lookouts in the loft, Pleasant and Swift
Eagle venturing for short distances to hunt what wild game they

could find. A day or so later, Meggi excitedly called from the loft
that a single Bluecoat was approaching from the east. The horseman was Major Easterwood. He stopped to rest in the trading
room, was friendly but sparing of words, and was soon on his
way to Denver.

During the next few days several more small parties of
Cheyennes made their way safely into the Ghost Timbers, the
news of their arrival being brought by Lean Bear, who made frequent night visits to obtain what meat or other rations those in
the trading post could spare. Aside from the shortage of food,
Lean Bear said, their greatest difficulty was concealment of
horses, which were growing in numbers with the arrival of each
group of fugitives from the south. He had seen Bluecoat patrols
far out on the Plains and he feared they might come closer and
discover the horses. If Big Star did not arrive soon, Lean Bear
thought, it might be best to start with the women and children
for the sandhills.

One afternoon Susa cried out from the loft that a Bluecoat was
approaching on foot from the west. Dane walked out to the trail
and soon recognized the limping man as Major Easterwood. Saddling a horse, he rode to meet him. The major barely had the
strength to mount behind Dane's saddle. His face was scratched
and bruised, his uniform encrusted with drying mud.

"My two wagons of rifles that I was bringing to Fort Starke
were ambushed by Indians," he told Dane.

"What Indians, what tribe?" Dane asked.

"I know nothing of your tribes. Their faces and upper bodies
were painted ferociously. Had they not slain my horse so that I
was plunged into a ditch and knocked senseless I am certain
they would have killed me as they killed at least one of my
drivers. When I regained consciousness one of my wagons and
its driver were missing. The other wagon was still there, but the
driver and both draft animals were dead."

Taking the two largest horses from the corral and a pony for
Major Easterwood, they started back for the site of the ambush.
On the way Dane wondered if one of Big Star's small parties
from Sand Creek had chanced upon the wagons and attacked

them, but he quickly dismissed the thought. The Cheyennes would have been accompanied by their families, they would not have wanted to be seen, and they certainly would not have been painted for war. He had heard of Oglala Sioux being in the area, but none had come as far as Fort Carrothers.

"You had only the two drivers and no soldier escort?" he asked Major Easterwood.

"I requisitioned a squad," Easterwood replied, "but the commander at Camp Weld assured me no escort would be needed."

Dane was puzzled. "The army always guards shipments of arms with several mounted men," he said.

"These people are not army," Easterwood answered dryly. "They wear the uniform, that is all."

They crossed a rotting bridge over a stagnant creek that turned and ran along the right side of the road. High grass and briers clogged each bank.

"The wagon's gone!" Easterwood cried.

In the road ahead lay a man and two draft horses without harness. Lying with half its body in the road and half in the brush-bordered creek was Major Easterwood's riding horse.

"They must have returned for the other wagon," Dane said, dismounting to study the tracks and other sign. He thought it odd that marks of wagon wheels led off into the creek. He picked an eagle feather from the dust; it was smeared with red paint. Two or three arrows were scattered here and there. The dead driver had not been scalped.

"Did they use arrows?" he asked Easterwood.

"I don't recall seeing any, but they may have." Easterwood pointed into a patch of thick briers that overhung the green-scummed stream. "That's where I was thrown. Lucky my head was out of the water."

"How were the Indians dressed?"

"It happened too quickly for me to see them well," Easterwood replied apologetically. "The nearest one to me wore buckskin leggings, and he had long hair. Black and red paint all over his face and upper body. I think it was he who killed my horse. I fired only a single shot at another who came up out of the brush on foot. He was shooting at the draft horses of the lead wagon. I remember seeing a flash of brass buttons along the sides of his pants. He stumbled and fell back, and then my horse went down and I lost consciousness."

Dane walked along the edge of the road, kneeled and looked at a cluster of small dark spots in the dust. "If he was about here," he said, "you must have hit him."

"Yes, it would have been along here." They both pushed into the brush. Dane reached the waterline and saw what appeared to be a green plant floating in the scum. He grabbed at it, caught slippery hair in his hand and pulled a human head above the surface. He dragged the body out into the road. The dead man's white skin bore faint markings of paint, not yet completely dissolved by the water. His sopping black velvet pants had brass buttons on the side.

Major Easterwood bent over to study the face. "I've seen this man at Fort Starke," he said. "He was a junior officer, a white man!"

"Most likely the others also were white," Dane said.

"Why would they attack their own wagons?"

Dane shook his head. "Maybe to sell the guns back to the army. Maybe to start an Indian scare. Is that not what you said Belcourt and his men want?"

"I can't believe they would go this far."

"They may already have reported an Indian attack. All they need is a rumor, and passing stagecoaches will spread it."

"Perhaps I can put a stop to their deviltries," Easterwood said. "Let's clear the road." Using their horses they pulled the dead animals into the creek. "Now, if you'll consent to lend me this pony and one of your horses," the major continued, "I'll take the two dead men into Fort Starke and report an attack on the wagons by renegades dressed as Indians."

42

Dane lifted his smoke-blackened coffeepot over to the rocking chair where Red Bird Woman sat motionless. "Was that same day you and your sons brought us wagon filled with guns?" she asked.

"That night, it was," Dane answered.

John Bear-in-the-Water, who had been listening intently, pointed a finger at Dane. "So your sons helped ambush the gun wagons?"

"Don't go outguessing me," Dane replied, hanging the pot carefully on its hook over the coals. "You see, after Major Easterwood rode off toward Fort Starke, I went to Sweet Medicine Woman and told her to get everything packed that we could carry on our horses. She did not want to leave her tipi with all of Amayi's designs and colors on it, but she knew her people had abandoned theirs at Sand Creek. It had to be done."

"But you lived in same tipi on Powder River," Red Bird Woman insisted.

"There you go now, like our young Crow friend, trying to get ahead of me," Dane scolded. "You see, it was in my mind to go to the Timbers and persuade Lean Bear to let me start the women and children north while he and his warriors waited for Big Star to come in. I knew we didn't have much time left before the Bluecoats would be on us.

"Darkness had just settled down when I heard the thumping of a slow-moving wagon across that stream from our tipi. At first I thought it was a Bluecoat patrol. Sometimes if they were in no hurry they'd burden themselves with a wagon. But in a minute or so, Pleasant and Swift Eagle came splashing across on foot. They were both grinning like raccoons with a secret.

"'Come over here and have a look,' Pleasant called when he recognized me in the dusk.

"Pulled up under a tree across the stream was the wagon, and hitched to it were the boys' riding horses. Pleasant lifted the canvas covering. The wagon was filled with wooden boxes of rifles and ammunition.

"I don't remember what I said to them, but it must have been a string of those old oaths I'd learned from Creek Mary. You see, like John Bear-in-the-Water here, my first thought was that my boys had been a part of that ambush. But it wasn't what it seemed to be. Pleasant and Swift Eagle were out hunting along the Lodgepole, with a little wooded slope between them and the stage road, when they heard gunfire popping over the rise. They crawled up in the high grass to the crest and saw the last part of the shooting. They were close enough to hear the attackers quarreling over whether they should abandon the wagon with the two dead horses. It was plain enough to Pleasant and Swift Eagle that the men in buckskins and feathers, with faces and bodies painted like no tribe they'd ever seen, were white men instead of Indians. Soon after the attackers rode away with the one wagon toward Denver, the boys saw Major Easterwood pull himself out of the briers. They waited until he limped on out of sight toward Fort Carrothers, and then they rode down to the trail.

"When they discovered that the abandoned wagon was filled with rifles, both agreed that the weapons were just what the Cheyennes at the Ghost Timbers needed to defend themselves. And so they took the harness off the dead team and hitched their horses to the wagon, hauled it along the bed of the shallow creek for a ways, and hid in a thicket until sundown.

"After Pleasant explained how they'd got the wagon, and was showing me the rifles, he grew very excited. 'They're Springfields,' he said. 'Same as the Union soldiers used at Elkhorn Tavern. And a good supply of cartridges and percussion caps.' He lifted one of them from a box he had broken open. 'I've fired four shots a minute with a gun like this. If we can get them to the Ghost Timbers, our warriors need not fear the Bluecoats.'

" 'We'll take the guns tonight,' I said.

"Before we left I told Sweet Medicine Woman to expect me and the boys back late on the following night, bringing the women and children with us, and for her to be ready to go. 'Through tomorrow's daylight, you and the girls stay inside the trading post,' I warned her. 'If you sight Bluecoats in any direction, hide in the root cellar.'

" 'Little Cloud is going with you?' she asked anxiously.

" 'We'll need him to ride guard for the women and children,' I said, but I did not tell her we also might need him to defend the gun wagon if we ran into a night patrol of Bluecoats.

"With Bibbs's help, we fastened gunnysacks around the wagon tires, hoping this would soften the sounds of the turning wheels and also confuse any trackers who might be looking for sign at next daylight. Pleasant took the lead, I drove the wagon, and Swift Eagle and Little Cloud rode far out on either side.

"Because of our late start, by the time we neared the Ghost Timbers the trees were already black shapes against the brightening eastern sky. I lashed the wagon team into a faster pace and Pleasant rode in ahead to tell the Cheyennes of the prize we were bringing them. Very soon, then, Lean Bear and his Dog Soldiers came galloping out to meet the wagon, shouting cries of victory and shaking their lances.

"The camp was already astir because of the arrival earlier in the night of Big Star's party from Sand Creek. We at once held a family reunion, Pleasant rushing to find Rising Fawn, and Big Star and Bear Woman embracing their grandsons, questioning them at length about their mother and sisters, and scolding me for not also bringing them from Fort Carrothers.

"Big Star had been the last to leave Sand Creek, and he was worried because the party ahead of him had not yet come in. 'War Shirt is the leader,' he said. 'All are Fox Soldiers with their families, some of them riding two on a pony.' Being a Fox Soldier myself, most of War Shirt's men were like brothers to me, and I knew they were the craftiest of the Cheyennes at throwing pursuers off the scent. Unless they'd run into bad luck, I was sure they'd reach the Timbers.

"Big Star, of course, was pleased by the windfall of Springfield rifles, and he took charge of distributing them and the ammunition to the best shots among the warriors. He then called a council and it was decided that if War Shirt did not come in by nightfall we would start north, leaving only the Dog Soldiers to wait for the overdue party. The council was just breaking up when one of the lookouts in a tall tree shouted a warning. With their new Springfields, the warriors hurried to the brush-covered sandpits. Some of the women gathered the children into dugouts, while others ran to the horse herd back in a willow thicket to keep the animals quiet.

"Swift Eagle and I joined Big Star and my brother-in-law Yellow Hawk behind the gnarled roots of a huge cottonwood. Two small dust clouds were rolling toward us across the plain.

"'War Shirt and his Fox Soldier people!' Yellow Hawk cried. 'Bluecoats behind them!'

"I shaded my eyes and tried to count the pursuing soldiers. Fifty or sixty at least. And they were fast closing the gap on War Shirt's small party, many of whom were riding double. They were my brothers, the Fox Soldiers, and I rose to my feet, wanting to ride to help them.

"About that time Lean Bear came bounding over to Big Star, begging the chief to send the Dog Soldiers out to save War Shirt. I added my words to Lean Bear's pleas. We had guns as good as the Bluecoats and we were better fighters. We could drive the soldiers away and then start for the north."

"Oh, but I remember that day," Red Bird Woman interrupted, and she began rocking back and forth with such agitation that she spilled coffee in the lap of her spotted dress. "A strange feeling come over me when I saw Lean Bear running back to the horse herd with Dog Soldiers. He looked big and handsome that day, shouting and laughing, but something was raging in his eyes, something I never saw before in Lean Bear's eyes. I ran to give him my medicine bag for protection, but he had his Dog Soldier sash and rattle and quirt. He was gone galloping like a ghost, waving his new rifle like it was more medicine than he ever carried before."

"We were all a little foolish that day," Dane said. "I saw Pleasant and his wife, Rising Fawn, go racing out side by side from the willows, with Little Cloud close behind them, and then Swift Eagle and Yellow Hawk and I, we all ran for horses. Red Bird Woman let me have her sorrel mare.

"The Dog Soldiers were singing their song of battle as they rode out. The same thought must have come to all of us when we saw the flashing sabers of the Bluecoats pursuing our brothers and their families. What right did the Bluecoats have to drive us from a country that the Maker of Breath gave us before the coming of the whites? By what right did they tell us we could not go where we pleased over our land rich in grass and buffalo?"

43

As soon as Lean Bear was clear of the Timbers, he signaled his Dog Soldiers into a V-formation. He rode at the point like the head of an arrow flying toward a low flat-topped rise that lay between the Bluecoats and War Shirt's hard-pressed little band. Strung out behind the Dog Soldiers were warriors of other soldier societies. Lean Bear halted his men on the rising ground, quickly forming them into two ranks facing the oncoming Bluecoats, and motioning the other warriors to fall in behind. When he saw that War Shirt's people were wheeling in confusion, he ordered some of the warriors in the rear to ride and escort them into the Timbers. Among those he sent were Yellow Hawk and Swift Eagle. They were reluctant to leave the war party, but Lean Bear was the war chief, and no one questioned his command.

The Bluecoats slowed their horses, the four platoons forming front into line at the command of a black-mustached captain. Far behind them was a smaller dust cloud, a mountain howitzer bouncing over sagebrush and grass hassocks like a live monster pursuing the frenzied horses that gave it motion. The captain's rapid commands, echoed by hoarse-voiced sergeants, reminded Dane of the barking of quarrelsome dogs. *Second and third platoons! As skirmishers! March! Prepare to fight—on foot! Into line! First and fourth platoons! Halt!* The clanking metal, the creaking leather, seemed unnaturally loud on the heavy morning air as the men in the center of the blue line dismounted and formed into ragged squads. They moved awkwardly, uncertain of what they were doing, and the Cheyennes could smell their fear.

Holding his horse steady a few paces to the rear of the Dog Soldiers, Dane saw the eagle feather in Lean Bear's hair angle backward. Lean Bear had lifted his chin and was holding his head rigid, alert for any sign of panic among the nervous recruits from the Denver saloons and gambling houses. He knew that fear was more dangerous than bravado among such men as these.

Lean Bear wanted no bloodshed. He had accomplished what he set out to do. War Shirt's party was safely entering the Ghost Timbers. Now all of Big Star's Cheyennes were together again, ready to travel north to the Powder River country where they would be out of the way of the Bluecoats. To Lean Bear it seemed reasonable that the Bluecoats would let them go. But first he had to make them understand that the Cheyennes must go north to keep from starving. He turned in his saddle, his eyes narrowing against the sunlight. "Dane!" he called out, motioning him to come forward.

Dane guided the sorrel mare through the close-packed mass of horsemen, each warrior watchful of the twelve-pounder howitzer that had been halted a hundred yards beyond the cavalry. The artillery horses were unhitched, the gun unlimbered. The black-mustached captain wheeled his mount, rode back a few paces, shouted something to the gunners, then turned and came back to take a position slightly to the rear of the dismounted cavalrymen. He stuck a long cigar in his mouth, clamping his teeth on it.

"I will make talk with the soldier chief," Lean Bear said to Dane. "You say the *Veheo* words. I do not want misunderstanding between me and the soldier chief."

"At this distance he may not hear clearly," Dane replied.

"We go closer." Lean Bear started his pony forward.

The Dog Soldier on Lean Bear's left, a young warrior named Porcupine, also put his pony into motion. Lean Bear gave him a sharp glance.

"I do not trust the hairy-mouth chief of the Bluecoats," Porcupine said. "My body will be Lean Bear's shield."

"Stay behind me," Lean Bear ordered roughly. "I am not a cringing coward like the Bluecoats there." He rode on, with Dane alone at his side. "Drop your rifle easy on the ground," Lean Bear said quietly to Dane. As both weapons slapped against the earth, Lean Bear clasped his hands before him in the peace sign. Then he lifted his left arm toward the sun, closing his fingers as though clasping the hand of the Great Spirit.

"Halt where you are!" the captain shouted.

"Tell him we come with peaceful hearts," Lean Bear said.

Dane put the words into English, calling them loud and clear across the twenty paces.

"You broke off my pursuit of reservation jumpers," the captain answered harshly. "By hostile action." His eyes were hard under the visor of his forage cap.

"Tell him those he was pursuing are our brothers," Lean Bear said. "Tell him we want only to go in peace to the north country. Tell him we will starve if we do not go north to the buffalo."

When he heard the English words, the captain lifted his saber, pointing it at Lean Bear. "You'll go where the army tells you to go!" he cried.

Lean Bear turned in his saddle, was surprised to see Porcupine just behind him, one of the new Springfields balanced in his arms. Four or five other Dog Soldiers had moved out from the front rank. Lean Bear motioned them back, and made a sign for all the warriors to lift their rifles high in the air. "Tell the Blue-coat chief," Lean Bear said softly, "to look upon the power of our warriors."

The captain shook his head angrily, sunlight flashing off the brass insignia of crossed sabers on his cap. "My orders are to kill Cheyennes where I find them!" he retorted. *Second and third platoons! Ready aim, fire!*

Dane saw thin puffs of blue smoke spurt from the rifle muzzles, heard an explosive rattle, felt fire burn the side of his head. Red Bird Woman's sorrel whirled beneath him, the earth spun, and in front of him he saw Lean Bear floating out of his saddle, his naked chest streaked with blood. Porcupine was facedown on the ground, the sorrel springing over his body. Dane slumped forward over the mare's neck, swaying loosely in the saddle, but his ears seemed stopped against sound. He tried to raise up but could not. His fingers gripped the sorrel's mane before he lost consciousness.

In response to the first volley from the dismounted troopers, the Dog Soldiers surged forward, firing at the Bluecoats before they could reload, and then used their ponies to scatter them. At the same time other Cheyenne warriors swept around the Dog Soldiers to engage the mounted cavalrymen on the left and right. These soldiers tried to wield their sabers, but fire from the Cheyennes' Springfields followed by use of lances and rifle butts drove the Bluecoats back toward the twelve-pounder howitzer. The captain hastily retreated to the artillery piece, and he was riding back and forth trying to block the disorganized flight of his men. He shouted angrily at a young bugler who was too frightened to blow more than a rasping note or two in his attempt at a rallying call. When two fleeing cavalrymen swept by him, the bugler threw his trumpet on the ground and joined the retreat.

"Fire the goddamned cannon!" the captain shouted. The boom and swish of the howitzer sent riderless horses scattering across the plain. Pellets of shot sprayed the empty flat-topped rise where the Cheyennes had been moments before.

Cursing angrily, the captain leaned from his saddle and slapped the artillery sergeant across the back with the flat of his saber. "Lower the barrel, you bastard! Point-blank!" The gunners fired once more, the shot tearing into a limping cavalry horse. To the right and left of the gun, the retreat was becoming a rout. The captain was no longer in sight. Without waiting for an order, the gunners quickly mounted and abandoned their useless cannon.

Furious over the killing of Lean Bear, the Cheyenne warriors pressed the fleeing Bluecoats relentlessly, giving them no chance to halt and make a stand. Because of the speed of the horses, few shots could be fired by either pursuers or pursued.

Among those who rode the hardest was Pleasant McAlpin. To him, Lean Bear was more than a friend; he was the father he had never found in Dane. When Pleasant saw the Bluecoats fire on Lean Bear and Dane, it was Lean Bear he burned to revenge. In hot anger he fired too quickly at the Bluecoat captain and missed. Pleasant was the first of the Dog Soldiers to reach Lean Bear, dismounting and bloodying his buckskin shirt when he tried to find life in the bleeding body, crying when he found no life, as he had cried at Poison Spider Creek beside his dead Appaloosa. On that day Lean Bear had been his father.

His eyes blurring with tears of anger, Pleasant turned then to discover what had happened to his real father. He was relieved to see Dane bent forward in the saddle of the sorrel that was galloping wildly for the Ghost Timbers.

In a single motion Pleasant remounted, one thought now fixed in his mind. He must kill the Bluecoat captain. Not until he swung his horse out and around the abandoned cannon was he aware that Rising Fawn on her fast-footed mustang was still beside him. Little Cloud and Lean Bear's young nephew, Spotted Shield, were close behind.

Several times Pleasant was able to load and fire his rifle, but he knew that from the saddle of a charging horse he was unlikely to hit any moving target. His hope was that the Bluecoats' mounts would tire before they reached Fort Starke, and as the sun rose higher in the sky he began to see signs of weariness among the cavalry horses.

"Listen!" Rising Fawn called suddenly, raising one hand. Above the sound of their hoofbeats came a louder drumming, and then ahead to the right, over the rim of an undulation in the plain, appeared a column of mounted Bluecoats, their bright pennons fluttering as they swept down the slope. One horseman remained on the crest, but even from that distance Pleasant could not mistake the hulking figure seated arrogantly in the saddle. "Belcourt," he said aloud, "with fresh mounts from Fort Starke." The exhausted Bluecoats in front of him began cheering, and he knew the chase was over.

Beckoning to Rising Fawn, he turned his horse. The Cheyennes were scattering in three directions, urging their spent ponies to one more burst of speed, seeking cover of high grass, hillocks, gullies, and streams.

Frightening off a pair of pursuing Bluecoats with a shot from his rifle, Pleasant found concealment in a weed-bordered dry wash. When he dismounted, his horse was wet with froth, its muscles trembling. He loaded his rifle to cover the approach of Rising Fawn's faltering mustang. Not a Bluecoat was in sight, but she slowed the pony and kept looking back.

"Hurry!" he shouted at her.

Anxiety was in her face when she dismounted beside him. "Little Cloud and Spotted Shield," she said. "The Bluecoats cut them off."

44

"All I ever knew about that fight was what I heard from Pleasant and some of the others," Dane said. He lifted one of his braids and showed me a scar behind his ear. "You might not think a scratch like that could put a man into the Darkening Land. Maybe I would still be there if Red Bird Woman had not brought me back to the land of the living."

"That old medicine man, Two Crows, he brought you back," Red Bird Woman insisted. "Two Crows kept shaking his deer-hoof sticks and a piece of buffalo tail over you till your eyes opened."

"When I opened my eyes," Dane said, "your mouth was on my wound sucking the blood out."

"Two Crows told me I must do that."

Red Bird Woman glanced at me, the white stranger, a flash of shyness in her eyes that made her face seem suddenly young again. "That was terrible day," she said. "When we first heard guns firing we ran to edge of willow thicket. I could see smoke of guns and then my sorrel mare come galloping to me with Dane flopping across its withers like dead man. The horse stopped running when it smelled me and walked right up to me. I pulled Dane out of saddle, but his hands would not turn loose of mane, like they was frozen there. Dane's legs hung loose and his face was pressed against sorrel's neck, and I had to pull each of his fingers loose from mane hairs.

"But that was not worst of that day. Worst was when they brought Lean Bear's bloodied body to me and told me he was dead." She turned to face me, her shyness gone now, her full wide mouth remembering a long-ago sadness, her fingers touching thin white lines across her unwrinkled forehead. "I too am scarred from that day. I gashed my forehead for Lean Bear, letting blood run into my eyes. If a high cliff had been near Hinta Nagi, I might of gone and jumped. I was Lean Bear's woman."

We all sat silent for a minute or more, and then Dane dropped a chunk of wood into the fireplace, making sparks fly and crackle. "By late afternoon," he said, "I felt strong enough to help in building scaffolds for the dead. Lean Bear, Porcupine, and four others. We left the dead Bluecoats where they fell. Because they acted so cowardly, no one wanted to take their scalps, but some of the women went out and cut the brass buttons off their coats. Most of our young men had not returned from chasing the soldiers, and we were all uneasy about what might have happened to them. The women and children were ready to start north, but it was long after dark before the Dog Soldiers and the other warriors came in. When they told us what had happened we knew we could not leave that night.

"Pleasant told me about it first. He and Rising Fawn stayed in the dry wash until the soldiers went back to the fort about sundown. The warriors came together then, intending to search for any who might be wounded or dead. Only Little Cloud and Spotted Shield were missing, and some of the Dog Soldiers told Pleasant they had seen the Bluecoats trap the young boys. They shot their ponies, but instead of killing the boys they tied them with ropes, and two men with stripes on their sleeves started off with them toward Fort Starke. Pleasant wanted to go at once and storm the fort, but the others told him they would all be killed by the big guns mounted on the walls."

Red Bird Woman made a soft sound in her throat. "Spotted Shield," she broke in, "was near to a son as I ever had. That night when they told me Bluecoats had made prisoner of Spotted Shield, I said it was just as well Lean Bear went to Land of Spirits. Lean Bear wanted a son but I could not give him one, and so he looked upon his nephew Spotted Shield like a son. Yes, he and Pleasant might of stormed that fort by themselves and both would been killed."

"We talked through the night," Dane continued. "Bear Woman and some others had found enough old lodgepoles to make a tipi frame, covering it with blankets and robes and pieces of clothing so the chief would have a proper place for councils. We sat there in the tipi—Big Star, Swift Eagle, Pleasant, Yellow Hawk, Spotted Shield's father and brothers, several of the women. My wound hurt and bled a little, but the medicine man told me it would heal quick if I did not cover it. Pleasant's anger had cooled by then and he knew as well as we that the Cheyennes could not recover the boys by attacking the fort. The Bluecoats would kill us all. None of us could guess why they wanted the young boys. 'Perhaps they want to trade them or sell them,' Big Star said. 'I have heard that the *Veheos* do these things.'

"'Trade them for what?' Pleasant asked.

"'Perhaps for the big gun they left when they ran away,' Big Star said.

"Pleasant thought this was a possibility. Big Star then told Yellow Hawk to go and call out his Fox Soldier brothers and roll the big gun into the Hinta Nagi so that we would have it in our possession if the Bluecoats wanted to trade the boys for it.

"I sat there most of the night listening to the others and wondering about Little Cloud and worrying about Sweet Medicine Woman, who I knew must be awake waiting for us to come as I had promised. Then I said to Big Star that the only thing to be done was for me to go to Fort Starke under a truce flag and find out what the Bluecoats might want in ransom for our boys.

"'This would be a dangerous thing for you to do, *Sanaki*,' Big Star replied.

"'That is so,' Pleasant agreed. 'Colonel Belcourt marked you that day he came to the trading post. He hates your dark Indian skin. If anyone goes to the fort, it shall be Pleasant McAlpin with my white man's pallor and blue eyes.'

"Big Star said he must think awhile on this undertaking, seek a vision. He was disposed to wait through one more day. Perhaps the Bluecoats would tell us what they wanted with our boys, but if they did not, the leaders must decide in council what we must do. 'The blood of my family runs in the veins of both Spotted Shield and Little Cloud,' Big Star said. 'Yet if they must be sacrificed to save the seed of this Cheyenne band—the women and children—then it must be done. We can risk waiting here but one more day.'

"We did not have long to wait. Before the sun was above the rim of the earth, our lookouts called a warning. Bluecoats, only a few, were approaching from the south under a truce flag. Before they reached the flat-topped rise where the fighting had started, they began lifting the dead Bluecoats from the ground and fastening their bodies to the backs of led ponies. Then they raised the white flag higher and started toward the Timbers, walking their horses very slowly. The officer in the lead was Major Easterwood. Most of the men with him were the gunners that our warriors had chased from their cannon.

"'I saw that Bluecoat chief in a dream,' Big Star said. 'I must dress in the dragoon uniform the *Veheos* gave me at Horse Creek.' He went into the makeshift tipi, and I mounted a horse and rode out with Pleasant and some of the Dog Soldiers to meet Major Easterwood. He was surprised to see me there, but made no comment other than to say that he had come to visit our chief.

"By the time we returned to the tipi, Big Star was standing very straight in front of it, a handsome old man with his white hair reaching the shoulders of the dark blue dragoon coat. Hanging over the brass buttons was the medal with the clasped hands of the treaty signers. He also held his copy of the scarlet-ribboned treaty.

"About twenty paces from the tipi, Major Easterwood halted his men, ordering them to remain where they were while he dismounted and limped slowly toward Big Star. I could tell that Easterwood was affected by the chief's military costume and his dignified bearing. 'I am Major Easterwood,' he said. 'I come from Fort Starke, commanded by Colonel Belcourt.'

"I had to interpret the words and when I finished, the major thanked me.

"'You have come here to talk about our young men,' Big Star said.

"Easterwood looked puzzled, uncertain as to what the chief meant, and so I spoke their names, Little Cloud and Spotted Shield. 'My son and a relative of the chief's,' I added. 'Why have the soldiers made captives of them?'

"'I have not come,' Easterwood said, 'to talk about the two young boys. My instructions from Colonel Belcourt are to recover the bodies of our dead and the mountain howitzer, and to order the chief to take his Cheyenne people back to their reservation below Sand Creek.'

"Big Star was angry when he heard these words. 'You have the bodies of your dead,' he said to Easterwood. 'Take them. But you will not take the big gun until you bring our boys to us.'

"Major Easterwood was silent for a while, looking first at me and then at Big Star. 'The two boys,' he said then, 'will be moved to Denver for a military trial. They are accused of ambushing wagons carrying army rifles.'

"'You know this is not true,' I shouted at him before interpreting the words for Big Star.

"His voice was almost a whisper. 'I know,' he said. 'But Colonel Belcourt wants it that way. The men who own Denver want it that way. There is nothing I can do.' He gave me a strange look. 'You have some of our rifles here. They were used against our men yesterday.'

"'They were the guns in the abandoned wagon,' I explained. 'If we had not had the fast-shooting rifles in our hands, the cavalry and mountain howitzer would have destroyed us.'

"When Big Star understood what was to happen to Little Cloud and Spotted Shield he had a hard time controlling his anger and his words. He unrolled the treaty and showed it to Major Easterwood. 'On this paper are the names of your soldier chiefs and agents of the Great Father,' he said. 'The name of Wannesahta, keeper of our sacred medicine arrows, is there for the Cheyennes. The white man's writing promised us land from the North Platte to the Arkansas, from the Great Mountains to the fork of the Platte, for hunting and traveling over as our fathers hunted and traveled over this country before the white men came here. Now you tell us we must live in the barren land below Sand Creek where there is nothing for us to eat. We want only to go away from you, to the north, where we can live in peace. Why do you not let my people go?'

"Easterwood's face showed the shame he felt in his heart. He shook his head. 'I know nothing of these things,' he said bitterly. 'I am only a messenger, a simple soldier from the East.' He looked at me, then quickly turned his eyes away. 'With your permission, my men will take that howitzer over there beyond the willow brush,' he said.

" 'When you give us our two young boys, you can take the big gun,' Big Star told him.

"Easterwood drew in his breath, sighed, and spread his hands. 'You are making a grave mistake,' he said. 'Colonel Belcourt . . .' Without finishing what he was going to say, he turned and limped back to his horse and mounted. 'If your people don't start for Sand Creek,' he called to me, 'I fear for the lives of all of you.' "

45

The dust of Major Easterwood's departing squad had scarcely disappeared on the horizon when Pleasant McAlpin and a dozen Dog Soldiers rode out of the Ghost Timbers in the opposite direction. After splashing through the shallow waters of the Platte, they followed a winding tributary, a small stream that eventually cut across the stagecoach road. No bridge had been built over this broad sandy crossing which rarely ran deep enough to wet the spokes of passing vehicles. Stagecoach drivers usually stopped briefly at the ford to let their teams drink before continuing the long run to the next station.

Fringing this crooked stream were growths of sandgrass, turning in late summer from green to gold, reaching higher than a man's head. Here the Dog Soldiers dismounted, two of them leading the ponies upstream until they were out of sight of the road. Pleasant and the remaining warriors then concealed themselves in the high grass and waited for the overland stage from the east.

The stagecoach was behind schedule that day, and it approached the ford with such speed that Pleasant feared it might not stop. Through his shield of grass he watched the driver anxiously, was relieved when he saw the man pull back on his lines, yelling *whoa* at the six-horse team. The stage was crowded, four men seated on the top, a woman beside the driver.

Pleasant waited until the driver dismounted. The man's black boots splashed in the water. He loosened the lines and unbitted the horses, patting their necks as they bent to drink. Sounding a shrill whistle, Pleasant stepped out in front of the team, his Springfield aimed at the driver. At the same moment five Dog Soldiers appeared on each side of the coach, one springing upon the top to knock a pistol from the hands of a startled male passenger, and to seize a rifle from another before either could be brought into action. During their raids against the invading *Veheos* in Kansas, these Dog Soldiers had learned from Lean Bear the value of surprise.

"We're carrying nothing but passengers," the driver said calmly to Pleasant. "Nothing you bucks would want."

Pleasant walked to the coach and jerked the door open, motioning the passengers to get out. Above him on the driver's seat, the woman began screaming. Two well-dressed men, a soldier with his arm in a sling, and three younger passengers stepped down on the wet sand. Pleasant studied the faces of the three young people. One was a boy of sixteen or seventeen, another a freckled red-haired boy about ten, and a blonde curly-haired little girl, perhaps seven or eight, who made him think for just a flash of his mother, Jerusha.

The oldest of the three was trembling with fright. The red-haired boy's eyes were big, but he was grinning with the delight that dangerous excitement sometimes brings to the young. The little girl spoke first: "Are you going to rob us?"

"No," Pleasant said. With his rifle barrel, he pushed the two younger children toward the farther bank of the stream. "Go and stand over there," he ordered.

"You ain't no Indian," the red-haired boy said.

Pleasant felt his anger rising. He was listening for the concealed ponies, but the woman in the driver's seat kept screaming. He shouted up at her: "Be quiet and no harm will come to your children."

"What do you want of them?" she cried.

"Your children will likely be in Denver sooner than you," he answered roughly.

Two Dog Soldiers were unhitching the stage team. Pleasant saw the holders bringing the Cheyenne ponies, their heads bobbing above the high grass. As soon as the ponies were in the road, the Dog Soldiers began mounting. Three of them led away pairs of the stagecoach team. Two others lifted the red-haired boy and the curly-haired little girl behind their saddles and started quickly off. The woman began screaming again.

"You harm them children, half-breed," the stagecoach driver said to Pleasant, "and you'll have every man in Denver after your neck. They're Tom Boyle's brats."

Keeping their rifles on the horseless stagecoach, Pleasant and the remaining Dog Soldiers danced their ponies back from it, whirled, and galloped toward the Platte.

When the Dog Soldiers returned to the Hinta Nagi, the two *Veheo* children they brought with them quickly attracted a crowd of Cheyennes. Big Star soon dispersed the adults, believing they might alarm the young hostages. "But they show no fear," Bear Woman said. This was true. The red-haired boy was curious about the mountain howitzer. He asked Pleasant where the Cheyennes had obtained the cannon and if they had fired it at soldiers. The little girl examined the clothing of the Cheyenne children gathered around Big Star's patchwork tipi and was puzzled because she could not understand what was said to her. Both she and the boy soon joined a playing circle for the *suhkpakhit* game. The children held hands with fingers interlocked, while one in the middle tried to break out of the circle. The red-haired boy volunteered to be locked in. He broke out with a loud whoop of triumph, but was quickly pursued and slapped to the ground, rolling and laughing in the leaves.

The question of who was to take the offer of exchange to Fort Starke had to be settled by Big Star. Pleasant and Dane were equally determined to be the message-bearer. Pleasant argued that he and the Dog Soldiers had captured the children and that it was his right to arrange the exchange for Little Cloud and Spotted Shield. Dane declared that he was the older and that only he could count on Major Easterwood as an ally against Belcourt in the event the colonel was reluctant to cooperate. Aware of Pleasant's quick temper, remembering his recklessness the day he helped bring the soldiers from Platte Bridge against the Cheyenne village, Big Star decided that Dane should go to Fort Starke.

"We shall both go," Pleasant insisted.

"No." Dane shook his head. "Those children are your responsibility. They can't make themselves understood with their *Veheo* talk to anyone here but you."

Dane started to Fort Starke late in the night, riding slowly so that he would arrive there soon after sunrise. This was the first time he had seen the new fort, and except that it was much larger, it reminded him of the Tennessee stockade in which a quarter of a century before he and his Cherokee kinsmen had suffered and died. A rectangle of tall poles connected four massive blockhouses at each corner. From the upper walls of the blockhouses, barrels of swivel guns pointed from long narrow loopholes. Between the north side of the stockade and the South Fork was a large corral crowded with hundreds of horses, dozens of wagons, high stacks of bagged grain, and a tented smithy.

As Dane approached, he wondered what mighty force Flattery

Jack Belcourt was in dread of. Who was it that he feared would raise up arms against him upon this lonely plain?

From the guard post above the gate a sentry challenged. "I come to talk with Colonel Belcourt," Dane called out. He heard voices inside, and then after several minutes the heavy gate slowly opened. Two guards held pistols pointed at him and told him to dismount. A third man searched him. He had come unarmed. The third man led his horse off toward the corral, while guards escorted him into a room at the base of the nearest blockhouse.

Flattery Jack was seated at a table eating breakfast, his shell jacket unbuttoned, his gray hair uncombed. He wolfed down a large piece of ham and glared at Dane.

"You! You again? Where have I seen you before, a long time ago. Why do you come to annoy me at breakfast time?"

"I bring a message," Dane said.

"From who, from where?"

"From Big Star of the Cheyennes."

Belcourt poured whiskey from a bottle into his china coffee cup. Dane could smell the fumes blending with the aroma of hot coffee.

"Two white children are in the Cheyenne camp at the Ghost Timbers," Dane said quietly. "They will be traded to you for the two young Cheyennes you hold in this fort."

"The ambushers of my rifle wagons! Why should I set free a pair of murdering thieves? You go back and tell Big Star that if he is not out of the Timbers with his people and on his way to Sand Creek by sundown, I'll exterminate every man, woman, and child in his tribe." Belcourt took a long swallow of his whiskey and coffee. "Who are these white children? From where do they come?"

"From Denver," Dane replied. "I believe their name is Boyle."

"Boyles of Denver? How old? Boys, girls?"

Dane described the red-haired boy and the blonde girl.

"Tom Boyle's younglings! Damn you! How in hell did—" Belcourt shouted at one of the guards standing in the doorway: "Corporal, get my adjutant in here!"

After the arrival of the adjutant, a lean sour-faced officer, Dane was ordered out of Belcourt's quarters. From where he stood, still under guard, he could see tents in the open space within the stockade. He also could smell meat cooking. Saliva flowed in his mouth. For two days he had shared the skimpy cold rations of the Cheyennes in the Timbers, and he felt an acute craving for food. While he waited he looked in every direction for Major Easterwood, wondering in what part of the fort he might be.

Belcourt and the adjutant came out. "On second thought," Belcourt was saying, "we'd better leave two companies here. You can't tell when some bunch of crazy drunked-up hostiles might try to take this fort." He turned to the guards. "Bring the redskin." The guards fell in beside Dane and marched him behind Belcourt across to the opposite blockhouse. A sergeant saluted the colonel and led the way inside a short corridor where there were two facing doors locked by metal bolts. Belcourt slid one of the bolts back and opened the door. "Outside," he said, and Little Cloud and Spotted Shield stepped cautiously into the corridor, their moccasins shuffling on the hard earthen floor, their eyes revealing uncertainty, searching for some meaning in the faces of those in front of them.

Suddenly recognizing his father, Little Cloud moved toward Dane, but Belcourt kicked the boy sharply in the buttocks, so that he stumbled past the guards. Then with one of his huge fleshy hands Belcourt pushed Dane into the emptied cell and closed the iron-bolted door upon him. "It was you," Belcourt shouted through the door, "who led the raid against my rifle wagons. And if you lied to me about the Boyle children, I'll bring these boys back to be put on trial with you in Denver."

46

"Being locked up in Fort Starke, I did not see the exchange," Dane said, "but Red Bird Woman was there. She can tell about it. And what happened afterward."

Her dark eyes regarded me as though she were dubious of my loyalties. She did not quite trust me, the white stranger. "Belcourt was evil spirit," she said slowly. "Some evil spirits have no fear, but that one was coward. He brought many Bluecoats close by Ghost Timbers, with two big guns on wheels. Then he sent his young men with stripes on sleeves to Big Star to talk about white children."

"Belcourt was afraid to come in himself?" I asked. "So he sent some enlisted men?"

"Yes, the young men with stripes on sleeves kept riding back and forth between Big Star and Belcourt. Belcourt was way out on rising ground with Bluecoats all around him like he in great fear of us.

"Then they brought doctor soldier. He said Belcourt want him to look at little girl to see if she been harmed. If she been harmed, Belcourt shoot one of our boys, Little Cloud or Spotted Shield, and trade his dead body for little girl. Doctor soldier took little girl in Big Star's tipi. Bear Woman went in with them. She said little girl cried when doctor soldier took her clothes off and put his fingers on her *san*. Doctor soldier seem surprised no harm been done to her.

"Soon after, Big Star and Pleasant and some other Dog Soldiers took children out to edge of Ghost Timbers, and Bluecoats with stripes on sleeves brought Little Cloud and Spotted Shield.

Little boy with red hair not want to leave us. He kept on begging Pleasant to let him stay and live with us. Little girl was crying and would not let doctor soldier carry her. Two Bluecoats then come in with horses and dragged big gun away.

"I thought Bluecoats go away after they trade us Little Cloud and Spotted Shield for children. They put children in wagon and it went along Platte in direction of ford, toward Denver. Then Bluecoats separated, some going one way, some another way, till Bluecoats around us in all four directions. Some more wagons come then from fort. They put up tent, and start feasting and singing. Pleasant told me tent was for Belcourt and one of wagons was filled with whiskey for Bluecoats to drink to drive away fear. I said it take much whiskey to make them not cowards, but I guess they had much whiskey.

"Late in day they start firing big guns at Hinta Nagi. Pieces of metal like hail tore leaves and bark from trees and stung our horses. All us except Big Star got into dugouts. Big Star was dressed in that Bluecoat uniform the *Veheos* gave him at Horse Creek. I thought Big Star's medicine must be strong because pieces of metal flying everywhere but nothing could hit him. Bear Woman was with me in sandpit nearby and she kept on lifting up tree boughs to see if Big Star all right.

"When daylight got like color of brown water in creek, just before dark, we heard bugles blowing all around us. The Bluecoats yelled all together, and then their horses started toward us from the four directions, their hoofbeats pounding, so many fast hoofbeats, like that time one summer we camped on the Nako and buffalo herd got scared of Thunderbird's lightning and ran right through our village. Buffalo herd ran on us from one direction, but Bluecoats come from four directions, firing guns and screaming like wolves gone crazy. When they come in on us, children and most women stay down in sandpits and dugouts. Some women like me and Bear Woman and Rising Fawn, we have guns instead of children and like warriors we rise up to shoot.

"Some of us got killed and bad wounded. Some of our children got frightened and tried to run and Bluecoats shot them like buffalo calves. I saw little girl not quite hid in sandpit. Two Bluecoats shot her with pistols and pulled her out of sand and dragged her. I saw woman trying to hide baby in her arms, but Bluecoat slashed it with saber and cut woman's belly open. But I think what happened to us at Ghost Timbers not so bad as happened later on to our relatives at Black Kettle's camp on Sand Creek. There Bluecoats waited till Black Kettle's warriors went off to hunt buffalo, and then they come and killed many women and children and old men. Bluecoats cut up bodies, cut off private parts, and wore them on hats. If we all stayed at Sand Creek, same might of happened to us.

"At Ghost Timbers we had warriors and good guns to fight with. Many Bluecoats so drunk they can't shoot straight. They rode horses into sandpits and dugouts, hurting selves and horses and some of our people. Our warriors shot many Bluecoats. After Bluecoats rode once through our camp, they not come back again, not even try to get their dead and wounded. Those Bluecoat scalps worthless, because such cowards nobody wanted scalps. But when we found Big Star lying dead in front of tipi, eyes open looking at sky, medal with white man's hand shaking red man's hand all covered with blood, and Big Star's fingers froze around that treaty paper, we all become crazy, we women crazier than men, and so we went and killed all Bluecoat wounded and scalped them. One of wounded Bluecoats had a pistol and he shot Rising Fawn."

47

The Fort Starke guardhouse room in which Dane was imprisoned was barely long enough for a man to lie on its earthen
floor. No light or air entered except through an unchinked crack
in the timbers, an opening that afforded him a narrow view of
the south side of the fort. From time to time he saw squads of
mounted soldiers hurrying around from the corral on the north
side. For an hour or so he heard shouts and commands. Occasionally a bugle sounded, and he knew from all the activity that
several companies of cavalry were moving out in the direction of
the Ghost Timbers.

Gradually the fort lapsed into quietness. Sometimes he could
hear voices through a thin wall and he guessed it faced a room
where the guards loafed while off duty. A bottle smashed with a
tinkle of glass followed by drunken laughter. He remembered
the time so long ago in the Tennessee stockade when the soldiers
locked him in the pine-slab privy too small to lie down in, with
the stench of excrement always in his nostrils. The same stench
came from a sinkhole in one corner of the cell.

In the dim light he could see that the timbers forming the base
of the blockhouse were deep in the ground and knew that escape
by digging would be a slow and difficult task. Nevertheless he
began gouging at the hard dirt, using his fingers and then a
small stone that he unearthed. The exertion made his head
wound bleed, and intensified his thirst and hunger, but no food
or water was brought him through the endless afternoon. At last
the sun went down and the light coloring the peaceful plain to
the south turned from yellow to rose to bronze, and then dark-

ness came. The voices of the soldiers on the other side of the wall became quarrelsome. Two swore loudly at each other, their dispute ending in a drunken fight, the plank wall shaking when a body fell or was pushed against it.

Although he had been able to excavate no deeper than the length of his hand, Dane was still digging when he heard the cavalry returning. Again commands echoed through the walls, followed by shouts and braying laughter. The sounds were more like those of a mob than an army, reminding him of the clamor of the Georgia Pony Guards when they were robbing the Cherokees at Okelogee. He waited, remembering the stoicism of Creek Mary when all control of action seemed lost, trying not to think of what might have happened at the Ghost Timbers.

After the soldiers swarmed through the gate, the interior of the fort became a bedlam, the noise gradually fading as the men moved toward the farther end of the stockade where the mess tents were. A few minutes later Dane heard a slight click of metal, an almost furtive scratching. A crack of light showed in the doorway.

"Anyone in here?" Dane recognized the low voice. He raised up, brushing his hands against his dusty jeans, and went to the door.

"Come on out," Major Easterwood said, holding up a lantern. "You and I are the only sober human beings in Fort Starke."

At the end of the corridor a sergeant lay sleeping in the shadows, his head lolling against the wall, his forage cap on the floor. Easterwood picked up the cap and put it on Dane's head. "The gate guards won't look twice at you in semidarkness," he said.

Easterwood held the lantern low while they passed between the two guards, both of whom saluted with their rifles, not even glancing at Dane. The air outside under the stars was sweet and clean after the long day in the fetid cell.

"I don't know where your horse is," Easterwood said. "Found you a lively pony though, bearing U.S. brands." He led the way into the corral. The pony was already saddled.

"What happened at the Timbers?" Dane asked.

"They made the swap. Then Colonel Belcourt ordered an at

tack, but it was more like a drunken brawl. Some of your people got hurt, more of ours." Easterwood's voice broke under his physical weariness. "I've been telling your people to go back to Sand Creek. Don't go there. Go on north, wherever it is you'll be out of reach of Belcourt and his kind. And go now. Belcourt sent a messenger to Fort Kearney to ask for a Nebraska regiment. Claims he was ambushed by a superior force of Cheyennes at the Ghost Timbers."

"I owe you my life," Dane said, settling into the unfamiliar army saddle.

"They would hang you in Denver and make a circus of it." Easterwood's voice turned bitter: "It's ironic that I, the only real army officer at this post, am committing a court-martial offense, aiding a prisoner escape." He offered his hand. "You'd better ride. Oh, one more thing. Belcourt is still out prowling with a troop of drunken men. Keep an eye out for them."

Dane pulled back on the reins. "What direction did they take?"

"When we left, I heard them splashing across the Platte."

Dane started the pony moving. He felt a cold chill at the back of his skull, the same icy dread he'd felt that night in the Cherokee Nation when he realized the danger threatening his Uncle Opothle. As soon as he reached open ground, he lashed the pony into a gallop. The forage cap lifted from his head and sailed across the plain behind him. Instead of turning north toward the Ghost Timbers, he angled westward for the Fort Carrothers trading post.

48

"It was the Moon of Dry Dust Blowing," Dane said. "When the sun first showed over the rim of the world it was the color of blood, and after full daylight the sky was yellow, clouds mixed with dust. *Soon it will rain,* I thought, *and wash the sky until it is clean and blue.* I remembered Grandmother Mary saying that.

"Above me I heard a hawk scream. I had to force myself to look up, and my heart stopped when I saw that it was blue-feathered, circling, circling, lower and lower, screaming until it flapped its wings and with the speed of an arrow soared out of sight into the yellow clouds. Then I saw the shine of the Platte, and galloped the tired army pony across the sandy shallows until I could see the trading post. Above it floated not hawks but black carrion birds, still high up, watching whatever it was below.

"Sweet Medicine Woman's tipi was gone. *Belcourt has burned it,* I thought, *as he threatened he would. But what has happened to Sweet Medicine Woman, to Amayi and Susa?*

"The pony rocked under me in its weariness. When we reached the creek behind the trading post, it wallowed in the water. I leaped into the stream and climbed the grassy bank expecting to see ashes and charred lodgepoles where the tipi had stood. Instead there was only a circle of bare earth ringed by stones, no sign of violence.

"I sighed with relief, yet I knew the place was too quiet. Bibbs should be making noises in the smithy. Smoke should be drifting from the chimney above Griffa's kitchen. Familiar voices should be sounding everywhere.

"I walked around the solid log wall at the east end of the trading post, and as soon as I turned the corner I saw three Bluecoats lying motionless on the hard-packed earth around the entranceway, two on their backs, the nearest one facedown in a pool of drying blood. I turned the body over with my foot. The three faces all looked alike to me, waxen now, but marked with animal coarseness, bearers of the Caucasian savagery that is akin to madness.

"The heavy door of the trading post stood ajar on one hinge, the wood battered by a pole that lay in front of it. A pair of boots, soles facing me, blocked the narrow opening. I shoved the door fully open and looked down on what remained of Bibbs's face. His muscular body was clothed only in a pair of thin cotton pants and the black boots. In the trading room lay two more dead Bluecoats. The arm of one of them was flung across the naked body of Griffa, lying spread-eagled on the floor, her eyes open and glassy in her pain-twisted face.

"Through the kitchen door I saw nothing but overturned furniture, and in only one bedroom did I find any signs of a struggle. In Meggi's room a washbasin, a shattered mirror, and a blanket were on the floor. The rumpled covering on her bed was spotted with blood.

"The connecting door to Bibbs's and Wewoka's quarters was wide open, and there I found two more dead, a Bluecoat with a Bowie knife driven in his armpit to the hilt, and Wewoka's half-clothed body beneath his. I rolled the Bluecoat to one side, hoping to find life in Wewoka, but she was dead, a cluster of purple marks on her olive throat where her attacker had crushed the breath of life from her. When I closed the lids over Wewoka's violet eyes, I remembered her fears of the wild Plains Indians when she first came to the trading post. All her dread-filled visions of hostile savages had come true, but in her case the savages were white men, not Indians.

"Five of my family and kin of Fort Carrothers were still missing, and I prayed that I would find them alive in the root cellar. I went to the kitchen, calling their names to reassure them with my voice. The heavy table that usually stood over the long entry boards lay on its side. I called again: Sweet Medicine, Amayi, Susa, Meggi, Young Opothle. I heard a whimpering then, like the soft wail of a lost kit cougar. I turned one of the boards, and there in a beam of light was Meggi's face, streaked with tears and dirt, looking up at me. I lifted her through the opening. She was clothed only in a blanket, and clung tightly to me, sobbing. 'Where are the others?' I asked. She tried to tell me, but 'gone away' was all I could understand. Then I saw Young Opothle pulling himself out of the root cellar, a great bloody welt on the top of his head, his eyes blank from shock.

"It was a while before I could make them tell me of the terrors they had lived through in that dark night. The Bluecoats had awakened them with shouts and curses and a loud banging at the entrance door. When the Bluecoats began pounding at the door with the pole, Griffa called Bibbs, and the two of them stood with their guns ready.

"'Were Sweet Medicine Woman and the girls with you?' I asked.

"'No,' Meggi said, 'they were in the tipi. It was they who drove away the soldiers.'

"When the door crashed in, Bibbs shot one of the Bluecoats, but the others killed Bibbs where he stood, and then placed the muzzles of their rifles in his face and blew it apart. They knocked Griffa to the floor, tore off her nightclothes, and raped her, several of them, while others raped Meggi in her sleeping room, and another met death when he went after Wewoka. Young Opothle tried to defend his mother, but was knocked senseless with the butt of a rifle.

"'Did you see Colonel Belcourt, the man who was here and threatened us?' I asked.

"Meggi shook her head. She was not sure. Through the wrecked entranceway she had seen the shadows of other soldiers on horses in the road. After Sweet Medicine Woman and Amayi and Susa began shooting at the soldiers in the road, the soldiers in the trading post ran out. 'Amayi told me that Susa killed two of them in the yard,' Meggi said, 'and then all the soldiers rode away very fast. Susa was hurt, and Sweet Medicine Woman and Amayi brought her in here.'

"'Where was she hurt?' I wanted to know.

"'All I remember is Sweet Medicine Woman saying Susa had a wound in her ribs. I was crying over my mother and Young Opothle. I thought he was dead, too. Amayi helped me and helped bring Young Opothle back to life, and then I remember hearing horses, many horses moving slow. We blew out the candles, and Sweet Medicine Woman went to look, and then she cried out that it was her people coming from the Ghost Timbers. The next I saw was Swift Eagle and Pleasant. Pleasant had a bloody rag around his head and was so weak Swift Eagle had to help him stand. They told us Little Cloud was dead and Pleasant's wife Rising Fawn was dead and Big Star was dead. They were carrying all the bodies north with them because they knew if they put them on scaffolds in the Ghost Timbers the soldiers would come and steal the medicine bundles and other things belonging to the dead.'

"Meggi also said Sweet Medicine Woman begged her and Young Opothle to go with the Cheyennes to the north, but they would not go. They promised her they would hide in the root cellar and wait for the stagecoach. Sweet Medicine Woman would not leave without her tipi and a travois to carry Susa. Amayi and Swift Eagle helped her dismantle the tipi and prepare two travois. She already had everything packed, and they all hurried away about the time the sun rose. As soon as they were gone, Meggi and Young Opothle hid themselves in the root cellar, where I found them.

"I knew that the eastbound stagecoach would soon be coming by, so I told them to get dressed in their best clothes and collect whatever things they needed to take with them. Then I took blankets from the beds and covered the bodies in the trading post. After that I dragged the three dead soldiers inside so the stage driver would not see them lying in the yard and want me to explain why they were there.

"I went in the kitchen and took a biscuit tin off a high shelf. Griffa kept the trading-post money in the tin box, and I was surprised at how much was there in greenbacks and gold and silver coins. I put aside enough to pay their stagecoach fares to Westport, and then stowed the rest in a leather pouch. As I was going where money was useless, I emptied my pockets of what coins I had and added them to the pouch. I gave the pouch to Meggi and told her not to turn loose of it until she could hand it over to her father.

"By the time the stagecoach arrived, Young Opothle was more in control of himself. He shook my hand, then put his arms around me and said he hoped we could all be together again after the war. Meggi fought to keep tears out of her eyes when she kissed me good-bye, but the stage driver was yelling at them to get aboard, and there was no time for tears. The last I saw of Meggi was her small hand waving at me from the coach window.

"As soon as the coach rolled away, I went back into the trading post. For a long time, fifteen years I think, Fort Carrothers had been a kind of center, a home, a meeting place for the children of Creek Mary's blood. Sweet Medicine Woman had always distrusted it, as a symbol of white man's greed. 'Maka-eta, money, it is bad,' she would say, and she would not have stayed one day of her own will anywhere near Fort Carrothers. Although she never spoke much about it, I knew that she sorrowed for me because I was afflicted with the white man's sickness for possessions. Sweet Medicine Woman wanted nothing more than happiness for me and her children, clothing and food, a shelter that was cool in summer and warm in winter, and she knew that from the buffalo she could have all these things. Why any living being would want more than that she could not comprehend. Goods were to be shared, not accumulated.

"I stood there in the trading room thinking about her, grieving for her because wherever she was she grieved for Little Cloud, the son I had saved and then lost. I thought about my grandmother, Akusa Amayi, how she had fixed into her memory the words of the great Tecumseh, who tried and failed to unite all the tribes against the *Unega* invaders. *Behold what the white men have done to your people! They seize your land, they cor-*

rupt your women, they trample on the graves of your dead. They must be driven back whence they came upon a trail of blood.

"I went into a little room at the back of the trading post, the room where Pleasant always slept when he stayed at Fort Carrothers. He and I kept things there that we no longer used. His Spanish coat of mail, showing streaks of rust, lay on a shelf. I started to put it in my saddlepack, but left it, knowing he would have taken it if he'd wanted it. In a battered parfleche box I found my old red breechcloth and a rawhide shirt. Beneath them was the horse bell that Sweet Medicine Girl gave me when I first parted from her at the end of that happy summer on the Hotoa, when we were young and unscarred by time. I put it in my saddlepack. Among Pleasant's things I found a buckskin bag containing tallow and red and black pigments. I stripped off every shred of my white man's clothing and painted my face and arms and body for the first time since I'd gone on the horse raid against the Crows. Then I dressed in the breechcloth and rawhide shirt.

"I went out to the smithy and brought Bibbs's jug of coal oil inside and poured it over the blankets of the dead. I heaped my white man's clothing underneath the thin wood of the trading counter, added straw and paper, soaked them with coal oil, and set them to blazing. Then I took my saddlepack and went outside and mounted the army pony and started following the marks left by Sweet Medicine Woman's travois. They cut across the trail, heading north along with hundreds of hoofprints of Cheyenne ponies. At the top of the first rise in the land, I looked back. Smoke and flames lifted skyward from each end of Fort Carrothers, and for a long time after that whenever I turned my face to the south I could see a gray streamer of smoke against the yellow sky. To me that smoke was a purge, burning away my past, and I felt like I was one with the People again.

"Not until the next day did I come to the burial place, a thicket of stunted trees high in the dry sandhills. In their flight the Cheyennes had not the time or means to build scaffolds or wrap wet buffalo skins around their dead. They hacked out enough space in the treetops for two poles and whatever coverings they had, blankets or robes lashed with rawhide strips, placed so the feet of each dead person pointed toward the rising sun. From the coverings and possessions left beneath I could name several of the dead who had been my friends and companions. Big Star was bound in his white buffalo robe, and beneath his tree was his lance and shield and his white horse, dead from arrow wounds.

"No other horses had been slain there, but I saw then a wooden horse hanging from the limb of a small thorny tree below a short blanket-wrapped body. It was the red-and-yellow rocking horse that Bibbs and Wewoka had made for Susa as a birth present, and the blanket wrapped around the body was Susa's, a red-striped Mackinaw that I'd brought her from Westport Landing. I wept then as I wept the day I first saw Grandmother Mary's grave. Twelve summers Susa had lived and already gone to the Darkening Land. 'Look for Akusa Amayi, your great-grandmother,' I whispered to her. 'Do not turn your face to this earth again.'

"Little Cloud and Rising Fawn both had been placed in a nearby tree. But I had no more tears to shed. I could hear my grandmother's voice speaking the words of Tecumseh: *Behold what the white men have done to your people! They must be driven back whence they came upon a trail of blood.*"

"Ah, those old times not good," John Bear-in-the-Water said. "We think we got it bad, fighting with words all time with Indian agent. You never told me about what happened to your sons and daughters, Dane." He slid on his buttocks away from the rising heat of the fireplace.

Red Bird Woman rocked forward and eased herself from the chair. She went over to Dane and put a hand on one of his shoulders. "That is enough looking at road behind us," she said. "Come show me where you want to put tipi for road ahead."

Dane glanced at me, his closed lips crinkling in a smile. "See, she gives me no peace. Look, I have this good cabin. What do I want with a tipi?"

She laughed. "A *Sanaki* stays always a *Sanaki*. Wants to stay inside wooden house that shuts out sun. Sweet Medicine Woman and me, we work all our lives to make Dane a good Cheyenne. Don't you know tipi is easier to keep clean? Warmer in winter—"

"And cooler in summer," Dane interrupted mockingly. "And all fresh air and sunshine. God damn, I can almost hear Sweet Medicine Woman's voice saying those words."

"Come on," Red Bird Woman said, moving toward the door. "You, too, John Bear-in-the-Water. We find good place, maybe put up some lodgepoles today."

Still smiling his thin smile, Dane beckoned me to come with them. Red Bird Woman led the way, lifting her skirts and showing her white deerskin boot moccasins as she stepped nimbly from stone to stone across the stream behind the cabin and climbed the embankment to a level place. "Can see butte to north, Dundee to south, mountains to west, sky to east. Creek never flood this high up. Good place." She frowned at John Bear-in-the-Water. "Where you put lodgepoles?"

"Wait," Dane protested. "This is where the coyotes come to sing and talk to me every night."

"Plenty room for coyotes here, too," she said. "Won't have to sing so loud close to tipi."

"God damn," Dane muttered. "John Bear-in-the-Water, go bring her the lodgepoles."

Book Three

THE SURVIVORS

49

During the years immediately following their flight from the Ghost Timbers to the Powder River country, the survivors of Big Star's band of Cheyennes saw many changes come into their lives. Afterward they always counted themselves lucky that they found Old Two Moon's Cheyennes near one of their former camping places on Crazy Woman's Creek. Two Moon's people had just returned from a summer's trading journey to posts on the Missouri River and they were rich in Hudson's Bay blankets, fine woolen cloth leggings, and stores of sugar, coffee, and flour. When Old Two Moon saw the condition of his relatives from the south, so poor they had only that one tipi brought by Sweet Medicine Woman, he summoned all his young men to join them in daily buffalo hunts. Then, as soon as the first hides were brought in, the women and girls from Two Moon's camp came to help in the fleshing and stretching and drying and smoking.

By the end of the Deer Rutting Moon, the fugitives from the south had enough tipis to shelter them from the coming cold and enough jerky and pemmican to last until springtime. They planned to spend the winter there, but Old Two Moon insisted that they go with his people to a creek valley across the Tongue. There the Bighorn Mountains and forests of tall lodgepole pines shielded them from bitter winds and heavy snows. After the anxieties, the violence, and sadness of their recent life, Dane and his little family felt that they had come at last into the real world.

Once the Cheyennes were settled for the winter, in tipis with thick inner linings, they began holding councils to choose new leaders to replace those lost in the fighting with the Bluecoats.

Some wanted Yellow Hawk to succeed his father as chief, but most thought he was yet too young, and so they chose War Shirt as chief of the band. Yellow Hawk then became the new leader of the Fox Soldiers, and to Dane's surprise the society members chose him as first subchief. The Dog Soldiers met in many councils before they agreed upon a war leader. The younger men admired Pleasant's daring and imagination, but he had been acting strangely since the death of Rising Fawn, keeping to himself and brooding, and the Dog Soldiers finally chose a hardbitten old warrior, Iron Crow, to be their war chief.

With the arrival of springtime, life became a procession of joyous days. They moved down the Tongue and then across to the grasslands of the Powder again, always camping near Two Moon's people. So many young men of each camp began courting young women in the other camp that it soon became apparent to the chiefs that someday the two bands might become one. Swift Eagle pledged himself to a girl in the Two Moon camp and went off on a horse-raiding expedition with other members of his soldier society, the Bowstrings. In a nearby camp of Oglalas, Pleasant discovered a *wiwazica*, a woman several years older than he, whose husband had been killed in a fight with Bluecoats on the Missouri River. After meeting this widow, Pleasant cast off his winter gloominess and spent much of his time with the Oglalas.

Young Two Moon, the old chief's nephew, paid frequent visits to Sweet Medicine Woman's tipi to admire the beauty of Amayi, but when he inquired of Dane if he might begin courting in earnest, Dane told him to wait another year; Amayi was still a child, late in forming into womanhood. As for Dane and Sweet Medicine Woman, they found themselves sitting close beside each other during the long evenings and making love through the nights as they had done in their first summer of wedded life.

The first shadow that touched them was the arrival of a band of Arapahos who had fled from the south after the massacre of Black Kettle's Cheyennes at Sand Creek. They told of the brutalities of the Bluecoats against the women and children and old men. Many of Black Kettle's people were relatives and friends, and the Cheyennes' newfound tranquillity was broken by days of mourning. Soon after that, hunting parties began bringing reports of white men traveling in wagons, so many they were making a rutted trail from Fort Laramie to the Powder, across Crazy Woman's Creek to the headwaters of the Tongue and on to the Yellowstone—right through the heart of the tribes' last hunting paradise.

The *Veheos* had found gold north of the Yellowstone, and in their madness for the yellow metal were swarming like gnats over a new road they called the Bozeman Trail. At first the Indians took no concerted action against these intruders. After all, the Horse Creek Treaty gave *Veheos* the right to travel across the Indian country. Many young men in hunting parties greeted the white travelers, offering to trade buffalo robes or moccasins for gunpowder and lead. But some of the gold seekers feared or hated Indians and fired on them if they came within range of their weapons. Some also began killing buffalo and other wild game in the wasteful ways of so many whites, leaving the carcasses to rot where they fell. Soon the Indians were retaliating with raids and ambushes, and then only well-armed and heavily guarded wagon trains ventured north over the trail to Montana. And eventually, because of the fury of the Indians, all travel stopped.

One day in the Moon When the Ponies Shed, Red Cloud of the Oglala Sioux rode into the Cheyenne camp on the Powder looking for Old Two Moon and War Shirt. With him was Big Mouth, a Brule Sioux who lived near Fort Laramie. Big Mouth had been sent north by the Bluecoat commander to summon the chiefs of all the tribes in the Powder River country to Fort Laramie for a council.

Red Cloud said that he and several other leaders of the Oglalas and Minneconjous were going, as well as Dull Knife of the Northern Cheyennes, Black Bear of the Arapahos, and Spotted Tail of the Brules. He invited Old Two Moon and War Shirt to accompany them. The chiefs would be taking along a number of their best warriors, Red Cloud said, so as to make an impression upon the *Wasicus* at Fort Laramie.

While the two Cheyenne leaders were considering the invitation, Red Cloud sought out Dane, finding him with his daughter Amayi. Dane was teaching her how to shape a bow. A dozen years or more had passed since Dane and Red Cloud had traveled together along the Platte, but they greeted each other with the warmth of old friends. Red Cloud complimented Dane for being blessed with so beautiful a daughter and commiserated with him over the recent ill-fortunes of the Cheyennes in the south. After explaining the purpose of his visit to the Cheyenne camp, Red Cloud said: "I do not think War Shirt will go to Fort Laramie with his warriors. He fears the Bluecoats would force his people back to Sand Creek. But you are not of Cheyenne blood. You may go there without fear."

Dane smiled. "I live as a Cheyenne, and under the treaty we have no right to be here north of the Platte."

"The treaty has been broken into many pieces by the *Wasicus*," Red Cloud said. "It is time for us to go to the fort on the Laramie with a treaty for them to sign. That is why I ask you to go with me. You understand the words of the *Wasicus*. They cannot fool you with their words."

Dane shook his head. "I have sworn to myself that I will never treat with the whites again. Their hearts and tongues are false."

"If we do not go to them they will bring their treachery and death to us," Red Cloud said. "How long can we live in peace in this land unless we show the *Wasicus* our power? Our warriors have stopped them from crossing our hunting grounds to shoot at our people and kill our animals. Now we must make them understand that this is Indian land forever in which no whites can make roads, build soldier forts, or intrude to hunt our animals."

Dane stubbornly resolved to have no part in the Laramie council, but during the feast that the Cheyennes gave Red Cloud before his departure, the Oglala leader became equally determined. "In the past we have always given to the white men," he said. "This time the white men must give something to the Indians." When he appealed to Dane as a patriot whose knowledge of the *Wasicus* was needed in the councils, Dane reluctantly consented to go.

This was Dane's first visit to Fort Laramie since the Horse Creek Treaty fifteen years before, and he was surprised to see log-and-adobe barracks and stables extending in all directions. He was also surprised to find commissioners from the American government waiting there for the chiefs. The Indians and their interpreters met with the commissioners in a large canvas tent outside the fort. Leading the commissioners was a Bluecoat chief, a great warrior named Sherman, and it was during the preliminary talks that Dane learned for the first time that the Civil War between the Bluecoat Yankees and Graycoat Confederates had ended in the East with a great victory for the Bluecoats.

The Great Warrior Sherman and Commissioner Edward Taylor told the chiefs that they had called the council to make a lasting peace with the Indians. "We do not want your land," Taylor said. "We want you to remember the treaty signed at Horse Creek, which gives us the right to make roads through your country so our people can go to the gold mines and make settlements in Montana Territory."

Red Cloud spoke first, and then other leaders joined him in complaining that the white travelers molested their people and disturbed the wild game. The commissioners promised that travelers would be forbidden to leave the line of the road or hunt animals while passing through the Powder River country. Red Cloud wanted to know how the commissioners were going to enforce the good behavior of white travelers through Indian country, and then he boldly proposed a new treaty that would set aside land for the tribes north of the Platte into which no white men could come for any purpose. Somewhat surprised, the commissioners whispered together for a few minutes and then replied that they would use the talking wires to counsel with the Great Father in Washington about Red Cloud's proposal. They then asked the chiefs to stay for another sleep at Fort Laramie. Before ending the meeting, the commissioners also dropped subtle hints that if the tribes continued to block the Bozeman Trail they would be considered hostile and barred from trading for powder and lead.

That evening Dane went alone to the sutler's store. He had brought with him from the Powder River camp two fine buffalo robes, and he traded them for red ribbons and peppermint candy sticks for Amayi, a bolt of brilliant-colored calico for Sweet Medicine Woman, and some gunpowder and lead for himself. As he was turning to leave the store, he almost collided with Jim Carrothers.

"Wa-agh!" Jim cried. "Bless me, Dane, they told me you was gone to the land of ghosts, burned up in my old tradin' post."

Dane told him what had happened, and then Carrothers gave him some news of his relatives in the Cherokee Nation. Carrothers had recently seen Jotham and Young Opothle in Westport, and learned from them about the troubles that had befallen the family. William had died during the last months of the Civil War, probably of a broken heart, Carrothers said, because of the turmoil in the Nation that had devastated the towns and farms and destroyed all of William's trade. Jotham had survived the war without a scratch, and with his son and daughter was now trying to restore the trading post near Park Hill.

"Jotham and I figgered we'd fired shots at each other in a night battle at Cabin Creek," Carrothers said. "He was leadin' rebel Cherokee cavalry and I was scoutin' for a Yankee supply train. The Cherokees whipped us good, and we had to run for it, leavin' enough arms and rations and whiskey to keep Jotham's boys goin' to the end of the war. Well, that's all over now."

"What brings you to Fort Laramie?" Dane asked.

"Scoutin' for the army. Need the pay to keep my family fed and clothed back in Westport. Since the war ended, this country out here is fillin' up with soldiers."

"They'll want to fight us, I suppose," Dane said.

"Mebbe so, mebbe no. I've signed on as guide for Colonel Carrington's regiment. They'll be campin' close by here tonight. Goin' north to open the Bozeman Trail, build some forts."

"They'll have to fight us for that country," Dane said. "It is all we have left."

Carrothers gave Dane a worried look. "I figgered so. That colonel is a greenhorn from back east, and his soldiers may be vet'rans but they're greenhorns when it comes to Indians." He tugged at the end of one of his long mustaches. "Colonel Carrington don't ask me for much advice, but I told him twicet that the army ought to make its road west of the Bighorns, away from the Powder River country. I know how much that country means to the tribes in there."

Dane had no desire to talk further on the matter. "We won't give the army the use of the Bozeman road unless they whip us," he said curtly.

"Hold on." Carrothers's aging face revealed his distress. "Mebbe Colonel Carrington will listen to me when he finds hisself in trouble in your country. After all, my wife's people come from there. I got friends in all the tribes."

"If you're a friend you'll try to keep the Bluecoats out," Dane said. "Not guide them in." He left the sutler's store, wondering where he could find Red Cloud to tell him about the Bluecoats' plans for marching north. But Red Cloud was not in the Oglala camp. He and Man-Afraid-of-His-Horses had gone down the river to see Spotted Tail and would not return until morning.

At dawn, off to the east of Fort Laramie, Dane saw an immense number of canvased wagons drawn into a hollow square. Inside the square, bluecoated soldiers were erecting tents in straight-lined rows.

On the Fort Laramie parade ground during the morning, soldiers from the garrison nailed together a small platform, and laid green-leafed boughs on a frame above the speaker's stand to screen the bright June sunshine. Then they brought several pine-board benches, placing them in front of the stand. The peace commissioners had decided that a tent would not be large enough for the important proceedings of that day.

As soon as the council ground was readied, the chiefs were invited to seat themselves on the benches. Commissioner Taylor mounted the platform, and in a hearty voice assured his listeners that the Great Father in Washington had agreed to set aside a tract of land, a reservation upon which no white persons except those authorized by the Indians "shall ever be permitted to pass over, settle upon, or reside in the territory to be described." The borders of this reservation would be decided upon later, the commissioner said.

Dane was seated with Red Cloud and Man-Afraid-of-His-Horses on one of the front benches. While Taylor was speaking, Red Cloud muttered to himself about the uncomfortable position in which he had to sit. He finally slid off the end of the bench and sat cross-legged on the ground. Man-Afraid called out in Lakota: "Why are so many Bluecoats camped nearby?" All the chiefs were restless, whispering among themselves, and looking inquiringly at Red Cloud.

Commissioner Taylor stamped one of his boots against the planking, calling for order. He beckoned to a bearded soldier chief who wore eagles on his shoulder straps. As Colonel Carrington stepped upon the platform, Taylor introduced him. "He comes here from the East as your friend," the commissioner's voice boomed cheerfully. "He will lead his soldiers up the Bozeman Trail to build forts to protect you. You no longer need fear mistreatment from travelers through your land. Colonel Carrington."

After the fort's interpreter translated Taylor's surprising statement, Carrington's bulging eyes peered nervously at the Indians, whose faces plainly showed their sudden anger. "It is my—" he began, but a loud chorus of disapproving *hunh-hunhs* drowned out his words. The interpreter leaned closer to the colonel and whispered something in his ear.

"Colonel Carrington wishes to hear first from the chiefs," the interpreter declared in a loud voice.

Most of the Indians looked at Red Cloud, who still sat motionless on the ground. Suddenly he arose and pulled his blanket over his shoulders. His straight black hair, parted in the middle, reached almost to his waist. "Dane," he whispered, "come with me to make my Lakota words burn in the ears of these *Wasicus*." Dane followed him to the platform, Carrington and his interpreter moving to the edge of the flooring to make room for them.

Red Cloud's wide mouth was fixed in an angry slit beneath his hawk nose, his dark eyes searching out the faces of the commissioners and the Bluecoat chiefs on the benches below. Phrase by phrase, as Red Cloud cried out in Lakota, Dane repeated the words in English: "You treat us like children. We are men. We are warriors. You summoned us here as though we were your children and pretended to counsel with us while behind our backs you bring soldiers to send into our country. The white men have pushed us into a small country north of the Platte, and now you want to send soldiers into our last hunting grounds. This land and its animals gives us our food, shelter, and clothing. If you take it from us, we will starve and freeze. For my part I will die fighting rather than by starvation. The Great Father sends us presents and wants to talk about a road through our country." He stopped and scowled at Carrington, his lips twisting as he glanced at the colonel's shoulder straps. "But you, White Eagle Chief, you come with soldiers to steal road before Indian says yes or no!"

Red Cloud abruptly turned his back on Carrington, tugged at Dane's sleeve while he was still translating his last words, and with a proud jerk of his head motioned to the other chiefs to follow him from the parade ground.

50

"That was the beginning of Red Cloud's War," Dane said. "For six or seven moons we gave Carrington's Bluecoats no peace, pestering and tormenting them while they built their fort at the Little Piney crossing of the Bozeman road. Then in the Moon When the Deer Shed Their Horns, Crazy Horse and Swift Eagle and their decoys led a hundred soldiers into our trap along Peno Creek and we killed them all."

We were seated on flat rocks overhanging the stream across from Dane's cabin, watching John Bear-in-the-Water driving his wagon down to the corral shed to bring the lodgepoles to Red Bird Woman. She was hunched forward, her white boot-moccasins crossed, resting her chin in one hand. "I remember, I remember," she said. "What heart-swelling times we lived in then. Two days we rode up Tongue River and never out of sight of tipis. Warriors come from everywhere."

"Yes," Dane said. "Camp after camp for forty miles. By that time, many Cheyennes from the south had come to join us, some of Black Kettle's people who would not let the Bluecoats drive them to Indian Territory. Yellow Woman, William Bent's Cheyenne wife, came with her half-blood sons. She swore she would never again live with a *Veheo*, and they renounced the blood of their father.

"Red Cloud would not rest until he brought all the Teton Sioux into war camps along the Tongue. He brought Brules up from the south, and Uncpapas, Sans Arcs, and Two Kettles down from the north. One day he met a hunting party of our old enemies, the Crows. His warriors could have rubbed them out, but Red Cloud escorted the Crows to our camps and invited them to join us in our war on the Bluecoats. The Crows said they would consider the matter, but they must have spent a lot of time considering, because they never came back.

"Red Cloud always treated the war chiefs as equal allies, but in the councils he decided when and where we would strike the Bluecoats, and which chiefs would lead the attacks and ambushes. I remember Sitting Bull of the Uncpapas was always wanting to set traps for soldiers guarding supply trains coming up from Fort Laramie. Oh, we had some great war chiefs—Black Shield and White Bull of the Minneconjous, Black Bear and Sorrel Horse of the Arapahos, Dull Knife of our Northern Cheyenne cousins, Roman Nose, who had brought a band of Dog Soldiers up from the south, Old Two Moon and Iron Crow of our people. Crazy Horse of the Oglalas was only a young boy then, but no one could match him as a decoy leader. Pleasant and Swift Eagle rode with him several times and in camp at night after the chases were over they would tell of Crazy Horse's daring, how he would badger the Bluecoat cavalrymen by leaping right out into the trail in front of them, shaking his red blanket to frighten their horses, and darting in and out of the brush until they foolishly followed him right into ambush."

"I remember Swift Eagle got pretty good, too," Red Bird Woman said, "decoying Bluecoats."

"We knew the fort was too strong for us," Dane continued, "but no *Veheos* could come or go on the Bozeman Trail without fear. Only one time did we let a white traveler go without hindrance. One morning Jim Carrothers rode out of the fort, alone, heading south for Fort Laramie. His shoulders were bent and he looked tired and beaten. We knew that old Jim had his craw full of the foolish White Eagle Chief. Old Jim was more our friend than the Bluecoats'. So we let him go. I heard afterward he went back to Westport and died.

"We were sure that if we could get Colonel Carrington's Bluecoats outside in the open we could beat them. To do this we had to make them crazy, like buffalo bulls pricked with lances until they run from the herd. Red Cloud chose the day for this to be done, and more than a thousand warriors rode up the Tongue to the fork of the Peno. We camped in three great circles—Sioux, Cheyenne, and Arapaho—no tipis, but saddle-blanket windbreaks and other shelters. Because we had used up most of our gunpowder and lead, and could get no more, most of us were armed with bows and arrows, lances and war clubs. It was very cold, with a fine powdery snow falling."

"*Aho-ya*, I remember that cold," Red Bird Woman said. "Night before battle when I kept you warm in my buffalo robe, our breath made icicles on the hair—" She stopped suddenly, putting both hands over her mouth, her eyes opening wide before she turned her face away from me.

Dane laughed. "She went to the battle camp with the warriors."

"Some other women, too," she added quickly. "Some without

men like me, and some not long married. I dressed like warrior. Arapahos thought I been changed into *he-e-man-eh*. But Dane, he knows better." Her body shook with silent laughter, the little folds of fat around her eyes squeezing them shut.

He shrugged. "Next morning Crazy Horse led one bunch of decoys down Big Piney on the north side of the fort and Swift Eagle took another bunch to the south side. Swift Eagle found a heavily guarded train of wagons going up the Little Piney to cut firewood for the fort. Swift Eagle's warriors began making feints against the wood train, just enough to anger the soldiers so they would fire their guns. The sound of the guns brought a rescue party of Bluecoats from the fort, and when they galloped out of the gate, Crazy Horse came down the slope of Lodge Trail Ridge and started tantalizing them. Colonel Carrington fired one of his cannons, and Crazy Horse's boys put on a show, jumping and yelling and darting back and forth on their ponies. Before long the wood train guard was chasing Swift Eagle's decoys, and another bunch of Bluecoats was after Crazy Horse.

"While all that was going on, our main war party moved up Peno Creek under the screen of Lodge Trail Ridge. The Sioux rode behind some big rocks on the east side of the Bozeman Trail, several remaining mounted, others leaving their horses and concealing themselves in high grass nearby the trail. The Arapahos and we Cheyennes took the west side of the trail. We waited there, about a thousand of us, for the decoys to bring the Bluecoats into our trap.

"The soldiers were cautious at first, firing at our little bunch of darting decoys, their anger rising because so few Indians dared challenge a hundred well-armed soldiers. At last the Bluecoats charged our decoys, chasing them over Lodge Trail Ridge and along both sides of the trail right into our trap. Cheyennes and Arapahos swarmed upon them from one side, Sioux from the other. It was like a buffalo surround. The air was filled with arrows, warriors on foot closing in, pony riders circling. The Bluecoats fought bravely and stubbornly, trying to break out of our ring.

"If we had not gone mad and killed with such fury, very few

of us would have gone to the Darkening Land or suffered wounds. But a craziness of desperation came over us. These Bluecoats symbolized death to us. As long as we could remember, the white man's soldiers had been pushing us always westward, taking our lands whether we resisted or not. Now there was no place left to go. When cavalrymen found cover among some rocks, warriors gave their lives to make certain that no one escaped. Toward the end of the fighting, Cheyennes on one side of the soldiers and Sioux on the other were so close together that Cheyenne arrows were striking Sioux warriors, and Sioux arrows were striking Cheyenne warriors. Then it was all over. Not a soldier was left alive. But we lost many, too.

"Then the scalping began. The Cheyennes who had come up from Sand Creek were the worst. They not only took scalps, they stripped off uniforms and mutilated the bodies of the soldiers in the same way the soldiers mutilated their women and children at Sand Creek.

"We left the battlefield then, believing that if we always fought as one tribe united we could defeat the Bluecoats with our bows and arrows. Many of us were certain that after our great victory Colonel Carrington would take his survivors out of our land and leave us alone. But instead the army took Carrington away because we had beaten his men and sent another soldier chief and more Bluecoats to fight us.

"For several more moons we raided and ambushed as we had done before, and then at last Brule messengers from Fort Laramie began visiting our camps to tell us that a new peace commission had come there to meet with the chiefs. The commissioners wanted to talk about the boundaries of a reservation within which the tribes could live without white interference. All those who signed the new treaty were promised presents, including gunpowder and lead, and the right to trade for them forever. We had heard all that before, of course, and the chiefs held together with Red Cloud, replying that they would not come to Fort Laramie to talk peace until all soldiers were removed from the Powder River country.

"At last, Red Cloud got what he wanted—except for one thing.

In the Moon of Red Cherries, the Bluecoats started leaving the fort, with white flags fluttering on their wagons, their long train crawling southward toward Fort Laramie. As soon as the last soldier was gone, Red Cloud led a number of warriors, heroes from all the tribes, down to the abandoned buildings and set them on fire.

"I was with him when he rode triumphantly to Fort Laramie with a thousand warriors to sign the treaty. After I read the treaty carefully, I advised him not to sign, but he would not listen. The boundaries of the promised land included the sacred Black Hills and extended to the Missouri River, but did not include our Powder River hunting paradise. When the commissioners promised him that his people would be given the right to hunt on any lands above the North Platte 'so long as the buffalo may range thereon in such numbers as to justify the chase,' Red Cloud signed, but I knew that we would soon lose our way of living forever. The boundaries of the Great Reservation were not meant to keep the white man out, but to keep the Indians locked in."

51

When Amayi was seventeen she made her first visit to Fort Laramie with Dane and Sweet Medicine Woman. The reason for the journey was a special council called by the peace commissioners for the Northern Cheyennes and Arapahos, who had not been included in the treaty with the Teton Sioux tribes. All the chiefs and warriors went, taking their families with them, so that for several days there was an enormous village of tipis along the Laramie River.

Not long after they returned to the Lower Tongue and made summer camp, Amayi started a calendar on a buffalo hide that Sweet Medicine Woman dressed soft and smooth for her. Using bright blue and red and yellow paints, Amayi drew tiny pictures of the things she had seen at Fort Laramie—the great tipi village, the soldiers, the buildings, and the big tent where the chiefs and her father parleyed with the *Veheos* who spoke for the Great Father in Washington.

What Amayi did not show in her Fort Laramie drawing was the apprehension of the Southern Cheyennes who were at the council. When the commissioners discovered that some of the chiefs were not northerners—such as War Shirt (Big Star's successor) and Big Shin (of Black Kettle's band) and two of the Southern Arapaho leaders—these chiefs were told that they must take their people south to the Indian Territory. Another treaty had been made for them at Medicine Lodge in Kansas, assigning all the Southern Cheyennes and Southern Arapahos a reservation in Indian Territory between the Arkansas and Cimarron rivers. None of the southerners, however, wanted to go back to the country in which they had suffered so much at the hands of the Bluecoats, and the night after they learned of the other treaty, they struck their tipis and hurried back north to the sanctuary of the sweet-watered Tongue. The southerners never forgave Dull Knife, Little Wolf, and the other chiefs for signing a treaty that gave only the northerners the right to roam and hunt north of the Platte, as well as a home in the same lands assigned the Teton Sioux. If Amayi had been able to forecast the future in her calendar drawings she might have depicted the irony of Dull Knife's and Little Wolf's Northern Cheyennes being driven south as prisoners to Indian Territory ten years later, while her own southern people were escaping to Canada.

Amayi was not a seer, however, but only a picture chronicler of the events of each passing moon in her young life. In her second moon-drawing she portrayed the Sun Dance held by the Uncpapas in which the neighboring Cheyennes were invited to participate. She drew a black buffalo bull seated atop the Sun Dance pole to represent Sitting Bull. He was defeating the sun by gazing steadfastly into it. She also painted figures of young women in bright shawls dancing, and several young men around a Sun Dance pole, tugging at leather thongs running from the pole to skewers in their bleeding breasts. The face of one handsome young man was turned toward the dancing girls.

Amayi kept her buffalo-skin calendar above her bed, fastened to the inner lining of the family tipi. Dane began to notice that in each moon-drawing there was usually a handsome young man in the foreground looking out of the picture. When the Cheyennes followed a buffalo herd west to Rosebud Creek and camped with the Oglalas, Crazy Horse was the young man whose face was turned to look out of Amayi's moon-picture instead of at the buffalo he was pursuing on horseback.

Then after they rejoined the Two Moon Cheyennes for winter camp, Young Two Moon's smiling round face began appearing in Amayi's drawings—in the foreground of the tipi village with large snowflakes falling around him, or leading his soldier society members off toward the tall lodgepole pine forest, or returning with a captured horse herd. Young Two Moon was courting Amayi in earnest that winter, but she seemed to be only amused by his overtures.

Her pattern of drawings changed somewhat the next spring when her half brother, Pleasant, paid them an unexpected visit, bringing along Maga, his Oglala widow, and entertaining everyone with his tales of wrecking one of the Iron Horses on the railroad. With a mixed band of Oglala warriors and Cheyenne Dog Soldiers, Pleasant had gone far down into Nebraska to raid wagon trains and stagecoaches. When they discovered that the railroad had penetrated into their old hunting grounds, they pried up some of the iron rails with an ax and waited nearby until the Iron Horse came puffing along. It ran off the track with a great noise, and some of the wagons on wheels behind it fell on their sides. Pleasant said they found many bottles of whiskey and bolts of multicolored cloth in one of the Iron Horse's wagons.

After Pleasant and Maga left, Amayi tried to draw a moon-picture of Pleasant's adventure, but she had never seen an Iron Horse and her drawing of a locomotive resembled a living monster breathing fire and smoke through its teeth. In this drawing, Pleasant was in the foreground looking out with smiling blue eyes above a tawny beard he had let grow during the winter. Amayi obviously did not care for the Oglala *wiwazica*, who stood on the edge of the picture appearing older than she was, a vulpine expression upon her profiled face.

One of Amayi's summer moon-drawings recorded the birth of her brother Swift Eagle's first son. Swift Eagle, his wife, Buffalo Calf Woman, and the baby wrapped in a cradle, were all smiling out of the picture. In the background was Buffalo Calf Woman's tipi that Amayi had decorated with figures of horses and antelopes, and the moon, sun, and stars.

Later in that year, while the Cheyennes were camping on the Bighorn River near Spotted Elk's Minneconjous, a handsome young man began returning to the foreground of Amayi's calendar drawings. In each picture, the figure and face were always the same, easily recognized by Dane and Sweet Medicine Woman because they saw the young man almost every evening. He was Bull Bear, a Minneconjou warrior with friendly eyes and a strong jaw, the handsomest of all the young men who paid court to Amayi or appeared in her drawings.

The last drawing that Dane remembered seeing on his daughter's calendar was of Bull Bear with his head shaved, vermilion rings circling his eyes, pendants of beads around his neck, copper bracelets on his wrists, and wearing a white cincture, beaded moccasins, and leggings decorated with porcupine quills. In the background were the dancers and musicians at the wedding of Amayi and Bull Bear, painted so that it was almost possible to hear the little bells on the dancers' skirts and the sound of the drums and tambourines.

When Amayi left her parents' tipi with Bull Bear, to go with the Minneconjous, she rolled up her calendar to carry with her. At the last moment of leavetaking, Dane warned her never to forget that her blood was the blood of Akusa Amayi. He had told her many stories of her great-grandmother, and now he begged her to keep Creek Mary's name always in her memory. As he spoke, Sweet Medicine Woman removed the silver Danish coin from around her neck, and placed it around the neck of her daughter. "Wear this in remembrance," Sweet Medicine Woman said. "It has been kept for you since the days of the old grand-mother."

Dane blinked, looking away because he did not want his sur-prise and pleasure to show in his face. He had said nothing to Sweet Medicine Woman about Creek Mary's gorget. He sup-posed that she must have read his thoughts. They both spent much time now in the world of dreams and magic where no unspoken thoughts could be kept hidden from another, and he had often thought strongly that his daughter Amayi should wear the silver coin when she went away from them forever.

52

"Mary Amayi always wears same breastpiece now," Red Bird Woman said. "Dane, you think Mary Amayi come back today from agency?"

"Before dark, I think," he replied, and tossed a small stone into the stream.

"You know agency never give her money for medicine house, don't you?"

He shook his head. "She had to go and find out, didn't she?"

"*Veheos* give us nothing. They only take. What we must do is give her your cabin for medicine house."

"Make my cabin into a hospital!" His thin lips parted, then opened wide as he broke into laughter.

"Why you think I build tipi for you up here?" Her eyes, half-closed by the tiny folds around them, flashed with a spark of exasperation at his slowness in comprehending.

He raised up on his knees, stood erect, and turned to look toward the west. "The agent promised to telegraph Washington," he said. "But you speak true, Red Bird. They'll give Mary Amayi nothing. We'll have to make the hospital ourselves, the way we got the money to send her to medical school." He looked at me then, as though surprised to find me still there. "My granddaughter does not wish to go to a city to doctor in a hospital for the white people," he explained in a soft voice. "She wants the bureau to build a hospital here for her people."

"And you don't think they will?"

"The bureau has our name on it, but it is not our bureau. They have some money that was paid for our land and the use of our land, but the bureau decides what is good for us. To them we are still children. The bureau does not believe children can doctor themselves." He did not smile.

"Thirty years ago I went to Washington as interpreter with a delegation of chiefs. Gold had been found in the Black Hills and the American government wanted to make a new treaty to take the Black Hills out of the reservation they had marked off for the Sioux only six or seven years before. Red Cloud sent for me in the Moon When the Geese Lay Eggs. His Oglala messenger found me in our first spring camp on the Lower Powder, and told me that Red Cloud wanted me to go with him to the Great Father's village. Red Cloud did not trust the government's interpreters, the messenger said, and wanted me to go and help him save the Black Hills from the white man's greed. If I could not come to the Red Cloud Agency on White Earth River I was to meet him at Fort Laramie early in the Moon When the Ponies Shed.

"I don't know whether it was because I felt it my duty to go, or because I was sixty years old that year and wanted the magic of a journey to Washington, the Great Father's village. I met

Red Cloud at Fort Laramie. He came in with about twenty subchiefs of the Oglalas, all dressed in their finest buckskins except for Red Cloud. He was wearing white man's clothes—a long-tailed black coat and trousers, a big black cravat knotted around a high white collar, a gold watch-chain hanging over his vest. Except for his Indian face he could have been a commissioner from Washington, and I told him so. He said the *Wasicus* gave him that fine clothing on his last visit to Washington.

"We had not seen each other for several years, but he said I appeared to be the same man except for my snow-white hair. Red Cloud had changed considerably. The fierceness was gone from his face, and he was full of petty complaints about things he would not have wasted his breath on when he was a war leader instead of the head of a reservation agency the American government had built and named for him. His voice almost had a whine in it when he complained about the presence of Bluecoats at Camp Robinson nearby his agency, the poor rations the government issued to his people, the unfriendly *Wasicu* agent, the willful young Oglalas who refused to stay on the reservation and ran off to live with Crazy Horse or Sitting Bull. He was especially provoked by Crazy Horse's refusal to go with him to Washington. 'Crazy Horse knows nothing of the white man's world,' he said.

"'He says he will never live on a reservation,' I replied.

"'The day will come when his people will be hungry. It is better to eat stringy beef than to starve.'

"'You speak like a *Wasicu*,' I said.

"He laughed then, and told me that my half-blood son, Pleasant, was happy living at Camp Robinson with the Oglala *wiwazica*. Pleasant had found employment as a scout for the army, wore a fine blue uniform, and earned enough money to live in a wooden house with glass windows and a wooden floor.

"Only once did Red Cloud show his old fire, and that was when he talked of the miners invading our sacred Black Hills. 'If the American government does not send Bluecoats to drive out the miners,' he said angrily, 'then the tribes must send warriors to drive them out. The treaty I signed here at Fort Laramie gives me that right. You will help me speak of this in Washington. The Great Father sent me a message on the talking wires, saying it is time for a new treaty.'

"Before we left Fort Laramie, we met Mr. Adam Beale, who had come from Washington to act as our escort for the journey. Mr. Beale was a lazy man whose clothes always seemed to be rumpled, and he liked to sit with his hands behind his head, his elbows thrust out, and his long legs propped up on something. His lips were large and loose and he was always licking them with his tongue. When he discovered that I could understand and speak English well, he directed many of his remarks to me. I suppose you might say Mr. Beale was a cynical man, not an old man though. He was lively and talkative after he'd been drinking whiskey and he seemed always to have a bottle at hand. He gave us clothing to wear on the journey. 'Passengers on the cars don't fancy naked Indians,' he said. 'Keep your cods covered with pants and your pods under buttoned coats so's not to shock the timid white ladies.'

"We rode in army ambulance wagons from Fort Laramie over to a new town on the railroad that was named for my adopted tribe. On the long journey to Washington I was to think often of how the white men not only stole our land but stole our names to put on the stolen land.

"Most of us had never seen an Iron Horse before, and when it came whistling in to the Cheyenne station, blowing smoke and steam, clanking and breathing as though alive, some of us would have found it far easier to run away than to stand still while the cars rattled to a stop alongside. But we were soon on our way, enjoying the feeling of flying past places where we had roamed and hunted in our younger days. When we grew weary and cramped on the hard seats, Mr. Beale passed his whiskey bottle around. Some refused to drink, and Beale pretended to be shocked. 'What!' he cried. 'You chiefs going to Washington cold sober? Can't have that. Wine, women, and song, that's what we do in Washington.' I soon found out that Mr. Beale had escorted many visiting groups of Indians to Washington, and in the course of his duties had developed gainful connections with hotel keepers, whiskey dealers, clothing merchants, and whores, putting government money into their hands, a part of which was returned to him.

"Cheyenne was where we started, and soon we passed Oglala, and then Pawnee Station. The rivers, the towns we passed, the states, kept singing to me with their Indian names—Niobrara, Omaha, Missouri, Iowa, Nishnabotna, Ottumwa, Osceola, Wapsipinicon, Mississippi, Illinois, Winnebago, Ottawa, Seneca, Chicago, Wabash. When the railroad men called the names they were like lost voices singing—Ohio, Muskingum, Chillicothe, Kanawha, Shenandoah, Susquehanna, Potomac.

"We arrived in Washington late in the day and rode in covered carriages to the Tremont House. Red Cloud, who had been grumbling throughout the journey because he had to sit on a seat like a white man, now complained because Mr. Beale had not taken us to the Washington House, where he had stayed on a previous visit. But Mr. Beale's bargain was with the manager of the Tremont and that is where we stayed.

"Next morning Mr. Beale escorted us through the crowded streets to the bureau, and there we were surprised to find other delegations of Sioux—Brules, Minneconjous, Yanktonais, all the subtribes who with the Oglalas owned the Black Hills as a part of the reservation that had been set apart for their 'absolute and undisturbed use and occupation,' as the treaty said. We knew that something big was afoot, or the government would not have brought so many delegations to Washington.

"In a room almost as large as the old Cherokee council house at Okelogee, several well-dressed white men sat around a big table smiling at us as we entered with Mr. Beale. Some of these men were the same commissioners we had seen at Fort Laramie. Mr. Beale whispered to me that the others were congressmen. One of them looked strangely familiar. His hair was as white as mine, he wore spectacles, and his face was flabbier and more mottled with whiskey veins than when I had last seen him at Fort Starke, but there was no doubt that the congressman was Flattery Jack Belcourt. Ah, but I should not have been surprised. I have since observed that you white Americans more often than not choose his sort to represent you in your representative form of government. Scoundrels, thieves, liars, betrayers of those who give them their power.

"The head commissioner, a handsome man with a gray-sprinkled beard, greeted us in that false cordiality of manner and hearty tone of voice that white men use when they wish to make Indians believe they are their friends. He soon came to the point. White miners had entered the Black Hills to dig for gold and were causing trouble for the Indians. The time had come for a new treaty that would remove the Black Hills from the reservation and so end the trouble.

"At this remark the response from his audience was a chorus of disapproving *hunh-hunhs* and a stamping of moccasins. The commissioner smiled his raccoon smile, and invited the chiefs to speak. Red Cloud tapped me on the shoulder, and I arose with him to face the table, my eyes watching Congressman Belcourt. Recognition of me came slowly upon his ravaged face, and for a moment I wondered if he would leap to his feet and demand my arrest as a fugitive from the army, but of course he did not. More than ten years had passed, and now Belcourt wanted something from us, the gold in the Black Hills, or such of it as he could contrive to turn to his pockets without digging for it. He averted his eyes from me when I began putting Red Cloud's words into English, words of anger and accusation. The Indians had not come to Washington to talk about giving away the Black Hills, Red Cloud declared, but to demand of the Great Father that he keep the promises of the treaty and shield the Black Hills from *Wasicu* invasion. 'When I speak I always call on the Great Spirit to hear me, because I always tell the truth. The *Wasicus* tell me lies, and I came to Washington to see the Great Father himself and to talk with him about the lies. I will speak no more until I see the Great Father.'

"He started to sit down, and then added: 'You were raised on chairs here in the East where the sun rises. I come from where the sun sets. I will sit as we do where the sun sets.' He lowered himself cross-legged to the floor, and this caused some laughter among the commissioners and congressmen.

"The head commissioner rose up, his false smile reappearing upon his bearded face. 'Your Great Father, President Grant, will be happy to see his children who came from the place where the sun sets. Tomorrow morning he will welcome you in his white house. Now I want you to hear from a gentleman who is a loyal friend to all red men. For many years his heart has been very warm toward the red men. Because of his high regard for you and his earnest efforts in your behalf, the Congress in its wisdom has made him chairman of its committee to see that justice is done about the Black Hills. Congressman Belcourt.'

"Well, I could not tell you what Flattery Jack said that day. His honey-mouthed words flowed out like sap from a gum tree, but they had no meaning for me, my eyes being filled with visions of his attempt to swindle Yellow Hawk and his friends at Bent's Fort, his trading for Red Bird Woman, his treatment of me at Fort Starke, and that awful morning when I came to Jotham's trading post and found the tortured dead and living. Whether he was there or not, Belcourt was the mover, as he had been at the Hinta Nagi, where my youngest son and some of my cherished friends died from the sabers and bullets of Belcourt's ruffian soldiers.

"Next morning we went with Mr. Beale to the White House, some of the chiefs wearing their buckskins and feathers for the meeting with the Great Father. We crowded into a large office room with an armed Bluecoat at each door watching us as though we were dangerous beasts. I had expected to see a tall man with a commanding figure, but the Great Father was shorter than most of the chiefs. He took a big cigar from his mouth and told us he was glad to see us, that he wanted his red children to be contented and happy, and he thought the best way to make certain of that was for us to give up the Black Hills. When Red Cloud had me say to him in English that we would never give up the sacred Black Hills, the Great Father replied: 'We know what is for your good better than you can know yourselves.' With that he dismissed us, saying he had many matters to attend to and that we should discuss our opinions with the head commissioner. Red Cloud was enraged, but Mr. Beale with the help of a soldier guard hurried him out before he could start a disturbance.

"During that afternoon Mr. Beale guided us on a tour of Washington. We visited the great council house of the Congress. Some congressmen slept in their chairs or read newspapers while others talked at great length. We climbed to the dome of the Capitol and looked out upon the great city. Then we went to the arsenal, where a giant cannon was fired for us down the river named for the vanished tribe that had lived upon its banks before the white men came there to destroy them to the last seed.

"After our dinner that evening, while I was resting on my bed and wishing that I was back on the Powder or the Tongue, Mr. Beale knocked on the door and said that Red Cloud needed me to interpret for him. We went along the hallway to a large room where we found Red Cloud and several other chiefs with the head commissioner, an army colonel, and Congressman Flattery Jack Belcourt. The air in the room was heavy with cigar smoke and the odor of whiskey. One by one, the three white men made their little speeches. The commissioner said it was true the Black Hills belonged to the Sioux, but that so many miners were invading the Hills that the government could not stop them. It was in the best interests of the Indians, he said, for them to give up the Black Hills and avoid trouble with the miners. Then the army colonel spoke, saying he had not enough soldiers to drive out the gold hunters, and as sure as the sun rose each day white settlers would soon be following the miners into other parts of the reservation. The colonel advised the chiefs to take their people south to Indian Territory, where they and their children would be always undisturbed among their own kind. Then Belcourt spoke, saying that Congress was ready to pay money to the chiefs to give up their rights to the Black Hills, money enough to make them happy and safe for the remainder of their lives.

"To all these remarks, Red Cloud had the same reply: 'I came to Washington to talk to the Great Father. When he is ready to talk to me, I will talk about the Black Hills.' The other chiefs said they must go home and consult with their people before talking about giving up Paha Sapa, the Black Hills. 'The Black

Hills,' the Minneconjou chief told Belcourt quite sharply, 'are not for sale.'

"The head commissioner and the army colonel then said that it was all right for the chiefs to return to the West and consult with their people. In a few weeks a peace commission would come and meet with them on White Earth River near the Red Cloud Agency to make a new treaty. The commissioner and the colonel then left, but Belcourt remained. Opening a large leather carrying bag, he gave each of the chiefs a box of cigars and a bottle of whiskey. Then from his pockets he took a handful of greenbacks, handing a roll of them to each chief. 'We congressmen always treat our friends right and we expect our friends to treat us right,' he said, and for the first time he looked at me with that cold yellow stare that meant I was not a friend. He knew by this time that I had no power to give away the gold of the Black Hills. Turning back to the chiefs, he said slyly, winking one eye: 'Any of you chiefs want a woman for the night? White or black. We could find no redskin girls for you. You want a woman, you just say the word to Adam Beale here and he'll see to it.' Flattery Jack picked up his empty leather bag. 'We'll talk again.' He bowed, said good night, and left the room.

"I don't know how many of the chiefs went with Mr. Beale. Red Cloud got drunk on his bottle of whiskey, roaming from room to room, keeping most of us awake until late in the night. The next morning he lay moaning in his bed, condemning the Great Father because he would not send for him, saying he would trade the Black Hills for enough Texas steers to feed his people for seven generations. He also wanted shelled corn and beans and rice and dried apples and saleratus and tobacco and salt and pepper for the old people, a wagon with a span of horses and six yoke of work cattle for each family, a sow and a boar, and a cow and a bull, a sheep and a ram, and a hen and a cock for each family, white men's houses with nice shiny black furniture, dishes to eat from, and a scythe and a mowing machine and a sawmill. Poor Red Cloud! He was beginning to love the things of the white man more than our sacred land. The

Wasicus had put blinders over his eyes. He would soon be like a grizzly bear with no teeth or claws.

"I asked him if he was ready to go home. He would wait one more day, he said, for the Great Father to send for him. That afternoon he spent Belcourt's greenbacks buying presents for his family and relatives, and when no message came from President Grant, he told Mr. Beale he wanted to go back to his agency.

"We left in the early light of morning. Mists were around the dome of the Capitol, so that it reminded me of one of those wind-carved rock formations I had seen in the deserts of Mexico —dreary, barren, heartless. I shivered in the dampness of the morning, feeling an evil power in the air I breathed, knowing that since I had come there I had seen too much of the darker side of the human heart.

"Many years had passed since my father, the Runner, had come to Washington from Okelogee to save his Cherokee Nation, only to return home embittered. I could hear his words: *The Congress has always claimed to own the Indian tribes, and if they get away with that, someday they will think they own all the whites, too.*

" 'What do you think of this place?' Mr. Beale asked. Standing beside me in front of the railroad station, he too was looking at the swirling mists around the marble dome.

" 'It is not what it was meant to be,' I replied.

" 'No,' he said, taking a flask from his coat pocket. 'They come here to fill their pockets and when they are full, they fill their hats, and then they say good-bye and go away.'

"A train whistle sounded, followed by a rumble of cars. Mr. Beale took a long swallow from his flask, licked his lips, and spat on the brick paving."

Dane picked up a flat stone and skimmed it over the surface of the stream. "That was thirty years ago," he said. "But nothing has changed." He looked at Red Bird Woman. "Here comes that Crow boy with the lodgepoles. Red Bird, I'll lend my hands to help you build the tipi."

53

In September 1875, the American government sent a commission composed of politicians, missionaries, traders, and military officers to the Red Cloud Agency "to treat with the Sioux Indians for the relinquishment of the Black Hills." Hoping to obtain representatives from the bands who refused to live within the boundaries of the reservations, the commissioners sent messengers to all the camps along the streams that flowed into the Yellowstone, inviting the chiefs to come in and receive presents from the Great Father. Sitting Bull and Crazy Horse both replied that they did not want to sell any land to the government, especially the Black Hills. Neither attended the council on White Earth River, but they sent observers, and they were pleased when their emissaries returned to report that Red Cloud, Spotted Tail, and other agency chiefs who met with the commissioners had resisted all efforts to entice them into giving up the Black Hills.

During the pleasant days of that Drying-Grass Moon, Dane and Sweet Medicine Woman's people were again with the Two Moon Cheyennes, traveling leisurely northward along the Powder. While Dane had been away on his long journey to Washington, both War Shirt and Old Two Moon had died. Yellow Hawk, Big Star's son, was now chief of the small band of former southerners, and Young Two Moon took his father's place as chief of the northern cousins. Through the years many intermarriages had occurred between the two bands, and several of the soldier societies had combined under one leader, but the older people still preferred to have separate chiefs instead of one. Fortunately Yellow Hawk and Young Two Moon were close friends, and they often joked about which one was the real chief.

Another event that occurred during Dane's absence was the birth of his first granddaughter to Swift Eagle and Buffalo Calf Woman. He and Sweet Medicine Woman spent much of their time with their two grandchildren, White Horn the boy and Sun Spirit Girl. Although he said nothing to Buffalo Calf Woman, Dane was disappointed that she had not named his first granddaughter after his grandmother.

Late in the Moon of Dry Dust Blowing, the Cheyennes turned eastward in pursuit of a buffalo herd and came upon Crazy Horse's summer camp on the Belle Fourche. It was a large village, with almost as many wickiups as tipis because there were so many young unmarried warriors there who had left the reservations to join Crazy Horse. Every few days Crazy Horse led a war party into the nearby Black Hills to harass the miners despoiling Paha Sapa. Dane and his son Swift Eagle joined one of these war parties, and they went deep into the Black Hills to attack a tent camp of miners. The war party spent four days among the pine-clad crags and canyons from which mysterious rumbling voices seemed to speak. Some of the Oglalas believed that Paha Sapa was the home of the Thunderbird and the Great Spirit, but for the Cheyennes this was the place of the Holy Mountain where their prophet Motzeyouf, the Sweet Medicine, had journeyed to learn the secrets of the Great Medicine. From the Black Hills the prophet brought to the tribe its four sacred arrows and the warrior societies that had since kept the Cheyennes strong. For the first time Dane came to fully understand the veneration of the Northern Plains tribes for Paha Sapa and their bitter hatred for the plundering white intruders.

At about this same time, events unknown to any of these free Indians were occurring in Washington. A report prepared by a high-ranking bureaucrat was attracting unusual attention among the politicians and government officials. It recommended that soldiers be sent against all tribes who refused to live on their assigned reservations, because they were "well-fed and well-armed and were a threat to the reservation system," a hindrance to the government's acquisition of the Black Hills. A few days after this report appeared, the Secretary of War announced that troops might have to be sent to protect miners in the Black Hills. This was quickly followed by a series of telegraph messages to the government's agents on the reservations, ordering them to send messages to all Indian tribes off the reservations warning them to come in and report by January 31, 1876, or a "military force would be sent to compel them."

The first that the Cheyennes heard of this threat was the arrival of a party of Oglala messengers from the Red Cloud Agency late in the Moon of Popping Trees. Yellow Hawk's and Two Moon's people were camped that winter along the Little Powder near where it ran into the Powder. The two chiefs met in council with the messengers and told them they did not want to become reservation Indians, but neither did they wish to fight the Bluecoats. Because it would be impossible to move travois and old people and young children during the Big Freezing Moon of January, they agreed to start for the agency on White Earth River as soon as the snow melted and the grass was green enough for their ponies to feed.

From Crazy Horse and Sitting Bull, whose winter camps were farther down the Powder, the messengers received virtually the same response. One reason the chiefs did not believe there was any need for hurry was the continual arrival of small parties of Sioux and Cheyennes fleeing the Red Cloud Agency in search of food. These fugitives said the rations doled out to them at the agency were rotten and filled with worms, and that their stomachs longed for fresh buffalo and antelope meat. An Oglala who brought his family to the Cheyenne camp told Dane that Red Cloud had asked the Bluecoat commander at Camp Robinson to come to the agency to inspect the food, but the day before the army officers came, the agent arrested Red Cloud. Red Cloud was put into the guardhouse with his hands tied and a wooden gag in his mouth until after the inspection was over so that he was unable to tell the officers that the food on display was not the usual daily fare offered the Indians.

None of the Indians in winter villages along the Powder knew that on February 7, 1876, the War Department ordered its commanders in the western forts to begin military operations against the "hostile" tribes who refused to report to their assigned agencies, or that one day later General Philip Sheridan notified generals George Crook and Alfred Terry to march their troops in the direction of the Powder, Tongue, Rosebud, and Bighorn rivers "where Crazy Horse and his allies frequented."

In the Moon of the Snowblind, Yellow Hawk's and Two Moon's Cheyennes were camped on the west bank of the Little Powder, about a hundred lodges including a few visiting Sioux, and a horse herd numbering seven hundred, all sheltered by bluffs from the wintry winds. Dane and Sweet Medicine Woman still lived in the tipi that Amayi had painted, though some parts of it had been replaced from time to time through the years, the representations of the family carefully coated with new paint. The two coyotes facing each other on each side of the entrance were still bright and sharply delineated.

Before daylight one morning Dane awoke suddenly. He was not sure whether he had heard something or felt something. Sound or movement, whatever it was, it did not belong there. He pushed aside the thick buffalo robe, sliding quietly off the willow bed-frame so as not to disturb Sweet Medicine Woman. Shivering in the cold, he pulled on his blanket-cloth leggings and then sat listening. It was still there, a faint reverberation in the air. He wrapped himself in the buffalo robe and raked coals together in the fire hole, laying two sticks of wood over them. Then he opened the entrance flap and listened. Horses' hooves on the snow, far away, he thought. All around the camp the snow cover had melted and frozen again. Now it was so cold that he could feel frost on his nose hairs when he breathed. He hurried to the top of a small knoll and looked toward the south. The late winter dawnlight was very pale, but he could see cavalry approaching at a steady pace, four troops, each mounted on horses of matched colors. The white-horse troop was in the lead.

Shouting an alarm, he ran back to arouse Sweet Medicine Woman and call his son Swift Eagle out of the adjoining tipi. Dane's carbine was in good working order, but he had only four

bullets left, and he knew that few others in the camp had ammunition for their weapons. While Dane armed himself with a bow
and arrows, Sweet Medicine Woman wrapped a buffalo robe
around her and fastened a parfleche bag to her back. Dane
pushed her outside, and tossed his carbine to Swift Eagle. "I'll
get the women and children up on the bluff ledge!" he cried.
Being one of the older men now, that was his duty—to save the
seed of the tribe before entering the fight.

The camp was swarming with movement when the white-
horse troop charged in, recklessly firing carbines and pistols. A
second line of Bluecoats on darker-colored horses struck from
the left, while a third swept toward the Cheyennes' horse herd
along the grassy flat. Dane lifted his young grandson to his
shoulders, hurrying the women ahead of him. Swift Eagle's wife,
Buffalo Calf Woman, had the little granddaughter in a cradle
and was also struggling with several packs. Sweet Medicine
Woman took the packs, and they started running up the icy
slope to the ledge. Behind them in the camp women were
screaming and children crying. The firing continued, bullets
whining in the cold air. Men shouted and cursed, ponies whin-
nied, a rumble of hooves came from the Cheyennes' stampeded
horse herd.

As soon as Dane was sure that his family was safe on the
ledge, he turned back to help the old people who were hobbling
up the slippery incline. Below, in the rear of the nearest tipi, he
saw an old woman with one small child in her arms, another
child clinging tight to her robe. All three were crying. The old
woman was attempting to conceal herself and the children in a
clump of leafless brush. A Bluecoat mounted on one of the white
horses sighted them, and wheeled to face them. He raised his
pistol but Dane had his bow up. He drove an arrow into the soldier's neck; the man fell, sprawling on his belly in the snow.
When Dane ran past him, he kneeled to jerk the pistol from the
man's tightening fingers. The riderless white horse was circling.
Dane tried and failed to catch the bridle. The second time the
horse came round he pulled the carbine from its bucket, and
then ran to help the old woman with the children.

By this time the Cheyenne warriors realized that they were too heavily outgunned to make a stand in their camp and began withdrawing to the ledge where their women and children had found refuge. From this position the warriors could pour enfilading fire down upon any soldiers attempting to pursue them. They could do nothing, though, to stop the Bluecoats from destroying their tipis. During the morning they watched everything except the clothing they wore go up in smoke. Sweet Medicine Woman wept when she saw flames licking at Amayi's painting, and others cried out over the loss of their blankets and bedding, their medicine bundles and saddles, the carefully hoarded winter supplies of food. The Bluecoats made useless even their kettles, pans, and other utensils by knocking holes in them.

In the withdrawal only four warriors were killed, but several suffered painful wounds. Swift Eagle's face was cut open from ear to eye, the bullet lodging in his cheekbone. Two Crows, the old medicine man, was prying a piece of lead out of the bone with a knife when Dane found his son with other wounded.

While the Bluecoats below were still destroying the tipis and everything they contained, Yellow Hawk and Two Moon decided their only hope of survival in the bitter weather was to reach Crazy Horse's village. By horseback the distance was two long days, and they had brought out only a dozen or so ponies from the camp. A few more that had scattered when the Bluecoats drove off the herd were being recovered by daring warriors, but hundreds more were needed. The final decision of the leaders was for half the warriors to go with the women, children, old people, and wounded, following the rock ledge to a coulee through which they could move northward toward Crazy Horse's village. While this was being done, the remaining warriors would watch the soldiers, distract them if necessary, and use any opportunity that offered to recover some of their ponies.

Late in the afternoon, the Bluecoats, after making a number of halfhearted attempts to drive the Cheyennes from the ledge, began withdrawing toward the south. As the winter light died, the warriors followed at a distance, tracking the cavalrymen to a tent camp in a grove of cottonwoods. They soon discovered what was left of their pony herd, penned in a cul-de-sac, with four army wagons blocking the entrance. Across a narrow gully, the picketed mounts of the white-horse troop looked like ghost horses frozen in the biting cold.

Dane was with these desperate horse hunters. He had defiantly refused to obey his brother-in-law Yellow Hawk's command to go on with the women and children. Not until they left the ledge to begin following the soldiers did he discover that the warrior wearing a buffalo-hair headdress and wrapped to the eyes in a maroon blanket—and who had stayed near him all afternoon—was Red Bird Woman. He scolded her until she reminded him that she had brought the Cheyennes good luck when she went with them to Peno Creek against the fort on the Little Piney.

"But by now you must have seen sixty winters," he said.

"And you more than that," she retorted.

Two Moon and Yellow Hawk gave the task of regaining the horse herd to old Iron Crow, who had succeeded Lean Bear as head of the Dog Soldiers. It was done speedily and almost silently. Iron Crow sent several warriors to work their way along the steep face of the ravine and then down into the rear of the herd. Then he and three of his Dog Soldiers with their usual competence dispatched the two Bluecoats guarding the wagon barrier. When Iron Crow heard what sounded like the distant yelp of a coyote, he signaled the remaining warriors out of the nearby gully and they quickly rolled the empty wagons aside. Meanwhile the warriors in the rear of the herd had mounted and were driving the animals before them. As the ponies rushed by, each warrior caught one and rode swiftly away.

In the confusion, Dane lost Red Bird Woman. He did not remember seeing her after he leaped out of the gully to help move the wagons. When carbine fire rattled suddenly behind him he turned and saw one of the white cavalry horses jumping the gully. Thinking that a Bluecoat was starting pursuit, he quickly drew the pistol he had taken that morning. As he raised the weapon he recognized Red Bird Woman's buffalo-hair headdress against the starry sky. She had stolen one of the mounts of the white-horse troop, and when she passed him like a streaking ghost her laughter was that of a gleeful young girl.

On their grim three-day journey to Crazy Horse's village, the Cheyennes lost more people from cold and exhaustion than they had lost to the Bluecoats. They had not been able to recapture half their stampeded ponies, and out of fear of another attack by the cavalry, they discontinued any further searches for lost animals. Consequently many had to walk, or take turns at riding, and progress was slow without saddles or bridles.

Temperatures below zero protected them from Bluecoat pursuit, but the weather was also a deadly enemy. On the second day, freezing rain coated their ponies and their clothing with ice, and made it impossible to keep fires going that night. The only food they had were tiny bits of dried buffalo meat from the small stores that the women had managed to carry away with them.

Without shelters everyone suffered, and on the afternoon of the third day they halted long enough to build makeshift scaffolds for the dead before going on to Crazy Horse's village. Among them was a tiny platform for Sun Spirit Girl. Dane and Sweet Medicine Woman had lost their only granddaughter. She died as Dane remembered the young McBee children dying on that long-ago exodus of the Cherokees—with a rasping of the throat and lungs, a choking, and then death.

When will this curse, this burden upon my people be lifted? he thought as he helped his wounded son lift the tiny blanketed form upon its scaffold. *When will the running stop, the flights be ended?*

Their sadness was lightened by the kindness of the Sioux, some of whom rode out from their village to welcome them. At every tipi they passed after they entered the camp circle, men and women and children stood outside in the cold to greet them: "*Hokahe*, brave Cheyennes, come and share food with us." Others brought blankets and robes, offering them in silence.

Crazy Horse, almost unnoticed in his simple buckskins, a red hawk's feather in his long unbraided hair, appeared out of the crowd to welcome Two Moon and Yellow Hawk. "I have heard," he said, "of the Bluecoats' savagery."

"We have no food or shelter," Two Moon answered, "and few horses."

"I am glad you are come," Crazy Horse said. "We Oglalas have more horses than are needed. We will share our food and shelter." He placed his hands on the shoulders of the Cheyenne chiefs, his eyes burning with anger. "We all will have to fight the *Wasicus* again." He recognized Dane, then, standing behind the chiefs. "Where is my old friend Pleasant?" he called out. Dane told him his half-blood son was at the Red Cloud Agency. Crazy Horse's face revealed his disapproval. "*Hoh!* With old Red Cloud and my uncle Spotted Tail, he eats the white man's leavings? But one day he will come and join us. Like us, Pleasant will find that he must live where the wind blows free. He will come, and so will many others."

Until the Geese Laying Moon of April, the Cheyennes lived with the Oglalas, slowly restoring their shattered world. For fresh meat, antelope were plentiful in the valley, but what they needed most of all were the life-giving buffalo—to replace their lost tipis and clothing and to replenish their stores of dried meat. The Oglalas also needed buffalo in the spring, and as soon as the grass was green and the ponies strong, both tribes moved west to the Tongue. There they found Sitting Bull with hundreds of lodges of Uncpapas as well as many others who had fled the reservations in search of freedom. The Uncpapas had heard of the disaster that had befallen the Cheyennes, and many came to offer ponies, blankets, tipi covers, bows and arrows, medicine pipes, anything that was needed.

During the days that followed, Sitting Bull's buffalo scouts began coming in with reports that herds were plentiful between the Rosebud and Little Bighorn. Instead of breaking camps on different days and taking different routes, the tribes and subtribes for the first time in anyone's memory moved westward as one great family, thousands of Uncpapas, Oglalas, Brules, Sans Arcs, Blackfoot Sioux, Arapahos, and Cheyennes.

Along the way they were joined by Spotted Elk's Minneconjous coming up from the southeast, and Dane and his family held a joyful reunion with Amayi and her husband, Bull Bear.

Amayi was more beautiful than ever, her skin bright with life, her glossy hair plaited with ribbons, her eyes and mouth always smiling. Dane was about to chide her for not presenting him with a grandchild, when he heard her whisper to Sweet Medicine Woman that she had suffered a miscarriage that winter but was fully recovered. Several of the Minneconjous had spent the winter at the Red Cloud Agency, and all vowed they would fight the Bluecoats rather than return to the constraints and deadly impoverishment of reservation life.

In the Moon When the Buffalo Bulls Are Fat, these last free Indians of the Northern Plains made their camp circles along the Greasy Grass (which the white men call Little Bighorn) to begin a busy summer of hunting, hide dressing, meat drying, robe tanning, and lodgepole cutting. On the morning of June 25 their chosen way of life was interrupted by the unexpected arrival of six hundred well-armed Bluecoats under the command of George Armstrong Custer. When the fighting ended, the tribes had won a great victory, but the triumph soon brought down upon them the wrath of mighty forces, and in the end they lost Paha Sapa, the hunting paradise of the Powder River country, and their cherished freedom forever.

54

"Mr. Teddy Roosevelt, your President," Dane said, "was always asking me to tell him about the fight on the Little Bighorn. He would not believe me when I told him I was there but saw only the finish of it from a long distance. He thought I was afraid to admit I might have helped kill Custer."

"Dane speaks true," Red Bird Woman said. "He was with me and Sweet Medicine Woman out on prairie digging breadroot when Custer's Bluecoats come shooting."

"Amayi was with us, too," Dane said, "and White Horn my grandson, six years old. Swift Eagle and Buffalo Calf Woman stayed in camp that morning, and my son-in-law, Bull Bear, was out with some Minneconjous hunting antelope. Our buffalo scouts had told us of Bluecoats prowling from the west, but we did not know about the column coming from the east—Custer's. And of course we did not know it was Custer until long after the battle."

"You had heard of Custer?" I asked.

"Oh, yes. The Cheyennes hated him because he killed Black Kettle and many relatives and friends on the Washita in Indian Territory. But we did not know Custer had come to kill us so far to the north."

He stepped down to the edge of the stream to help John Bear-in-the-Water bring one of the lodgepoles across. After the young man turned back to the wagon for another, Red Bird Woman asked in a loud whisper: "You going to let Mary Amayi marry that Crow boy?"

He shrugged. "Mary Amayi knows her own heart. These times are not like the old times, Red Bird."

"The Crows rode as scouts for Custer," she said, glancing at me.

He laughed. "They didn't stay around long after Crazy Horse and Gall and Two Moon started chasing them. The Crows did us no harm. As I said, I was far out on the prairie. It was covered with wild flowers, wide sweeps of yellow and red and blue and white, and I was wading with my little grandson in melted snow-water, too cold to teach him to swim. I was drying his legs and feet with dead grass when we heard the guns popping far off toward the south end of the long camp where the Uncpapas had their circle. From the first sound of the firing I knew it was Bluecoats attacking, and I started running for the north end where the Cheyennes were camped. Soon in the distance I saw many people moving around our horse herd, women helping with saddles, and warriors riding off toward the Little Bighorn.

"Custer brought his men right down to the edge of the Little Bighorn across from the Cheyenne camp, and my brother-in-law, Yellow Hawk, told me that if Crazy Horse had not come with his Oglalas, many Cheyenne warriors would have died there in the river. The Cheyennes all alone had to stop Custer from reaching their tipis and then Crazy Horse came, and also Gall, after the Uncpapas drove the eagle chief Reno and his men upon that high bluff.

"By the time I got to our Cheyenne tipis, Custer and all his men were lying dead on the slope across the river. Sitting Bull always said the fight did not last long enough to light a pipe.

"I found Buffalo Calf Woman safe at her tipi, and soon afterward Swift Eagle came riding in, blood dripping down his Frenchman's nose from his unhealed scar. He held out his lance to me, and I saw the blond hairs of a fresh scalp fastened to the shaft. 'I did not want to fight the Bluecoats today any more than I wanted to fight them when I was a boy, the day they fired their big guns at us on that place called Pea Ridge,' he said, and dismounted. 'The Bluecoats were coming to destroy our tipis again, so I took the scalp for Sun Spirit Girl. When we pass her burial scaffold I will leave it there.'

"All that night we kept Reno's soldiers trapped on the high hill, but we could not get at them and they were afraid to come down and fight us. Before daylight our scouts came in to tell us of many Bluecoats coming from two directions. The chiefs held council with Sitting Bull, and they decided our great family should break apart again, each tribe and subtribe going in different directions, traveling fast so that the Bluecoats would have a hard time finding any of us. So Sweet Medicine Woman and I had to say good-bye again to Amayi and Bull Bear, who went off with the Minneconjous.

"Several chiefs took their people toward the Bighorn Mountains to hide in the forests, but we Cheyennes knew we could not live long without grass for ponies and buffalo for food, shelter, and clothing. And so we went across the Yellowstone and down to where the Tongue flows in. Sitting Bull must have felt the same way we did because we soon discovered the Uncpapas camped near us.

"For a few moons we lived as we had lived before, but then the Bluecoats began to come from all the four directions. We would run this way and run that way, trying to keep our tipis and our lives, seldom camping in one place for more than a day. Once on the Powder we met Sitting Bull and his people running from one bunch of soldiers while we were running from another bunch. 'The Bluecoats are angry because we beat them,' Sitting Bull said. 'We did not fight them until they came to fight us. What have we done that the *Wasicus* want us to stop? We have been running up and down the country but they follow us from one place to another.' He told us that Crazy Horse was farther up the Powder, and that his people were hungry because they could not stop running long enough to hunt buffalo.

"Not long after that we had a skirmish with some Bluecoats, and during the fighting our little band—Yellow Hawk's—got separated from the Two Moon people. In our flight we caught up with the Uncpapas. Sitting Bull welcomed us, but he was angry because he had discovered Bluecoats building a new fort right where the Tongue ran into the Yellowstone. We all knew that soldiers prowling from there would make it impossible for us to live peaceably in what was left of our hunting paradise. We were being squeezed from all sides, and now the Bluecoats were going to stab us in the heart.

"Sitting Bull sent one of the French half-bloods in our camp to arrange a meeting with the commander of this new fort. In the Falling-Leaf Moon of October, I went as interpreter with the chiefs to meet the Bluecoats' star chief. All our warriors formed into a line facing a line of Bluecoats, and the chiefs and a few warriors and I walked out to meet the star chief and a few of his officers.

"We named him Bear Coat because he was wearing a fur hat and a long bearskin coat. He was General Miles. The town that grew up there later was named for him—Miles City.

"Bear Coat pretended to be friendly, but Sitting Bull would not smoke a pipe with him. 'Why will you not be my friend?' Bear Coat asked.

"'I am not for the *Wasicus*,' Sitting Bull replied, 'but neither am I your enemy. I want only to be left alone.'

"'What are you doing in the Yellowstone country?' Bear Coat then asked.

"'I am hunting buffalo to feed and clothe my people,' Sitting Bull answered. 'I do not want to fight you. I have never fought the *Wasicus* until they come to fight me. There will be no more fighting if you will take your soldiers and forts out of our country.'

"Bear Coat's smile turned to a scowl. His hard eyes glared at each of us. 'There will be no peace for you,' he said, 'until you go to the reservation we have made for you.'

"I could feel the anger growing in Sitting Bull. He turned his head and looked back at our line of poorly armed warriors facing the line of Bluecoats with their shiny new rifles. He knew the *Wasicus* sometimes violated truce meetings. If Bear Coat chose to do so, he could kill or capture all of us in the council group. 'The Great Spirit made me an Indian,' Sitting Bull said quietly, 'but not a reservation Indian. I do not intend to become a reservation Indian.' He glanced at Yellow Hawk and me. '*Aban!* Look out, be careful. It is ended.' He turned his back on Bear Coat, and we all walked without hurrying to our line of warriors and mounted our ponies. From the Bluecoat line came the sound of clicking rifle hammers. Sitting Bull waved the warriors into the trees. Two or three shots were fired behind us, the bullets whining over our heads, and then we heard Bear Coat bellowing a command to cease firing. At least he had honored the truce meeting.

"That night the chiefs held a council and Sitting Bull said the *Wasicus* had taken our land and there was no longer room enough for us to live in the Great Father's country. If we stayed where we were we could hope for nothing but imprisonment or death. The only thing left for us was to go to Canada, to the land of the Grandmother, Queen Victoria. Before we left, Sitting Bull and Yellow Hawk sent messengers south along the Tongue and Powder to find Crazy Horse and Two Moon and ask them to go with us to the Grandmother's Land. But the messengers found only a few scattered bands fleeing from soldiers, and no one knew what had happened to Crazy Horse and Two Moon.

"And so we went to Canada, and there we became prisoners of the redcoated Mounted Police. They did not want to kill us and they treated us kindly, but we were outcasts forbidden to wander or hunt buffalo. We had nothing to do but sit in our canvas tents day after day, remembering our lost homeland and waiting for the Mounted Police to feed and clothe us. Survival was all we had to live for.

"This is the way life is. Things may be going well for you, then one day something happens and you are finished. Remember, it can happen to you, too."

55

Sergeant Pleasant McAlpin, Indian Scout, buttoned his dark blue uniform blouse and buckled on his pistol belt. Listening for the bugle call, he tiptoed to the door of the tiny bedroom. Maga, his Oglala wife, lay in a drunken stupor on the bed, a blanket twisted between her naked legs. A whiskey bottle rested at an angle against the clay wall. He went inside and picked it up, saw liquor in the bottom, and drained it into his throat, relishing the sweet warmth, hoping it would drive the aching from his head.

The bugle sounded then, and he hurried out into the dry morning chill of Camp Robinson, facing the towering white cliffs on the north where the sun was already lighting the pine trees. When he brought his horse from the grazing ground, he saw infantrymen far across the river to the south putting up rows of gray canvas tents, and for the first time he truly believed that Crazy Horse was bringing his people in to surrender.

With the other Indian Scouts he rode around the cavalry barracks to the parade ground. There he formed the scouts into a squad at one end of Lieutenant Clark's regular cavalry company. Lieutenant Clark wasted no time that morning, and they were soon moving out, the lieutenant in the lead, the ten scouts ranked behind him, the cavalrymen in a column of fours. Less than half an hour after leaving Camp Robinson they sighted the Oglalas coming down the valley from the northeast. Lieutenant Clark shouted an order for the cavalrymen to form a line front, and as they continued at a slow walk Pleasant saw that the Oglalas were advancing in a similar formation. Crazy Horse was out front on a white-faced mustang, ten subchiefs riding behind, then a thin line of warriors, and in the rear a mass of women and children with a large pony herd. They had not one travois, which meant they were without shelter of any kind. The lieutenant and Crazy Horse halted almost simultaneously, not more than twenty paces apart.

The Oglala warriors were hollow-eyed and lean-fleshed, their clothing worn to scraps, the bones of their ponies pressing against loose folds of hide. Yet the warriors held themselves proudly while Crazy Horse dismounted and came forward to meet the lieutenant and the interpreter from Camp Robinson. Crazy Horse's gaze passed contemptuously over the faces of the ten Indian Scouts, and Pleasant wondered if his old companion of daring decoy exploits on the Little Piney had recognized him under his broad-brimmed army hat.

From where he sat in his saddle, Pleasant could hear the slow talk, Crazy Horse's soft-spoken Lakota words rendered into crude English phrases. Crazy Horse offered his left hand to Lieutenant Clark, explaining that his heart was on the left side of his body and he was giving his heart to the *Wasicus*. He wanted to sit on the ground while he smoked a pipe with the

Little White Chief because the earth they sat upon would make the peace solid. He was surrendering, Crazy Horse declared, because he had been promised a reservation in the Powder River country, a place of his choosing. Pleasant knew this was a lie; the army officers had invented the promise to ensnare the last of the great Sioux war leaders.

Pleasant wanted to shout to Crazy Horse that the promise was a lie, to tell him to turn and flee to safety, but he knew there was no place of safety left this side of the Canadian border. Two Moon, who had already surrendered his Cheyennes, had told Pleasant that Dane and Sweet Medicine Woman were in flight to Canada with Yellow Hawk and Sitting Bull; that is, if they were still alive. But no one knew if they were alive. He felt that old pain of loneliness smothering him again. His throat was dry and he craved the dreams he could find only in a bottle of that craw-rot whiskey the sutler sold from a wagon hidden up the willow-bordered river. He was certain that his mother, Jerusha, was dead. He had written three letters to her in the Cherokee Nation but no reply ever came. He ached with a loneliness that Maga, his wife, could no longer relieve because she too sought her own dreams from the bottle, spending on whiskey the money she earned as a laundress for the soldiers, weeping when sober for the old days of freedom, cursing the log walls of the cubicle that imprisoned her with Pleasant.

Lieutenant Clark was on his feet, shouting orders to the Indian Scouts and cavalrymen. They spent the morning counting and disarming Crazy Horse's people, searching the 217 men and 672 women and children for hidden weapons, finally collecting 84 worn-out rifles and 33 pistols. Pleasant was glad when it was finished. He did not like the way the warriors and the women looked at him when they saw who he was, and he felt like crying when he looked at the children. When he had known them they were always running and laughing. Now they were as solemn as old men and women, many coughing painfully, pus running from their noses and eyes.

Then the procession began. Along the valley, with the high white bluffs on their right, the remnants of the last free Oglala

Sioux moved toward the bend of White Earth River, skirting Camp Robinson. On both sides of the river thousands of reservation Sioux and Cheyennes were gathered to honor Crazy Horse, their voices rising in rhythmic chants and songs, wailing old forgotten battle cries. Not since the victory against Carrington on Peno Creek, eleven years past, had Pleasant heard such a crescendo of pulsating voices.

They crossed the narrow river and rode on to the canvas tents that were set in straight military rows instead of in a camp circle. Here, as the Oglalas dismounted, their ponies were led away by the Indian Scouts and added to the herd. Before nightfall Sergeant Pleasant McAlpin and the scouts had the two thousand half-starved ponies of Crazy Horse's people safely corralled on the west side of Camp Robinson. In the days to come these animals would be slaughtered and fed to their former owners, who were now prisoners of the United States Army.

A week passed before Pleasant could steel himself for a visit to Crazy Horse. He feared that his former warrior comrade would refuse to speak with him, or, if he did so, would condemn him as a mercenary, a traitor. All of Camp Robinson buzzed with rumors of the strange man of the Oglalas, and it was plain to Pleasant that Crazy Horse's presence was disturbing to the higher army officers. The noisy demonstration by the agency Indians had alarmed them. Even though Crazy Horse and his warriors were now without arms or horses, he remained a symbol of freedom, a danger to the reservation system. Pleasant heard whispers of plans to send him far away where he could no longer be a threat.

Early one evening after Pleasant was relieved from duty, he dressed in his buckskins and waded the river, walking at a rapid pace until he reached Crazy Horse's camp. The Oglalas had rearranged the tents into a circle, so that he had no trouble finding Crazy Horse. He was seated on a horse blanket beside his tent, gazing into the setting sun, lines of melancholy ridging from his nose to the sad corners of his mouth. He looked much older than his thirty-five years. Pleasant approached him from the side, expecting him to turn at the sound of footsteps, but he seemed oblivious of everything but the sun.

"Tashunka Witko," Pleasant said softly.

Crazy Horse looked at him then, his face remaining grave, but he stood up, offering his hand. "Iron Shirt Pleasant," he said, with the faintest flicker of a smile. Crazy Horse still wore the red hawk's feather in his hair. Holes were worn at the elbows of his buckskin shirt.

"You saw me the other day," Pleasant said. "In my bluecoat uniform I was ashamed for you to look upon my face."

"*Hna!*" Crazy Horse grunted. "We both have done things to shame ourselves, Iron Shirt. But wait a little, wait a little. You and your wife Maga can come and live with me where buffalo are still plentiful. The *Wasicus* have promised me a reservation in the Powder River country."

The promise is a lie, Pleasant thought. *I must tell him they lie.* Instead he asked: "Have they named the moon when you will go there?"

Crazy Horse made a growling sound. "They say I must first go to Washington to see the Great Father. I tell them I will go to see the Great Father after I see the reservation. They wait. I wait. They tell me my people must become civilized. I tell them my people *are* civilized, that we want to live as our fathers lived and their fathers before them. We must now look to the *Wasicus* for food, shelter, and clothing. In this way they will destroy us. We do not want the civilization of the *Wasicus*. They do not understand me. I do not understand them."

They talked until darkness fell, and then Pleasant left without telling Crazy Horse of the lie, knowing that without the lie his friend would have nothing, nothing, nothing—not even a dream from a bottle.

On another evening he asked Maga to go with him to see Crazy Horse. Some of her relatives were in the camp. But she refused. "I could not bear to see them the way they are now," she said, "or for them to see me. Crazy Horse and his people have always been wild and free. They will all die soon in this place."

She began weeping soundlessly, and he went alone across the river.

This time he and Crazy Horse talked mostly about the old days, the hunts and wars along the Tongue and Powder, the great victories at Peno Creek and the Little Bighorn. "It is all finished," Crazy Horse said abruptly, his lean body shivering with the realization of the present, the false world that surrounded him.

Pleasant took out a bottle from the lining of his coat. "This is my deliverance," he said, offering it to Crazy Horse.

"What good is this firewater of the *Wasicus?*" Crazy Horse cried scornfully. "It makes a man like a bear who has lost his senses. He growls, he scratches and he howls, he falls down as if he were dead." He pushed the bottle away, a queer look coming into his eyes as he stared hard at Pleasant. "Did the Bluecoats send you to me, Iron Shirt?" he asked.

"No!" Pleasant drew away, hurt by the accusation.

"I have learned to trust no one since coming to this place. They tell lies about me over in Red Cloud's agency and in your soldier camp."

During the weeks that followed, Pleasant scouted with a company of cavalry up the North Platte, searching for a rumored band of "hostile" Arapahos. He did not want to find the Arapahos, but they found them, seventeen frightened men, women, and children, and herded them back to Camp Robinson like Longhorn cattle. As soon as he returned he noticed that the Crazy Horse camp was gone. The army, fearful of the magic of the Oglala leader, had moved him and his people a few miles farther south to put more distance between him and the Red Cloud Agency.

Around the sutler's store and in the adjutant's office where Pleasant made his reports, he heard much talk about Crazy Horse. Long before, he had discovered that the army officers looked upon the Indian Scouts as useful animals, capable of understanding commands but no more likely than their horses to comprehend or communicate gossip or rumors spoken in English. The officers would say things in their presence they would never have whispered anywhere near the white enlisted men. After a few days, he learned enough to know that Crazy Horse was in great danger. Using the false promise of a buffalo hunt, the Bluecoats planned to bring him into Camp Robinson, put him in irons, and take him to the railroad under cover of darkness. The journey would end at Dry Tortugas, an island off the coast of Florida. Crazy Horse would die there, surely.

After dark one evening, Pleasant rode to Crazy Horse's camp. This time he wore his uniform, because he had learned that agency Indians were forbidden to visit the Oglala camp. An old man was hovering over the coals of a tiny fire beside Crazy Horse's tent. He was the war leader's father. "My son has gone far out on the prairie," he told Pleasant.

"He must never return here," Pleasant said.

"Crazy Horse will not desert his people." The old man stirred the coals with a stick. "He related to me something that he dreamed. He was standing on top of the high white cliffs. A great eagle soared above him, floating in the blue sky. All at once the eagle folded its wings and began falling. It fell straight down, landing at the feet of my son, and when he looked upon it he saw that the eagle was himself, pierced through with an arrow, without life."

"I too have such dreams," Pleasant said.

"My son has traveled far out on the prairie to seek the meaning of this dream."

Pleasant turned toward his horse. "Old man," he said as he mounted, "tell your son he must not come into Camp Robinson."

The next morning eight companies of cavalry, with several chiefs and Indian police from the Red Cloud Agency, marched out of Camp Robinson to arrest Crazy Horse. The Indian Scouts did not go, perhaps because their officers did not trust them, perhaps because—as they were told—they were needed at Camp Robinson to keep the agency Indians from entering the camp to await the arrival of Crazy Horse. Throughout the day Pleasant and his scouts circled the outer walls of the buildings and the connecting high board fences, warning a steadily enlarging assemblage of Indians to stay away. Until long after dark the crowd remained, and then singly or in small groups they departed. By daylight next morning they began returning, and the commandant sent out a company of cavalrymen to drive them away. But as soon as the cavalrymen rode back inside the fence, the Indians again gathered around the perimeter of the military post. All day this game of approach and withdrawal continued, and then just as the sun was setting the watchers sighted a dust cloud on the eastern horizon. For a while there was silence, and then the murmuring of voices was like a wind in a pine forest, rising and falling. Pleasant led the Indian Scouts to a wide gate between the officers' quarters and the infantry barracks. They forced the crowd back, opened the gate, and used their horses to form a passageway for the approaching column to enter.

The soldiers rode in quickly, a squad of cavalry first, and then a major with Crazy Horse and two chiefs from the agency followed. As Crazy Horse passed by, Pleasant called out his name above the rapid pounding of hooves. *"Aban!* Be careful!" Pleasant shouted, and made the sign for danger. Crazy Horse bowed his head, and was swept along by the cavalrymen in his rear.

As soon as the column was through the gate, Pleasant closed it and posted the scouts along the fence. He then led his pony into the parade ground. A cavalry squad was drawn up around the adjutant's office. In the dimming light of dusk he saw Crazy Horse dismount. Two infantrymen with bayoneted rifles and an Indian policeman from the agency surrounded him. Instead of leading Crazy Horse into the adjutant's office they turned him toward the guardhouse.

Pleasant climbed into his saddle and started slowly across the parade ground. He was halfway to the adjutant's office when he heard Crazy Horse cry out, a wailing protest from deep in his throat, and Pleasant knew that his friend had seen the iron bars of the guardhouse and perceived in them the reality of the *Wasicus'* lies that had tricked him into a final indignity. The four shadows—Crazy Horse, the two infantrymen, and the Indian policeman—scuffled in a wild dance while a voice shouted *Kill the son of a bitch, kill the son of a bitch!* A soldier's bayonet went twice and deep into the lean body of Tashunka Witko, piercing entrails and kidneys.

Within moments the thousands of his kinspeople gathered outside knew, and they waited into the darkness until he was dead, and they then went away.

Sergeant Pleasant McAlpin could not go away. He went to the cubicle in the log building, longing for Maga to comfort him, but she was not there. For a while he sat in a chair staring at the empty whiskey bottle leaning against the log wall beside the bed, lusting not for dreams but oblivion. He started searching then, lifting the loose boards of the floor until he found a bottle that Maga had concealed in the sandy clay. He drank in quick swallows, retching and wiping his mouth, and swallowing again. After a while he took off his uniform, dropping the blouse and pistol belt and trousers on the flooring. Stuffed in a wooden box under the bed, he found musty-smelling unwashed blanket-cloth leggings and an old war shirt. He put them on and painted half his face black. From his belt on the floor he took his pistol, removed the cartridges, and flung them against the wall. He thrust the empty weapon inside his shirt, took a long gulp from the bottle, and went out into the darkness.

The parade ground was quiet, but the night guard had been doubled and he could smell the uneasiness in the air. Lantern light bathed the front of the adjutant's office in pale yellow, glinting off the bayonets of two guards posted there. Pleasant walked unsteadily toward them, and as he appeared out of the shadows both guards came quickly alert. He swayed toward the nearer man. "Tashunka Witko," he muttered. "Who killed him?"

"What're you doin' inside here, half-breed?" the guard demanded. "Pack off, or into the guardhouse with you."

Pleasant moved closer. When the guard brought his rifle to port arms, Pleasant reached out as if to seize it, but the guard shoved him roughly away with the weapon. "Pack off!" he repeated angrily.

Regaining his balance, Pleasant thrust a hand inside his shirt for the empty pistol, quickly aiming it at the guard and drawing back the hammer.

"Look out!" the second guard shouted. "He's armed—"

The first guard fired, and the last thing that Pleasant saw on earth was a flash of orange light against the log wall of the building in which Crazy Horse died.

The official report stated that Sergeant Pleasant McAlpin of the Indian Scouts came to his death "in a drunken brawl." The United States Army buried him on the bank of White Earth River, marking his grave with a wooden shingle which soon rotted and was blown away by the wind, leaving his bones lost and unremembered, as were the bones of his Cherokee great-grandfather, the Long Warrior, on the bank of the Tallapoosa at Horseshoe Bend.

56

"Maga told me how Pleasant died," Dane said. "I found her at Pine Ridge with the Oglalas after we came back from Canada and I started searching for lost members of my family. For a long time, however, I could find no trace of my daughter Amayi or her husband, Bull Bear, among the Minneconjous. When the army drove all the Sioux from the agencies on White Earth River into Dakota, the subtribes were scattered to different places— mostly Oglalas at Pine Ridge, but I found Minneconjous at Rosebud with the Brules, at Cheyenne River with the Sans Arcs and Blackfoot Sioux, and at Crow Creek with the Two Kettles and Yanktonai. None of them knew what had happened to Bull Bear and Amayi, and I feared they might have lost their lives in the last running fights with the Bluecoats.

"The Sioux were all having a hard time on the Dakota reservations, worse than the Cheyennes suffered after we came back to Tongue River."

Red Bird Woman made a scoffing sound. "*Aho-ya!* We almost starve that first summer. Nothing to eat—only plums and cherries and serviceberries. We all sick."

"We were all sick before we left Canada," Dane said. "If Yellow Hawk and Swift Eagle had not made their way across the border and found Two Moon scouting for the army at Fort Keogh, we all would have gone to the Darkening Land. One more winter in the canvas tents and never enough meat would have finished us. Some days in Canada we were so hungry we were glad when we found one of our ponies frozen to death so we could eat it."

"You came back here to the Cheyenne reservation?" I asked.

"There was no reservation when we returned," he replied. "But so many Cheyennes came and lived along the Tongue that after two or three years the American government took pity on them and gave them a reservation there. But I never lived on it. By that time I was alone in the world. Sweet Medicine Woman died of the lung disease she fell ill of while we were in Canada. Swift Eagle's little boy, White Horn, the only grandchild I had left, suffered the same illness and died soon after. Then that old wound of Swift Eagle's began suppurating, got into his bones. I took him to the contract surgeon at Fort Keogh, but all that army doctor knew to do was pour burning liquids into it. Swift Eagle lost the sight of his eye and then died in great pain. I am certain that if a healer like Mary Amayi had been among us she could have saved all of them. Oh, it was a dark time for me. I felt the way Creek Mary did when the Cherokees were penned up in the Tennessee stockade and the Maker of Breath kept taking the younger people to the Darkening Land and leaving her and old Stalking Turkey to burden the survivors.

"I was about seventy years old then, but I was strong enough to drive an army freighting wagon for Fort Keogh. Then the railroad tracks were built, and they didn't need freighting wagons anymore, so I worked as a blacksmith for an old Scotsman who owned a livery stable in Miles City.

"As I've always said, Scotsmen and Cherokees are like blood brothers. After this man I worked for died, a lawyer came and told me the livery stable belonged to me. There I was, all alone in the world or so I believed, a wild hostile Indian who was a man of property. For a while I considered selling out and going to the Cherokee Nation to die among my blood kin. I thought I might find Jotham or his children, perhaps Jerusha; I'd heard nothing from them for many years.

"And then one day, who do I see coming into my livery stable in a two-seated wagon? Red Bird Woman and Yellow Hawk and his wife and two or three others of my old Cheyenne friends, up from Tongue River with a load of moccasins and beadwork things to sell or trade!"

"First time ever I saw tears in old Dane's eyes," Red Bird Woman said. "Next day he didn' want us to leave."

"Soon after that," Dane added, "I rode down here and found this little piece of ranchland so I could be nearby what real friends I had left. Sold the livery stable and built that little cabin over there that Red Bird wants me to give up for a tipi."

"You must have found your daughter Amayi," I said, "or else how—"

"Oh, yes, if I had not come here, most likely I never would have found Amayi, never would have known my granddaughter Mary Amayi. At that time the Cheyennes had a kindly agent, a Quaker man named Talcott. I got acquainted with him when I went over to the reservation to see the pony races. One day I told him I still had hopes that my daughter and son-in-law were alive, but I did not know how to find them. Mr. Talcott promised to have their names searched on the Minneconjou rolls in Washington, and the next time I went to the agency office he informed me that Bull Bear and his wife, Amayi, were living on the Cheyenne River Reservation in Dakota. His words passed from my ears into my heart, making it beat strong for knowing that I was not the last of the red blood of Creek Mary.

"We had no courier mail then, and I was not sure a letter would ever find its way to Amayi. So I filled my old saddlepack with dried meat and hard crackers, rolled a blanket, and started out on horseback in the Moon of Black Cherries. Two hundred miles or more I had to ride. By day the hot sun warmed my old bones, and for the first time since losing Sweet Medicine Woman I slept sound through the chilly nights. It was like the old days, following streams through piny canyons, and then down the Cheyenne River with meadowlarks calling all around me. I was like a young man again, and I felt like singing when at last I saw their house on a low plain above the river. It was a good solid house of barked logs with glass-paned windows and heavy shutters to close against the winter blizzards, but it was then summertime and as I rode up the slope I could see the green leaves of a brush arbor hung from the front eaves, and under it a table, a big man seated next to the door, three children around it, a woman with braided hair standing facing me with a large spoon in one hand and a pot in the other. She was looking at me and I was looking at her, and as I dismounted she came running toward me. '*At-é! At-é! At-é!* Father! Father! Father!' Swinging between the braids over her breast, on a silver chain, was Creek Mary's Danish coin. We laughed and wept and hugged each other. 'Three children?' I finally managed to say. 'Yes, three grandchildren for Grandfather Dane,' she cried, drying her eyes with her sleeve.

"Amayi and Bull Bear had tried to find me the way I found them, but my name was not on the Cheyenne rolls, and they could find no trace of me. Amayi had learned of the deaths of her mother and brother and nephew, but we did not talk much of these sad things. For me all the magic that had gone out of my life was restored when I looked on the faces of my grandchildren—two boys, seven and nine, and the little girl of five. Amayi had named her Mary Amayi to please me. Her eyes were the young eyes of my old grandmother, constantly searching the great world with wonder.

"When I would take the two boys out to teach them to play Cherokee racket ball, Mary Amayi was always there with us, running so hard after the deerskin ball that her cheeks were like bright little apples. She would swing the crude ball sticks I made for them with all the determination of a grown-up. She put a spell upon me, and I could not bring myself to leave, as I knew I must. I asked Bull Bear to come and bring his family to live with me on this little ranch. Although they were very poor, living mainly on rations doled out to them by the agency, Bull Bear was a leader in the tribal council, and he said his place was with the Minneconjous on Cheyenne River. At the beginning of the Drying-Grass Moon, when Bull Bear took the boys to a boarding school near the agency, I knew it was time for me to leave them."

"You went back there more times," Red Bird Woman said. "Seem like every day I come here to see you, you gone to Cheyenne River." She stood up, groaning, and stretched herself. John Bear-in-the-Water brought the last lodgepole across the stream and placed it carefully on the grass.

"How many dressed buffalo skins you say you have?" Dane asked.

"Seven, maybe eight if Ohona gives me one she promise."

"That's only half enough. Only one of us can live in half a tipi. I tell you this, Red Bird, we are too old to live under canvas covers."

"Two Moon says our buffalo herd on Lame Deer big enough now so we can kill seven or eight. He promise me all hides if Mary Amayi need your cabin for medicine house."

Dane blew his breath sharply between his teeth. "God damn, you are a scheming woman, Red Bird."

He looked quickly across the stream. A one-horsed buggy with the top raised against the sun was crawling around the bend in the trail beside his corral. A bearded white man was driving. The box behind the seat was piled high with tools—picks, shovels, and drills. The driver glanced briefly at us as he passed, but he did not acknowledge our presence, although both Dane and Red Bird Woman raised their hands in salute.

"Not even a nod," Dane said, watching the dust cloud spinning behind the buggy.

"Who that *Veheo?*" Red Bird Woman asked.

"He is the man looking for gold," John Bear-in-the-Water volunteered.

"Not gold," Dane said. "He is looking for coal. When he finds it, others will come and dig up our earth."

Red Bird Woman walked over to the row of lodgepoles and rolled three of the longest ones aside. "Where is tie rope, Bear-in-the-Water?"

"I got it here," the boy answered.

"Come on, Dane," she said. "You help with first three, I'll do others."

57

In the late spring of 1890 when Dane visited his daughter Amayi's family, she greeted him with a piece of surprising news. She had recently seen her cousin, Opothle Kingsley. "More than twenty years have passed since we last parted from each other at old Fort Carrothers," Amayi said, "but we knew each other at first sight."

"Creek Mary's blood," Dane declared. "I suppose there's no mistaking it, even in Young Opothle."

Opothle had become a Christian minister, the head of a church at Pine Ridge, and he traveled occasionally to other Dakota reservations to preach his beliefs. Amayi had heard his name mentioned as being at the Cheyenne River Agency, and she rode over to see him. Their meeting was brief because she arrived just as Opothle was preparing to travel on to Standing Rock, but he promised to come and visit her on his next circuit, which would be in the autumn.

Dane also found Bull Bear greatly concerned over the apostle of another religion—Kicking Bear and the Ghost Dance. Kicking Bear, a Minneconjou medicine man, had recently returned from a journey far to the west, where he had gone with several other Sioux and Cheyennes to investigate rumors of an Indian messiah who lived near the Sierras. Kicking Bear claimed to have seen this Son of the Great Spirit, who had given him a message and a Prayer Dance to bring back to Cheyenne River.

"Many of our people are leaving their livestock unattended," Bull Bear said. "They do no more work on their little farms. Some have taken their children from the mission schools to spend their days and nights listening to Kicking Bear and dancing the Ghost Dance. They believe they can bring back their dead relatives, the great buffalo herds, and make everything the way it was before the *Wasicus* came. I too would like to believe these things, but I cannot. Our agent is growing angry, threatening to stop issuing rations."

A few days after Dane's arrival, the time came to take eight-year-old Mary Amayi to the girls' boarding school. The four of them rode over in Bull Bear's new wagon, and then went on to the boys' school to visit Dane's two grandsons, who were now almost into their teens, very handsome and very bright. Dane wished that he could bring Creek Mary back from the Land of the Ghosts for a few minutes so that she could see them.

On the way back home, as they were crossing a little creek, they saw about twenty wagons drawn up as though in a camp circle along a dusty flat beside the stream. Off toward a low ridge were a few tipis covered with canvas and pieces of aging buffalo skins.

"Kicking Bear must be starting a new Ghost Dance up here," Bull Bear said, a disapproving tone in his voice.

"Let's stop and see what is the nature of this dance," Dane suggested.

Bull Bear showed no enthusiasm, but he hawed his team to the left and stopped the wagon on the outer rim of the circle. "Look," he said, "there are some Uncpapas from Sitting Bull's Standing Rock reservation. The Ghost Dance is spreading everywhere."

It was late in the afternoon, the weather turning colder with a biting wind as the sun lowered. Everyone was wrapped in blankets, some standing, some on horseback, some sitting in the wagons, all waiting for Kicking Bear. He appeared suddenly from one of the tipis and came striding down the slope. He was wearing a dark red blanket gathered round his waist by a large brass-buckled belt. Around his neck was a bright crimson scarf. His long hair fell over his shoulders. As he began orating, he walked around the inner circle of wagons, gesturing with thumb and forefinger, his eyes burning with a strange fever. He told of how he had traveled to the far mountains to see the Son of the Great Spirit.

"Long, long ago," intoned Kicking Bear, "the Great Spirit made this earth and then sent his Son to teach the people how to live, but the *Wasicus* treated him badly, piercing his side with a lance, driving nails into his hands and feet, and so the Son returned to the Upper World. Now the Great Spirit has sent his Son back to earth as an Indian, to make the earth as it was before the *Wasicus* came here. For twelve moons we must dance the Ghost Dance, and then the Great Spirit will send a whirlwind to destroy all the *Wasicus*, leaving a new land covered with sweet grass and clear running water and trees. If we dance and pray every day through these twelve moons, we can bring back our dead relatives and friends, we can bring back the lost buffalo, and herds of wild horses. While the whirlwind is passing, the Great Spirit will take the Ghost Dancers up in the sky, and when it has passed, they will be set down upon the new earth where only Indians will live."

Kicking Bear called to the spectators to join him in the Ghost Dance. They left their wagons slowly at first, mostly old men and women, then children, and a few young men and women, until more than a hundred formed into a dance circle. Kicking

Bear told them to stand with their hands placed on the shoulders of the person in front of them, and he repeated for them a chant that would be used instead of a drum to mark the rhythm of the dance.

"Father, I come!" Kicking Bear chanted, and the dance began, a slow shuffle forward, the circle constricting and then enlarging, the dancers' moccasins kicking up little spurts of dust. "Mother, I come," the voices called. Following Kicking Bear's example, they raised their arms above their heads, praying to the Great Spirit. "Brother, I come," they chanted. "Father, give us back our arrows!"

The dancing went on and on, until the shadows of the wagons fell long and black across the ground. Some of the older dancers would shriek out the names of dead relatives and then fall trance-like into the powdery dust, lying there unnoticed while the others continued to dance.

Amayi shivered under her blanket. "Let's go home," she said. "They are calling the ghosts to come back."

"I think Kicking Bear tells big lie," Bull Bear said, and clucked his team into motion. For a long time they could hear the deep rhythm of chanting above the grating of their wagon wheels.

With no grandchildren left at the house, Dane grew restless. He told Amayi that he wanted to see Young Opothle, and so he cut his visit short and instead of returning straight westward, he followed the Cheyenne River down to the Badlands and then rode toward Pine Ridge.

He had thought that Kicking Bear's dance was an occurrence limited to the Cheyenne River Reservation, but after he reached White Earth River he passed several small groups of Oglala Ghost Dancers. Along a creek not far from Pine Ridge, he saw more Oglala dancers wearing ghost shirts made of cheap muslin, with bright-colored figures of thunderbirds, eagles, buffalo, and arrows painted upon them. The haranguer at this dance told his listeners that the holy shirts were invulnerable to the bullets of the *Wasicus*, and he led them in a chant:

It is I who makes the Sacred Shirt
Says the father, says the father.
The shirt will cause you to live
Says the father, says the father.

Dane rode on, pitying the believers, knowing they were driven to believe because they had nothing else in which to believe. They lived in a time without spirit, in a time of despair.

Late that afternoon he sighted Opothle's church, the tall white steeple visible far across the bleak treeless plain, with a scattering of small log houses and a few shabby tipis beyond it. As he rode up to a hitching rail, he saw two children playing in the churchyard. "Opothle Kingsley," he called out to them, and they ran inside the back door of what appeared to be living quarters appended to the main church building. A minute or so later a rotund man in a black suit filled the doorway. He wore wire-rimmed spectacles too small for his fleshy olive-skinned face, and his eyes blinked uncertainly as he watched Dane dismount.

"Uncle Dane!" he cried suddenly, and lumbered forward in the same awkward way that Dane remembered Young Opothle walking as a boy.

They had much to talk about, seated by a tall cast-iron stove that took the chill off the spring evening. After Dane met Opothle's wife and two children, he learned that both Jotham and Priscilla had been dead for more than ten years. "Aunt Prissie was the one who led me to my calling," Opothle said. "She was always very religious, you know."

"Jerusha Crookes?" Dane asked. "What happened to Jerusha?"

Opothle did not know. He thought that the Reverend Crookes and his wife had left the Cherokee Nation after the Civil War, but he did not know where they went. "There is someone here," he added, "who remembers you. My stepmother. After father died, she became a part of my family." He stood up. "She's growing frail now and naps in the afternoons. I'll see if she's awake." He went down a passageway and after a minute or so returned with a narrow-waisted woman of about Dane's age. Her iron-gray hair was clipped short, her eyes much friendlier than when Dane had last looked into them more than forty years past on a rainy leaden morning in Cane Hill, Arkansas.

"Saviah Manning," he exclaimed. "Dr. Saviah Manning."

"Saviah Kingsley," she corrected him, laughing as she extended a slender but strong-fingered hand.

During the Civil War, Saviah Manning had joined Jotham's Cherokee regiment as an unofficial surgeon, and after the war ended they married. "She was a ministering angel to Meggi and me," Opothle said, "helping us to cleanse the horrors of Fort Carrothers from our minds." Through the family supper, and into the night they talked—of Fort Carrothers, the war years, the happy times and the sad times, of births and deaths and marriages.

Next morning Opothle insisted that Dane stay a month, at least a week, with him and his family, but Dane explained that he was hoping to start a beef herd before the weather turned too warm and he had to be riding on to Montana. As he was preparing to leave, he asked Opothle if the Ghost Dance craze was affecting his church activities.

"It has come so quickly," Opothle replied, shaking his head in bewilderment. "The older people seem most drawn to the Ghost Dance, although the teachings are pernicious to me, as a Christian. I don't know where the belief could have come from."

"It came from you and your fellow preacher men," Dane said. "The Ghost Dancers are throwing the Resurrection and the Last Judgment back at you Christians, from their point of view."

"You can't be serious." Opothle stared at Dane through the heavy lenses of his wire-rimmed spectacles. "You always were a great teaser, Uncle Dane."

"If you don't believe me, go and listen to the chants." Dane tightened the fastenings on his saddlebags, and then quickly mounted. "You should have preached to them of the Maker of Breath."

Opothle was still shaking his head when his stepmother came

out through the back door, making her way determinedly toward the hitching rail. "My recollection of you, Dane," she scolded, "is of one who always runs away from me before sunrise."

She offered her hand, and when he leaned from the saddle to take it, she whispered: "I remember, I remember. What an arrogant young female fool I was."

"No more a fool than I." He reached for his reins.

"You will write to us," Opothle called. "With the new mail courier, letters go quickly between the agencies."

"I'll write if you'll write." Dane raised his hand in good-bye. "We're the last of the old blood, and we must not lose track of our separate pathways again."

During the late summer and autumn, Dane received letters from both Amayi and Opothle. Each described at length the turmoil brought on by the Ghost Dance on their reservations. In his replies, Dane complained that they had written more about the Ghost Dancers than about their children. "As for the Ghost Dancers," he wrote, "I can tell you all about them. My poor Cheyenne neighbors do nothing else these days but spend all their waking moments at wild dancing and chanting. The Crows, on the other hand, will have nothing to do with this Ghost Dance. Like me, they are skeptical of prophets."

In November an alarming letter came from Amayi. The Cheyenne River boarding schools had closed because so few pupils remained. Most of the teachers had fled in fear, the trading posts were locked and shuttered, and soldiers summoned by alarmed white settlers were patrolling the borders of the reservation. Worst of all, Bull Bear had received warnings and threats because he would not join in the Minneconjou Ghost Dances.

For some days Dane heard nothing more except wild rumors of many soldiers marching in the Black Hills, and then one dawn he was awakened by the sound of hoofbeats. Through his misted window he saw a troop of cavalry passing slowly down the road toward Dundee. After that, he rode to the agency every two or three days to see if Mr. Talcott might have a letter for him from Amayi or Opothle.

He was saddling his horse one morning when he saw Red Bird Woman approaching across the plain from the west. The old mare she was riding snorted as though with indignation because Red Bird Woman forced it into a canter over the last lap of the ride. As she crossed the stream, Red Bird Woman held up a white envelope. "Mr. Talcott sent letter," she explained.

He reached for it. The envelope was marked *Urgent* in Opothle's stilted handwriting. Before he could open it, she said: "Sitting Bull has been killed."

"Sitting Bull! At Standing Rock?"

"Mr. Talcott say he killed few days ago. Ghost Dancers will mourn for him tonight."

"Sitting Bull would never believe in Ghost Dancing." He ripped the envelope open and hastily read Opothle's short letter. Amayi had sent Opothle a verbal message by a government courier. She and Bull Bear and their children had been forced to leave their home and take refuge at the Cheyenne River Agency. They had their wagon and some household goods and were starting to join Spotted Elk's Minneconjous at Cherry Creek. From there they hoped to make their way with other fugitives to the safety of Pine Ridge.

"I must go to Pine Ridge," Dane said, turning toward his cabin. While he was packing his saddlebags, Red Bird Woman came in to help, gathering blankets from the bed. "Pack enough jerky for two," she said. "I go with you."

"You're too old," he answered her.

"No older than you."

"We're in the Big Frozen Moon," he said. "There'll be snow for certain going through the Black Hills."

"All more reason you need Cheyenne woman to keep you warm, *Sanaki.*"

Red Bird Woman went with him, and he was glad for her company, although he would not tell her so. Snow fell on them twice, but not heavily, and they did not suffer from the cold until the last day, after they left Horsehead Creek and faced into a bitter east wind off the rolling plain. They were almost frozen when they rode up to Opothle's church in the dismal December darkness.

Light filtered from the sharp-pointed side windows, so that they appeared to be yellow arrows aimed at the black sky. The wind made a horizontal line of the smoke pouring from a brick chimney behind the steeple. Banked against the long hitching rail were several long high-backed benches, pews that had been removed from the church.

As Dane dismounted, the door under the peak-roofed entranceway opened, and he saw the silhouette of a man framed there against the lamplight. He caught a faint scent of carbolic acid. Red Bird Woman was blowing on her fingers, trying to warm the numbness out of them so she could tie her horse to the rail. Dane reached out and tied the rope for her, and then guided her toward the church entrance. The man who had come outside stopped to peer at them through the dim light. "*Hau*," he said, and Dane saw the vapor of his breath.

"Opothle Kingsley?" Dane asked. "Is he in the church?"

"You have relatives?" the man replied in Lakota.

"Reverend Kingsley is a relative," Dane said, and the man moved aside for them to reach the doorway.

When Dane pulled the door open, he was surrounded by a wave of humid air, heavy with the odors of antiseptics, human bodies, and putrefying flesh. Straw covered the floor of the church, and along both walls lay thirty or more Indians—men, women, and children—on blanket beds. Wreaths and long pendants of pine greenery, Opothle's Christmas decorations, still hung from walls and ceiling, the streamers coming to a point over the pulpit. Mounted to the chancel wall on opposite sides of the altar were two banners with letters cut from red and green paper: GLORY TO GOD IN THE HIGHEST and ON EARTH PEACE, GOOD WILL TOWARD MEN.

"*Aho-ya*," Red Bird Woman moaned, and had she not been there beside him Dane was certain that he would have believed himself trapped alone in a vision of unbearable desolation. He saw Opothle then, seated on an old straight-backed chair beside one of the blanket beds, a child on his lap, and the child was eight-year-old Mary Amayi. Stumbling over the strewn hay, Dane reached for his granddaughter, and saw dangling from her delicate throat Creek Mary's Danish coin on its silver chain. "Where is your mother?" he whispered, and then he looked down and saw the face of Amayi framed against the straw, a blanket drawn to her chin. Her eyes were closed, her beautiful mouth twisted in a pain more powerful than sleep.

"It happened at Wounded Knee Creek," Opothle said, his voice weak from weariness.

Mary Amayi's head rested against Dane's shoulder, and he could feel the muscles of the child's thin body slackening into complete repose.

"Amayi?" Dane asked. "How bad . . ."

Opothle shook his head. "Very bad. All very bad. Those who were able to run fled down the creek. Your grandchild is the only one without a scratch."

"Bull Bear and my two grandsons?"

"We don't know. They were not brought in on the wagons."

"Let me warm the child," Red Bird Woman said, and she took Mary Amayi from Dane's arms and carried her to the red-hot stove in a corner of the church. Dane saw Saviah Kingsley moving slowly from one blanketed form to another, offering water from a tin pitcher to an old woman, soothing a whimpering child. He waited until she glanced up and saw him, and then he went to her.

"Your daughter was shot through the hips," Saviah said softly. "The army surgeon gave us some morphine. It dulls the pain, but she cannot live, Dane." She touched the back of his hand gently, and then a little girl raised up on the straw behind them, calling in Lakota for water. Saviah held a tin cup to the child's mouth. She swallowed a long gulp of water, but most of it flowed in a pale red stream down the front of her dress, from a hole in her throat. "Nor can she," Saviah added bitterly. "Have they determined to destroy us all, Dane?"

58

"Amayi lived through that night of howling winds," Dane said, "with sleety snowflakes spitting against the church windows. Opothle's Oglala friends kept bringing more blankets for the wounded, and sticks of wood so that we could keep the stove red-hot, but the cold crept in like an invisible biting monster. Soon after daylight the storm stopped and a pale sun showed in the dull sky. Opothle and some of the young Oglalas went off with the soldiers to search for dead on the battlefield. Late that morning, while they were gone, Amayi died.

"When Opothle returned he told me as gently as he could of that hideous field of death, snowswept, with frozen bodies lying as they had fallen, of how they found many women and children who had been wounded but were able to crawl for more than a mile up gullies and ravines only to die in the blizzard. Several small children found their way to cabins down the creek and were taken in by Oglala families. They are still there, most of them, grown up now. The American government never made any move to help those children who had been orphaned by its army, leaving them to be fed, clothed, and sheltered by the poor people of the reservation.

"Opothle found Bull Bear and my two grandsons all lying facedown, frozen beside a frozen horse, as if they had been hiding there when the bullets struck them.

"I have seen that place many times in my dreams, and have heard many stories of how and why the shooting started. The soldiers say the Minneconjous fired first, and the few Minneconjous who survived say the soldiers fired first. Mary Amayi does not remember anything but the noise of guns and the stench of powder smoke, of her mother running with her up a little ravine, and then both of them falling to the ground and lying there a long time while the guns kept firing. After a while her mother raised up and took the Danish coin from her neck and put it around Mary Amayi's neck. Then Mary Amayi saw blood soaking through her mother's dress. A long time later a wagon stopped beside them and some soldiers picked them up and put them in the wagon. I am thankful to those soldiers, but if the soldiers had not been there, no one would have died.

"I know that my warrior people would never fire guns to provoke armed soldiers while their own women and children, the seed of the tribe, are in a place of danger. The whites say the warriors were wearing ghost shirts and believed the soldiers' bullets could not harm them, but only a few, maybe none, of Spotted Elk's people were wearing ghost shirts. Most of them were running away from the turmoil of the Ghost Dancers, the frightened white settlers, and the soldiers—their urgency increased because of the assassination of Sitting Bull. Perhaps some believed that a new earth was coming, but they never saw the promises of Kicking Bear's messiah, the sweeping waves of sweet grass, clear running water and trees, and great herds of buffalo and wild horses. Instead they saw the only thing your people have ever given my people—pain and desolation and death.

"The Maker of Breath left to me only Mary Amayi, the last of Creek Mary's red blood, and when Opothle and his wife out of kindness offered to take her into their family, I refused them with such rudeness that I fear they have never forgiven me."

"He was like old she-cougar with dried dugs," Red Bird Woman said. "Shielding the last of its young." She took down one of the long lodgepoles she had lifted into place. "Door pole too long," she announced. "John Bear-in-the-Water, go get Dane's ax."

The framework of poles was a black conical skeleton, a promise against the afternoon sky.

"I took Mary Amayi to the Blackrobes' school," Dane said, "but she would run away and come back here, I don't know how many miles, no matter what the weather. The last time she ran away, two of the sisters came out here to talk to me about her. They said she would have nothing to do with other people, young or old, that she was interested only in animals. She had told them she could talk to animals and that animals talked to her. They wanted me to give them permission to keep her locked up so she could not run away again. I would not do so. Mary Amayi stayed with me and we talked with the coyotes every night.

"In the daytime she wandered up and down this stream, talking with the beavers, I suppose, and the birds and jackrabbits. One day she found a young eagle with a broken wing and brought it home. I thought the eagle would die surely, but she mended its wing and found food for it, and one morning she brought it up here, right here on this little rise, and turned it loose. It circled and soared into the sun, and for days afterward Mary Amayi sang about the eagle and its freedom.

"One thing she could not bear, and that was the sound of a gun firing. Even the smell of gunpowder smoke would set her to trembling. One evening I saw several antelopes feeding in the willows up there along the stream. I took my rifle and shot one, and when I went back in the cabin she was lying on the floor, holding her hands over her ears, crying and calling her mother's name. After that I did no more shooting anywhere near the place when she was here.

"The next year Red Bird Woman helped me persuade her to go to the contract school. She lived with Red Bird and her sister, nearby the school, and she liked the teacher, who knew a great deal about animals and plants. Sometimes when she came to visit me, she would ask me to tell her what I knew about the leaves and roots of plants that healed animals and people. So I told her about the roots of beggar's-lice and wild senna, the juice of milkweed and skullcap, the leaves of ferns and tassel flowers, and what they would heal. But most of these were medicine plants that Creek Mary told me about when I was a boy in the old Cherokee Nation, and they do not grow in this country."

"I told her about balsamweed for loose kidneys," Red Bird Woman said, "and black root for snakebites. My sister told some others, I forget what they are."

John Bear-in-the-Water returned with the ax, and Red Bird Woman showed him where to chop the end of the lodgepole.

"In one of my letters to Opothle I wrote about Mary Amayi and her healing plants," Dane went on, "and I suppose Opothle must have read the letter to his stepmother, Saviah. Anyway, Saviah wrote me to bring my granddaughter to Pine Ridge so that she could teach her to be a healer. When I told Mary Amayi about Dr. Saviah Kingsley and the invitation, she could hardly wait for summer to come.

"That was six or seven years ago, but my old bones ached all night after the first day's ride to Pine Ridge. After that I was all right. Red Bird Woman made Mary Amayi a buckskin riding dress for the horseback journey, and when I would look at her riding along the wild trails through the Black Hills she was so much like Sweet Medicine Girl when I first knew her that I felt like I was a young man again.

"Mary Amayi stayed through the summer with Saviah, and when I went to bring her home I found that she had suddenly grown into a young woman, proud and smiling and beautiful to look upon. What she was proudest of was an old medical saddle-bag filled with vials and a kit of surgical instruments, a present from Saviah. 'Mary Amayi knows all that I know about healing, and more,' Saviah said. 'I would trust her with my life.'

"After we returned home, Mary Amayi told everyone that she was a healer, but she was so young the Cheyennes would let her treat only their animals at first—sick dogs, horses with rubbed sores, and steers that had got their hides cut on barbed wire. While they were building the railroad through here, she found a fawn lying by the tracks with a broken leg. She begged me to take my wagon down there and bring the fawn back to the cabin. I told her we ought to put the fawn out of its misery, but she made me help her strap it down so she could put splints on its leg, and damned if she didn't heal that fawn. Kept it in the corral for a while and then turned it loose with four good legs. Everybody around here knew about that fawn, and when one of Buffalo Horn's little boys caught his foot in a steel trap, they brought him over here to Mary Amayi. Some of the boy's bones were crushed and the cuts were deep, and after she did everything she knew to do, she made Buffalo Horn take him to Miles City. The doctor there said the little boy's foot was fixed just right, and sure enough in a week or so he was hopping around on it. After that, well, everybody around here with hurts and ailments was coming to see Mary Amayi. Old Bear-in-the-Water, John's father, was the first of the Crow ranchers to come. Broke a splinter off in his hand and the flesh was all swollen up purple, driving him crazy with pain. She got the splinter out and used some of Saviah's medicine, and the swelling went right down.

"Must've been around that time that Mr. Teddy Roosevelt, who is now your President, came riding up to my cabin early one afternoon in company with a pale-faced young man some years younger than he was. I'd never seen either one of them before, and at first I thought they had got themselves lost and were going to ask me for directions. They were mounted on splendid riding horses and were leading two spare ponies loaded with tents and all kinds of expensive trappings, rich shining leather and fancy gunstocks and such.

"Mr. Roosevelt was wearing a wide-brimmed hat, a fringed jacket, short leather leggings, and a big belt with a sheathed hunting knife on one hip and a holstered pistol on the other. 'How!' he called out in a high rasping voice, raising one hand the way some whites think they are supposed to do when greeting Indians.

"'Good afternoon,' I said to him.

"'Are you Dane?' he asked.

"When I told him I was, he dismounted and pulled a long

brown envelope out of his jacket. He handed it to me, naming my lawyer friend in Miles City as the sender.

"As I soon came to find out from the letter, the pale-faced young man with Mr. Roosevelt was a Mr. Jefferies, a New York lawyer who was related to my friend in Miles City. Mr. Roosevelt had learned from my friend that the Cheyennes had a small herd of buffalo somewhere along Tongue River, and he had come down to ask permission to kill one.

"'I want only the head,' he said. He spoke very fast, telling me how eager he was to mount a buffalo head on the wall of his house in New York. 'A wild buffalo,' he said, showing his big white teeth. 'Imagine, Jefferies, the head of a *wild* buffalo in my study. I thought they were all gone, except for the tame ones in parks and zoos.'

"I explained to him that the buffalo were the property of the Cheyennes, that the herd was very small, and the tribe allowed only a few to be killed each year. 'But you know the chief,' he insisted, his small eyes piercing me through the thick glass of his spectacles. 'You will intercede for me.'

"There was nothing to be done but ride with Mr. Roosevelt and his friend over to see Two Moon. I did not expect Two Moon to allow them anywhere near the Cheyennes' secret herd on the Lame Deer, and he did not. What he did was send some of the young men down there to drive out a worthless old bull they were going to kill anyway. The young men herded the old bull up into a blind coulee, and then Mr. Roosevelt—after paying Two Moon about five times what it would've cost him for a good steer—rode out to the coulee and got his buffalo head.

"I never expected to see Mr. Roosevelt or Mr. Jefferies again, but after camping out somewhere that night they came up to my cabin soon after daybreak and called me outside. Mr. Roosevelt wanted me to go with them to the Bighorn Mountains. He craved a grizzly bear's head to put on his wall with the buffalo head. I told him I had some beef cattle to look after and could not go. I suppose if I'd known what a big man he was, soon to be the President of the United States, I'd have gone along anyway, but he looked like any other *Veheo* to me.

"He asked me if I could draw him a map of the main trails into the Bighorns, and after I did so, he and Mr. Jefferies rode off toward the Tongue Valley, leading their spare ponies loaded with all those fine leather trappings and saddlebags and tents and the buffalo head wrapped in canvas.

"Two or three days passed and they'd gone out of my thoughts, and then one rainy morning Mary Amayi called me to the window. Like ghosts out of the gray mists and sheets of rain blown by the wind, two men in pommel slickers came riding slowly up the road from Dundee. When they turned in toward my cabin, I opened the door to invite them out of the wet.

"Mr. Roosevelt, who was in the lead, called out to me: 'Where's the nearest doctor?'

"'A long day's ride,' I answered him.

"'Don't they have an infirmary and a doctor on the reservation?' he asked.

"'No. The Cheyennes come here to see my granddaughter. She's our healer.'

"He did not know what to make of that, but he decided the first thing he should do was get his friend Jefferies out of the driving rain even if he had to bring him inside an Indian's cabin. Mr. Jefferies was leaning forward in his saddle, his wet face ashen as death, his lips pressed tight together. On the day before, his horse had shied at some darting animal, Mr. Roosevelt explained, unseating Mr. Jefferies. He had taken a bad fall into some jagged boulders and broken a leg. They had been riding all night through fog and rain.

"We brought Mr. Jefferies inside, and Mary Amayi spread a blanket for him on the floor in front of the fireplace. 'What a neat, clean place,' Mr. Roosevelt said, looking around as if he'd expected to find us living amidst grime and squalor. He watched Mary Amayi slip a thermometer into his friend's mouth. Then with her surgical scissors she cut away the lower part of Mr. Jefferies's trousers, so that we could see the broken leg. The shinbone appeared to be twisted to one side, and the flesh was badly discolored. 'I can ease his pain,' Mary Amayi said, looking at Mr. Roosevelt, 'with your permission.'

"'Not with some kind of mumbo jumbo and black magic,' he cried.

"She went and brought one of the vials of medicine that Saviah had given her, and he peered at the label through his thick glasses. 'You know the dosage?' he asked suspiciously, and then he showed the vial to Mr. Jefferies. 'Let her treat me,' Jefferies moaned.

"'She's a full-blood Indian,' Mr. Roosevelt said.

"'Let her treat me,' Jefferies repeated in a piteous tone.

"We then had to decide who was to ride for the doctor. Mr. Roosevelt wanted to go, but he also was afraid to leave his friend in the power of two full-blood Indians, one of whom he still suspected of being a female witch doctor. So he gave me his rain slicker and I rode for the doctor. By midmorning I was out of the storm and under clear skies, and late the next day, after some hard riding, the doctor and I reached the cabin.

"We found Mr. Jefferies sitting up in my bed, drinking soup from a bowl that Mary Amayi was holding for him. Mr. Roosevelt was frisking about, showing his big teeth in a grin, and bragging about how he and Mary Amayi had set Mr. Jefferies's broken shinbone. The doctor had to have a look, of course. He scissored off the bandages and splints and felt around with his fingers. 'Damned good,' he said, and started rebandaging the leg.

"'It's bully,' Mr. Roosevelt said. 'Bully!'

"Well, they stayed in the cabin another day or two, and then Mr. Roosevelt hired Old Bear-in-the-Water to haul Mr. Jefferies up to Miles City in a wagon, lined and upholstered with blankets and buffalo robes. I could see that Mr. Jefferies did not want to leave Mary Amayi. With his big pale-blue eyes he kept looking at her the way a calf looks at a mother cow. He kissed her hand and promised that he would remember her until the day he died. 'You will hear from me,' he said as we loaded him into the wagon.

"And we did hear from him, some weeks afterward, a long letter from Mr. Jefferies informing us that upon his recommendation Columbia Medical College was admitting Mary Amayi as a trial student at the beginning of its next term. The costs of her journey east and all expenses while in attendance would be borne by him, Mr. Jefferies wrote. At first, Mary Amayi said she had no intention of going east to a medical school and leaving her people without a healer, but soon I could tell that she was thinking hard about the matter. One day she asked me what I thought my grandmother Creek Mary would have done if she'd had a chance to go to a medical school and become a real doctor.

"'If she wanted to become a doctor,' I replied, 'she would go even if it meant leaving her people.'

"'But she would return to her people afterward,' Mary Amayi said. 'If I become a medical doctor I would not need to send anyone to Miles City. I could have a hospital on the reservation.'

"'All right,' I told her. 'If you want to become a doctor, then go.'

"She was still troubled in her mind about something, however, and after a day or so she let me know what it was. Red Bird Woman was over here that day, and Mary Amayi started talking about Mr. Jefferies and the medical college. She wanted to be a doctor, she said, but she could not bear the thought of being indebted to a *Veheo*, not even a kind young man like Mr. Jefferies.

"Red Bird Woman kept quiet while Mary Amayi was talking, but she was nodding her head and whispering: '*Nihini, nihini.*' And then she said: 'Your granddaughter is a wise one, *Sanaki.*'" Red Bird Woman placed the shortened lodgepole into place and turned to face us. "That *Veheo* try to buy Mary Amayi," she said. "Like that evil one, Belcourt, bought me from the Apaches."

"Mr. Jefferies was not like Belcourt," Dane said.

"All same, he try to buy your granddaughter." She put her hands on her wide hips and frowned at him. "You too thick-headed to see, *Sanaki*. So I have to show you how we Cheyennes send Mary Amayi to doctor school." She turned her back on him to examine the tipi frame again.

"How did you do it?" I asked.

Dane shaded his eyes against the lowering sun to look toward the west. "Everybody gave something," he said. "The women made moccasins and necklaces and took them to Miles City to sell and trade. They sold all their old buffalo robes. After the trains started running through here, the children sold beads to the passengers through the coach windows."

"They sold beads to white people?" I asked. "Glass beads?"

"The boys sold arrowheads and arrows," John Bear-in-the-Water said. "Sometimes the train would start up before they gave us money. We would run along on the cinders beside the train until it was going too fast for us, and the mean ones would laugh at us and keep our arrows and not give us money."

"Little girls sold their dolls same way," Red Bird Woman said. "But most money for Mary Amayi come from beef cattle."

Dane laughed. "That's the truth. Red Bird went to everybody who was raising cows and threatened them until they sold one beef for Mary Amayi."

"My old man sold two for her," John Bear-in-the-Water said proudly.

"You would not think a Crow do that, would you?" Red Bird Woman said, winking at me.

Dane pointed across the plain to a horsewoman riding toward us. "There she comes," he said. "I can tell the way she rides, they gave her no help for the hospital."

59

John Bear-in-the-Water trotted on foot to meet her, and I could hear her contralto voice returning his greeting as he reached for the halter of her pony. He led the pony up the slope toward the tipi skeleton, and they were etched against the sky like one of those old medieval tapestries showing a hostler leading the caparisoned steed of a knight's lady or a princess in from the hunt.

She dropped easily from the saddle, adjusted her divided riding skirt, and stood looking at the tipi frame while Dane and Red Bird Woman moved toward her.

"So you've started the tipi," she said. Red Bird Woman embraced her, speaking softly in Cheyenne.

"No," she said. "They refused to help."

"You had to find out," Dane said. "You'll have to start in the cabin."

"You can't give up your cabin," she answered him strongly.

"I'll live in the tipi," he said. "It's warmer in winter and cooler in summer."

"And easier to keep clean," Red Bird Woman added.

"No," she said. "For a hospital we'll need beds and instruments and medicines. Cost too much *maka-eta*."

"We get medicine house things same way we make you a doctor," Red Bird Woman said. "Everybody share."

"I got six steers," John Bear-in-the-Water said. "I will sell all of them for you. My old man will sell two."

"*Nohetto!* Now then!" Red Bird Woman's hands gripped Mary Amayi's shoulders. "If Crows help like that, think what Cheyennes will do."

Dane turned her toward me, whispering something. Noticing me for the first time, she smiled, and I could feel an impulse of life, that driving force I had felt the day I saw her at Teddy Roosevelt's luncheon in the White House. In some romantic fashion, I suppose, I thought of her as the essence of America, the Lady of Cofitachequi and Hernando De Soto, Muskogean blood and Spanish blood, and the Long Warrior and the blood of the *Ani-Yun-Wiya*, the Real People, the magic of the Cherokees mixed with that of the Tall People, the Cheyennes, and the unnamed Frenchman, the *voyageur*, whom I saw as a young man of noble blood bearing a magnificent nose, fugitive from the French Revolution, and then the Minneconjous of the Teton Sioux, the mighty Dakotas. Warriors they all had been, male and female, warrior survivors. What was she, if she was not America?

I felt her strong hand in mine and looked into her eyes and knew the heritage of all those strains of blood, and when she drew away I saw the Danish coin, larger than I had imagined it to be, silvery against the tawny risings of her breasts. She was Creek Mary, the reason for my being there, the sun lowering behind her reminding me that I was only a sojourner there, an outsider, and I said something about the train I must board.

"You ride in wagon to Dundee station with me and John Bear-in-the-Water," Red Bird Woman said.

I could have stayed forever. I wanted to see the unfolding of the dream, but this was not my world to live in.

When I looked back from the wagon seat, waving, her hand was resting on her grandfather's shoulder, and he was smiling with his thin lips closed, the ends of his smile extending into the wrinkles of his aging face. And then the wagon jolted over a hump in the land and there was only the framework of the tipi sinking slowly out of view.

The wagon seat was not wide enough for the three of us, and John Bear-in-the-Water crouched forward of Red Bird Woman's wide girth, slapping the lines and urging the team to move faster. "He want to get back to Mary Amayi in big hurry," she said, blinking at me.

"I would be in a hurry, too," I replied.

"I glad you there today."

"Why?"

"Easier for me to make Dane give in for tipi with you there." Her body shook against me as she laughed. We were already nearing the brown-stained railroad depot. The wagon swung with the turning of the road, the wheels spinning up dust. John Bear-in-the-Water sawed at the lines, whoa-ing the team to a jarring halt. I reached behind the seat for my bag, and stepped down, thanking them for the ride. "See you sometime," he said. Red Bird Woman said nothing. She just looked at me with her young-old eyes that had seen more pain and grief and injustice and hate and love and farewells than I could imagine. As the wagon started rolling away, she turned and placed her fingers on her lips and blew me a *Veheo* kiss. I returned it.

From the rear the depot appeared to be deserted, but when I turned the corner onto the cindered platform I found a man seated on an iron bench facing the tracks. He looked up at me in surprise. "By God, you startled me," he said. "Seldom see a white man around here."

He was the bearded man who earlier in the afternoon had passed Dane's cabin without acknowledging our presence, the man who Dane said was looking for coal so that miners could come and dig up the Indians' earth.

"Going to catch the eastbound?" he asked.

I told him that I was.

"I'm waiting for supplies coming on the baggage car," he explained. "You one of the ranchers hereabouts?"

I told him I was a traveling newspaperman from Washington.

"Roving correspondent, eh? Not much going on here, is there? Nothing but Indians. I'm a geologist. Work for a coal company."

"What are the prospects?" I asked.

"God, this country is rich in coal, close to the surface, easy to mine, just scrape the worthless earth away. Most of it's on reservation land, though. The government gave the land to the Indians because it looks so damned worthless, arid and scrubby. But there are fortunes underneath when the time comes to mine it. Someday we'll have to move these Indians out of here. They wouldn't know what to do with coal, any more than they know how to do anything else for themselves. They stand in the way of progress, you know. Got all these strange notions about land being sacred—"

The hoarse whistle of the approaching train overrode his words, the locomotive bearing down upon us, its black smoke pluming across the tall grass. Somehow it metamorphosed into the drawing described to me by Dane of his daughter Amayi's calendar depiction of an Iron Horse breathing fire and smoke through its teeth. The cars swept by us, the geologist rising from K22 the bench and clumping angrily along the cinders in his high-laced miner's boots toward the distant baggage car.

A blue-uniformed conductor dropped down from the first passenger car and motioned me to board. Before I fell into a plush seat and faced eastward, the train was moving again. Through the dingy window I watched the daylight fade, and then I quickly pressed my forehead against the glass. For a moment a line of low irregular hills seemed to shape themselves into the silhouette of a woman supine, gazing up at the indigo sky, Creek Mary's Sleeping Woman materializing on the Western Plain. It could have been a trick of the light and the motion of the train, or some magic in the landscape of Montana.